John Burgoyne
of Saratoga

Books by James Lunt

Charge to Glory

Scarlet Lancer

The Barren Rocks of Aden

Bokhara Burnes

From Sepoy to Subedar (ed.)

The Duke of Wellington's Regiment

16th/5th The Queen's Royal Lancers

General John Burgoyne, by Reynolds

John Burgoyne of Saratoga

JAMES LUNT

Harcourt Brace Jovanovich

New York and London

Library of Congress Cataloging in Publication Data

Lunt, James D   1917–
John Burgoyne of Saratoga.

Bibliography: p.
Includes index.
1. Burgoyne, John, 1722–1792.   I.   Title.
DA67.1. B8L86   973.3'41'0924   [B]   75-15699
ISBN 0-15-146402-2

First edition

B C D E

To Alex

Contents

Calendar of Important Events in the Life
of John Burgoyne   xiii

Part One. The Making of a General

1. The Burgoynes of Sutton   3
2. Love, Marriage, and Exile   12
3. Breaking Windows with Guineas   19
4. A Colonel of Light Dragoons   28
5. Burgoyne's Light Horse   37
6. A Clubbable Man   45
7. Honourable and Gallant Gentleman   55
8. A Triumvirate of Reputation   65
9. Fifth Wheel of the Boston Coach   80

Part Two. The Breaking of a General

10. Carleton's Deputy in Canada   99
11. Confusion Worse Confounded   114
12. Preparing for Disaster   132

Contents

13. "I Have Beat All the Americans" 147
14. The Dividing of the Ways 161
15. The Beginning of the End 178
16. Bennington: The Futile Foray 189
17. "This Army Must Not Retreat" 202
18. The Decisive Battle 216
19. The Gamester's Throw 231
20. Convention—Not Capitulation 250
21. Qui s'excuse, s'accuse 269
22. Scapegoat 291

Part Three. Life Still Had Much to Offer
23. Politician and Playwright 313

Epilogue 327

Appendixes
1. Order of Battle—the Expedition from Canada—1777 333
2. Articles of Convention between Lieutenant General Burgoyne and Major General Gates 335

Bibliography 339

Source Notes 344

Index 357

Maps
The British Advance from Canada 151
The Battle of Freeman's Farm 223
The Battle of Bemis Heights 241

Acknowledgments

THE WRITING of this book has placed me in the debt of many people, but above all my thanks are owing to Alexandra Ward, my research assistant. Her scholarly interest has acted both as a spur and as an encouragement, and I feel therefore that it is entirely appropriate that *John Burgoyne of Saratoga* should be dedicated to her—with her permission. I must add, however, that she is in no way responsible for errors of fact, imperfections of style, or the opinions expressed. Here the responsibility is mine alone.

I owe a special debt of gratitude to D. W. King, formerly Chief Librarian of the Ministry of Defence Whitehall Library, and his staff, who provided me with ample opportunity for research; and I acknowledge with thanks the assistance I have been given by the Earl of Derby; the Earl of Courtown; John Brooke-Little, Richmond Herald, College of Arms; Professor D. T. Wright, University of Waterloo, Ontario, Canada; Denis Lyonson, Librarian, and Agnes Rose, Acting Librarian, at Knowsley; Mrs. Thomas Lape, Librarian at Fort Ticonderoga, N.Y.; J. A. de Fonblanque; Major-General E. B. de Fonblanque; William Seymour; Professor Alastair Smart; John Fleming; John Carleton; Lieutenant-Colonel J. R. Palmer; General Sir Antony Read; the Librarian of the U.S. Military

Acknowledgments

Academy, West Point; and the Director and staff of the National Army Museum, London.

Brigadier-General Sam Griffiths, U.S.M.C. (retired), of Freeport, Maine, was kind enough to share with me the results of his research into the operations of the British Army during the American War of Independence. This has been a kindness to which I am not entitled and is all the more appreciated for that reason. Finally, I must thank William E. Meuse, of the U.S. National Park Service, and Lucy, his wife, for so kindly showing me round the Saratoga battlefield, and for so patiently answering my many questions. I am sincerely grateful to them both.

JAMES LUNT

Calendar of Important Events in the Life of John Burgoyne

Feb. 4, 1723   Born in Park Prospect, Westminster, London

1737   Appointed sub-brigadier in the Horse Guards

1744   Appointed cornet in the 1st Royal Dragoons

c. 1751   Sold commission and eloped with Lady Charlotte Stanley

1754   Daughter Charlotte Elizabeth born

1756   Reconciled with Lord Derby, his father-in-law, returned to England, purchased captaincy in 11th Dragoons

1758   Appointed captain-lieutenant and lieutenant-colonel in 2nd Foot Guards

1759   Appointed lieutenant-colonel commandant of 16th Light Dragoons

1761   Elected member of Parliament for Midhurst (Sussex)

1762–63   Served in campaign in Portugal

1763   Appointed colonel of 16th Light Dragoons

1764   Daughter died

1768   Elected member of Parliament for Preston (Lancashire)

1769 Appointed governor of Fort William, Scotland

1772 Named chairman of parliamentary committee to investigate affairs of East India Company

1772 Promoted to major-general

1774 *Maid of the Oaks* produced at Drury Lane Theatre

1775 Sent to Boston

1776 Sent to Canada as deputy to General Carleton

June 5, 1776 Death of Lady Charlotte Burgoyne

Mar. 26, 1777 Appointed to command expedition from Canada

July 6, 1777 Captured Fort Ticonderoga

Aug. 16, 1777 Action at Bennington

Aug. 29, 1777 Promoted to lieutenant-general

Sept. 19, 1777 Battle of Freeman's Farm

Oct. 7, 1777 Battle of Bemis Heights

Oct. 16, 1777 Convention of Saratoga signed

May 13, 1778 Returned to England

1779 Resigned colonelcy of 16th Light Dragoons and governorship of Fort William

1780 *The Lord of the Manor* produced at Drury Lane Theatre

1782 Appointed commander-in-chief in Ireland

1782 Appointed colonel of 4th (King's Own) Regiment

1782 Son (later Field-Marshal Sir John Fox Burgoyne) born to him and Susan Caulfield

1784 Resigned command in Ireland and retired from army

1786 *The Heiress* produced at Drury Lane Theatre

Aug. 4, 1792 Died

Part One

The Making of
a General

*"Every man thinks meanly
of himself for not having
been a soldier...."*
—Samuel Johnson, April 10, 1778

Chapter 1

The Burgoynes of Sutton

When Robert Benson, the first Lord Bingley, died on April 9, 1731, he left behind him a handsome fortune. He also provided posterity with an intriguing scandal, which was to delight the gossip-mongers for many years to come. It was alleged that he was the father of John Burgoyne, later to distinguish himself as soldier, politician, and playwright, and no one was more assiduous in propagating this story than Horace Walpole.

Lord Bingley was a time-serving politician who had inherited from his father ("an attorney, and no great character for an honest man"[1]) a handsome estate in Yorkshire and £1,500 a year. He managed to build up his fortune and entered Parliament, but his main interests were money, women, and the embellishment of his estate at Bramham and his splendid mansion in London's Cavendish Square. His peerage came as a reward for his services to Robert Harley, for many years Queen Anne's first minister.

Bingley married Lady Elizabeth Finch, who was both eccentric and something of a virago. On her death she left part of her large fortune to a footman, on condition he hang her fourteen cats. She bore Bingley one daughter, Harriott, who inherited £100,000 on her father's death, but according to

1. Source notes are on pages 344–356.

Horace Walpole there was little affection between husband and wife. Although unattractive in both appearance and character, Lady Bingley must have found her husband's interest in other women hard to endure; he owned to at least three illegitimate daughters. There was also the attractive Anna Maria Burgoyne, who caused Lady Bingley much concern.

She was the wife of John Burgoyne, the spendthrift second son of Sir John Burgoyne, third Baronet of Sutton, in the county of Bedfordshire. The Burgoynes were a long-established country family whose estates had been granted to them in 1387 by John of Gaunt, if there be any truth in the old rhyme

> I John of Gaunt
> Do give and do graunt
> Unto Roger Burgoyne
> and the heirs of his loyne
> All Sutton and Potton
> Until the world's rotten.

However, the Burgoynes had to wait until 1641 before a baronetcy was conferred on the family, by King Charles I, although they had been granted the right to bear arms as far back as the reign of Henry VII. They managed to retain their estates during the bitter years of fighting between king and Parliament.

John the second son of the third baronet was born in 1684. He entered the army, in which he acquired a passion for gambling and a taste for high living, but little else. In 1714 he married Anna Maria Burnestone, daughter and coheiress of a rich Hackney merchant, who brought with her a handsome dowry, most of which was gambled away by her husband. She bore him a son on February 4, 1723,* and on the following day the baby was carried by his father to be baptized John in St. Margaret's, Westminster, a stone's throw from the Burgoynes' lodgings. Lord Bingley was a godfather.

---

* Burgoyne's birth is sometimes shown as 1722. This is in accordance with the old calendar. For this book, 1723 has been chosen as being more accurate.

The Burgoynes of Sutton

The Burgoynes were friendly with Bingley, who owned the house in Park Prospect, overlooking St. James's Park, where the Burgoynes had been living for some years. John Burgoyne was forced to borrow money from Bingley to stave off his creditors, and in Bingley's will, drawn up in 1729, he was specifically released from his debts to Bingley. Not that this act of kindness was of much use to Burgoyne. He continued to gamble heavily until he was lodged in the King's Bench Prison by his creditors, where he remained until he died.

Bingley's notorious interest in women and Anna Maria's beauty, as well as the problem of her ne'er-do-well husband, caused tongues to wag. One of the most venomous was Lady Bingley's, and she is supposed to have begun the story that the baby baptized on February 5 had not been fathered by John Burgoyne, but by his godfather, Lord Bingley. Fuel was added to the flames of this story by the publication of Bingley's will after his death in 1731.

He left his wife only his house in Westminster, so long as she remained unmarried, plate and earrings for life, and a coach and horses (except those at the Nunnery, Cheshunt). To Anna Maria Burgoyne, he left £400 a year for her separate use "notwithstanding couverture," which was presumably intended to keep her husband's hands off it; the Nunnery, Cheshunt, and "all freehold and copyhold estate in Hertfordshire, furniture and effects, ready money bills, coach horses and other personal estate at the Nunnery"; and also the house at Park Prospect for her life, provided that the lease continued that long. This was a handsome legacy, but Bingley did not forget his godson. He specified that in the event of his daughter Harriott's premature death, and the death of his natural daughter Mary Johnson, the residue of the Bingley estate should go to John Burgoyne, "son of John Burgoyne of Park Prospect," on condition that he take the name Robert Benson.

This must have confirmed Lady Bingley's suspicions, and the story she spread gained credence with the years. On Sep-

[5]

tember 25, 1823, the *Morning Herald* commented: "It is curious that a man of such celebrity as a writer, a senator, and
an officer as the late Lieutenant-General John Burgoyne,
should be found among the number of those of whose youth-
ful days no memorial has been preserved. Neither the time,
place, nor circumstances of his birth are known. Even his
parentage is doubtful. He is said, though upon what authority
does not appear, to have been a natural son of Lord Bingley,
who died at an advanced age in 1774." [2]

The editor of the *Morning Herald* would have taken more
trouble to check his facts if the law of libel in 1823 had been
as stringent as it has since become. It would have soon become
apparent that at least some of the facts as stated were incorrect.
Reference to the register of St. Margaret's, Westminster, would
have established the time and place of birth, as well as John
Burgoyne's parentage. Not much more research would have
shown that the Lord Bingley who died in 1774 was the second
Lord Bingley, husband of Lady Harriott Bingley, for whom
the peerage was revived in 1762. It had been in abeyance since
the death of her father in 1731. These obvious inaccuracies,
as well as the slur on the family name, infuriated a Miss Warburton, whose mother, Lady Elizabeth Warburton, was a
daughter of the eleventh Earl of Derby, and General Burgoyne's sister-in-law. On September 25, she wrote a letter to
Mrs. Caroline Parker, who was herself a natural daughter of
John Burgoyne:

> I must take a folio sheet to vent my rage (not at you but) at
> the *Morning Herald* of today, in which there is an article relat-
> ing to your father that moves my ire, and which I think we might
> contrive to have contradicted in some parts, and cleared up in
> others. . . . You would suppose from what is said that his birth
> was obscure; and it alludes to a report that he was a natural son
> of Lord Bingley, in which there is not one word of truth. . . . It
> happened that when your father was christened, Lord Bingley
> was one of the sponsors; upon which Lady Bingley raised a story
> to poor Mrs Burgoyne's disadvantage, which at a later period, in

some minds gained a footing, in consequence of Lord Bingley bequeathing your father a handsome legacy as his godson. But Mrs Carr (my old friend) assured me there was not the slightest truth in the story. . . .[3]

Miss Warburton's defense of her relative's parentage may not be conclusive, since she conveniently does not mention the handsome legacy bequeathed to Anna Maria Burgoyne by Lord Bingley, but she fills in several gaps and specifically accuses Lady Bingley of starting the rumor. This would also explain how Horace Walpole came to hear of the matter, since he conducted a violent feud with Lady Bingley, whom he particularly disliked.

It would seem, on balance, that John Burgoyne was not the natural son of Lord Bingley, although there is some reason to assume that, either before or after his birth, his mother was Lord Bingley's mistress.

John Burgoyne, former army captain, rake, and gambler, sent his son John at the age of ten to Westminster School, in the shadow of the great abbey. From his mother the boy had inherited attractive features and a handsome appearance; from his father a passion for gambling. Westminster, the most highly political school in England at that time, was to add an interest in politics and the smattering of a classical education, which did not go much deeper than a ready use of Latin tags. It was a school with an ethos all its own. Sir Robert Walpole never visited the school when he was prime minister for fear of the boys' reception and always expressed an aversion to Westminster products. A list of them during the first half of the eighteenth century makes formidable reading: Warren Hastings, Edward Gibbon, Admirals Howe and Keppel, Lords Rockingham, Portland, and Germain, to name but a few. Not all of them were contemporaries of the young Burgoyne, but one who was, and who became his closest friend, was Lord James Strange, only son of the eleventh Earl of Derby, and heir to one of the greatest patrimonies in the realm. Strange was five years older than Burgoyne, but the friendship begun at Westminster endured until his death. It was as a result of this friendship that Burgoyne met Strange's youngest sister, Lady Charlotte Stanley, who was to become his wife.

Burgoyne attended Westminster School as a day boy, at a cost of a guinea a quarter for tuition. This was paid directly to the tutor, and there were, in addition, an entrance fee of a guinea, thirty shillings a year for books, and presents at Christmas for the masters. The curriculum provided a good grounding in Latin and Greek, taught mainly by repetition; there was hardly any note-taking, possibly because paper was so expensive. In the only classroom, even mathematics was taught in Latin. Divinity, the Hebrew classics, and ancient history were also studied, but little or no attention was paid to the learning of English. There were no organized games, though there was a good deal of horseplay. Justice was rough, punishments were Draconian, and life was hard. The boys were mercilessly birched for the slightest transgression of the disciplinary code, and there was also much bullying. A boy had to be able to defend himself against physical assault both in school and outside, where the narrow stinking streets were infested with pickpockets and footpads. Young men-about-town found it amusing to push their more sober fellow-citizens into the sewage channels that ran down every street, and most men carried a stout stick with which to defend themselves. A man who could not, or who would not, defend himself against attack had to put up with a great deal.

Westminster School possessed "a court of honour, to whose unwritten laws every member of the community was amenable, and which to transgress by any act of meanness, that exposed the offender to public contempt, was a degree of punishment, compared to which being sentenced to the rod would have been considered as an acquittal or reprieve." [4] Men were particularly conscious of their personal honor at that time, finding insults where none were intended, and were prepared to fight to the death with pistols or swords to avenge some imagined slight. In later years, John Burgoyne was to talk much about honor—a word often on his lips—and some of the reason may be traced to his schooling at Westminster.

He did not make much impression on his contemporaries, and Westminster School certainly does not count him among its great alumni. He did, however, receive as good an educational grounding as could be found anywhere in England at that time, and the friendship he made with Lord Strange was to stand him in good stead in the future. The house of Stanley, to which Strange was the heir, was one of the greatest in the land, owning vast estates, which at one time included even the Isle of Man. Created earls of Derby in 1485, the Stanleys were one of those families, like the Cecils, the Russells, and the Bentincks, that provided Britain with generation after generation of statesmen and politicians. To possess entree to such an exclusive circle was an immense benefit to any ambitious young man, and without any doubt the most important part played by Westminster School in the life of John Burgoyne was to bring him together with Lord James Strange.

The young Burgoyne went straight from school into the army—at the age of fifteen. The *Gentleman's Magazine* of August, 1737, records a Mr. "Burgoyns" as being appointed sub-brigadier in the 3rd Troop of Horse Guards. Three months later the same publication reported the death of "Mr Burgoin, Sub-Brigadier in the Life Guards . . . who eight weeks ago gave £1,800 for the place." There is some justification for supposing that despite the difference in spelling the reference is to the same person, but the Life Guards and the Horse Guards were quite different regiments. Since British Army records are very inaccurate until 1754, when an annual Army List began to be produced, it is difficult to prove that John Burgoyne began his career in the Horse Guards, but it is reasonably certain that he did so. The fact that he was only fifteen is of no consequence; infants of much more tender years had commissions purchased for them for the same reason that parents buy them savings bonds today.

From the reign of Charles II until the middle of Queen Victoria's reign the British officered their army in a way both complicated and incredible. "Advancement was made easy for those whose way was smoothed by wealth. Commissions were bought and sold like shares on the exchange. . . ."[5] Fortunes were made by brokers who specialized in this form of activity, and advertisements by them appeared frequently in the newspapers.* Apart from the Artillery and the Engineers, all officers' commissions and steps in rank up to lieutenant-colonel had to be purchased, and although there was a regulation price for each rank, this was as likely as not to be exceeded. Both George I and George II were strongly opposed to the system, but they did not succeed in abolishing it. Purchase made money, rather than merit, the criterion for military advancement, and the system is hard to defend. Those who did so argued that at the worst it gave the officer a financial stake in the army, and at the best it ensured that all officers were gentlemen.

Sub-Brigadier John Burgoyne's first commission must have cost his mother a good deal of money—certainly around £1,000—because the Horse Guards was an expensive regiment. He was not required in return to devote much time to military training, other than to learn his drill and how to handle his weapons. The soldiers spent most of their time patrolling the roads and streets of the capital, dealing with highwaymen and footpads, while their officers cut a dash in smart society. They paraded only on ceremonial occasions, leaving the dull routine of military life to their noncommissioned officers. It was a form of existence calculated to appeal to a young man of handsome appearance with a taste for gambling. And it was during his

---

* "TO BE SOLD/AN ENSIGNCY in General Cornwallis's Regiment, now lying at Gibraltar. The lowest price is £360. For further particulars enquire of Mr J. Shave, Bookseller in Ipswich, of whom may be had the greatest variety of Paper-hangings." —*Ipswich Journal*, September 3, 1763.

early years in the Horse Guards that Burgoyne acquired his skill with the cards that was to earn him a somewhat dubious reputation.

In November, 1741, for reasons that remain obscure, Burgoyne sold out of the Horse Guards, and, according to one of his biographers, retired from the army.[6] The pace of London's social life may have been too hot for his purse, or he may have decided to purchase his way into a regiment more likely to see active service than the largely ceremonial Horse Guards. He came from a family with military traditions * and certainly had plenty of ambition. The one thing certain is that he was not long out of the army, because he is recorded as serving as a cornet with the 1st Royal Dragoons at Lessines Camp in Flanders in April, 1744.

It has been claimed that he purchased a cornetcy in the 13th Dragoons before transferring to the "Royals," but this is incorrect; Burgoyne never served in the 13th Dragoons. Instead, under the Duke of Cumberland, he served with the Royals against the French in the War of the Austrian Succession, which brought little glory to any of the contestants. So far as the British were concerned, it was rudely interrupted by the Jacobite Rebellion of 1745, and most of the British regiments were recalled home. Before this happened, Burgoyne was presumably present at the battle of Fontenoy, in which the Royals charged repeatedly, losing 48 men and 104 horses. The British retreated after the battle to Lessines, and by the end of the year the Royals were back in England forming part of the protective screen around London. Burgoyne, now a captain, at the age of twenty-two, had had his first taste of active service.

* Burgoyne's first cousin Major-General Sir John Burgoyne, with whom he is sometimes confused, succeeded to the baronetcy in 1780 and died in 1785 while serving in Madras. He joined the army at an early age (he was born in 1739), and in 1780 received a warrant to raise the 23rd Light Dragoons for service in India. There is a painting of him, by Romney, wearing the uniform of that regiment, in the Holborne Museum at Bath.

Chapter 2

Love, Marriage, and Exile

ONCE the Jacobite Rebellion had been crushed and the army had returned to peacetime duties, John Burgoyne settled down to enjoy himself in London. He acquired a reputation for being as successful in the boudoir as he was at the gaming tables, and there must have been occasions when Anna Maria Burgoyne wondered whether her son was following in his father's footsteps. The fact that he did not do so may in some measure have been due to Lord Strange.

Strange was an attractive and sensible man (even Horace Walpole spoke well of him), and Burgoyne spent much time in his company. The principal Derby estates were in Lancashire, where the family spent part of the year at Knowsley Hall, between Liverpool and Preston, but among their other properties was a mansion in London. The youngest of Lord Derby's six daughters was born in 1728 and was christened Charlotte. She was five years younger than Burgoyne, and when first they met he was a schoolboy and she was still in the nursery. But as the years passed they developed a mutual affection, which in Charlotte's case turned into love.

There is a story that the young couple first met and eloped in 1743, when Burgoyne was supposedly quartered in Preston with his regiment. There is no evidence, however, that Burgoyne was ever stationed in Preston, and his regiment, the Royals, was in Flanders from 1742 to 1745. On his return he lived the life of a typical young man-about-town, pursuing many women, including one of the reigning beauties, Miss Frances Poole, who years later married Lord Palmerston. Burgoyne wrote an ode * for the Palmerston wedding that makes it clear that Frances preceded Charlotte in his affections, and Miss Poole was only ten in 1743, the year in which he is reputed to have eloped with Lady Charlotte.

Burgoyne and Charlotte did elope, to escape the wrath of Lord Derby, but the most probable date for this romantic act is sometime in the spring of 1751. Burgoyne himself implied this when he wrote on three separate occasions in 1775 and 1776 of their twenty-four years of marriage, and there is no reason to question his arithmetic. Charlotte was twenty-three in 1751, Burgoyne twenty-eight, and both were old enough to know their own minds, but a clandestine marriage was necessary because Charlotte's father was bitterly opposed to the match. It is likely that Lord Strange was in on the secret, because he later played an important part in reconciling the Burgoynes with Lord Derby. This did not happen for several years, however, and the angry earl's furious reaction to the elopement was to cut off his youngest daughter with the proverbial shilling.

John and Charlotte could not have expected otherwise, though Lord Derby's action put them in a difficult situation. Charlotte had her jewels and some clothes but little else. Burgoyne probably had nothing but debts and the miserable pay of a captain. There was only one sensible course open to

---

* 'Twas mine to see each opening charm,
New beauties rise—new graces charm;
'Twas mine to feel their power;
Nature and morals just and pure,
For that had made the fruit mature,
Since I adored the flower.

After hard conflict passion cool'd;
Discretion, honour, reason ruled;
O'er the subsiding flame;
Till Charlotte to my vacant breast,
With kindred charms and virtues blest,
A sweet successor came.[1]

them: to realize their only capital, Burgoyne's commission; to pay off their more pressing creditors; and to flee with what was left to the Continent. On October 31, 1751, Burgoyne sold his troop to Lieutenant Robert Hinde, of the 10th Dragoons, and soon thereafter he and Charlotte took ship for France. Their exile had begun.

The Burgoynes possessed one advantage over most other English couples in their situation: Lady Charlotte's lineage. The French aristocracy were the most snobbish in Europe, and the daughter of an English earl could expect many doors to open to her. John Burgoyne could also make a contribution. He was handsome, elegant, and well-mannered, all of which counted in his favor in French society. Moreover, he was an accomplished gambler at a time when gambling was considered to be the "gentleman's disease." It was not long before the Burgoynes were being made welcome in the most exclusive *salons* in Paris, but it is not easy to explain how they fared for money. Though she had her jewels to pawn should the need arise, and he had what remained from the sale of his commission, it is likely that Lord Strange and Burgoyne's mother sent them money. They never appear to have been short of cash.

Soon after their arrival in France the Burgoynes became acquainted with the Comte de Stainville.* Both men had taken part in the War of the Austrian Succession, but in quite different capacities; Stainville was a lieutenant-general, whereas Burgoyne had been only a subaltern. They shared an interest in military and foreign affairs. For most of their stay in France, it has been said, the Burgoynes lived at Chanteloup, Stainville's estate in Touraine. This is improbable, because Stainville acquired Chanteloup only in 1761, by which time he had become a duke; but there is evidence to show that Burgoyne and Stainville were well acquainted. Miss Warburton, in the letter in which she defended Burgoyne's parentage, informed Mrs.

---

* Étienne de Stainville (1719–1785) acquired a great fortune when he married Louise Crozat. Soldier, diplomat, and statesman, he was created duke of Choiseul in 1758.

Parker: "Here commenced the intimacy of your father and my aunt with the Duke and Duchess of Choiseul, which ceased only with their lives. They went together on a tour of pleasure into Italy; and at Rome Ramsey [*sic*] took the portrait of your father, which Mrs Horton afterwards had. . . ." [2]

Miss Warburton muddled her facts a little. Stainville arrived in Rome ahead of the Burgoynes, to take up his appointment as ambassador to the Vatican. The Burgoynes, following after, stayed en route at Aix, where they fell in with Robert Adam, the young Scottish architect, who was also on his way to Rome. Adam dined with the Burgoynes on several occasions at Aix and commented later on the fact that Burgoyne gambled every night. "Nothing but gaming goes forward," he wrote, "in which all the ladies, both young and old are wholly engrossed, playing from 5 to 12 or 1. . . ." [3] The young Scot, still to find fame and fortune, lamented his inability to join in the fun, but, alas, he knew none of the games.

Adam went on to Rome, but the Burgoynes tarried longer in Aix, to allow Charlotte to recover from the birth of a daughter, the Burgoynes' only child, in either October or November of 1754. The baby was christened Charlotte Elizabeth. Her mother was sufficiently recovered "to take a twirl" around Florence in Robert Adam's coach when the Burgoynes caught up with him there in time for the carnival in February, 1755. Adam recorded that Lady Charlotte "did not like foreigners," nor did she enjoy her stay in Italy, if her letter to Lord Palmerston ten years afterward is any guide:

I shall be glad to hear how you like Italian society, though, I think, in general, it is very agreeable to most men. To me it was detestable. The turn of all women in that country is gallantry, and if one is so unfashionable as to have some notions of honour and virtue one has but a bad chance of passing one's time the least agreeably. I have no idea how anybody can live in Italy that does not give themselves wholly to passion. . . . [4]

She was a woman who believed in speaking her mind; she complimented Adam on his clothes, apart from his "red suit," which she disliked. A woman of strong views and firm loyalties, she had proved her love for John Burgoyne by her willingness to elope with him. She remained devoted to him throughout her life, and he likewise to her, but this did not prevent him from enjoying the company of other women. There is, however, no hint of scandal about him in Robert Adam's correspondence from Italy, and Adam's ears were alert for the slightest rumor.

Adam went to Italy to perfect his style and to obtain fresh ideas. He also hoped to acquire the patronage of the many wealthy English who included Italy in their tour of the Continent. One of his future patrons was Burgoyne, who later employed him to decorate his house at 10 Hertford Street in London, and who introduced him to Lord Derby. The earl provided Adam with several commissions.

Allan Ramsay, the artist, was another member of the Burgoynes' circle in Rome. He had gone to Italy to reappraise his approach, and during his three years' stay he perfected the style by which he is best remembered; this was despite Adam's disparaging comment in one of his letters, "As for his painting Cardinals, I never heard anything of it & indeed all he has painted since he left Edin[burgh] to this day are, His wife, Mr Wood, Abbé Grant, Mr Burgoyne & myself, of which the first two only are finish'd, the others half done so that he has properly come to Italy to have the name of it." [5]

Ramsay's portrait "General John Burgoyne as a Young Man" depicts him in classic pose, leaning negligently against a wall with the sunlit ruins of the Colosseum forming the background. The face is strong and intelligent, the features handsome, and the general impression is one of relaxed elegance. The portrait was finished in 1756 and it has been claimed that "the portrait . . . occupies a unique position in Ramsay's *oeuvre* in that it belongs, as no other portrait by him does, to that well-known fashion which has so great an appeal in the second half of the eighteenth century to the English milord making his Grand Tour, whereby he would be represented as standing, or sitting in studious mood, against some piece of Roman antiquity. . . ." [6] The Burgoynes had left Rome for France before the portrait's completion, for Adam records on May 24, 1775, that they would be leaving within a week or two.

Burgoyne's exile enabled him to become fluent in French, which was to stand him in good stead later. The French were then the leading military nation, and a knowledge of French was essential for the study of both military strategy and tactics. Burgoyne still had ambitions as a soldier, despite the premature ending of his army career, and much of his time in France was spent discussing and reading about military matters. It must have seemed unlikely when first he fled from England that he would ever again be able to rejoin the British Army, but his father-in-law's anger cooled as the years went by. With Strange's loyal assistance the young couple became reconciled with Lord Derby, and they returned to England either late in 1755 or early in 1756.

Presumably Lord Derby helped them with the debt problem, and he certainly helped in other ways. Reconciliation with his influential father-in-law meant more to Burgoyne than just family amity and financial security. It was important during the eighteenth century for any ambitious young man to possess "interest"; even the writer, scribbling in his garret, would find his way smoothed had he a wealthy patron. John Burgoyne, now that he could count on Lord Derby's support, could have chosen almost any career, but the army was his first love. Soon after his return from exile he set about organizing his return to arms, though this turned out to be rather more difficult than he had anticipated. He was unwilling to begin again at the bottom of the ladder and was, in any case, too old to be acceptable to any regimental colonel as a cornet or an ensign. King George II had had some success in tightening the regulations for the purchase of commissions, and therefore the secretary-at-war was less willing than formerly to oblige applicants. It is unlikely that Burgoyne would have achieved his object without the Derby "interest" to support him. Eventually he obtained a captaincy in the 11th Dragoons, at the cost of £1,000. His commission was dated June 14, 1756, his exile having cost him nearly five years' seniority.

It was the right time for a man ambitious for military glory to join the army. War had broken out with France, and it was to continue for seven years. The British had an empire by the time peace was signed, but the war brought them little cheer in its early stages. As in most of Britain's foreign conflicts, the beginning of the Seven Years' War was a catalogue of disasters—retreats, lost battles, and surrenders. The army was undermanned, badly trained, and hopelessly mismanaged. New regiments were hastily raised, mostly by the great landowners, who persuaded their tenants to enlist by promising they would not be sent to serve overseas. The government, worried about Gibraltar, which was threatened, drove the protesting recruits aboard transports, battened down the hatches, and shipped them off to the Rock. This arbitrary action dried up the flow of recruits and left the government with no alternative but to call upon the king's Hessian and Hanoverian regiments to defend Britain from the expected French invasion. Such a monstrous decision brought William Pitt from his sickbed to persuade Parliament to rescind it. He was defeated by nearly three to one. The country was in a ferment, fearing the French would descend upon the coasts, while defense depended more on German than on British troops. Leadership was lamentably lacking, and it was not until after the disasters of 1757 that a leader was found. He was William Pitt the Elder, who was to become John Burgoyne's most powerful patron.

Chapter 3

Breaking Windows with Guineas

JOHN BURGOYNE's military enthusiasm soon waned when he discovered the effect on his army career of his five years' exile. It had flattered his ego to discuss strategy with a lieutenant-general of France, but Burgoyne was a civilian at the time; it was quite another matter to be a mere captain when his contemporaries in the 1st Royal Dragoons were majors and lieutenant-colonels. He made his feelings plain in a letter which he sent to his commanding officer, Major Warde, on November 23, 1757:

I cannot help saying that the circumstances of serving *under* so many men I had commanded appeared so disagreeable to me, when my friends proposed my entering a second time into the army, that I should not have suffered any application to be made for me had I not had good assurances that I should not long continue a captain, and had I not flattered myself that my situation would have procured me in that rank in the regiment as many indulgences as could be made consistently with the good of the service. I have great reason to believe that I shall not be disappointed in the first of these expectations, and I return you a thousand thanks for the manner in which you deal with me in regard to the last.[1]

This was Burgoyne at his most unlikable. His letter was both a complaint and a request for special treatment; it also contained the veiled threat that if Major Warde was prepared to do nothing for him, there were others far more influential than Warde who would. Warde would have known, of course, of his new captain's important connections, and he probably wished that he had been spared such an importunate officer. But as luck would have it, he was to be rid of Captain Burgoyne much sooner than he could have expected. The light troop of the 11th Dragoons was required for a special operation, and Warde assigned Burgoyne to command it.

There was a change in British strategy when Pitt replaced Newcastle as the king's chief minister. Pitt was a great believer in carrying the war to the enemy, although those he employed to execute his grand designs were often incompetent, and sometimes even cowardly. In the autumn of 1757, Pitt decreed that there should be joint operations against the French coast, the aim being to cultivate an offensive spirit and to keep the French on the *qui vive*. Charles James Fox contemptuously described these raids as "Breaking Windows with Guineas," but there was more to them than that. Unfortunately, they were badly planned and executed, partly because the commanders were inept, and partly because of jealous rivalry between the Royal Navy and the Army. After a miserable failure in September of 1757, Pitt, nothing daunted, ordered another operation for May in the following year. The objective was Saint-Malo, and the troops for the operation were concentrated on the Isle of Wight. There were thirteen infantry regiments, the light troops of nine dragoon regiments, and a sizable body of artillery.

The commander of the expedition was the third Duke of Marlborough, an amiable nonentity with none of his great ancestor's genius for war. He was, according to Walpole, "an easy, good-natured gallant man . . . without any military experience or the common habits of a man of business, or indeed capacity for either, and no force of character whatever." [2] These were not the qualifications required of a general selected to command one of the most difficult operations of war—an amphibious assault on a defended enemy coast. But, Walpole said, "The Duke of Marlborough commands, and is in reality commanded by Lord George Sackville." [3] Sackville, by contrast, was arrogant rather than amiable and irritable rather than good-natured. As for Sackville's gallantry, it was found to be wanting when tested at the battle of Minden in August, 1759.

Major-General Lord George Sackville (or Germain, as he became known in 1770) was to figure prominently in Burgoyne's later career. He was forty-two in 1757, a younger son of the Duke of Dorset, and a secretive and ambitious man. He had fought at Fontenoy, where he was wounded, and had played a prominent part in hunting down the fugitive Highlanders after the battle of Culloden. He had been at Westminster School, but ahead of Burgoyne, and his career from then onward had been in the army. Wealthy, and with powerful connections, he had bought his way rapidly through the ranks without in any way distinguishing himself as a soldier. In this respect he was unlike another officer taking part in the Saint-Malo expedition whose career, like Burgoyne's, was later to be wrecked by Sackville. This was William Howe, whose reputation for personal bravery was already firmly established. Howe and Sackville disliked each other from the start; Howe's dislike was shared by his brother, Commodore Richard Howe, who commanded the naval side of the expedition. It was hardly a good augury for co-operation between the two services.

The troops were embarked on June 1 and were landed five days later at Cancalle Bay. They marched the eight miles to Saint-Malo preceded by the dragoons, who surprised the French garrison and set fire to the vessels lying in the harbor. The cavalry's success should have been rapidly exploited, but Marlborough, fearing that his retreat would be cut off by the now alert French, hastily withdrew to Cancalle Bay, where he re-embarked his troops. After making futile demonstrations against Cherbourg and Le Havre, the expedition returned home, having achieved precisely nothing, unless it was to intensify the navy's contempt for the army. But John Burgoyne had enjoyed himself with his dragoons, and his appetite for military glory had been increased.

"If they send a patch-box to Lord George Sackville, it will hold all his laurels," commented Walpole on the expedition's return; and also, "It was said that Lord George Sackville was not among the first to court danger." [4] Walpole was probably referring to a lampoon circulating in London that compared Sackville's conduct adversely with that of Brigadier-General John Mostyn, referred to in the lampoon as the "Brig":

> All pale and trembling on the Gallic shore
> His Lordship gave the word, but could no more;
> Too small the corps, too few the numbers were,
> Of such a general to demand the care.
> To some mean chief, some Major or a Brig,
> He left his charge that night, nor cared a fig;
> 'Twixt life and scandal, 'twixt honour and the grave,
> Quickly deciding which was best to save,
> Back to the ships he ploughed the swelling wave.[5]

Sackville had had his fill of amphibious operations and was shrewd enough to realize their complicated nature and the uncertainty of success. He therefore intrigued for a senior appointment with the British troops serving in Germany under Prince Ferdinand of Brunswick. His request was granted, and he joined his former master the Duke of Marlborough, whose failure at Saint-Malo had been rewarded by the command of the largest body of British soldiers serving overseas at that time.

By no means all those who had been involved in the Saint-Malo fiasco regretted their participation. Burgoyne, among others, was anxious to try his hand once more against the French. Nor was Pitt to be deflected from his purpose by the failure of his generals. Another operation was planned, this time against Cherbourg, a more important and more heavily defended port. Surprisingly, Marlborough was offered the command, with the offer of Sackville as his deputy, but he wisely declined the honor. Then, as if determined to wreck the operation before it was launched, the government picked Lieutenant-General Thomas Bligh to command the expedition. Bligh was "an old General routed out of some horse armoury in Ireland," [6] and his main claim to command was longevity in the service. He was seventy-three, crippled with rheumatism, a martyr to gout, and disinclined to anything demanding the slightest physical exertion. Commodore Howe again commanded the naval support.

The expedition sailed from the Isle of Wight on August 1, 1758, and included in it was Burgoyne's troop of the 11th Dragoons. The weather was fair, the fleet arrived off Cherbourg unopposed, and the town was bombarded on August 6. Bligh, encouraged by the absence of any French reaction, then sailed to Saint-Marais Bay, six miles from Cherbourg, and began disembarking his troops. Cherbourg was attacked two days later from the landward side, and the town was surrendered after little resistance. The capitulation was followed by an orgy of looting, raping, and burning, all control being lost for a time. The dragoons, of which there were nine troops, were not involved in the town; instead, they terrorized the surrounding countryside, demanding provisions at saber point and doubtless doing their own share of raping and looting. It was a disgraceful business.

Order was at last restored, the docks were destroyed, the shipping burned, and the troops re-embarked. Two hideous weeks of seasickness followed as the expedition tacked up and down the French coast, the weather being too foul for a landing. When the wind slackened on September 3, the fleet put in to Saint-Lunaire Bay, twelve miles east of Saint-Malo. Bligh's plan seems to have been to storm Saint-Malo from the landward side, but he drowned many of his soldiers by landing them through heavy surf. The troops had barely gained the shore when Howe told Bligh that Saint-Lunaire was too dangerous an anchorage. Thereupon he sailed to Saint-Cast, a few miles westward, leaving Bligh with no alternative but to follow him along the coast. The French were meanwhile massing their troops, and Bligh's advance guard encountered some of them disposed along the far bank of the River Equernon. "It speaks volumes for the incapacity of Bligh and his staff," wrote Sir John Fortescue, "that the passage of the river was actually fixed for six o'clock in the morning, though that was the hour of high water." [7] By the time of the ebb it was late in the afternoon, and the British had to fight their way across through waist-high water. On the following morning, September 10, the British met and drove in the advanced French pickets, but Bligh was then informed that the French were 10,000 or more in strength. He decided to retreat and sent word to Howe that he would re-embark his troops next day at Saint-Cast.

The story of the re-embarkation was of a piece with the rest of the expedition. It was essential that it should be carried out swiftly and secretly, but the British drums beat the "Assembly" at dawn on the eleventh, thus warning the French. Moreover, the troop formation ordered for movement to the embarkation point was single column, which needlessly prolonged the time required to reach the ships' boats. It also gave the French time to establish themselves on the heights overlooking the bay. Burgoyne has provided an excellent account of the events that followed.

Lord Howe, as soon as it was day, had brought the bomb-ketches and frigates as near the shore as possible in a circular bay, about an English mile in extent; the right bounded by a steep hill, with a village on the top; the left by a range of high rocks, which stretched a considerable distance from the sea. On the top of the beach ran a breastwork, cannon-proof, that had been formerly thrown up to oppose the descent; beyond this was a plain of about a quarter of a mile, terminated by a range of hills on the side of which were two works and the village of St Quest [Cast]. By the time the rear brigade of the army had gained the beach, the first column of the enemy appeared on top of the hill. We began embarking as fast as possible, beginning with the Dragoons and the youngest [junior] regiments. The Guards and the Grenadiers of the Line, who were to cover the retreat, were drawn up close to the breastwork, and stretched from one end of the bay to the other. About nine o'clock our bombs began firing, and the first shells that were thrown took effect on top of the hill with some success. When the enemy began to descend, which was about nine o'clock, all the frigates gave him their broadsides, and from this moment it was continual fire until all was over. About ten the enemy opened a battery of cannon on the top of the hill, which did not hurt us very much.

Burgoyne goes on to describe how he prevented the entire embarkation from being overrun by the enemy.

Soon afterwards, C. and myself, who were upon the right of all, perceived a large body pushing with great expedition upon the hill on the right, in the intention to flank us. Of this we immediately informed the Generals, but received no order how to act, and were obliged to determine upon our own authority to wheel the divisions we commanded so as to front the enemy. A short time afterwards I received orders to lead 300 men up the hill, but this was countermanded before I had got forty yards, and the whole battalion was ordered to occupy the rocks upon the left, towards which another column of the enemy was advancing. About twelve the enemy poured down from the village of St Quay [Cast] and from the hill on the right, in the face of all the fire from the frigates and the bomb-ketches. The fire of our Grenadiers did great execution while they were forming, but they advanced with resolution, and the ammunition of our men being wholly expended, they were obliged to quit the breastwork. During the whole of these proceedings the embarkation had been going on with all the expedition possible, but from the moment the breastwork was forced all was confusion. It was the lot of our regiment to get on board before the dismal part of the scene began. Those left behind were part of the 1st Regiment and all the Grenadiers of the army, on the whole amounting to between 1,700 and 1,800 men. Our people ran up to the neck in the sea; some pushed to the rocks on the left, but the French had now gained the opposite side of the breastwork, where they were safe from the fire of the ships, and were able to fire upon our defenceless men.[8]

Saint-Cast was yet another British disaster; it would have been worse had it not been for the conduct of a few officers like John Burgoyne. The French fire was so hot that the sailors were only kept at their oars by Commodore Howe's personal example. General Alexander Drury, commander of the rear guard, was killed, and the British casualties amounted to 750. The administrative arrangements had been chaotic throughout, and Burgoyne recorded that only three wagons were landed as transport for a force of 10,000, although "the sick and wounded alone could not have been contained in a dozen." There had been rioting and looting, but nothing was done to punish the offenders. At the crisis of the re-embarkation, when all was confusion, the expedition's quarter-master-general was to be seen sitting calmly on the beach reading a copy of the latest *Gazette*.

Bligh had to bear the brunt of his government's displeasure. He was stripped of all his appointments. If Burgoyne learned anything from such a mismanaged affair, it was probably the same as had the Duke of Wellington, whose first campaign as a young officer was equally disastrous. When asked many years later what he had learned, the duke replied: "Why—I learnt what I ought not to do, and that is always something." Burgoyne's own conduct had been favorably noticed; he had been cool under fire and dashing in action. Reports reaching London spoke well of him and were seized upon by his friends for dissemination in the right quarters. His reward was transfer from a not particularly distinguished regiment of dragoons to one of the *corps d'élite* of the army, the 2nd, or Coldstream, Regiment of Foot Guards, which would certainly bring the gallant captain to the notice of the Court. An additional advantage was that every officer in the household troops held double rank. For example, every lieutenant ranked as a captain in the army, and every captain as a lieutenant-colonel. Every captain was on the general list for promotion to lieutenant-colonel in strict order of the date of his commission as a captain. He could also exchange with a lieutenant-colonel of a line regiment should the occasion offer.

Chapter 4

A Colonel of Light Dragoons

In 1759, Pitt's *annus mirabilis*, John Burgoyne was thirty-six and Lady Charlotte thirty-one. It was a year when it was wonderful to be alive and British. Guadeloupe, in the West Indies, had been captured; the French had been defeated at Minden, in Germany, and at sea at Quiberon Bay. But the greatest victory of all had been won in Canada, where Wolfe had defeated Montcalm outside Quebec, and where William Howe had led the stormers up the Heights of Abraham. More than 200,000 men wore the red coat of the British Army, and the Royal Navy was at its peak in numbers of ships and efficiency. "I am sure that I can save the country, and that no one else can," Pitt had said, and he had made good his boast.

It is remarkable that he had been able to do so considering the feebleness of the instruments at his disposal when first he came to power. The navy had been neglected and was short of ships and men; the army was in an even worse state. When the imminent threat of a French invasion caused the secretary-at-war to examine the country's defenses, it was discovered that the forty-six guns defending Pendennis Castle were served by a master-gunner over ninety, with but a single assistant. In Saint Kitts, the 38th Regiment could muster only forty per cent of its strength as fit for service, and they lacked hats, shoes, cartridge boxes, and swords. Gibraltar's guns lacked both range and carriages. Discipline was bad and morale was low. Officers did more or less as they pleased, and their soldiers were not slow to copy them.

The Duke of Cumberland headed the army, and, in spite of civilian obstruction, did much to improve matters. The "Butcher of Culloden" was a capable military administrator who was "as angry at an officer's infringing the minutest precept of the military rubric as at his deserting his post, and was as intent on establishing the form of spatterdashes and cockades as on taking a town or securing an advantageous situation." [1] He was a martinet who brought to heel the more recalcitrant officers, and he did much to advance the careers of the more meritorious ones, like James Wolfe. What Cumberland had started, Pitt continued. His influence in the army was not direct, but it was certainly far-reaching. He believed in picking good officers, leaving them to get on with the job, and supporting them loyally if they ran into trouble. He adamantly refused to interfere with the running of the army and took great care to protect it from meddlesome interference by members of Parliament, many of whom were serving officers with their own axes to grind. Although the influence of Cumberland and Pitt did not long outlast them, the immediate effect on the army was wholly good.

King George II, the last British monarch to take the field in person,* had a keen interest in the army. Though approaching the end of his life in 1759, he strongly supported a proposal that the British Army should follow the example of other European armies and add light cavalry regiments to the military establishment. Two regiments were authorized to be formed, one by the government and the other by any suitable applicant willing to undergo the trouble and expense of raising a regiment. They were to be called "Light Dragoons" and numbered 15th and 16th. A distinguished cavalry officer,

* At the battle of Dettingen in 1743.

Major-General George Eliott, was selected to raise the 15th, but it was not easy to find someone to raise the second regiment. There was a financial risk attached, and many an English nobleman had had his fingers burned by allowing his feeling of patriotism to outweigh his care for his purse. The regulations were so obscure, the chicanery of War Office clerks so notorious, that men, however rich and powerful, thought twice before volunteering for such an undertaking.

No such considerations deterred John Burgoyne from coming forward to offer his services. He was eager for military distinction, ambitious for promotion, and bored with the dull routine of London duties. Moreover, he was professionally interested in the employment of light cavalry. With the support of his powerful Derby connections, he applied for the appointment of commandant of the 16th Light Dragoons. There were those who doubted the wisdom of entrusting such an undertaking to an officer so junior and relatively inexperienced. Lord Barrington, the secretary-at-war, was opposed to the choice of Burgoyne, but his arguments failed to convince the king. On August 4, 1759, Lieutenant-Colonel John Burgoyne received the king's commission to raise the regiment, and this was to prove to be the watershed of his military career.

He was directed to raise it in the area of Northampton and posted off immediately to that town, where he made himself known to the local gentry by a series of banquets. A new regiment usually had little difficulty in obtaining officers, because it provided the opportunity to purchase steps in rank; soldiers were another matter. The army was unpopular, even in times as stirring as 1759, and colonels were provided with little help from the government in drumming up recruits. Some were forced to offer bounties to induce men to enlist; others did not scruple to impress men into the ranks. Burgoyne chose another method. He placarded Northampton and the surrounding villages with posters emphasizing the glory and the glamour of life in a light cavalry regiment.

You will be mounted on the finest horses in the world, with superb clothing and the richest accoutrements; your pay and privileges are equal to two guineas a week; you are everywhere respected; your society is courted; you are admired by the fair, which, together with the chance of getting switched to a buxom widow, or of brushing a rich heiress, renders the situation truly enviable and desirable. Young men out of employment or uncomfortable, "There is a tide in the affairs of men, which, taken at the flood, leads on to fortune." Nick in instantly and enlist.[2]

It worked. Men flocked in to join, and within a few months the 16th Light Dragoons had not only been raised but also had so many applicants that a further two troops were authorized. Much of this success was attributable to Burgoyne's own efforts, since he personally supervised the recruiting arrangements instead of leaving the business to recruiting sergeants. He also used all his influence to obtain the officers he wanted. Within six months of the regiment's formation there were twenty-one officers on the regimental list; they included three honorables and three baronets, as well as Horace Walpole's cousin, who was to turn out to be a failure. By February, 1760, the regiment was considered to be sufficiently fit to be sent to Scotland for a short stay, from where it returned to Hertfordshire to prepare for foreign service.

Burgoyne became totally absorbed in his new regiment, abandoning his former gambling haunts and the social round in London. He drew up a code of instructions for his officers which was years ahead of its time.[3] Some of the instructions derived from his observations of the French Army during his exile, but mostly they expressed his own views of military life. He reminded his officers that they were "as much particularized by their youth and inexperience as by their rank and fortune." It was not his intention "to offer anything in the following sheets as the orders of a commanding officer, but as the sentiments of a friend, partly borrowed and partly formed upon observation and practice." He did not favor anything so radical as commissions from the ranks—"corporal and sergeant should be considered as the most signal honour that a man from the ranks should attain"—but this was no reason why there should not be friendly relations between officers and soldiers.

Consider the Prussian and French armies, he told his officers. In the former, men were trained "like spaniels, with the stick"; the French relied upon "the point of honour in the place of severity." The Prussians were probably the best disciplined and the French the worst in Europe. In Burgoyne's opinion "a just medium between the two extremes [was] the surest means to bring English soldiers to perfection," and he was convinced that "an Englishman will not bear beating so well as the foreigners in question." These were radical views at a time when the British Army relied almost entirely upon the lash for enforcing discipline. Burgoyne believed that equally good discipline could be maintained if the soldiers were treated as "thinking beings." His officers should obtain an "insight into the character of each particular man," and there was to be no swearing at the soldiers in the 16th Light Dragoons. He even advocated a little familiarity between the ranks: "There are occasions, such as during stable or fatigue duty, when officers may slacken the reins so far as to talk with their soldiers; * nay, even a joke may be used, not only without harm but to good purpose, for condescensions well applied are an encouragement to the well disposed, and at the same time a tacit reproof to others." There is good evidence to show that Burgoyne practiced what he preached in this respect, and it is therefore not surprising that he evoked much more personal loyalty from his soldiers than most other commanding officers of his time. It also goes a long way toward explaining the nickname bestowed on him by his soldiers—"Gentleman Johnny." †

Relations between officers were as important as those be-

* This provides a good illustration of the more usual officer-man relationship in the British Army at that time.

† George Bernard Shaw uses "Gentlemanly Johnny" in *The Devil's Disciple*.

tween officers and soldiers. Gentlemen were touchy about their honor and were quick to draw swords to defend it. Dueling between officers damaged a regiment's reputation and reflected adversely upon its commanding officer's. Officers should therefore strictly observe proper subordination to rank when on duty, but at all other times there should be complete social equality. This particular precept has been strictly observed in Burgoyne's regiment during the 200 years of its existence, sometimes to the bewilderment, sometimes to the disapproval, of officers accustomed to more formal relationships.

Officers should also devote time to the study of their profession. "A short time given to reading each day, if the books are well chosen and the subject properly digested, will furnish a great deal of instruction." They should learn French, because the best military treatises were written in that language, and study mathematics, essential for their profession. "An officer ought to write English with swiftness and accuracy." "If a man has a taste for drawing, it will add a very pleasing and useful qualification; and I would recommend him to practise taking views from an eminence, and to measure distance with his eye. This would be a talent peculiarly adapted to the light dragoon service."

Stable management should not be neglected. English gentlemen rode from infancy and usually managed their horses well,* but few of them troubled with the stable side of the business; that was better left to grooms and ostlers. This was not good enough for an officer in Burgoyne's regiment. "I hope I shall not appear finical," he told them, "if I recommend to officers sometimes to accoutre and bridle a horse themselves until they are thoroughly acquainted with the use of each strap and buckle." Lest they should feel that such chores were beneath their dignity, he inquired "whether a reproof from a field

---

* Apart from, perhaps, Cornet Duperron, whom Burgoyne was forced to dismiss from the 16th Light Dragoons because he was such "an incorrigible bad horseman."

officer, or, what is perhaps worse, a criticism from a judicious spectator, would not give them more pain." They should also learn something about farriery and interest themselves in the feeding of their horses.

These instructions, drafted in Burgoyne's own hand, were so far in advance of their time that there was to be nothing to compare with them in the British Army until Sir John Moore set about training his troops at Shorncliffe Camp at the beginning of the nineteenth century. Moore is rightly considered to be one of the British Army's greatest reformers, but many of his ideas on man management had been put into practice in the 16th Light Dragoons many years before. It can certainly be claimed for John Burgoyne that he, too, was a military reformer.

His success in raising the 16th Light Dragoons so efficiently and quickly was not to be denied, but unfortunately some of the methods he used were bound to arouse criticism. He was, in modern terms, a "go-getter," with an acute awareness of the main chance, seizing every opportunity to advertise John Burgoyne and his regiment of light dragoons. Sooner or later this was certain to bring him into conflict with the War Office, which regarded itself as the constitutional protector of military tradition. No one felt this more strongly than the secretary-at-war, who was prejudiced from the outset against brash young officers who believed that their use of influence could drive a coach and horses through well-established military procedures. Burgoyne, early in their relationship, was so unfortunate as to fall foul of the formidable and conservative Lord Barrington. The cause of the quarrel was Burgoyne's request for the provision of a chaplain and musicians. Denied when he applied through official channels, Burgoyne then wrote direct to Barrington, emphasizing, as he had done previously to Major Warde, the fact that he had influential connections. Barrington's reply, written on October 27, 1759, is worth quoting at length, partly because it demonstrates the personal fashion in which the British Army was administered in those days, and partly because it shows that Burgoyne, although junior in rank, was a man to be reckoned with.

There is so little regard for the public to be found in mankind that I must neither be surprised or offended that you do not give me the least credit for any thing of that sort in my transactions with you. . . . I will state the reasons, which have obliged me to adhere to your own establishment, as given into the War Office by yourself in your own hand-writing; and to reject your subsequent demands of a chaplain, hautboys, and additional levy money for each horse. I think these are the only articles in which we differ. As you claim a chaplain and hautboys, because they are allowed in regiments of British cavalry, and particularly in Elliot's [15th Light Dragoons], I must state what you seem to have entirely forgotten, viz: the essential difference between a regiment of dragoons raised by the public in the usual way, and one which you proposed to raise yourself, and for yourself, on certain conditions, every one of which I have made good.

Major-General Elliot, an officer of long uninterrupted service, after commanding a corps of cavalry with great reputation for many years . . . obtained the command of a new regiment of dragoons. . . . Mr Burgoyne, one of the youngest Lieutenant-Colonels in the service, after a series of favours of which the army does not furnish a precedent, and to which with all his amiable and valuable qualities as a man he had not the least claim as a soldier, obtains at his own solicitation and desire permission to raise a corps of dragoons on certain conditions. . . . Has Lieutenant-Colonel Burgoyne a right to every *douceur* which General Elliot may expect? or can he demand more than his bargain? Is a chaplain more necessary to six troops than to four? Are hautboys more necessary to each troop when there are six than when there are four in a regiment? You know that a chaplain never attends in England, and that hautboys never exist in any corps of dragoons but are considered as so much additional pay to the Colonel. A regiment of dragoons, [even] without the *douceur*, is a very great thing for any man who was a captain a year and a half ago. . . .

You think it hard that any new public economy should begin

where you are concerned: where can it begin so properly as in a regiment commanded by a man who was a captain a year and a half ago? I come next to your demand of £15 instead of £13 levy money for horses. . . . Your bargain was positive to undertake the business at £13 a horse. If they have cost you more, must the public make it good? If they had cost you less, would you have accounted to the public for that saving? I believe you are £400 out of pocket by this article. . . . Let your officers make it good among them. . . . If you cannot prevail on them to pay this trifle divided among so many, would it be very unreasonable that a commandant of dragoons, who was a captain a year and a half ago, should pay that small fine for what brings him in from a thousand to fifteen hundred pounds per annum?

If an officer, by the length or merit of his services, has a claim for preferment, he should have it *gratis*; but when a young gentleman, who has no such pretension, is put over the head of older and better soldiers, he should *buy* it. In short the public should be paid in services or in savings. . . . There is one part of your letter which renders it impossible for me to relax in these articles, if I were ever so much inclined. You threaten me with the House of Commons, in case I am what you call partial against you. . . . This is not the way to influence me. . . . After saying so many truths which perhaps you will dislike, I shall finish with some that will be more agreeable; though I might be excused from any thing of that kind in reply to the least courtly letter that was ever written by an officer to a Secretary at War.

Your regiment has been raised with surprising expedition. I am told and believe it will be a good one. You are a man of sense, honour and merit. I am persuaded you will deserve hereafter, in some other corps, emoluments which I cannot at present allow you in this. When that time comes you shall have my best assistance, however you may speak or write about me. [4]

Chapter 5

Burgoyne's Light Horse

BURGOYNE was little disturbed by Barrington's tirade; he was far too busy preparing the 16th Light Dragoons for service overseas. But he got his chaplain, the Reverend John Smith, and even the hautboys arrived in due course. It was astonishing what influence could do. With all set fair for death or glory, it was a blow when the orders for active service were canceled. Instead of the full regiment, only two troops of the 16th Light Dragoons were ordered to embark at Spithead in March, 1761. They formed part of an expedition intended to capture Belle-Île, off Saint-Nazaire, but Burgoyne was too senior to take command of only two troops. He nominated Captain Sir William Williams to command the detachment, and volunteered to accompany the expedition in some other capacity. This led to protests from Lady Charlotte, which Burgoyne attempted to soothe by some flowery verse.

> The power that formed my Charlotte's heart,
> Thus tender, thus sincere,
> Shall bless each wish that love can start,
> Or absence foster there.
> Safe in the shadow of that Power,
> I'll tread the hostile ground;
> Though fiery deaths in tempest shower,
> And thousands fall around.[1]

In fact, Burgoyne's poetic fancies were not all that far from reality. Belle-Île turned out to be a bloody affair, the British losing more than 700 men. Among them was Captain Williams, who lost his way on a reconnaissance and was killed by a French sentry. "He had some papers and two of Drummond's notes of £100 each in his pocket," [2] which were returned the next day by the French. The *Annual Register* noted that Williams was "the third gentleman of fashion whom in this war the love of enterprise had brought to an honourable death in these expeditions to the coast of France." William Cole, on the other hand, wrote that Williams was "wild and extravagant and not having an estate equal to the greatness of his condition, it is said that he went on the expedition to Belle Île with a formal design not to return home again." [3]

In Williams' death Burgoyne lost both a friend and a patron. He had assisted in the formation of the 16th Light Dragoons and had been active in promoting Burgoyne's parliamentary ambitions. But there was little time to grieve, because Burgoyne's advice was being constantly sought by Major-General Studholme Hodgson, the commander of the Belle-Île expedition. His position as a volunteer did not permit Burgoyne to distinguish himself as conspicuously as did William Howe, who commanded a brigade, but he did well enough to draw attention to himself in London. Burgoyne was avid for military fame and pushed shamelessly for opportunities to acquire it; if Belle-Île had not satisfied all his expectations, it had nevertheless been better than maneuvering his regiment around Wimbledon Common.

He had hardly returned home when Spain entered the war on the side of France, largely due to the diplomacy of Burgoyne's old friend the Duke of Choiseul. Spain had no desire to attack Britain but had scores to settle with Britain's oldest ally, Portugal. With a large Spanish army concentrated on the frontier, King Joseph I, of Portugal, appealed for British assistance. The prospect of yet another front won little support in the House of Commons, but Pitt was at his most persuasive. "I do not mean that we should carry the King of Portugal," he said, "but only that we should set him on his legs and put a sword into his hand." [4] A few advisers and some financial aid were all that was intended, and since war by proxy has appealed to politicians throughout history, Pitt won his point. He was soon to be disillusioned by Lord Tyrawley, whom he sent to Lisbon in the dual capacity of ambassador and commander-in-chief. "Ten thousand disciplined troops might take their choice whether they would march upon Lisbon or Madrid," [5] reported James O'Hara, Viscount Tyrawley, who then proceeded to quarrel with Pombal, King Joseph's chief minister.

Tyrawley was replaced by the Count of Lippe-Buckeburg, a German soldier of fortune and possibly the foremost artillerist of his age. He was also reputed to be a bastard son of George I. He was a capable soldier, and his first action after arriving in Lisbon was to demand reinforcements. Appalled by the state of the Portuguese Army, he warned Pitt that more would be required than just a few advisers. In the event, the British dispatched 7,000 men under Lord Loudon to Portugal in May and June of 1762. The 16th Light Dragoons formed part of the expeditionary force, being joined later by the two troops from Belle-Île. On this occasion Burgoyne took his wife campaigning with him and established her in a house in Lisbon before joining his regiment at Abrantes. Since the 16th Light Dragoons were the only cavalry in the British contingent, Burgoyne was the senior cavalry officer present and was therefore made a local brigadier-general. Two Portuguese regiments were brigaded with the 16th Light Dragoons.

Lippe must have been relieved when the British arrived. The Portuguese Army was in a sorry state and was chronically underpaid. Officers served as waiters in their spare time, and their wives worked as laundrywomen. The standard of marksmanship of the artillery was so poor that Lippe offered a prize to the first gunner who succeeded in hitting the flagpole outside the commander-in-chief's tent; to add zest to the occasion he chose to start the competition on the day when he was giving a banquet for the Portuguese generals. There was nothing basically wrong with the Portuguese soldier, but corruption and nepotism had destroyed his morale. Fortunately, the Spanish Army was in little better shape, and Lippe was provided with the time he needed to reorganize and deploy his troops. The Spanish advance on Lisbon ground to a halt at Almeida in August. The troops then began to concentrate at the frontier fortress of Valencia de Alcántara. Lippe determined to disrupt this concentration, and he selected Burgoyne's brigade for the task.

Valencia de Alcántara was strongly garrisoned, but Burgoyne could only muster about 3,000 men, mostly Portuguese, apart from the 400 sabers of the 16th Light Dragoons. Speed and surprise were therefore essential for success, and in his orders Burgoyne emphasized the need for boldness in action. The 16th led the advance, crossing the Tagus at midnight on August 23. They pressed on through the night for forty-five miles, to Castel da Vida. The cavalry so outpaced the infantry that the dragoons were forced to dismount from time to time and give up their saddles to the British and Portuguese grenadiers who made up the rest of the advance guard. The remainder of the brigade struggled on through the dust miles behind the cavalry, and it soon became apparent to Burgoyne that it would take several days for them to catch up with the advance guard. By then all hope of surprise would be lost. He therefore decided to make a sudden dash at Valencia de Alcántara, using only the advance guard for the purpose.

His plan was to approach the town under cover of darkness, block the escape routes, and attack simultaneously from three sides. The assault was timed to go in at dawn on the twenty-sixth, but it took longer than planned for the troops to be deployed.

My guides had greatly deceived me with regard to the distance [he later wrote]. Contrary to my expectation I found the day coming on fast, and the sun would be risen before the foot could possibly reach the town. I thought it therefore expedient to lay aside entirely my first disposition, and carry forward the light dragoons, who by a brisk gallop might possibly still effect a surprise, or at worst stop the avenues [of escape]. I accordingly went with that corps at three-quarters speed without molestation, and the advanced guard, consisting of forty men . . . finding the entrance clear pushed into the town sword in hand. The guards in the square were all killed or made prisoners, and the ends of the streets were possessed with very little resistance.[6]

The plan was a daring one, and in Burgoyne's opinion it was a proper use of light cavalry. The gamble succeeded, and that was all that mattered. "By the time the body of the regiment was formed in the square, a few desperate parties attempted an attack, but all perished or were taken. The only firing that remained was in single shots from windows, which did not continue long after the grenadiers came up. . . . I detached the dragoons into the country to pick up all who had escaped. . . ." Among the prisoners was Don Miguel de Irunibeni, the Spanish general commanding the garrison. Burgoyne also took prisoner most of the Regiment of Seville, together with its colors, and there was a large haul of arms. Count Lippe was delighted when he heard the news, and he issued a eulogistic order of the day. The Marquis de Pombal sent Burgoyne his felicitations, and King Joseph I added a diamond ring, "*comme un petit souvenir de l'action de Valence, que vous avez si bravement conduite. . . .*"[7] It had been a gallant affair.

The Spaniards, however, soon recovered from their temporary setback. They began once more to advance into Portugal, and Burgoyne's brigade covered Lippe's withdrawal. By early October the Spaniards had captured Villa Velha, on the Tagus, and were threatening Lisbon. Desperately needing time to prepare defenses, Lippe called again on Burgoyne, to impose a check on the enemy. This time the odds were so great that it might well amount to sacrificing the brigade, but Lippe assured Burgoyne that he would have no need to fear for his reputation if he was overwhelmed. Lippe would accept full responsibility.

Burgoyne decided to repeat his tactics of Valencia de Alcántara and attack the enemy where least expected. Villa Velha was to be the objective, and a picked body of troops would endeavor to surprise the enemy. The commander was to be Lieutenant-Colonel Charles Lee, serving as a volunteer with the British contingent in Portugal, and Burgoyne gave him a troop of the 16th Light Dragoons, some Portuguese cavalry, and about 250 infantry, most of them British. The raiding force was to ford the Tagus at night, make its way through the hills to Villa Velha, and attack the enemy at dawn. Villa Velha was a small village, dominated by two ruined Moorish castles, and was strongly held.

Lee was a very strange man. He had joined the British Army at the age of fourteen, and had been with the 44th Regiment under Braddock when that general was disastrously defeated near Fort Duquesne in North America. The 44th lost so many men that it had to be recruited locally, and it became almost an all-American unit. Lee fought with it at Louisburg, Ticonderoga, and Montreal. He admired American soldiers and enjoyed the American way of life. He lived for a time with an Iroquois woman, from whom he acquired some knowledge of the language, and returned from America with the reputation of being an excellent soldier. Unfortunately, he was a difficult colleague, moody, sarcastic, and lacking in polish. He came from a good family, but dressed and behaved like a cartman. Lee could not have been more unlike Burgoyne in appearance and manners, but the two men developed a high regard for each other's military abilities. Burgoyne certainly chose well when he selected Lee to lead the raid on Villa Velha.

The Tagus was crossed during the night of October 5, and the objective was reached before daylight. Surprise was complete; most of the Spanish soldiers were cut down in their tents before the alarm could be raised. Some enemy cavalry, attempting to make a stand, were charged by the dragoons. Six cannon were captured, and the Spanish magazines were blown up. Lee suffered few casualties, and brought his wounded back safely. It had been little more than a raid, but it had been well planned and, above all, well led. "So brilliant a stroke speaks for itself," wrote Lippe to the British prime minister. It certainly served to check the Spanish advance for several weeks. By then the winter rains had begun, and the tracks were almost impassable. It was no time for campaigning, so the Spaniards withdrew. Burgoyne enjoyed a pleasant winter with Charlotte in Lisbon. By the time a new campaigning season could start, the Seven Years' War was over. Burgoyne and his 16th Light Dragoons returned home, well satisfied with their exploits.

The campaign in Portugal has been dismissed as being "so trifling and of so short duration that [it is] unworthy of detailed mention." [8] This may be true, but military reputations are often made in minor campaigns. John Burgoyne had become something of a popular hero because the conduct of his 16th Light Dragoons, now commonly referred to as "Burgoyne's Light Horse," had aroused the public imagination. This was perhaps as well, because he had again clashed with the secretary-at-war, on this occasion Charles Townshend. The quarrel had been about promotion, Burgoyne claiming before he went to Portugal that he was entitled to promotion to colonel. This had been refused on the grounds that he was too junior, but Burgoyne had argued that the only reason for refusing him promotion was that he lacked "interest." He had reminded Townshend that he, too, had powerful friends, such as Lord Strange, who was about to become a minister, and regretted that his lack of success was calculated to cause Strange more pain than it would himself.

Townshend tried to wriggle out of the difficulty, protesting

his admiration for Strange and his support for Burgoyne. But
the truth was that the king carefully controlled all senior promotions, even though he had at this date been less than two
years on the throne, and Townshend, however much he may
have wished to help Burgoyne, could not do so without the
king's agreement. Burgoyne had therefore to leave for Portugal
in his rank of lieutenant-colonel, but his conduct there provided the opportunity to make amends for the earlier refusal.
Bute, the prime minister, wrote personally to Burgoyne on
November 2, 1762, informing him of his promotion.

I hope you will excuse my not answering your letter sooner.
I thought the most agreeable manner of doing it was by procuring you the rank you wished, which His Majesty very readily
consented to, out of regard to Lord Strange, and your own
merit; permit me, sir, to congratulate you on the very brilliant
manner in which you have conducted yourself ever since your
arrival in Portugal; and on the success that has attended it. Count
Lippe has indeed done you ample justice; and his Excellency's
letter was of no small use in procuring what I so much wished.
I am happy to observe, sir, how your own gallant behaviour has
in the eyes of the army justified the mark of favour His Majesty
has conferred.[9]

This was a remarkable piece of condescension from a prime
minister to a mere colonel of light dragoons, and is ample evidence of the truth of Burgoyne's boast that he could call upon
the assistance of powerful friends. He had risen from captain
to colonel in less than four years. A further mark of royal
favor was bestowed on him on March 18, 1763, when he was
gazetted colonel of the 16th Light Dragoons. This was an
appointment he might expect to hold for life, and it carried
with it many financial advantages. A regiment was its colonel's
property to some extent, and was worth at least £3,000 a year.
For a man who spent as lavishly as John Burgoyne, the
colonelcy of his regiment was far more valuable than a pension.

Chapter 6

A Clubbable Man

ON HIS RETURN from Portugal, Burgoyne must have believed that his military future was assured. There had, moreover, been an improvement in his finances, not only because of his colonelcy, but also because Lady Charlotte had inherited some money. He could now afford to turn his attention to another important matter—his membership in the House of Commons. He had been elected a member for Midhurst, in Sussex, in 1761, through the assistance of his friend and brother officer Sir William Williams, who owned several pocket boroughs, but the campaigns in Belle Île and Portugal had intervened before he could take his seat. When the time came for him to do so in 1763, he was received in Westminster as a hero and was given the thanks of the House for his gallant conduct in Portugal.

The regulation that prevents British officers from being at the same time members of Parliament dates from as recently as 1927. There used to be nothing unusual in a combination of parliamentary and military duties, doubtless to the detriment of one or the other, and it was "an undoubted and lamentable fact that colonelcies of regiments were freely given as rewards for political service." [1] Edmund Burke, complaining in 1774 of the "huge increase of the military establishment," [2] warned that twenty new regiments meant twenty new colonels with seats in Parliament. For some strange reason, the British, much as they disliked the concept of a standing army, apparently did not object to officers involving themselves in politics, and a seat in Parliament was a valuable acquisition for an officer with ambition. Burgoyne certainly considered this to be so and was as anxious to make his mark in the House of Commons as on the battlefield.

He was often on his feet, speaking on a variety of subjects and usually at great length. Indeed, one member, bored to distraction by his oratory, muttered loudly that Burgoyne seemed to him to belong "rather to the heavy than the light horse." Walpole thought him "a pompous man whose speeches were studied and yet not striking," and considered that he "had more reading than parts"; [3] this may have been an allusion to Burgoyne's irritating habit of sprinkling his speeches with Latin quotations. But Walpole was not predisposed toward Burgoyne, possibly because his cousin in Burgoyne's regiment, who appears to have been both idle and inefficient, had fallen foul of his colonel and was in the process of being removed from the 16th Light Dragoons. Walpole apart, it is clear that Burgoyne, although he became a popular, and in some ways an influential, member of the House of Commons, was always considered to be unnecessarily verbose, and on occasions unduly pompous.

A parliamentary career had its pitfalls for a military man. Since the Court controlled higher promotions in the army, those military members who did not support the king's friends in government had only themselves to blame if the plum appointments went elsewhere. Burgoyne, at the outset of his parliamentary career, stood well with the king, despite the fact that his political affiliations were basically Whig. George III, like all the Hanoverians, had a passion for military ceremonial and was never happier than when reviewing his troops. The 15th and 16th Light Dragoons were particular favorites in this respect, and hardly a year passed without a review, usually on Wimbledon Common. In May, 1766, the king commanded that the two regiments be known as the King's and the Queen's Light Dragoons, respectively, bringing Burgoyne into even closer contact with the Court.

Burgoyne's early years in Parliament coincided with one of those events that arouse political feelings to the highest pitch and convulse the House of Commons. It concerned John Wilkes, the notoriously radical member for West Middlesex. Wilkes, whose libertarian views were anathema to the Court, had been arrested under a general warrant in April, 1763, and the Whig party rallied to his support. When Sir George Saville and Sir William Meredith offered a motion in his support in February, 1764, declaring general warrants illegal, Burgoyne was faced with either following his conscience and voting for the motion, thereby losing favor at Court, or abstaining from a crucial vote. His own views on Wilkes are not known, but Charlotte made hers plain in a letter to Lord Palmerston in November, 1763.

You have perfectly cleared yourself with me in regard to having an intimacy with, or friendship for, Mr W[ilkes]. Indeed, I was persuaded before I had it under your hand, that you could have no connection with so vile a man. . . . I hate the very name of Wilkes, and will not let him employ more of my time at present, nor will I ever mention him unless to say he has been made an example of which I hope soon to hear of. . . .[4]

It is not clear from the above whether Charlotte's dislike of Wilkes was founded on his political opinions or on his reputation as a libertine and gambler, but Burgoyne could not have been unaffected by his wife's views. He attempted to dodge the issue in a letter to the prime minister. "I take the liberty to communicate to you that I have considered the question of tomorrow's debate [on the legality of general warrants]," he wrote to Grenville, "& am very earnest in my wishes to avoid the decision of it at this juncture. I am also very desirous . . . to speak my sentiments in the House, &

I humbly offer myself to second any motion for postponing the question." [5] But Grenville, who had already refused Burgoyne the chief secretaryship of Ireland, for which he had lobbied, saw through his game and made it clear that this was a time when the king's friends must stand up to be counted. Burgoyne understood the message, sacrificed principle for prudence, and voted against the motion. It may not have added to his political reputation, but at least he had avoided the fate of General Henry Conway, who was dismissed from all his appointments for voting with the Ayes.

Most of Burgoyne's correspondence has disappeared, but many of his wife's letters still remain, and they show her to have been both an observant and a witty woman. One of her chief correspondents was the second Viscount Palmerston, and in 1763, when he was making the Grand Tour of the Continent, he was kept up to date with the social and political scene in London by Lady Charlotte's regular bulletins. She wrote in one of them:

Her Majesty is so perfectly recovered that our enquiries after her health ceased last Sunday. St James's has been a most admirable coffee house, where everything resorted that was in town and as the hours from seven to nine suited me extremely well I used to go almost every night, and am really sorry it is at an end. What little amour was going forward one might see there, and indeed Lady B[olin]g[bro]ke and Lord G[ower] afford the town no little conversation; that connection was begun before you left England, and it goes on finely. I cannot feel sorry for Lord B[olin]g[bro]ke, he deserves to be ornamented, and I am only sorry it is not Lord C[o]v[entr]y that does him so great a favour. . . . The Duchess of Ancaster has finished herself the most complete figure of affectation and absurdity I ever saw. She can now scarcely walk without shaking off her head,* and as to her rouge, it is as deep coloured and as thick laid on as e'er a Duchess in France. . . .

* Absurdly large wigs were then the fashion among the *haut ton*.

Is it not strange that we must be so very fond of French fash-
ions that we must even imbibe their vices. I verily believe, in a
very little time, we shall be as remarkable for gallantry as they
are. . . . Though I love the French very well and like to live
among them I own I am quite angry at our nobility spending so
much money in the kingdom. We shall very soon enrich them
and are absolutely furnishing them with arms against ourselves,
for depend upon it as soon as ever they get up a little again, they
will find a pretence for more quarrels and I expect war again in
two or three years, which touches me so nearly that I own I hate
to hear of so many English people being in France. I dread the
consequences. . . .[6]

She was to prove an accurate prophetess and clearly did
not approve of her husband's martial ardor. Nor does she
seem to have shared his outspoken admiration for William
Pitt. In writing to Palmerston, she said:

Very anxious everybody here is to know who is to succeed
Egremont [joint secretary of state]. His sudden death, I suppose,
would not atall surprise you, for he was the sort of man to expect
it from. . . . Mr Pitt I hear has behaved very insolently to His
Majesty and has determined not to accept the post of Secretary
of State, without every man that voted for peace was turned out.
. . . I am sorry to find he holds himself up in that manner. Sure
he has no pretensions. . . .[7]

Charlotte Burgoyne's correspondence also shows her to have
been a woman of character, loyal to her husband, family, and
friends, and possessed of a nice sense of humor, which only
occasionally becomes malicious. She had been deeply in love
with her handsome cavalry subaltern when she braved the
wrath of her father to run away with him, and she remained
in love with him ever afterward. In his way, he remained in
love with her, but it was an age when men and women of
fashion thought little of sharing their beds. Charlotte clearly
did not approve of this, but if there be any truth in rumor,
her husband was not so strait-laced. There was never any
scandal apparently—or Horace Walpole would have reported

it—and the one cloud on the Burgoynes' marriage would seem to have been the death of their only child.

This occurred on March 7, 1764, when Charlotte Elizabeth Burgoyne was in her tenth year. There is nothing to show the cause of death, but the child had been well enough in the previous January to accompany her mother to a special performance at the Opera to celebrate the marriage of the king's sister, Augusta, with the hereditary prince of Brunswick. The Burial Book of Westminster Abbey shows that Charlotte Elizabeth was buried in the North Cloister and that the funeral expenses amounted to £12. 17s. 2d.

It was not until the following October that Charlotte wrote again to Palmerston, telling him of the Duke of Devonshire's death—"a great loss to the world in general and particularly to his party." By the end of that year Palmerston had returned home, his Grand Tour completed, and was a frequent guest at the Burgoynes', then living in Chesterfield Street. When out of London, he was kept in touch by Charlotte's regular letters.

The little political news I have heard since I came to town is chiefly in the newspapers [she wrote in July, 1765], except this with regard to Mr Pitt, which you may depend on being true. . . . That he is in no way connected with the present administration, nor does he intend it and that it is very displeasing to him to have hints thrown out everywhere as if he gave his advice. They further add that the Duke of G[rafton] * went one day to make him a visit and produced some papers which he said he was come to consult him upon and show him the plan on which he purposed acting. That Mr Pitt's answer was that he was always very happy to see his Grace, and had much too great a regard for him to shut his doors to him, but he must excuse him if he shut his lips. . . .⁸

She was certainly well informed, writing on the following day: "Mr B[urgoyne] has just heard an express has been sent

* The Duke of Grafton (1735–1811) headed the administration from 1768 to 1770.

to you to offer you something. From what you wrote, I suppose I may guess at your answer, I wish however that that or anything else might bring you to Town. . . ." [9] It might be inferred from her obvious eagerness to see Palmerston that there was more to Charlotte's letter-writing than merely the interchange of social and political gossip, but nothing can be found to substantiate this suspicion. Palmerston was on equally friendly terms with her husband, and he was, in any case, busily engaged in wooing the beautiful Frances Poole, who had been the object of Burgoyne's attentions many years previously. Where Burgoyne had failed, Palmerston succeeded, and the two were married on October 7, 1765.

The Burgoynes returned to the Continent in the following year. The plan was to visit Prussia, Austria, and France and to study their respective military organizations. Burgoyne ensured that he was provided with the right introductions. Among those he approached for them was the great William Pitt. The "Great Commoner" was all affability, and willingly complied. "Accept, dear sir," he wrote, "many warm wishes for your health, pleasure, and satisfaction in the tour you are going to make; wherein you will, agreeably to yourself, and usefully to your country, add to the rich stock of military treasures already your own, fresh matter of present contemplation and of future action. . . ." [10]

The tour took several months. On his return Burgoyne recorded his impressions in a paper, *Observations and Reflections upon the Present Military State of Prussia, Austria and France*, of which a copy was sent to Pitt. This was gratefully acknowledged in a letter dated December 14, 1766, in which Pitt assured Burgoyne that "I count the minutes while indispensable business deprives me of the pleasure of seeing you." [11] This may be attributed to mere politeness, but equally it can be taken to show that Burgoyne's reputation, both as a soldier and as a man, stood high in the opinion of the greatest English statesman of his age.

The *Observations* began with a report on the Prussian Army, which Burgoyne had visited in the field. He considered the Prussians' success to be as much due to their training, which turned every man into an obedient automaton, as to the military genius of Frederick the Great, and Prince Henry, his brother. Drill had been simplified until the stupidest man could grasp it, and the discipline was Draconian. "In an army thus composed," wrote Burgoyne, "it is wisdom and sound policy to sink and degrade all intellectual faculties, and to reduce the man as nearly as possible to machinery. . . . The first principle of the Prussian army is subordination, and the first maxim 'not to reason, but to obey.' " [12]

Although Frederick's system had made his infantry the most formidable in Europe, with his artillery not far behind, Burgoyne believed it depended entirely on the king and his brother. "Prussian officers, by length of time and experience, only become more expert artificers to prepare and sharpen a fine weapon, diligent and proud to put it in the hands of their master in the most perfect order, awkward and ignorant if compelled to employ it themselves." As for their master, Frederick, "his designs are not within the fathom of common conjecture, nor is his character to be attempted upon common observation. He is jealous of prying eyes in all his employments. If he means to manoeuvre ten thousand men in private, he shuts up the country as effectually as his palace; at *Sans-Souci* * his retirement is so strict that sometimes for a month together he is seen only by his *valet de chambre*." [13]

Surprisingly, the Austrians, despite their poor showing against Frederick the Great, impressed Burgoyne. The officers and soldiers were good, but "the troops have been ill paid, ill appointed, and ill disciplined; the military plans have been unwisely concerted in the cabinet, and the commands injudiciously conferred in the field." It was, however, expected that the new emperor, Joseph II, would introduce reforms. Bur-

* Frederick the Great's palace at Potsdam.

goyne tried to visit the Arsenal in Vienna but was refused permission. He did get a glimpse of some guns called "cannon for cavalry"; "it is pretended that they will cross ditches, or pass the most uneven ground without turning." [14] These guns were presumably the genesis of horse artillery, which was soon to be introduced into most European armies.

Many of the best Austrian generals were of Irish extraction, debarred, as Roman Catholics, from serving in the British Army. Burgoyne felt this to be a waste of splendid material, observing "that every Roman Catholic service in Europe abounds with this race, full of the same spirit and the same passions; and should means be found in future times of exigency to open a door without danger to the state to receive these emigrants into British pay . . . those who have conversed with them abroad will not hesitate to foretell that they will flock to your standard, and bring home a stock of military acquirements highly desirable to any power." [15] He was undoubtedly right, but fifty years were to pass before Roman Catholic subjects of the king were to be considered suitable recipients of his commission.

The French Army was in the process of reorganization. The minister of war was Burgoyne's old friend the Duke of Choiseul; he is described as being "a man of lively talents and sanguine temper—vigilant, secret, ambitious, enterprising, with activity often resembling precipitancy, and perseverance that may sometimes be termed obstinacy." Burgoyne shared some of his friend's characteristics, but he was critical of some of the ideas Choiseul was introducing. He agreed that the French Army's failure in the late war had been due to "a want of subordination and discipline," but he did not consider a slavish copy of King Frederick's methods would produce the right answer. The older officers doubted whether the system suited the French temperament, and "among common soldiers it is received with repugnance that causes an incredible desertion." The French cavalrymen, on the other hand, were undoubtedly the best in Europe, although the same could not be said of their horses. "It is with exultation," wrote Burgoyne, "that a Briton observes that our breed of horses is not only superior to any the French have, but to any they can have, unless they draw from our stock." [16]

His final conclusion was that Europe was again preparing for war. A reopening of hostilities between Austria and Prussia could not long be delayed. Therefore "the wisdom, the vigilance, and the spirit of his Majesty's counsels [should] continue unshaken [in order] that, while the ambitious or restless States of Europe become partially formidable, England may be found universally formidable." [17]

Chapter 7

Honourable and Gallant Gentleman

THE FIRST RUMBLINGS of the storm that was about to burst in the North American colonies began to be heard some eighteen months before Burgoyne set out on his Continental tour. George Grenville succeeded Lord Bute as prime minister in April, 1763, and found the country plunged in debt as a result of the Seven Years' War. He instituted stringent economies and at the same time looked for ways of increasing revenue. Among the latter was a stamp tax in North America, expressly intended to help defray the cost of the British garrison stationed there to protect the colonies. There was an immediate outcry, both in the House of Commons and in the colonial legislatures; hitherto taxes levied across the Atlantic had been raised indirectly, but the stamp tax was the first example of direct taxation. The idea of "no taxation without representation" spread, and the Whigs came out strongly as champions of the colonists.

From outraged protests in the American assemblies, and hot words exchanged across the floor of the House of Commons, the situation rapidly deteriorated until oratory in the legislatures was accompanied by rioting in the streets of Boston. What had begun as a grievance was transformed into a struggle for liberty, in which men on both sides of the Atlantic took sides and resolved never to capitulate. As a Whig, as an admirer of William Pitt, the colonists' champion, and as a boon companion of Charles James Fox, Pitt's ablest lieutenant in the House of Commons, Burgoyne should have expressed support for the colonists; but Grenville's measures had the king's support, and it thus behooved an ambitious soldier to act cautiously. He left for his tour without committing himself to either side.

When Grenville resigned, the Whigs came in under Rockingham, who was regarded as merely acting in place of Pitt, whose health was rapidly deteriorating. The new administration repealed the Stamp Act by a handsome majority, but not before passing a bill declaring the right of Parliament to tax the colonies. Only Pitt opposed the latter, but Burgoyne, somewhat surprisingly, voted against the repeal of the Stamp Act. Whether this was owing to conviction or to self-interest can be only a matter of conjecture.

Burgoyne was a member of Parliament for more than twenty years, and was a regular attender in the House of Commons, but his record was not particularly distinguished, if Sir Nathaniel Wraxall is an unprejudiced witness. "General Burgoyne," he wrote, "would not deserve any place in this list, if respect were had only to his parliamentary talents." [1] He implies that Burgoyne owed whatever standing he enjoyed in the House to his friendship with Fox, and he certainly was indebted to Fox for the fact that he kept his seat after the contested election in Preston in 1768. This was *cause célèbre* at the time and did little to enhance Burgoyne's reputation as a parliamentarian. Even though political corruption and gerrymandering were both then accepted and tolerated, the Preston election stank in the nostrils of most decent men.

Preston, in North Lancashire, had always enjoyed a reputation for independence and truculence. It contained many Roman Catholics and had made Prince Charles Edward welcome when he came there with his Highlanders during the

1745 rebellion. The country seat of the earls of Derby was close to Preston, and successive earls regarded it as their right to nominate the town's representatives in Parliament. This had never been accepted by the burgesses, and it was not again in the general election of 1768, when Lord Derby proposed the names of Sir Henry Hoghton and Colonel John Burgoyne for Preston's two seats. The town, always more High Tory than Whig, exploded with fury. The Corporation of Preston had long claimed an exclusive franchise within their borough, although a committee of the House of Commons had previously decided that the mayor and burgesses did not possess this exclusive right. Parliament had declared instead that "all the inhabitants" of Preston were entitled to vote, thereby conferring universal suffrage on Preston long before this applied elsewhere. The Corporation contested this ruling, and in 1768, as formerly, they determined to assert their rights by nominating their own candidates—on this occasion Sir Peter Leicester and Sir Frank Standish—"and be damned to the Earl of Derby!"

Burgoyne little knew what lay in store for him when he gave up his comfortable pocket borough of Midhurst and set off north to contest the Preston election. Contested elections were always occasions for lawlessness and were usually accompanied by intimidation and violence. Preston was no exception. Hooligans roamed the streets, fighting drunk from the liquor provided by the contestants; shops were looted, citizens molested, and the candidates' meetings interrupted by shouting and fighting. "The contest here is attended with imminent danger," wrote one of the citizens; "I have just escaped with many friends." The four candidates had to be protected by bodyguards, and Burgoyne went to the poll with a loaded pistol in each hand; he required them as protection, he claimed, although his opponents insisted that he carried them in order to intimidate people into voting for him.

The excitement and the danger appealed to the dramatic side of Burgoyne's nature. He wore his regimentals and went about with a military guard, partly for protection, but also to enhance his importance. He and Hoghton were elected by a handsome majority, but the Corporation persuaded the returning officers to declare that all votes cast other than by "freemen" of the town did not count. This brought in the Corporation's two candidates, and Lord Derby immediately appealed to the House of Commons. The House could only uphold its previous ruling on Preston's universal franchise, which gave the seats to Burgoyne and Hoghton, but the Corporation was not finished yet. It indicted Burgoyne and his supporters for incitement to violence.

The trial, which took place in the Court of the King's Bench before Mr. Justice Joseph Yates in April, 1768, engendered considerable interest. It did not proceed at all along the lines expected by Burgoyne and his friends. The proceedings in the House of Commons, which had ended in Burgoyne's favor, had been largely influenced by Fox's arguments in the select committee appointed to consider the Preston election result, but Yates was not open to such pressure. He found Burgoyne guilty of intimidation and fined him £1,000, a very large sum in those days. Some of his supporters were fined £100, and three sergeants and drummers went to prison, "but no fine, being poor." Many people considered that Burgoyne should have gone with them.

Political opponents were not slow to make capital out of Burgoyne's discomfiture, and not least the anonymous "Junius," whose vicious polemics contained just enough truth to cause people to wonder whether there was not more to them than might immediately appear. Junius involved Burgoyne's name in an attack on the Duke of Grafton, whose administration had replaced Rockingham's. On December 12, 1769, Junius, in his letter number 34, accused Grafton of "selling a patent place" for £3,500. The money was paid to Burgoyne, with Grafton's connivance, "to reward him . . . for the decency of his deportment at Preston or to reimburse him, perhaps, for the fine of £1,000 which, for that very deportment, the Court of King's Bench thought proper to set upon him. It is not often that the Chief Justice and the Prime Minister are so strangely at variance in their opinions of men and things. . . ."

Junius was not content to leave it at that; he went on to attack Burgoyne personally.

Perhaps the noble Colonel himself will relieve you [Grafton]. No man is more tender of his reputation. He is not only nice but perfectly sore in everything that touches on his honour. If any man, for example, were to accuse him of taking his stand at a gaming table, and watching with the soberest attention for a fair opportunity of engaging a drunken young nobleman at piquet, he would undoubtedly consider it as an infamous aspersion upon his character, and resent it like a man of honour. Acquitting him therefore of drawing a regular and splendid subsistence from any unworthy practices, either in his own house or elsewhere, let me ask your grace for what military merits you have been pleased to reward him with a military government? He had a regiment of Dragoons, which one would imagine was at least an equivalent for any services he ever performed. Besides he is but a young officer, considering his preferment, and, except in his activity at Preston, not very conspicuous in his profession. But it seems the sale of civil employment was not sufficient, and military governments which were intended for the support of worn out veterans * must be thrown into the scale to defray the extensive bribery of a contested election. Are these the steps you take to secure to your sovereign the attachment of his army. . . ? [2]

Junius, secure in his anonymity, seldom pulled his punches, but on this occasion he hit harder than on most. The prime minister was accused of jobbery; and, even worse, that elegant man-about-town Colonel Burgoyne was being termed a card-sharper. The venomous jibes would scarcely have worried

* At a period when pensions, if granted, were so small as to be barely worthwhile, it was the custom to reward good service in the army and navy, and even political service, by the award of sinecure appointments such as the governorships of out-of-date fortresses. Burgoyne, so far as is known, never visited Fort William.

the third Duke of Grafton, an idle and pleasure-loving nobleman whose chief passion was horse-racing, but they hit Burgoyne hard indeed, and the mud slung in 1769 has stuck ever
since. They may have contained a grain of truth, but nothing
has been found to substantiate the charge of cardsharping.
The governorship of Fort William, in Scotland, was, however,
another matter. It was worth £300 a year, and Burgoyne was
given it early in 1769. It was undoubtedly a political "job,"
Grafton having recommended Burgoyne's "fair pretensions"
to "an early mark of royal favour, on account of an expensive
attack he had made in a part of the country the least affected
to Government [*i.e.*, Preston], and which has cost him a sum
which I dare hardly name." ³

Burgoyne was understandably furious at the outcome of
the trial, but there was little he could do about it. Some time
later, in Parliament, Solicitor-General Wedderburn, engaged
in argument with Burgoyne over the conduct of Lord Clive
in Bengal, slyly advised him to try a little self-reformation
before he tried reforming others. This touched Burgoyne on
the raw, and he leaped to his feet, clutching his sword. "I am
now personally marked," he thundered, "and I rejoice in the
opportunity [to reply]. I have long groaned in secret for an
occasion of venting myself against those scandalous persons;
and if that wretch Junius is lurking here in any corner of this
house, I now tell him to his face he is an assassin, a liar, and a
coward!" ⁴ But in vain; Junius' anonymity remains secure to
this day, and Burgoyne was never able to clear his honor.
Wraxall even referred to the charges in his *Historical Memoirs*,
saying that "these aspersions, which never received any public
answer, did not prevent his [Burgoyne] occupying a distinguished place in Fox's regard. . . ." ⁵

It is hard to believe, too, that they did anything to reduce
Burgoyne's passion for gambling. Brooks's in St. James's, the
favorite haunt of the Whigs, saw much of John Burgoyne,
and there he spent many a night gambling, drinking, and talking politics with Charles James Fox and his friends. The Bur-

goynes were then living at 10 Hertford Street,* a comfortable stroll from Brooks's, and were clearly not short of money, since they employed Robert Adam, then at the height of his fame, to improve and redecorate the house from cellars to attics. Although Charlotte's health was failing, perhaps as a result of her daughter's death, her husband was out much in society. He was a regular attender at the Green Room of the Drury Lane Theatre, as well as "at the dinners of the Thursday Night Club, at the Star and Garter, at every place of amusement where the gay, the witty, and the well-bred of London were gathered together." [6] His interests were many, and numerous his friends, among them David Garrick and Sir Joshua Reynolds. Reynolds painted Burgoyne in 1767, in dramatic pose, wearing the regimentals of the 16th Light Dragoons and clasping his saber. He looks a fine figure of a man with, alas, just the beginnings of a paunch.

It is hard to know whether Burgoyne's ambitions at this time had been switched from the army to politics. There was no war in which a soldier could distinguish himself, and the management of the 16th Light Dragoons could safely be left to the commanding officer and the regimental agent. The House of Commons rather than the barracks was his place of work. He still tried to avoid identifying himself too openly with the Opposition, though, lest this should damage his chances of promotion. He did fall foul of the prime minister, Lord North, when he voted against the government in the dispute with Spain over the Falkland Islands. The incident was a minor one, which North sought to play down, but his opponents clamored for war. North got his way, which the king considered very creditable, but he also thought "the seeing Colonel Burgoyne's name on the side of the minority appears so extraordinary that I almost imagine it was a mis-

---

* It is in Mayfair, just around the corner from the London Hilton. Burgoyne died there. Richard Brinsley Sheridan bought the lease three years after Burgoyne's death.

take." [7] Burgoyne doubtless took the hint, if indeed it was passed on, because he came out strongly in favor of the Royal Marriage Bill, a measure dear to George III's heart. When North duly informed him of Burgoyne's support, the monarch remarked that it was just as well, since otherwise he would have been obliged to find another governor for Fort William. It seems likely that North passed this on, too.

Burgoyne lost a powerful patron in 1771 when Lord Strange died, at the early age of fifty-four. He had been greatly respected, and Walpole considered him to be the best speaker in the House of Commons. Fortunately for Burgoyne, Strange's death did not lessen his ties with the Derby family, since Strange's son, Lord Stanley, was a devoted admirer of Burgoyne and became one of his closest friends. This was as well, because Charlotte was fast becoming an invalid, and it seemed increasingly likely that Burgoyne would outlive her. He would have need of the powerful Derby interest in the struggles for preferment that lay ahead.

He was consolidating his position in the House of Commons, where he made the affairs of the Honourable East India Company his particular concern. The company was in deep financial water, partly as a result of maladministration, and partly on account of the venality of its servants, who went out to India paupers and returned as rich men, or "nabobs," as they were scornfully described by those who regarded them as parvenus. When Parliament could no longer ignore either the company's plight or the accusations being leveled against the company by men like Burgoyne, it set up a select committee of enquiry, on April 13, 1772. Burgoyne was the chairman, and among the members were Fox, Germain, and Clive. Sir George Saville declined to serve, declaring his opposition to everything connected with India, and not least to "many of the importations, tea especially," as "being destructive of the healths of the people of England." [8]

It early became clear in the committee's deliberations that the main subject of inquiry would be the conduct of Lord

Clive, the greatest and the richest of all the "nabobs." Burgoyne made a dead set against Clive, accusing him of all manner of crimes, including the abuse of the power with which he had been entrusted. This was not calculated to improve Burgoyne's standing at Court, where Clive's services in India were highly regarded; and there were others who found something repugnant in this hounding of a distinguished public servant who had done great things, if on occasion some others of a less praiseworthy nature. Moreover, Burgoyne's pompous oratory alienated some of the select committee members, whereas Clive's defense, part indignant, part humorous, part contemptuous, attracted to him that sense of fair play that has for so long been a feature of the House of Commons. "I have been examined by the Select Committee more like a sheep-stealer than a member of this House," he complained, and since no one had been more assiduous in hunting him down than the deputy chairman of the East India Company, he had a proposal to make: "As the Heads upon Temple-Bar have tumbled down, and as there is no probability of their being replaced, I would propose that my head, by way of pre-eminence, be put upon the middle pole; and his Majesty having granted me these honours, it is proper they should be supported; what think you then of my having the late Chairman and Deputy on each side?" [9] The House laughed for a full ten minutes after this sally.

Clive's speech was a great one, and, apart from the defense of his own enormous fortune, a convincing one. Most honest men knew that without Clive there could no longer have been an East India Company. Finally, with an eye on the select committee's chairman, whose use of the word "honor" was well known to the House, Clive came to the peroration of his speech. "Before I sit down," he said, "I have but one request to make to the House, that when they come to decide upon my honour, they will not forget their own." [10] The debate that followed lasted far into the night. Clive was indeed censured for abusing his powers, but this was mild when compared with the original motion proposed by Burgoyne; and after it was carried, Wedderburn rose in his place to move "That Robert Lord Clive did, at the same time, render great and meritorious services to this country," and with that no man could disagree. It was passed unanimously, there was no impeachment, and the select committee was dissolved. It had brought Burgoyne some passing fame, which was not appreciated by the king, and it had to some extent vindicated Clive. But the East India Company had been warned to set its house in order, and that, presumably, was what the business was all about.

Burgoyne does not appear to have borne any personal animus against Clive, but he could have chosen his language more carefully. Clive felt deeply humiliated, and Wedderburn's motion proved little solace. A moody and neurotic man, his constitution damaged by his years in India, he was a slave to opium, and probably mentally ill. Eighteen months after the proceedings in the House of Commons, he was found dead in his handsome Berkeley Square mansion, and the gossip was that he had died by his own hand. When in due course it was Burgoyne's turn to be placed on the rack in the House of Commons, he was to prove of tougher metal.

Chapter 8

A Triumvirate of Reputation

In May, 1772, John Burgoyne was promoted to major-general. He was a few months past his forty-ninth birthday, and therefore somewhat older for his rank than some of his contemporaries. But considering his exile he had not done too badly, and it looked as if the time was approaching when Britain was going to need her admirals and generals again. For the question of the hour was the political situation in New England, where matters were getting worse month by month. A grievance had been allowed to fester until it had become an open wound, and hot and wild words across the Atlantic were being matched by equally extravagant language at home. Boston, in Massachusetts, was the center of dissension, and the government reluctantly decided to reinforce the garrison. But when the troops were eventually dispatched, they were too few in number to restore the situation but too many to be accommodated in the existing barracks. Civilian accommodation had to be requisitioned, exacerbating the tensions still further, and adding to the gloom of Lieutenant-General Thomas Gage, the commander-in-chief. He had asked for 20,000 men. Lord Dartmouth, the secretary of state for the colonies, had replied that such a figure was impossible without putting the army onto a war establishment, and he doubted whether such a serious step was justified.

The House of Commons was sharply divided between those who believed that the colonists should be brought to heel by force if necessary, and those who championed their cause, of whom the leading exponent was William Pitt, Earl of Chatham. Burgoyne, as usual, tried to steer a middle course, which could not have been easy for him with his patron, Pitt, so loud in the colonists' support. Moreover, Charles James Fox was equally active on the colonists' side; when it was decided to reinforce the Boston garrison, Fox declared "he could not consent to the bloody consequences of so silly a contest, about so silly an object, conducted in the silliest manner that history or observation had ever furnished an instance of, and from which we were likely to derive nothing but poverty, disgrace, defeat, and ruin." [1] Burgoyne's views may have been the same as his friend's but he did not dare to be so outspoken, for the leading "hawk" in London was George III himself.

Burgoyne attempted to make his position clear when he opposed the motion for the repeal of the duty on tea on April 19, 1774. "I look upon America as our child," he said, "which we have already spoilt by too much indulgence. It is said that if you remove the duty, you will relieve all the grievances in America: but I apprehend that it is the right of taxation which they dispute, and not the tax. It is the independence of that country upon the legislation of this for which they contend." [2] It was not far from the truth, and whether by accident or design it happened to coincide with the views of the king and his ministers. However, Burgoyne did add his hope that the colonists would be "convinced by persuasion, and not by the sword"; although, if this hope turned out to be illusory, he would certainly support the use of force.

It is not uncommon for ministers, when they cannot bring themselves to provide adequate reinforcements, to choose instead to send more generals. Early in 1775 the king and Lord North hit on this solution as a way out of their difficulties. They had lost confidence in Gage, a mediocre character whose advice ran counter to their own opinions, and they therefore decided to bolster Gage by sending him three generals, who although junior to him in rank were far superior to him in caliber. They failed, however, to take into account the fact that Gage commanded too few soldiers to provide worthwhile employment for three such senior officers; and that he had in any case restricted any possible sphere for their activities by withdrawing his outlying garrisons into Boston the previous October. Gage was now a general under siege, but this fact does not seem to have penetrated to London, where, in February, Major-Generals William Howe, Henry Clinton, and John Burgoyne were assigned to service under Gage in Boston. They were ordered to embark as soon as possible.

They did not welcome the order. Howe had long connections with North America, having fought under Wolfe; his eldest brother, who had been killed at Ticonderoga, was a hero figure, commemorated by a statue erected by the Bostonians. Clinton, too, had connections with America, having been reared on Manhattan Island when his father was governor of New York. Burgoyne had both political and domestic objections to service in North America: his Whig friends condemned the mere idea of war; his wife was a very sick woman. Civil war, for such it would be, has seldom appealed to the professional soldier. Many of Burgoyne's contemporaries resolutely refused to fight against the colonists. Admiral Keppel declared he could not go; "Although professional employment is the dearest object of my life I cannot draw the sword in such a cause." [3] Lord Effingham resigned his commission rather than accompany his regiment to North America. Howe, Clinton, and Burgoyne had undoubtedly the same feelings, but in the end either a sense of duty or ambition prevailed. It would be charitable to assume that it was the former. They agreed to go.

Burgoyne's unaccustomed silence during the frequent debates on North America was explained on February 27, when he told the House that he had abstained from speaking once he had received his orders. He declared that he had not sought the appointment.

> I will take leave to say on the part of my colleagues, it was sought by none of us, but it was accepted with that submission which is due from servants of the crown, and with that sense of gratitude to his Majesty which the importance of the trust required. I feel an additional call of gratitude on my own part, for the honour my name receives in being classed with those distinguished officers to whom I have alluded. I will trespass no longer upon the time of the House; with the sentiments I have expressed I take leave of all American questions, with these sentiments I shall take leave of my country; I shall endeavour to maintain them in arguments if admitted to any intercourse in America. I shall enforce them to the best of my power if called upon to act in the line of my profession. . . .[4]

The government's decision had a mixed reception on both sides of the Atlantic. "Howe was one of those brave and silent brothers, and was reckoned sensible, tho' so silent that nobody knew whether he was or not," wrote Walpole. "Burgoyne had offered himself to this service; he was a vain, very ambitious man, with a half understanding that was worse than none. Clinton had not that fault, for he had no sense at all." [5] The gibe was cheap and ill-founded. Howe had more battle experience than any other officer in the army, and although indolent by nature, he was interested in his profession. Clinton had distinguished himself on the staff in Germany, and Burgoyne had no cause to be ashamed of his record. That he did not seek the appointment would seem to be firmly established. As for the story that Lord North, when he heard of the appointments, wondered out loud, "I don't know what the Americans will think of them, but I know they make me tremble," [6] it cannot stand up to investigation. It was, after all, North who headed the ministry that made the appointments.

Burgoyne's term for his colleagues and himself was a "Triumvirate of Reputation." An American view was provided by Arthur Lee, confidential agent in London for Massachusetts, who wrote to John Dickinson in Philadelphia on April 25, 1775:

> The first [Howe] is an honorable man, respected in the Army, & trained in the late American war. He goes reluctantly. The second [Clinton] is a man of very fair character. He served all the late war in Germany. His abilities, tho not brilliant, are yet respectable. General Burgoyne is of a very different character. A man of dark designs, deep dissimulations, desperate fortunes, & abandoned of principles. He is closely connected with the Bedford Party in this country. No Banditti were ever bent on blood & spoil, & on more desperate principles than this Bedford Party. . . . They are as ready to sacrifice this country as America to the arbitrary views of a tory, tyrannical court. Among the worst of their party is Gl. Burgoyne. You will see his character well drawn in the Letters of Junius. . . . To finish his character of dissimulation tho an abandoned & notorious gambler & engaged in every scene abhorrent from true religion & virtue, he has always effected to be exemplary in religious worship. . . . You will judge however from what I have said, that he is a dangerous character; & therefore be on your guard. If he is solicitous to commune with you, it will be to betray you.[7]

Lee's portrait is unflattering, relying mainly on gossip, but it emphasizes the unhappy effect of the Preston election on Burgoyne's reputation. He may have aligned himself temporarily with the group around the Duke of Bedford, who, in their search for places, rallied to the support of Lord North in Parliament, but Burgoyne was a Whig at heart and could not have expected to retain Fox's friendship if he reneged to the Tories; or, for that matter, his membership of Brooks's, which he clearly retained. Lee's alarmist letter aroused no concern in America, where a lampoon was soon circulating.

> Behold the *Cerberus* * the Atlantic plough,
> Her precious cargo, Burgoyne, Clinton, Howe,
> Bow, wow, wow! [8]

* The three generals had sailed from Portsmouth on April 18, 1775, on board the warship H.M.S. *Cerberus*.

Fortunately, Burgoyne wrote a detailed account of how he came to be selected for the Boston appointment, and it is clear from this that he did *not* lobby for an American assignment in the first place.[9] It is equally apparent, however, that once his selection had been confirmed, he made every effort to secure a more attractive post in America than the one in Boston. If North America it had to be, he had no wish to play second fiddle to Gage, Howe, Clinton, or anyone else, and it is worth studying his account in some detail for the interesting slant it throws on his character and his capacity for intrigue. It also shows that although Burgoyne obviously valued his talents highly, and in some respects justly when compared with his fellow-generals', this opinion was by no means shared by all the ministers, and possibly least of all by Lord North.

The first hint that he was being considered for an appointment in North America came in January, 1775, from Charles Jenkinson, a junior member of the administration, close to the king. He told Burgoyne that he wished Burgoyne was serving in North America; and Burgoyne, realizing he was being sounded, replied, "Every soldier must go where he is ordered." He did enter the caveat that "in the present state of things, *that* service would not be desirable to any man." In a subsequent conversation with Jenkinson, Burgoyne discovered that he was the man who had first put Burgoyne's name forward, though not in a subordinate capacity. Jenkinson had thought to replace Gage by Burgoyne as commander-in-chief.

On February 2 Burgoyne was summoned by Barrington, the secretary-at-war, and was given the king's command. As he wrote in a memorandum:

The manner of breaking the business appeared to me at the time rather singular. As soon as I was seated, his lordship began upon the American debate the preceding day in the House. "We sat late; it was very tiresome," and a few other common chit-chat observations of that sort; till at once, with a sort of abruptness . . . he "hoped and did not doubt that everything in America would mend, when I and the two other Generals for whom he was to make out letters of service, should arrive there." The perfect indifference of his countenance, the tone of voice, and whole manner of opening to me one of the most important . . . most unexpected . . . and *most disagreeable events of my life,* suited the idea I had ever entertained of his lordship's feelings.

Barrington's indifference may have been due to his dislike of Burgoyne, or to his disapproval of the government's policies in North America, but it obviously came as a shock to his listener. Burgoyne inquired whether he had been chosen by the king, or was he merely being asked to volunteer? In the latter case there were several personal reasons that would make him decline the appointment. If, however, the king had singled out "the last [most junior] and humblest of his list of Generals," Burgoyne would "forego every consideration of private interest or happiness." Barrington was complimentary—"it is a language in which he is always ready"—and made it clear that the choice was the king's alone. Indeed, the king "had expressed himself decisively in regard to Generals Howe, Clinton, and myself [Burgoyne], and he [Barrington] was persuaded the whole kingdom would applaud his decision." Barrington had already seen Howe and Clinton and was pleased to discover that "we exactly agreed in principles of duty, and almost in the expression of them."

Burgoyne could still have declined, on grounds of conscience, but to have done so would have wrecked his career. The fact that Howe and Clinton had already accepted may also have influenced him. There was nothing for it but to make the best of things, and perhaps the most distasteful part of the whole business would be breaking the news to the ailing Charlotte. "To separate for a length of time, perhaps for ever, from the tenderest, the faithfullest, the most amiable companion and friend that ever man was blessed with—a wife, in whom during four and twenty years I never could find a momentary act of blame," would be hard indeed. It would be harder still if he never returned from North America.

The narrow circumstances, the distressed state in which she might find herself at my death, added severely to my anxieties. To supply the requisites of her rank, to reward the virtues of her character, I could only bequeath her a legacy of my imprudences. My intimates, even those of most sensibility, acquainted with the levities, the inattentions, and dissipations of my common course of life, might have wanted faith in my sincerity; and I even suffered my dearest Charlotte herself—not, I hope, to doubt that I felt—but rather to be ignorant [of] how much I felt, than expatiate on a subject that would be so afflicting to her in the tender and delicate state of her mind and health.

Burgoyne was to make his anxieties plain to the king before his departure, but in the meantime he busied himself in trying to obtain a North American post more congenial than Boston. Lord North was the obvious man to approach, although unfortunately he had had his differences with Burgoyne. There was a "coldness" between the two men, to which Burgoyne had added by his opposition in Parliament to several of North's measures. "Nothing short of professed enmity could place me farther than I found myself from the confidence of this minister," wrote Burgoyne, but he decided to pocket his pride and ask for a meeting with the prime minister, adding somewhat disingenuously that he did so only in the public interest and not for any personal advantage.

North received him, listened to him civilly, and bore patiently with his laborious explanation of how he had so often found himself opposed to the prime minister in Parliament. He expressed satisfaction at Burgoyne's expressed intention to carry out the government's policies in North America and commended such admirable devotion to duty. Burgoyne, thus encouraged, then came to the real purpose of the interview. This was the governorship of New York. William Tryon, the current governor, was in England; he was unpopular and was believed to have connections on the side of rebellion. His deputy was elderly and feeble. Burgoyne wondered whether "a military man, clothed with that character only, going in his station at the head of three or four regiments, might with equal talents or with less talents than Mr Tryon possessed, find more facility in negotiation." There was, of course, no desire to interfere in the proper chain of military command, and the only reason for raising the matter, he said, was his desire to be employed for the best advantage of his country. He trusted that Lord North would mention the matter to the king, since an appointment of this kind would make better use of his abilities than "the bare superintendence of a brigade."

North was noncommittal, but promised to raise the matter with the king. Burgoyne bowed his way out. Next, he proceeded to drum up more support for his being given the governorship of New York, lobbying with, among others, Mr. Jenkinson and Lord George Germain. Germain had not yet succeeded Dartmouth as secretary of state for the colonies, but he was intriguing hard for the post. He willingly received Burgoyne, and what he had to say was music in Burgoyne's ears. "He had more information about the subject, more enlarged sentiments, and more spirit than any of the ministers with whom I had conversed," recorded Burgoyne. "He acknowledged that he was in all consultations upon American measures; that indeed his warmth [interest] had led him almost to offer himself to Lord North. . . . He even told me he had for a long time goaded every part of the administration upon the neglect of New York; that he knew not where they could find a more proper person than myself to send there. . . ."

Burgoyne was impressed by Germain and counted on him as a powerful ally, a man who knew what needed to be done to put things right in North America and was longing to put his plans into effect. Burgoyne cannot be blamed for failing to realize that this ambitious and imperious man would turn out to be his country's evil genius in the struggle with the colonies, quarreling with each of his generals in turn and continuing the war long after most reasonable men had concluded that it was lost. Now, he seemed a mine of energy when compared with the rest of Lord North's cabinet, and his support was certainly worth cultivating. And so was Sir Gilbert Elliott's, a leading "hawk" in Parliament and a confidant of the king's. Elliott assured Burgoyne that there could be no question of sending General Howe to New York—his place was in Boston—and left Burgoyne to infer that he could reckon on Elliott's support for the governorship.

Burgoyne next tackled John Pownall, the senior civil servant dealing with North American affairs, who happened to be a distant relation of Burgoyne's. "I only expressed in general terms my desire to be known to Lord Dartmouth," wrote Burgoyne, "as a man having had the lot to be appointed to the American staff, was anxious to render government every service in his power." Pownall's response was discouraging. "He entered into a long, formal, and sometimes unintelligible discussion of American affairs." Moreover, he infuriated Burgoyne by his air of conscious superiority. "He talked to me as I imagined he might be accustomed to do with men really inferior to him in information. . . . Gentlemen in trade and other situations in life, which set them at a distance from great men in office, or even from the subalterns and apes of official greatness, diffident of their own judgment, and believing men in power to be better informed because they ought to be so, are generally patient hearers, and hence a secretary is very apt to contract an air of supercilious or ministerial importance." Burgoyne had no intention of being patronized by Pownall, and neither man made any headway. "He was guarded—mysterious—obscure," complained Burgoyne. "I acquired by the conversation (as I thought) some lights into his character, but none into American affairs."

Pownall did, however, procure Burgoyne a meeting with the well-meaning but ineffectual Dartmouth, who proved no more forthcoming than his secretary. "I . . . found what I had expected from his general character, *much* politeness and benevolence of mind, *too* much attention to his secretary whose parts appeared to me to be inferior to his own, and a good deal of caution in committing an opinion on nice subjects, though not more of it than was excusable in a minister conversing with a perfect stranger." There was nothing to be gained from Dartmouth, but Burgoyne continued indefatigably with his lobbying. General Haldimand, Gage's second-in-command, was returning home to make way for Howe, and Burgoyne learned there were many ministers who favored his own appointment to New York. Dartmouth was an exception; he considered that Governor Tryon was the proper person to conduct negotiations with the Americans in that province. Burgoyne felt this was mere prevarication on Dartmouth's part, because Tryon was delaying his departure for New York. Since Dartmouth was determined not to commit himself, Burgoyne next attempted to enlist the support of General Howe.

I thought it a point of honour to mention this subject to General Howe [he wrote], that I wished myself employed in some more active station than the mere inspection of a brigade; that I should not think of interfering with him in any military competition, but that New York opened up another line of business; that possibly I was thought of for that distinction during the absence of Mr Tryon, though I would not accept the government with any stipend that could be allotted to it.

Howe's reply was friendly, but noncommittal. He said he would prefer not to go to Boston. "I knew the reason given publicly by all his friends was the obligation his family owed to the Bostonians, who had raised a monument to the late Lord Howe, and particularly complimented the general. However I very soon discovered that the secret and real reason was the low opinion he held of the commander-in-chief [Gage] as a soldier. . . ."

A hint of exasperation now appears in Burgoyne's memorandum.

Some time passed without any overture of consultation between the ministers and the major-generals. I knew there was equal reserve to us all, and I began to feel regret at being selected merely to make up a triumvirate of reputation, and to foresee the irksome situation of being placed at the head of a small brigade without confidence, without detached command, or a mixture of civil negotiation, which it had been hinted in the House of Commons, and was become the general expectation of the world, was designed for us.

It was time to look elsewhere for support. "I made use of Sir John Blaquière," he wrote, "who I knew had an inclination to serve me, and power to do so; a head excellently turned for ministerial intrigue, an established intimacy with Lord North, and an uncommon confidence with [Lord Rocheford]." The Earl of Rocheford was secretary of state for the Southern Department from 1770 to 1775, and as such had some responsibility for American affairs. Blaquière put Burgoyne in touch with him, and, according to Burgoyne, he was immediately admitted into Rocheford's confidence. He learned from Rocheford that the king was well disposed toward him, but in the Cabinet, Lords Dartmouth and Suffolk were staunch supporters of Howe. The other ministers, including possibly Lord North, preferred Burgoyne, if there was any question of negotiations having to be conducted. "General Howe's friends were, nevertheless, indefatigably at work," commented Burgoyne.

Burgoyne also seems to have felt that the time had come to take a public stand on the subject of the colonies. He spoke in the debate of February 27, 1775, and appears to have made a distinct impression on the House.

I spoke from the heart, and to that cause I impute its success. It was uncommonly well received by the House. Lord North professed at every table, that it had done more essential service to Government than any speech of the year. Copies were much desired. Lord Gower read one to the King, who ratified the general strain of encomium by the most obliging expressions to me upon the subject at his levée, and in his closet, where I introduced myself for the declared purpose of asking the royal consent to my nephew going a volunteer to America; but not without a view to express my sentiments upon affairs of that country, were a favourable opening given to me.

The king was gracious, the atmosphere was cordial, the interview lasted a long time, but, alas, "no opening that I could avail myself of with propriety."

Lord George Germain was frequently visited by Burgoyne during these frustrating weeks prior to embarkation. Germain considered it surprising that Howe, Clinton, and Burgoyne had not been consulted prior to the government's drawing up instructions for Gage. He felt that the generals ought to be invited to express their views, and he trusted this could be done informally, preferably at a dinner attended by the ministers rather than at the council table. "He had often observed," he told Burgoyne, "that the surest means of collecting matter from professional men, especially if they were modest men, were to employ convivial hours for that purpose." Soon afterward Burgoyne and his colleagues were invited to dinner at Lord Dartmouth's:

There were present all the Cabinet, and moreover Lords Sandwich and Barrington [first lord of the Admiralty and secretary-at-war], and General Harvey [adjutant-general], Governor Hutchinson [Gage's predecessor in Massachusetts], and Mr Secretary Pownall; and to the whole was added (I could never guess for what purpose) the Earl of Hardwicke. I did not conceive much expectation of business upon the sight of so numerous and motley a company, and except for a short conversation between Lord Suffolk, General Howe, and myself, who sat near each other at table, and which Lord Suffolk expressed a desire to extend upon some other occasion, we talked of every subject but America. It was at this dinner that Lord Dartmouth, in the name of the whole Cabinet, and he added that of His Majesty, desired that I would permit my speech to be printed, in order to its being dispersed in America.

It is surprising that Burgoyne should have attached any significance to soothing expressions of approval. Had he been a plain, blunt soldier, more accustomed to the tent than the *salon,* he might be excused for his ingenuousness, but he should have known the world of politics too well to be fobbed off in this fashion. That this was not so is shown by the concluding sentences of his memorandum:

Such repeated professions of obligation from all parts of the ministry I thought entitled me to press my claims of separate employment more pointedly than I had done before. I represented in repeated conversations with Lord North, how different I found the state of things as my embarkation approached, from what I had expected at my appointment; that at that time I had not conceived, nor I believe had any other person, that I was taken from the last of the roll merely for the inspection of a brigade—*to see that the soldiers boiled their kettles regularly;* that nothing bore the appearance of any further intention towards me, nor indeed towards my colleagues; that we were totally in the dark upon all the plans of Government for the campaign; that willing and zealous to forego all private interests if placed in a state of confidence or of action, I felt the hardship of being called upon to make such sacrifices only to attain the character of a cypher; that the general voice was in my favour for New York, and that as it was not a military but a political competition, I hoped his Lordship would allow me to urge my pretensions; that I looked upon their success or disappointment as a test of the real opinion the King's servants had of me.

North was gracious but he did not yield an inch. He preferred to leave General Gage to dispose of his distinguished reinforcements as he thought best. "I shook my head at that insinuation," wrote Burgoyne, "and requested his Lordship to do me at least the honour to treat me like a man not totally ignorant of the world; that I knew General Howe was using every engine of interest for the preference, and it was preposterous to suppose that a private hint would not be given to General Gage where to give it." The embarrassed prime minister then admitted that certain promises had been earlier made to Howe by the king, and that therefore there were certain problems regarding New York. However, he would do his best for Burgoyne, and with that Burgoyne had to be content.

He had expended much time and energy in furthering his case, but in the end he was still assigned to Boston.

His last act before sailing was to write a letter to the king, to be delivered only in the event of his death. He commended Lady Charlotte to the royal protection and told the king: "I received your Majesty's commands for America with regret, the first sensation of that nature I ever experienced in a call for service, but I have not less a sense of duty. . . ." [10] The letter is dated from Portsmouth, April 18, 1775, and on the same day H.M.S. *Cerberus* hoisted sail to carry the "Triumvirate of Reputation" to North America.

Chapter 9

Fifth Wheel of the Boston Coach

In the five weeks that it took the *Cerberus* to cross the Atlantic the situation in Boston deteriorated alarmingly. War seemed inevitable, and it would be a war for which neither the British nor the Americans were prepared. "If you think Ten Thousand men sufficient, send twenty," Gage had advised Lord Dartmouth. "If one million is thought enough, give two; you will save both blood and treasure in the end. A large force will terrify, and engage many to join you, a middling one will encourage resistance, and gain no friends. . . ." [1] Dartmouth's reaction was to urge Gage *to do something*—anything, rather than remain supine in Boston. "It will surely be better," he argued, "that the conflict be brought on, upon such ground, than in a riper state of rebellion." [2] The result was the fighting at Lexington and Concord, on April 19, 1775. Less than a month later, Ethan Allen, with his Green Mountain Boys and accompanied by the New Haven merchant Benedict Arnold, captured Ticonderoga and Crown Point on Lake Champlain, severing Gage's land communications with Canada.

A disconsolate commander-in-chief welcomed his three distinguished reinforcements on May 25. As he had foretold, thus it had happened. Lord Percy could describe the colonists as "a set of sly, artful, hypocritical rascalls, cruel and cowards," [3] but the noble lord could not deny that this contemptible crew had halted the advance of a body of British troops and had driven them back in demoralizing retreat. Howe, Clinton, and Burgoyne were horrified by the situation they found in Boston; it was much worse than they had been led to expect, although Burgoyne still held to his view that the problem was primarily a political one. The more blood that was shed, the harder it would be to negotiate a sensible way out of the impasse.

But the time for negotiation had already passed. Owing to his reluctance to precipitate a clash, Gage had allowed himself to be bottled up in Boston by a rag, tag, and bobtail militia. British morale was low, and desertion was prevalent. New England seethed with rebellion, but Gage was unwilling to proclaim martial law. British soldiers were therefore at the mercy of the local courts, which made no secret of their partisanship. Now, the commander-in-chief could prevaricate no longer, for the three generals had brought with them in convoy a substantial body of reinforcements. Gage proclaimed martial law throughout Massachusetts, offering free pardons to all who returned peaceably home, except for the notorious agitators Sam Adams and John Hancock.

Burgoyne drafted Gage's proclamation, which was dated June 12. It spoke of the "infatuated multitude" and warned that such a "preposterous parade" could not expect to hold the British Army besieged. This pompous manifesto, now hectoring, now pleading, succeeded only in arousing derision, and it was at once proposed that the rebels should issue their own proclamation, pardoning, in their turn, the British government. It was a great pity that Burgoyne in his choice of language should have so underrated the intelligence and misunderstood the feelings of the colonists. His aim was sensible— to try to divide the bulk of the population from the more fanatical leaders—but he hopelessly failed in this intention. Still, Gage's proclamation would probably have failed no matter how skillfully drafted.

It may have come as a shock to Burgoyne and Clinton, neither of whom had served previously in America, to find British soldiers besieged by what they must have regarded as untrained militia; but Howe, who knew Americans, should have found it easier to understand. Many of the colonists had fought in British units against the French, and they were as capable as any British soldier of handling their muskets and laying and firing cannon. They were hardy, self-reliant, and pugnacious, and fiercely determined to stand up for their rights. Gage's main advantage over them was the better discipline of his regulars. Paradoxically, there were Americans serving in British units, and Englishmen, newly settled in New England, shouldering muskets in the rebel ranks. On June 17, the colonists were to show how well they could fight when Gage attempted to drive them from Breed's Hill and Bunker Hill, which dominated Boston harbor.

Howe commanded the British troops. Clinton played a minor part toward the end. Burgoyne, to his chagrin, was only a spectator, as he commented bitterly in a letter to Lord Palmerston written a week after the battle.

I take the first opportunity of a safe conveyance of my letter to acquit myself of the duty you enjoined, and which I owe to your friendship. But after informing you I am perfectly well, a circumstance from which I am sure you will receive satisfaction, I know not where to find one, which will not give you pain. Our prospects on the side of the enemy are gloomy. Enthusiasm, a combination of artifice on one side, perhaps mismanagement on the other, and accident or both, have produced a crisis that my little reading of history cannot parallel. The British Empire in America is overturned without great exertions on your side of the water. If the confederacy on this continent is general, as I incline now to believe it, and you determine to subdue it by arms, you must have recourse to Russia or Germany; such a pittance of troops, as Great Britain and Ireland can supply will only serve to prolong the war, to create fruitless expense, and insure disappointment.

It had taken less than a month to convert Burgoyne to Gage's point of view, but he had more to tell Palmerston.

You will hear by these dispatches of a victory of our troops [Bunker Hill], and perhaps government will be elated with the account. It is glorious to the troops, and important to the nation, inasmuch as the disgrace of the 19th of April [Lexington] is erased, and the superiority of the King's troops over a rebel army is confirmed. . . . But our victory has been bought by an uncommon loss of officers, some of them irreparable, and I fear the consequences will not answer the expectations that will be raised in England. . . .[4]

He referred Palmerston to Lady Charlotte for a more detailed picture of the battle. He had not himself been personally involved other than "in the superintendence of a cannonade." It had been a terrible scene to observe, and the casualties had been unusually heavy. Indeed, Clinton recorded in his journal on the night after the battle: "A dear-bought victory; another such would have ruined us"; [5] and Gage wrote to Barrington: "The loss we have sustained is greater than we can bear." [6] However despicable the proud Lord Percy might think them, the American militiamen could certainly fight.

Burgoyne resented his minor role and perhaps was more critical than he would have been had he taken a more active part; but the interesting aspect of his letter to Palmerston is his statement that the rebellion was more widespread than he had imagined before leaving England. He had also reached the conclusion, long before most of his colleagues, that Britain did not possess the military resources required to defeat the Americans. Foreign troops would be required, and he repeated this opinion in a letter to Lord Rocheford. Stressing the confidentiality of the correspondence, his only desire being "to convey truth to the King," he told Rocheford that if he appeared critical of Gage, it was as a soldier, and certainly not as a man. He wrote:

I arrived at Boston, together with Generals Howe and Clinton, on the 25th May. It would be unnecessary were it possible, to describe our surprise or other feelings, upon the appearances which at once and on every side, were offered to our observation. The town, on the land side, invested by a rabble in arms, who flushed with success and insolence, had advanced their sentries to pistol shot of our outguards; the ships in the harbour exposed to, and expecting a cannonade or bombardment; in all companies, whether of officers or inhabitants, men still lost in a sort of stupefaction which the events of the 19th of April had occasioned, and venting expressions of censure, anger, or despondency.

He defended the decision to seize the arms at Lexington and Concord, surprised that this had not been done earlier, but criticized the poor planning of the operation and the lack of intelligence. Boston, he would have thought, was ideally situated for the collection of supplies and warlike stores, but nothing had been done. The failure at Lexington had aroused the countryside and encouraged the malcontents. It had led directly to the investment of Boston. "A paltry skirmish," as he described Lexington, had resulted in consequences as considerable as the battle of "Pharsalia," * and had led to "the colours of a fleet and army . . . not wrested from us, but without a conflict, kicked out of America." These views were shared, he assured Rocheford, by Howe and Clinton. They had done their best to persuade Gage to act more vigorously, although Burgoyne had to admit that Bunker Hill had proved Gage's wisdom in not acting until he had received reinforcements. So far as that battle was concerned, Burgoyne's role had been "almost a useless spectator. . . . In the general regular course of business in this army, Major-Generals are absolute cyphers." He was himself placed in "a motionless, drowsy, irksome medium, or rather vacuum, too low for the honour of command, too high for that of execution."

Burgoyne then provided Rocheford with a thumbnail sketch of Bunker Hill. "Turn your eyes first, my Lord, to the behaviour of the enemy. The defence was well conceived and

* Pharsalia, better known as the battle of Pharsalus, 48 B.C., where Julius Caesar decisively defeated Pompey.

obstinately maintained; the retreat was no flight; it was even covered with bravery and military skill, and proceeded no farther than to the next hill, where a new post was taken, new intrenchments instantly begun, and their numbers affording constant reliefs of workmen, they have been continued day and night ever since." Here was no peasant rabble led by down-at-heel attorneys and innkeepers, but a well-armed body of men led by officers with an eye for ground and a good understanding of tactics. It was high time that gentlemen in London revised their opinion of the American rebels.

View now, my Lord, the side of victory; and first the list of killed and wounded. If fairly given, it amounts to no less than ninety-two officers,* many of them an irreparable loss—a melancholy disproportion to the number of the private soldiers—and there is a melancholy reason for it. Though my letter passes in security, I tremble while I write it; and let it not pass even in a whisper from your Lordship to more than *one* person; † the zeal and intrepidity of the officers, which was without exception exemplary, was ill seconded by the private men. Discipline, not to say courage, was wanting. . . .

Burgoyne made it clear that this serious accusation did not apply to all the troops engaged, nor did it mean that those who had failed in their duty lacked heart. They lacked training and good morale. If they were to improve, they required training "under such generals as Howe and Clinton," but even if better trained and led, what could they accomplish from Boston?

Look, my Lord, upon the country near Boston—it is all fortification. Driven from one hill, you will see the enemy continually retrenched upon the next; and every step we move must be the slow step of a siege. Could we at last penetrate ten miles, perhaps we should not obtain a single sheep or an ounce of flour by our laborious progress, for they remove every article of provisions as they go. . . . Count our numbers, my Lord; any officer will

* Fortescue gives the officer casualties as 19 killed and 70 wounded.
† Presumably the king.

tell you that in such a country, and against such an enemy, who in composition and system are all light troops, they are not more than requisite to secure our convoys and communications between the army and the great deposit of magazines; or if that difficulty were got over by great and active genius, look into our state once more, and you will find us totally unprovided with bread waggons, hospital carriages, bat-horses, sufficient artillery horses, and many other articles of *attirail* indispensably necessary for an army to proceed by land to a distance.

The logistic problems were much as Burgoyne described them, and as he was to experience them himself two years later, but he was ignoring the problems of the enemy, which were in many ways more difficult. A determined effort, accepting the risks and damning the consequences, might have restored the situation in New England, but it would have required bold and ruthless leadership. Gage was fit only, according to Burgoyne, to govern in quiet times, and lacked the character to rise to great exertions. But the blame did not lie only on Gage's side. He had been kept so short of money that he had been unable to build up supplies; nor had he managed to establish an efficient system of intelligence. "We are ignorant not only what passes in Congress, but want spies for the hill half a mile off. And what renders the reflection truly provoking is that there was hardly a leading man among the rebels, in council, or in the field, but at a proper time, and by proper management, might have been bought."

He proposed alternative plans for overcoming the impasse in Boston. There were about 5,200 British troops there—"if you, in England, reckon upon more, you are mistaken"—and a part of this force should be employed in making Boston secure. About 2,000 men should be embarked, provided with a strong naval escort, and be used as an amphibious force to threaten landings anywhere along the New England coasts. The immediate enemy reaction would probably be to reduce the numbers of Americans investing Boston; Connecticut men, for instance, would want to protect their own homes. This might provide the opportunity to break out of Boston and reopen communications with the rest of Massachusetts. The amphibious force would meanwhile sail southward, dealing with Rhode Island en route, land on Long Island, and bring the New Yorkers back to their allegiance. On the subject of New York, Burgoyne trusted he would be forgiven if he reverted to the governorship: "That province is lost for want of management, and a proper force to second it." He could only lament that he had not been appointed governor, since he was still convinced that the conflict should be resolved by negotiation rather than by force.

He then turned to psychological warfare. His advice had been to treat American prisoners with kindness. They should be admonished: "You have been deluded; return to your homes in peace; it is your duty to God and your country to unde-ceive your neighbours." He had personally interviewed many prisoners. They were, on the whole, sensible men, deluded by their leaders, and expecting to be hanged. If they were set free, it might produce a favorable impression: "Should it fail, it will at least serve to justify acts of a different nature here-after; and you are no further the dupes of it in the meantime than by adding about thirty men now in your power to a stock of many thousands who are out of it." This was sound com-mon sense if one believed, as Burgoyne did, that the problem was still negotiable. But if he was wrong, then there was no alternative, he felt, to a massive amphibious operation, accom-panied by wholesale requisitioning of transport and animals. Selected towns should be razed as a warning of the wrath to come, but he warned there could be no question of subduing the rebels with the troops then available. He proposed, instead, "a large army of such foreign troops as might be hired, to begin their operations up the Hudson river; another army composed partly of old disciplined troops and partly of Cana-dians to act from Canada; * a large levy of Indians and a

---

* This is the first mention by Burgoyne of the plan that later was to come to grief at Saratoga.

supply of arms for the blacks, to awe the southern provinces conjointly with detachments of regulars; and a numerous fleet to sweep the whole coast, might possibly do the business in one campaign." [7]

In sum, first try negotiation; if unsuccessful, war *en outrance*, with no holds barred, to ensure it was finished quickly. If the prospect of the latter appalled the government, half-measures would not be a substitute. There was no other option but to come to terms.

Lord Rocheford was not the only recipient of Burgoyne's confidences from Boston. General Edward Harvey, the adjutant-general, received a letter criticizing General Gage.[8] Only a strong man, backed to the limit by the government, could cope with the situation, he wrote. The king's troops in Boston were in a lamentable state, short of transport, horses, and supplies. Worse, there was a chronic shortage of money. Gage had requested £40,000; he had been sent £10,000. Burgoyne and his two colleagues had been promised £500 to set themselves up in Boston, but not a penny had been forthcoming, despite Pownall's assurances that he would write to Gage on the matter; Gage "cannot even supply us with personal pay. . . ." The generals had been advised to write to their London bankers for the necessary cash, but in the meantime were they presumably expected to live on air? He took leave to wonder what had happened to the money voted by Parliament for the prosecution of the struggle, but hastened to assure the adjutant-general that his and his colleagues' "zeal for the King's service will not be impeded by our personal resentment against any persons whatsoever."

This assurance could have brought little relief to the harassed Harvey, struggling, like most British principal staff officers at the beginning of every war, to make bricks without straw, and having to compete with the government's wishful thinking. "Taking America as it present stands," Harvey had written to General John Irwin in June, 1775, "it is impossible to conquer it with our British Army. . . . To attempt to conquer it internally by our land force is as wild an idea as ever controverted common sense." [9] He believed, as did everyone else with any knowledge of strategy, that the colonists should be brought to heel by the employment of sea power, and not by a campaign on land. "Unless a settled plan of operations be agreed upon for next spring," he wrote to Howe in July, "our army will be destroyed by damned driblets. . . . America is an ugly job . . . a damned affair indeed." [10]

Burgoyne would have agreed with Harvey. Indeed, he deemed it his duty to return to London to argue the case in person. On June 14 he wrote to Lord North complaining of his embarrassing situation in Boston, and asking to return home once the campaigning season was over.

Burgoyne's pen was kept busy in Boston. He wrote a farce called *The Blockade of Boston*, and the prologue to a performance of *Zara*, acted by the officers of the garrison. He wrote to Germain, complaining of "fatal procrastination," and asserting that the British had drifted into war without any of the requisites necessary for its successful prosecution. "It may be asked in England, 'What is the Admiral doing?' I wish I were able to answer that question satisfactorily; but I can only say what he is *not* doing." He then listed the deficiencies of Admiral Thomas Graves: "*not* supplying us with sheep and oxen," "*not* defending his own flocks and herds," "*not* defending the other islands in the harbour," "*not* employing his ships to keep up communication and intelligence," not retaliating for the numerous insults suffered by the British from raiding parties and privateers.[11]

More important, perhaps, Burgoyne spent much of his time attempting to suborn his comrade of Portugal days, Charles Lee. Lee's republican views and cantankerous temperament had made him one of the first British officers to offer his services to the American Congress, although his wholehearted loyalty to the cause remained in doubt throughout the war.

After the Seven Years' War he had joined the Russian service, where, as he wrote, "I am to have command of Cossacks and Wollacks, a kind of people I have a good opinion of. I am determined not to serve in the line [infantry]; one might as well be a churchwarden." [12] He soon tired of European warfare and returned to England, convinced there was no faith in princes. This belief was further reinforced when he was received in audience by the king, who regretted his inability to promote him. "Sire," replied Lee, "I will never give your Majesty an opportunity of breaking your promise to me again," [13] and, abruptly resigning his commission, he set off for North America, where he was farming in a desultory fashion when the troubles began. He offered his services to Congress on condition that he should be indemnified "for any loss of property which he may sustain by entering into their service," but he proved his worth time and again during the early days of the British investment in Boston. He was one of the few on the American side who understood the importance of discipline and military organization, and he had the force of character to drive the lesson home. "General Lee is a perfect original," wrote Jeremy Belknap in August, 1775, "a good scholar and soldier; and an odd genius, full of fire and passion and but little good manners; a great sloven, wretchedly profane, and a great admirer of dogs, of which he had two at dinner with him, one of them a native of Pomerania, which I would have taken for a bear had I seen him in the woods." [14]

Lee was no ordinary soldier. Like Burgoyne, he had thought a great deal about his profession. He despised the conventional officer, and never doubted that the American soldier, properly trained and led, would be more than a match for the products of the British barrack-square. His commander-in-chief, George Washington, considered him "the first officer in Military knowledge and experience we have in the whole army . . . but rather fickle and violent . . . in temper," [15] but Washington was essentially conventional in outlook and upbringing.

Lee was a born irregular, with all the strengths and weaknesses of the breed.

He began his correspondence with Burgoyne on June 7, 1775. "We have had twenty different accounts of your arrival in Boston," he wrote, "which have been regularly contradicted the next morning, but as I now find it certain that you are arrived, I shall not delay a single instant addressing myself to you." He told Burgoyne he owed this to their friendship and to the "many testimonies of esteem and affection" he had received from Burgoyne. "I entreat and conjure you therefore, my dear Sir, to impute these lines not to a petulant itch of scribbling, but to the most unfeigned solicitude for the future tranquillity of your mind, and for your reputation. . . ." He regretted that men of "such a stamp" as Howe and Burgoyne should have been seduced by a "wicked and insidious court and cabinet," and that Burgoyne had already stated his opinion of the dispute in Parliament. In Lee's view, Parliament did not possess the right to tax the North American colonies, and it was some relief to know that Burgoyne had not sought a command in North America. However, he found it alarming that men of "sense and integrity" should have felt it incumbent upon them to obey the mandates of a court, "be they ever so flagitious." In his view this only went to strengthen his opinion "for the total reduction of the army." Lee was in fact opposed to the concept of a standing army, as a danger to liberty, and preferred a militia, a view that was later to bring him into conflict with Washington.

He doubted whether Burgoyne would be any the wiser from anything that Gage might tell him. He would deceive Burgoyne, as he had deceived himself. "I do not say he will do so designedly . . . but his mind is so totally poisoned, and his understanding so totally blinded by the society of fools and knaves, that he no longer is capable of discerning facts as manifest as the noon-day sun." Gage had no conception of the depth of feeling in North America, and consequently his advice to the government was "one continued tissue of misrepresentation, injustice, and tortured inferences from mis-stated facts." Lee was concerned lest Burgoyne and his colleagues should be similarly misled. There were better places for their military talents than America. No one knew the situation better than Lee. He had traveled through all the colonies and talked with high and low. He asserted that all felt the same; "not less than a hundred and fifty thousand gentlemen, yeomen, and farmers, are now in arms, determined to preserve their liberties or perish. As to the idea that the Americans are deficient in courage, it is too ridiculous and glaringly false to deserve a serious refutation." He had fought with them in the war against the French, and they had behaved as well as British troops.

Lee hoped Burgoyne would acquaint Howe with his sentiments. He found it particularly hard to understand why Howe had accepted an American command—"the brother of him, to whose memory the much injured people of Boston, erected a monument. . . ." He assumed it was because loyalty to the king overrode all other moral obligations, which only went to show "that power cannot be lodged in worse hands than theirs [courts and princes]; and of all courts I am persuaded that ours is the most corrupt and hostile to the rights of humanity." This alone would justify Lee's determination to take up the sword, for America was "the last asylum of persecuted liberty." [16]

Burgoyne valued Lee as a soldier but he doubted his judgment. However, Bunker Hill was fought before Burgoyne had time to reply, and the result bore out Lee's assessment of the American as a fighting man. Discussions with those Americans still living within the British perimeter had also convinced Burgoyne that peace through negotiation was still possible. His old acquaintanceship with Lee might provide the opportunity to open negotiations, and with Gage's blessing he replied to Lee on July 8, thanking him for his kind remembrances, which were warmly reciprocated, but regretting his inability to agree with him. The supremacy of the king in

Parliament was a vital British constitutional principle. Burgoyne declared his undying opposition to republicanism, and defended the right of Parliament to tax British subjects wherever they might live. These views, he assured Lee, were endorsed by the majority in Britain, including Lord Thanet, for whom Lee had long entertained the warmest feelings. Thanet had, through Burgoyne, forwarded a letter. He told Lee he had also brought a letter from Charles Danvers, but he did not enclose them because he hoped to deliver them in person.

"The place I would propose for our meeting is the house upon Boston neck, just within our advanced sentries, called Brown's house," wrote Burgoyne. He guaranteed Lee's safety, and by the same token required Lee's assurance that "no insult" would be offered to Burgoyne. Lee was left to name the day and hour, and was assured of the compliments of Generals Howe and Clinton, and Lord Percy, all of whom had read his letter, and who concurred with Burgoyne's reply to it. The meeting never took place, because the Massachusetts legislature, to whom Lee submitted Burgoyne's letter, refused to permit it. Perhaps they feared for Burgoyne's persuasive tongue and were none too sure of Lee's loyalty; perhaps Arthur Lee's description of Burgoyne's character had made them suspicious; perhaps a bit of both. On July 11 Lee replied:

General Lee's compliments to General Burgoyne. Would be extremely happy in the interview he so kindly proposed. But as he perceives that General Burgoyne has already made up his mind on this great subject; and it is impossible that he [General Lee] should ever alter his opinion, he is apprehensive that the interview might create those jealousies and suspicions so natural to a people struggling in the dearest of all causes, that of their liberty, property, wives, children, and their future generation. He must, therefore, defer the happiness of embracing a man he most sincerely loves, until the subversion of the present tyrannical ministry and system, which he is persuaded must be in a few months, as he knows that Great Britain cannot stand the contest. He begs General Burgoyne will send the letters which his Aide-de-Camp has for him. If Gardiner is his Aide-de-Camp he desires his love to him.[17]

It came to nothing—Lee's hopes of winning over the most intelligent general on the British side; Burgoyne's hopes of suborning Lee, whom he described to Lord North as "late half-pay major, and incendiary in the King's service." Burgoyne went to some pains to make public, and explain, his share in this exchange; it would never do to be thought to be trafficking with the enemy. Charles Stuart, son of former prime minister Lord Bute, had written home saying he had read Burgoyne's letter to Lee, and thought he had protested too much. Major Webb, writing to his American compatriot Silas Deane, warned him against Burgoyne. "He is as cunning and subtle as the Devil himself, and writes as if he were on the right of the question, like a man of his abilities, but his wickedness is to be seen in every sentence of his letter." [18]

The best of intentions can be misconstrued, although it is doubtful whether Burgoyne's were as honorable as Lee's. In his letter of explanation to North, Burgoyne makes it clear that he intended to suborn Lee, touching on "his pride, interest, and ambition." He believed Lee's contumacy stemmed from disappointment at failing to obtain preferment. Where the king had failed to secure his loyalty, Burgoyne thought he might succeed. "Were he secretly bought over, the services he might do are great; and very great, I confess, they ought to be to atone for his offences." [19] Burgoyne's main fear was that the king might misunderstand his intention in corresponding with Lee, and he trusted North to make the position clear.

At the same time, he enclosed another letter from Lee, in which the latter expressed concern that the British would enlist the aid of the Indians. Should not action be taken to turn this threat into reality, inquired Burgoyne. And what of Lee's other assertion, "that France and Spain are ready to accept the Colonies"? North would know more of the truth of this than Burgoyne, but if untrue, should not Lee's statement be published, in order either to brand him as a liar or to compel him to disclose the source of his information?

Burgoyne's letter-writing continued, sheet after sheet containing wise observations on the state of things in Boston, interspersed with self-pitying remonstrances on the inadequacy of his own situation. A second letter to Rocheford was more outspoken about Gage, and critical of his naval colleague, Graves.[20] Gage was toying with the idea of transferring the Boston garrison to New York, which made sense to Burgoyne, but it could succeed only if carried out with the greatest secrecy. It would be wrong to leave the port of Boston intact, but Gage was too kindhearted to destroy it. If the army remained in Boston for the winter without supplies, it would die of hunger or perish from lack of fuel. Burgoyne had already warned Germain, in August, that the rebels were gaining strength, and that their leader, Samuel Adams, was "as great a conspirator as ever subverted a state." It would be a mistake to underrate him. "Be assured, my Lord, this man soars too high to be allured by any offer Great Britain can make to himself or to his country. America, if his counsels continue in force, must be subdued or relinquished. She will not be reconciled." [21]

Lord George Germain, busily intriguing for the colonial secretaryship, would have found Burgoyne's letter of unusual interest. He was certainly more articulate on paper than any of his colleagues. Perhaps he was a general who could be more usefully employed. On December 10, 1775, Germain achieved his *immediate* ambition and succeeded Dartmouth as secretary of state for the colonies. Burgoyne sailed for home the same month, in H.M.S. *Boyne*. Gage had preceded him, ostensibly for consultation, but in fact to be quietly shelved. The British fortunes in America were now in the hands of the brave, indolent, popular, but indecisive Howe, whose brother, the Viscount, took over the naval command.

Captain Evelyn, writing home at the time of Burgoyne's

departure from Boston, said: Burgoyne "appears from the line he has taken here to have been intended rather as a negotiator than to be active in the field. He is a man of great abilities and power of language." This probably summed up British opinion in Boston: an agreeable man, more politician and diplomat than general, who could turn his hand to drafting proclamations and writing plays, but whose military qualities were less evident. It would not have pleased Burgoyne.

Part Two

The Breaking of
a General

"*Il y a beaucoup de puérilités
dans la guerre.*"

—Samuel Johnson, May 16, 1778

Chapter 10

Carleton's Deputy in Canada

BURGOYNE arrived home in late December to find Lady Charlotte's health much worse. He also found a marked change within the government. Lord George Germain had lost no time in making his presence felt in an administration that, until his arrival, had opted for drift rather than drive. His determination to bring the American rebels to heel, and the zeal with which he proclaimed his intentions, made him a man after the king's own heart.

Lord North's reluctance to assert himself made it inevitable that a man with such authoritarian tendencies as Germain had would soon assert leadership, and in doing so his energies would not be confined to the political direction of the struggle in America. He involved himself with equal vigor in military matters, which were the responsibility of the secretary-at-war; but since the latter was not a member of the Cabinet, he played little part in formulating strategy. Barrington, moreover, positively disapproved of the war, and "had distinctly informed his brother ministers as early as 1774 that he disapproved of the whole policy of coercing the colonies, and that he believed the military enterprises which he organized could lead to nothing but disaster." [1] He repeatedly asked to resign, and pointedly refrained from involving himself in anything other

[99]

than military administration. This was as well for Burgoyne, because he and Barrington were always at odds; with Germain, on the other hand, his relations were good.

Burgoyne had hardly set foot in London when he was waiting on his lordship, and what he had to tell of his recent experiences in Boston was much in accord with the views already formed by Germain. Things were going badly, and there had been even worse developments in Canada. After their successful capture of Ticonderoga and Crown Point, the rebels had bypassed Montreal, and by November of 1775 were laying siege to Quebec. They were led by men of rare quality: Benedict Arnold, a natural soldier; Richard Montgomery, an inspiring leader; Daniel Morgan, well schooled in Indian fighting; and the swashbuckling Ethan Allen. It was less than ten years since the bells had rung out in celebration of Wolfe's capture of Quebec. Now it looked as if the bastion of British power in Canada was about to fall.

The commander-in-chief in Canada was General Guy Carleton (knighted in 1776), whose character was well described by one of his officers, Lieutenant Digby, of the 53rd Foot. General Carleton "is one of the most distant, reserved men in the world, he has a rigid strictness in his manner, very unpleasing, and which he observes even to his most particular friends and acquaintances . . . he was far from being a favourite of the army." [2]

History may have concluded that Carleton was a better statesman than soldier, but he nevertheless possessed the one attribute without which no general can expect to win battles—luck. Before he found himself besieged in Quebec, at the head of a weak and dispirited garrison, he had narrowly escaped capture by the Americans. Arnold, on reaching Quebec, lay outside the walls waiting only for the arrival of Montgomery to deliver the *coup de grâce*. Reserved or not, Carleton had a soldier's eye for ground, and the ability to inspire his troops. When, on the last day of 1775, the assault was launched, Montgomery was killed early in the action, and Arnold was wounded in the leg. The rebels failed to penetrate the lower town, and Quebec was saved. The siege continued until small-pox came to the aid of the British, and decimated the besiegers.

There was a long-standing feud between Carleton and Germain, which went back at least as far as Germain's unfortunate conduct at Minden. Toward the end of 1775, with Carleton besieged in Quebec and the likelihood of all Canada being lost, Germain was more inclined to listen to Burgoyne than he would ever have been to his commander in Canada.

During his passage home, Burgoyne had drafted a plan of campaign for the following year. By the time he reached London, it was rumored that Quebec had fallen, but he did not allow this to interfere with his recommendations for the 1776 campaign. His *Reflections upon the War in America* contained much good sense, and almost as much wishful thinking. His first recommendation was for a more effective blockade of the North American coast. This would require a larger fleet and a more enterprising commander than Admiral Graves to direct its operations. There was also the problem of the organization and equipment of the army. Burgoyne was a staunch protagonist of mobility. The formalized warfare of the North German plains had no relevance in the vastly different conditions of North America. What was required, he felt, were lightly equipped and highly mobile bodies of light infantry; not just one company per battalion, but complete light battalions.

Burgoyne had definite ideas about the American style of warfare.

Composed as the American army is, together with the strength of the country, full of woods, swamps, stone walls, and other enclosures and hiding places, it may be said of it that every private man will in action be his own general, who will turn every tree and bush into a kind of temporary fortress, from whence, when he hath fired his shot with all the deliberation, coolness, and certainty which hidden safety inspires, he will skip as it were, to the next, and so on for a long time until dislodged either by cannon or by a resolute attack by light infantry.[3]

The Americans must therefore be dislodged by artillery fire. The guns must be highly mobile to compete with the conditions of forest warfare, and their devastating cannonade must be followed up by swarms of lightly armed infantry, trained to beat the colonists at their own game. The well-dressed lines, carefully controlled volley-firing, and meticulous drill expected of infantry fighting in European conditions would have to be abandoned. This was an original concept, and no general of Burgoyne's time attached more importance to artillery.

Having dealt with tactics, Burgoyne turned his attention to strategy. He demonstrated the impossibility of breaking out of Boston and advancing into Massachusetts. Since the British lacked the strength and the requisite supplies and transportation, he recommended instead a two-pronged attack—one force moving south from Canada and another force advancing north to join it. Herein lies the basis of the plan adopted for 1777. At the time Burgoyne was drafting his *Reflections*, it was believed in London that Quebec had fallen. In Burgoyne's view this would not affect his proposals. "Quebec being in the hands of the rebels will prove no impediment to our armies passing above it," he wrote; "the experience of the year 1759, when our fleet and navy pushed past it, leaves all doubt upon that matter fully decided." [4] The main thrust should be from Canada; the supporting movement could best be made from New York.

While Burgoyne's proposals were being pondered by Germain, and discussed with the king and such of his ministers as could be persuaded to take an interest, Carleton was grimly defending Quebec and Howe was similarly beleaguered in Boston. Whereas in Quebec the Americans were operating at the extreme limit of their supply line, with cold and disease making daily inroads in their strength, in Boston there had been the welcome reinforcement of the cannon captured at Ticonderoga. By immense efforts, these cumbersome pieces had been transported across New England, and Washington now possessed the means to pound his way through Howe's defenses. Counterbalancing this, he had his troubles holding together a collection of men who by no stretch of the imagination could be described as an army. "Such a mercenary spirit pervades the whole," he wrote on November 28, 1775, "that I should not be surprised at any disaster. . . . Could I have foreseen what I have experienced and am likely to experience, no consideration on earth would have induced me to accept the command." [5]

Washington, however, shared with Carnot the genius of being an "organizer of victory." A better strategist than tactician, he was, above all, a superb improviser. He also possessed that magnetic quality of leadership which is given to few men to possess. He held the British penned within their lines partly as a result of his success in shoring up gaps in his own wherever they occurred, and partly because Howe displayed so little enterprise.

In March of 1776, Howe, yielding to Washington's pressure, decided to evacuate Boston, and, for want of sufficient transports, he was compelled to abandon large quantities of supplies and many guns. He sailed for Halifax, leaving Boston to the rebels.

Germain had disliked Howe ever since the two men had served together in the Saint-Malo expedition in 1757. The antipathy was mutual, although Germain could not deny Howe's reputation as a fighting general, and at the outset of Germain's assumption of office the exchanges between the two men were unctuously polite. But Germain did not find it easy to condone Howe's abandonment of Boston, any more than he could approve Carleton's conduct of operations in Canada, and his views were well known to the king.

The British Army was, and is, well used to disasters. It has emerged victorious from few of its wars without having had to survive defeats at the outset. In America, the story was different. What began with near-defeat ended in the fullness of time in complete disaster. No single man was more responsible for this misfortune than the man who seemingly believed himself predestined to restore the king's authority throughout his North American dominions.

He now had at hand a general after his own heart—polished, at ease in the anterooms of the great and at Court, connected by marriage with a family no less distinguished than Germain's own, and, above all, a general with ideas. Burgoyne's *Reflections upon the War in America* could not have received a more sympathetic reading. The king was enthusiastic; the Cabinet, acquiescent; and it was left to Germain to draft the instructions for the 1776 campaign. Howe, supported by his naval brother, was to seize New York; Clinton was to conduct an amphibious operation against the Carolinas; Carleton was to be reinforced, in order to drive the Americans from Canada. Carleton was also to be provided with an energetic second-in-command in whom both the king and Germain had full confidence. They chose Major-General John Burgoyne.

A single general, however highly thought of, was not sufficient to provide Carleton with the strength he needed to drive the Americans from Canada, but the British Army was short of men. The total strength at the outbreak of the war was around 48,000. Several regiments were required in the United Kingdom to support the civil power, for there was no proper police force. As many were required in Ireland, where a sullen and truculent peasantry had always to be overawed, and frequently coerced. The islands of the West Indies, from which Britain drew much of its wealth, had to be garrisoned, as had the other overseas possessions. When to these inescapable commitments there was added the numbers required by Howe and Carleton, it is not surprising that General Harvey should have groaned aloud. "Recruiting as bad as ever. Ireland produces nothing whatever," wrote the adjutant-general in November, 1775. "Something must be done if possible to correct this fundamental want." [6]

Little was done. Regiments competed with each other for the available recruits. Some recruited invalids and pensioners, unfit for anything other than sitting on a bench in the sun; others scoured the poorhouses to persuade the unemployed, or unemployable, to take the king's shilling. Even Roman Catholics were enlisted in Connaught and Munster. Yet the numbers fell far short of those required. The king was persuaded to approach the Empress Catherine of Russia to obtain a levy of Russian troops, but her eccentric majesty indignantly refused. "The letter of the empress is a clear refusal," wrote the king mournfully to Lord North, "and not in so genteel a manner as I should have thought might have been expected of her. She has not had the civility to answer me in her own hand, and has thrown out some expressions that may be civil to a Russian ear but certainly not to more civilised ones." [7]

There was, however, plenty of cannon fodder in Germany, where the peasantry had long been accustomed to arbitrary enlistment. Moreover, Germans had been hiring themselves out as mercenaries generation after generation. George III was also king of Hanover, and there were good reasons why such potentates as the Landgrave of Hesse and the Duke of Brunswick should be willing to come to his assistance. Some 18,000 troops were hired from Brunswick and Hesse-Cassel, and individual Germans were also recruited.

On March 1, 1776, Lord George Germain wrote a letter of instructions to John Burgoyne.

I have proposed to the King that you should embark at Spithead with the first division of the Brunswick troops; that the artillery should sail at the same time; and that the regiment at Plymouth, instead of going to Cork, should join you as you pass through the channel. Lord Sandwich says Captain Pennel commands the *Blonde*, and is one of the convoy, and he says he is persuaded he will, upon your applying to him, receive you with pleasure on board his ship. It seems he is rich and you need not fear putting him to expense. I likewise mentioned again the affair of your rank; the King wishes to antedate as far back as you desire; it is now with Lord Barrington, and I have sent him word that the King inclines that his lieutenant-generals should command Knyphausen [a Hessian officer commanding the German troops destined to join General Howe], and that his Lordship will contrive to do this with as little impropriety as possible, so that this point will be settled to your satisfaction. The King enquired anxiously about Lady Charlotte and you, and I trust I did not inform him wrong when I said I had heard she was something better.[8]

Burgoyne must have received this letter with mixed feelings. He would have been gratified by his selection to serve as Carleton's second-in-command in the forthcoming campaign, but Germain had been wrong about Charlotte's health. She was worse, and Burgoyne was unhappy to leave her. He accepted the king's commands because of the importance he had always attached to a soldier's duty, and possibly because he now knew that his wife's condition was beyond cure. He clearly did not expect to see her alive again; shortly after his arrival in Canada, he wrote to Clinton describing her as "that truest friend, amiable companion, tenderest, best of women and of wives." [9] Only his sense of duty brought him to leave her, and certainly his appointment as Carleton's second-in-command was unsought for—or so he said.

He landed at Quebec in early May of 1776, bringing with him in convoy seven infantry regiments. There were also 4,300 Brunswick troops. In the same convoy traveled two senior officers whose fortunes were to become closely linked with his own. One was a German, Baron Friedrich von Riedesel, age thirty-nine and a subject of the Duke of Brunswick; he commanded the Brunswickers. The other, Major-General William Phillips, was a veteran of Minden, where his handling of his guns had received universal commendation. Phillips was not the easiest officer to deal with, having a savage temper and a short manner with those he disliked or despised. Some years later he was described by Thomas Jefferson as "the proudest man of the proudest nation on earth." As an artillery officer he was not entitled to hold field command, but Burgoyne came to value his services so highly that he managed to circumvent this.

If Burgoyne had expected that his arrival with reinforcements would raise the siege of Quebec, he was disappointed. Three British vessels had slipped upstream a few days previously, splitting the American besieging force camped on both banks of the Saint Lawrence. American morale was poor; Arnold had recovered from his wound, but had again damaged his leg by a fall from his horse. He was sent back to Montreal, and Major General John Sullivan took over command at Quebec, bringing some reinforcements. But the American blockade had been broken. Carleton could now muster nearly 1,000 troops, and there were more on the way. He sallied out from the walls and defeated Sullivan's ragged, dispirited force. The Americans melted away, and Carleton had the situation well in hand by the time Burgoyne arrived. All that remained was to clear Canada of the American invaders.

Burgoyne, who held the local rank of lieutenant-general, found Carleton easier to work with than Gage. Carleton's austere manner did not overawe him, and the two men got on well. It was in some ways an advantage that their characters were so dissimilar, for Burgoyne gained by the comparison in the eyes of the army. Digby, who was critical of Carleton, admired Burgoyne. He wrote:

From having seen a great deal of polite life, he possesses a winning manner in his appearance and address (far different from the severity of Carleton), which caused him to be idolized by the army, his orders appearing more like recommending subordination than enforcing it. On every occasion he was the soldier's friend, well knowing the most sanguine expectations a general can have of success, must proceed from the spirit of the troops under his command.[10]

Success in battle is the most certain way of ensuring good morale, but no general can expect always to be successful. The ability to make men give of their best in good times and in bad is perhaps of more significance in the military profession than in any other. If the opinions of those who served under him are any guide, Burgoyne possessed this ability in full measure. He may not have been a Great Captain, but he certainly possessed the confidence and affection of his troops.

Carleton, on the other hand, was a cautious general. Quebec had been saved by his exertions and example, and he had no intention of throwing away his victory by a reckless pursuit. He landed his reinforcements and reorganized his force before pushing on upriver. The advance was led by Brigadier-General Simon Fraser, a scion of the Lovat family from the Highlands of Scotland, with a fine reputation as a soldier. He had begun soldiering early, and was forty-five when he went out to Canada with his regiment, the 24th Foot. Fraser reached Trois-Rivières, where he was attacked by the Americans, who had received reinforcements up Lake Champlain. The rebels were bloodily repulsed and their commander taken prisoner. The advance then continued almost to the head of Lake Champlain, where Carleton would need to take to the water if he was to continue the pursuit. The last American to quit Canadian soil was Benedict Arnold, still lame. He had commanded the rear guard with skill, and before stepping on board the boat that was to take him across the lake, he shot his horse to prevent it falling into British hands. With a typically grandiloquent gesture, he then bade farewell to Canada, swearing he would soon return. It was not due to any lack of courage or leadership on his part that the Americans had failed to take Quebec.

Burgoyne wished to take a more active part in the pursuit than Carleton would allow. One of those energetic men whose minds are always fertile with schemes and plans, he became impatient as Carleton plodded on. It would take time, Carleton pointed out, to construct a fleet sufficiently strong to defeat the one already assembled by the Americans at Crown Point. Then why not allow him, expostulated Burgoyne, to take part of the force across Lake Ontario and cut in behind the Americans via the Mohawk valley? This would undoubtedly expedite the American withdrawal, enable Carleton to move more rapidly against Crown Point and Fort Ticonderoga, on Lake Champlain, and also be of assistance to Howe, who had landed on Staten Island on July 3, the day before the American Congress declared the colonies' independence. With a British force established in the area of Albany, Howe's advance up the Hudson valley from New York would be greatly facilitated.

Carleton would not take the risk. He may also have wondered whether Burgoyne was entirely stable at that particular time. Lady Charlotte had died on June 5, 1776, and, despite Walpole's subsequent sneers, Burgoyne was plunged in grief. Writing to Clinton, himself a widower, Burgoyne described himself as "an unconnected cypher in the world— The partner lost which made prosperity an object of solicitude— Interest, ambition, the animation of life is over." [11] We can disregard the extravagant expressions as being characteristic of that age, but Burgoyne was as affected as any husband would be at the loss of a wife with whom he had lived happily for nearly twenty-five years. At such a time it is normal to seek action in order to overcome melancholy. He told Clinton that his wife's death left him nothing but "the honour" of being "finished in a professional grave." Carleton had no intention of obliging him by sending him off on a wild adventure up the Mohawk which could have had disastrous consequences.

It was several weeks before the British could assemble a fleet on Lake Champlain. Sailors and marines had to be brought from the Saint Lawrence to man the ships; guns had to be dragged to Saint Johns, on the Richelieu river, which led from Lake Champlain; and gunboats had to be knocked apart, carried around the ten-mile portage near Chambly, and then reassembled at Saint Johns. When, finally, Carleton was ready to try his fortune as an admiral, it was the end of August, and the bitter winter months were approaching. The Americans had had time to entrench themselves at Crown Point, and to strengthen Ticonderoga's already formidable defenses. It must have been infuriating for a man of Burgoyne's temperament to stand by and watch, as he conceived, time being frittered away. At least, he supposed, Carleton would not be content with a purely naval action, but would embark part of his force to take immediate advantage of what he assumed would be a total naval victory. Here again Carleton demurred. One thing at a time. Burgoyne was left behind in command of the troops while Carleton raised anchor and sailed off in search of the American fleet, commanded by the formidable Benedict Arnold.

Arnold put up a tremendous fight. Off Valcour island on October 11, Carleton, with a greatly superior force, hammered the American fleet to pieces. In the end, Arnold was forced to abandon his flagship, *Congress*, and the only four other boats remaining afloat. He burned them to the waterline before leading the survivors to the American lines at Crown Point. He had done all that man could do, but Carleton was now master of Lake Champlain.

The British occupied Crown Point on November 3, the Americans having withdrawn to Ticonderoga, and Carleton anxiously scanned the sky. He knew better than Burgoyne what a Canadian winter meant. He was reluctant to move any farther south, and resisted proposals that he should assault Ticonderoga, at the bottom end of the lake. He remembered the losses of the British when they wrested the fortress from the French. Now, Major General Horatio Gates, who had served in the British Army, commanded in Ticonderoga, and Colonel Kosciusko had employed his engineering talents to improve its defenses. Carleton persuaded Burgoyne that an assault would be foolhardy, but he was not so successful with some of his other officers. On October 23, Phillips wrote bitterly to Burgoyne from Crown Point, criticizing Carleton's caution, and in particular his decision to abandon Crown Point and withdraw to Canada for the winter. It would have been better, he said, to remain at Crown Point, or at least to have had a shot at taking Ticonderoga before deciding to withdraw. He believed it quite possible that a feint at Ticonderoga would have scared the Americans into abandoning the place.

. . . I wish this army might have been allowed the share in the war which it should, in my opinion, have had. I write my mind freely to you and repose my griefs in the bosom of a friend. . . . I do not talk to the folks here thus; my pride at soldiership forbids it. The army here seems distressed and hurt at the langour which governs every movement. I still fear a dreadful winter. . . .[12]

By the time Burgoyne received this letter he was preparing for his return to England. He had received permission to return home during the noncampaigning season. He has been criticized for quitting the seat of war once winter set in, but this was a common practice at that time. He could plead urgent private affairs, as a consequence of his wife's death, that demanded his attention. He had yet to visit her grave in Westminster Abbey, where she had been buried beside her daughter on June 14. He had also his parliamentary duties to attend to, as well as family affairs to discuss with the new Lord Derby, who had succeeded his grandfather as twelfth earl in February. And there were important matters that could be discussed only in the secrecy of Germain's closet.

Burgoyne did share Phillips' concern over Carleton's decision to abandon Crown Point. "I must honor Carleton's abilities and judgement," he wrote to Clinton; "I have lived with him upon the best of terms and bear him friendship— I am therefore doubly hurt that he had taken a step in which I can be no otherwise serviceable to him than by silence." [13] The criticism was sharp, but it was unjust. Carleton bore the burden of command, and his prime responsibility was the defense of Canada. Only he could be the judge of how that best should be done, and no one bears less responsibility in the military hierarchy than a second-in-command or deputy. He can only advise, but seldom command, and do the latter only in the absence of his chief, and in accordance with that chief's instructions. "A secondary station in a secondary command" is how Burgoyne described his own position.

This was no kind of employment for a soldier burning with ambition, as he explained to Germain on December 10. Germain agreed. Carleton's withdrawal had angered the secretary of state, as he hastened to inform the king.

Lord George Germain has the honour to send to your Majesty Sir Guy Carleton's letter by which your Majesty perceives he has abandoned Crown Point. Genl. Burgoyne was strongly in opinion against that measure. Lord George is glad your Majesty will permit him to make his report on what pass'd between him and General Burgoyne before your Majesty honors him with an audience.[14]

George III had a good opinion of Carleton, and he knew that much of Germain's ill will stemmed from personal enmity. He wrote to Lord North:

That there is a great prejudice perhaps not unaccompanied with rancour in a certain breast against Governor Carleton is so manifest to whoever has heard the subject mentioned, that it would be idle to say more than it is a fact, perhaps Carleton may be too cold and not so active as might be wished . . . but should the proposal be to recall Carleton or censure his conduct that would be cruel and the exigency cannot authorize it.[15]

It was as well that Carleton had such a friend at Court, because both Germain and Burgoyne were undermining his reputation. Germain may be forgiven for this; as the responsible minister, he had lost confidence in Carleton. But Burgoyne had no such excuse. Carleton had made him welcome and had listened carefully to his advice. He had given him leave to return home, not to criticize his commander-in-chief, but to deal with his own affairs. Yet Burgoyne, although he was later to repudiate any charge of self-interest, was outspoken in his criticism of Carleton's caution and dilatoriness. He had probably been told that, but for contrary winds, he might have had the command the previous summer, when Germain wrote to order Carleton back to Quebec, leaving Burgoyne in command of the army. Had the ship carrying Germain's dispatch not been forced to turn back, Burgoyne might have been master of Ticonderoga in the fall of 1776.

It is hard to decide at this distance, and in the absence of conclusive evidence, whether Burgoyne was merely allowing his enthusiasm to run away with him or whether he was in fact intriguing to supplant Carleton. If posterity has concluded that it was the latter, Burgoyne has only himself to blame for the misconception.

Chapter 11

Confusion Worse Confounded

GEORGE III, in a letter to Lord North of December 12, 1776, cautioned him against being influenced by Germain's ill-concealed dislike for Carleton, but the king agreed that the general lacked the drive for operations of the kind contemplated from Canada. A more enterprising general was needed. Carleton's role would be to secure Canada; for this a minimum of 3,000 troops would be required. Any advance from Canada into the rebellious colonies should be a two-pronged one. One part of the force should use as its axis of advance the Lake Champlain–Hudson valley route; the other should make a right hook up the valley of the Mohawk river. Albany should be the junction point. "Burgoyne may command the corps to be sent from Canada to Albany," concluded the king.[1]

John Burgoyne has been credited by some historians with the responsibility for this strategic concept, and in some instances has even been thought to have originated it. This is incorrect. As far back as April, 1775, Lord Dartmouth was anxious to launch an operation designed to cut off New England from the rest of the colonies. A year later Howe was writing that the seizure of New York would facilitate a joint operation with Carleton, utilizing the Hudson valley as its axis. In his early letters from Boston, Burgoyne did no more than endorse the views of his colleagues. New England was the seedbed of rebellion; only isolate New England from the rest of the colonies, and the rebellion would wither on the bough. As soon as Canada could provide a secure base for an advance from the north, and New York the same from the south, the stage would be set for the campaign intended to end the war.

Like all strategic concepts founded on seizure of territory, rather than on the destruction of the enemy army, the proposed strategy for 1777 overlooked the fact that so long as the American army remained in being, the war could continue. There was no certainty that Washington would allow himself to be crushed between the two advancing British armies. However, when strategic concepts win acceptance, they frequently become sacred cows. The king thought the strategy was correct; so did Germain; and so did most of the generals. When all involved were so convinced, it would be wrong to pin the blame for future disaster on any one of them.

Howe, goaded by Germain into taking more positive action, had written on November 30, 1776, with proposals for a more aggressive policy the following year. He would require massive reinforcement (no fewer than 15,000 men), with which he proposed to form two armies, each 10,000 strong. One of these, commanded by Clinton, would operate from Rhode Island. The other, commanded by Howe himself, would move up the Hudson river to make a junction with Carleton, advancing south. The balance of Howe's available troops would be needed to cover New Jersey and secure his base.

Germain received this letter a month after its dispatch. By the time of its receipt Burgoyne had arrived with Carleton's proposals, and had been seen by both Germain and the king. His views, as well as Carleton's, fitted in well with Howe's suggested plan, which received Burgoyne's enthusiastic endorsement. Germain was less happy about Howe's request for more troops. "When I first read your requisition for a reinforcement of 15,000 rank and file," he wrote on January 14, 1777, to Howe, "I must own to you that I was really greatly alarmed, because I could not see the least chance of my being able to supply you with the Hanoverians or even the Russians in time." [2] He managed to salve his conscience by obtaining the figures of all troops shown on Howe's establishment, including the sick in hospital, men listed as deserters or under confinement, and those employed on detached duties. These added up to a grand total of 27,000, which, deducted from Howe's stated requirement of 35,000, left a balance of only 8,000 to be found. This was mere juggling with figures. It nowhere represented the numbers requested by Howe, but Germain was able to convince himself, and presumably his colleagues, that 8,000 reinforcements were all that Howe required. Howe was furious when he received this communication.

In the meantime, he had changed his mind. His problem was basically one of time and space. Even supposing Germain could supply the reinforcements he considered he needed, there was bound to be a time lag of many months before they could arrive in North America. Similarly, Carleton would need reinforcement before undertaking an advance from Canada. It would be at least September before a junction could be made. Thus the best months for campaigning would be wasted while he waited to launch his operation up the Hudson river. Howe therefore proposed an alternative plan, with Philadelphia as the objective. There were, in his opinion, both military and political advantages to be obtained from this. First, it could be assumed that Washington would do his best to defend the rebel capital; there was therefore a fair chance he could be brought to battle and destroyed. Second, an advance across New Jersey would in itself provide protection for his main base, thereby enabling him to reduce New York's garrison to a minimum. Third, the loss of their capital, from where they had so resoundingly declared their independence, must inevitably strike a severe blow at the enemy's morale. A further advantage of this plan was that it would require far fewer troops than the operation originally proposed.

Howe, in proposing this plan, had clearly decided to treat Carleton's advance from Canada as a secondary operation. Carleton had, after all, very nearly captured Ticonderoga the previous fall. In many people's view, he had failed to do so only through lack of enterprise; Burgoyne believed so, and had so told Clinton. If men like General Phillips were critical of Carleton's decision to withdraw from Crown Point, it is reasonably certain that their subordinates felt the same. They would have had friends in Howe's army who knew of their criticism. Why, therefore, should not Carleton, taking advantage of better campaigning weather, complete in 1777 that which he had so lamentably failed to do in 1776? Surely he could advance as far as Albany without more than token support from Howe? Once he was in Albany, with Howe secure in Philadelphia, it would be comparatively easy to plan the next phase of the campaign. In any case, Carleton was unlikely to be in Albany before September, by which time Howe was confident that Philadelphia would have been taken, and Washington probably defeated. Howe was, of course, underrating the fighting ability of the American generals and the resolution of their troops. It is a poor basis on which to found a plan of campaign, but better generals than Howe have fallen into similar traps.

Burgoyne had meanwhile taken himself off to Bath to restore his health. He had had a trying year in Canada, and a tragic one domestically. The gaiety, the glitter, the smart society of Bath, coupled with the restorative effects of its waters, should set him back on his feet again.

It has been suggested that he was not well received by Germain when first he returned from Canada. The secretary of state may have been irritated by Burgoyne's return from the seat of war without his authority. "I am surprised at Clinton's coming home. Burgoyne will not be sorry to see that he is not the only General, second in command, who takes that liberty without the King's leave," he wrote to his under-secretary, William Knox, on December 31.[3]

Burgoyne's first reception may have been chilly, but his assiduous attendance on Germain, and his unconcealed criticism of Carleton's withdrawal from Crown Point, soon restored him to favor. He was received in audience by the king, and was to be seen riding in the park alongside his majesty. He laid himself at the king's feet for whatever employment "he might think him worthy of," [4] and undoubtedly discussed the 1776 campaign and how this might be improved upon in 1777.

Burgoyne also reverted to old habits that took him back to old haunts. He was in Brooks's on Christmas Day, with Charles James Fox, who was at that particular moment opposed to Burgoyne's military role in North America. There he wagered Fox fifty guineas that he would be "home victorious from America by Christmas Day 1777." Fox is said to have replied, "Burgoyne, be not over-sanguine in your expectations: I believe when next you return to England you will be a prisoner on parole." [5]

Fox's comment would have been more significant if Burgoyne had already known he was to receive an independent command in North America. He may have heard that the king had already stated his preference for Burgoyne as commander of the expedition from Canada in 1777, but he was too familiar with the ways of government to place much credence in rumors, and there was General Clinton to be considered.

Clinton had returned home at the end of 1776 an angry man. His unsuccessful attack on Charleston the previous May, as published in the *Official Gazette*, was an implied criticism of his conduct. He had since captured Rhode Island and had been largely responsible for Howe's victory on Long Island. Smarting under a strong sense of injustice, he returned to rally his friends, and with resignation also in mind. His record of his interview with Germain is interesting:

His L.ship began by saying that the other day being with the King, he asked his Majesty whether he had come to any determination in regard to the time of my going back to America; that the King made answer he had come to no determination, that he understood I was still hurt, that he had ever declared his public & private approbation of my conduct on all occasions. Ld. G. told me, he then said to his Majesty, that if I had his Royal approbation he submitted whether it would not be right to give me some immediate publick mark of it, that he knew of none so proper as the red ribbon; * that my Family, Rank, & Character intitled me to it. The King said he had no objection, therefore desired it might be signify'd to me, that notwithstanding there was no vacancy, I might be invested with it immediately. I told his L.ship that nobody could be more sensible than his Humble Servant of the King's most gracious goodness on all occasions. His L.ship said the King seemed to doubt whether Sr. William Howe might not be offended at the Ribbon being given to me in so particular a manner, upon which I looked very glum; & his L.ship told me his answer was, that Sir W. H. would of course be pleased, that an officer he approved of, should receive such a mark, besides which, Mr. H. had no right to monopolize all the red ribbons nor anything else. . . .[6]

Clinton agreed to return to America. The minister then asked him a few questions about the Americans, most of which Germain answered himself, and, according to Clinton, wrongly. Clinton did his best to disabuse him of his contempt for the Americans. He was then asked if he would consider commanding the northern expedition, but he declined on the grounds of his great respect for Carleton. Germain may even have hinted at the governorship of Canada, because Clinton later recorded in his papers: "It is true, indeed, that I was offered a very high command. . . . I could not by any means accept before the very able General in possession should think proper of himself to resign." [7]

The two men took leave of each other with "a thousand civil one two threes, & I as many polite four five sixes." Ger-

* The Order of the Bath, carrying with it knighthood.

main had lost the confidence of yet another of his generals; Clinton, for his part, lost respect for his failure to resign. "General Clinton was pacified by a super-numerary red ribbon—a paltry way of retrieving his honor, which he had come so far to vindicate," commented Walpole, doubtless repeating club gossip.[8] This could account for Burgoyne's strange refusal of the red ribbon some weeks later.

While Burgoyne was at Bath, he began work on a planning paper entitled *Thoughts for Conducting the War from the Side of Canada*. This was in draft only when Germain saw Clinton, and was not submitted to Germain until February 28. There was still no clear indication that Burgoyne would be chosen to execute the plan if it was accepted. Indeed, the king wrote on February 24 to Lord North, saying, "Lord George Germain will tomorrow propose Clinton for Canada and Burgoyne to join Howe. I thoroughly approve of this." [9] But three weeks later, by which time Burgoyne's paper had been read and studied, the scenario had changed. William Knox told Thomas Hutchinson that Burgoyne would get the command of the army in Canada, though possibly this was not decided until after Clinton had been approached and had declined.

Burgoyne's paper went into considerable detail. He did not minimize the difficulties. He thought that Ticonderoga would be strongly defended and that therefore a strong body of artillery would be required for its reduction. According to Fortescue, he "indicated the purely military difficulties and risks of an advance to Albany from Canada by land so clearly, that a wise man might well have hesitated to incur them." [10] This is fair criticism, but Burgoyne did propose ways of overcoming the difficulties. However, like every British general in North America, with the possible exception of Carleton, he underrated his enemy, and overrated the "loyalists," or "Tories." He thought it probable that he would be able to rally the loyalists as he advanced, and ignored the problem of enlisting Canadian support. This was inexcusable, because he had served in Canada and knew the attitude of the French-Canadians.

Given the premise that Burgoyne was not putting forward a plan that depended solely for its success on the operations of the force advancing south from Canada, there was nothing basically unsound about his strategic aim. It was:

to operate against the heart of the rebellion, to cut off the New England States by occupying the line Ticonderoga–the Hudson and holding it by block-houses. Next, to conquer New England, and then, should the Southern States still remain in arms, to fall upon them. Strategically, its greatest recommendation was that, except for a break of a few miles between Lake George and the Hudson, water transport could be used all the way from Quebec to New York.[11]

Although the logistic difficulties of an advance through 200 miles of virtually roadless wilderness were formidable, the fact that the expedition's communications were dependent for the most part on the use of water transport went quite a long way toward overcoming them. At the same time, Burgoyne explicitly stated the aim of the northern expedition. Its sole purpose was "to effect a junction with General Howe, or after cooperating so far as to get possession of Albany and open the communication to New York, to remain upon the Hudson's River and thereby enable that general [Howe] to act with his whole force to the southwards." [12] Surely, the aim could not have been more clearly stated.

Burgoyne recognized that his plan must include alternatives. "Should the strength of the main American army be such as to admit the corps of troops now at Rhode Island remaining there during the winter, and acting separately during the spring, it may be highly worthy of consideration," he wrote, "whether the most important purpose to which the Canada army could be employed, supposing it in possession of Ticonderoga, would not be to gain the Connecticut River." [13] There was, too, always the possibility that the army in Canada could not be reinforced in sufficient strength to provide a reasonable chance of success. In such circumstances there was "the alternative . . . of embarking the army at Quebec, in order to effect a junction with General Howe by sea, or to be employed separately to cooperate with the main designs, by such means as should be within their strength upon other parts of the continent." [14]

The expedition ought not to consist of fewer than 8,000 regular troops, he wrote. A considerable amount of artillery should be provided, as had already been listed by Carleton. The guns would be required initially to reduce Ticonderoga; thereafter, in accordance with Burgoyne's already stated views, they would be employed to blast the Americans out of their field defenses and permit the British infantry to use their bayonets to full effect. "A corps of watermen, two thousand Canadians, including hatchetmen and other workmen, and one thousand or more savages" would also be required.[15]

Ticonderoga would be the first objective. It should be taken by the early summer, and would then provide the base for further operations.

The next measure must depend upon those taken by the enemy, and upon the general plan of the campaign as concerted at home. If it be determined that General Howe's forces should act upon Hudson's River, and to the southward of it, and that the only object of the Canada army be to effect a junction with that force, the immediate possession of Lake George would be of great consequence, as the most expeditious and the most commodious route to Albany.[16]

If the enemy was too strong to be dislodged from Lake George, "the route by South Bay and Skenesborough might be attempted, but considerable difficulties may be expected, as the narrow parts of the river may be easily choked up and rendered impassable, and at best there will be a necessity for a great deal of land carriage for the artillery, provision, etc., which can only be supplied from Canada." [17] In view of what was to happen later, it is significant that Burgoyne should so clearly have foreseen the logistic difficulties of a land advance southward from Ticonderoga.

Burgoyne also adopted the idea of a right hook, to confuse the enemy, and also to reduce opposition to the main advance. There should be a diversionary force directed on Albany by way of Lake Ontario, Oswego, and the Mohawk river. This "would be highly desirable, provided the army should be reinforced sufficiently to afford it." [18] He emphasized that this diversion should not be provided at the expense of the main army. He had himself suggested just such a diversion during the 1776 campaign, but at that time the situation was different because the limit of advance was Crown Point and Ticonderoga. The 1777 plan envisaged a much more extensive operation, necessitating the protection of much longer lines of communication. For these reasons, Burgoyne advocated a specific allocation of the proposed reinforcements to the Mohawk valley force.

This planning paper reached Lord George Germain at the end of February, and no time was lost in its consideration. The king's comments were sensible and to the point.[19]

As sickness and other contingencies must be expected, I should think not above 7,000 effectives can be spared over Lake Champlain, for it would be highly imprudent to run any risk in Canada.

The fixing of stations of those left in the province may not be quite right, though the plan proposed may be recommended. *Indians must be employed, and this measure must be avowedly directed.* . . .

As Sir William Howe does not think of acting from Rhode Island into Massachusetts, the force from Canada must join him at Albany.

The diversion on the Mohawk River ought, at least, to be strengthened by the addition of 400 Hanover Chasseurs.

The provisions ought to be calculated for a third more than the effective soldiery, and the General ordered to avoid delivering these when the army can be subsisted from the country.

Burgoyne certainly greatly undervalues the German recruits.

The idea of carrying the army by sea to Sir William Howe would certainly require the leaving a much larger part of it in Canada, as in that case the rebel army would divide that province from the immense one under Sir W. Howe. I greatly dislike that idea.

There is another memorandum included in the king's correspondence, unsigned but in his handwriting, which was probably intended for General Lord Amherst. Dated March 5, 1777, it reads: "As Sr. W. Howe seems to think that he can't act in the Massachusetts from Rhode Island, it may probably be the most advisable to Force to Albany and Join at that place, Instead of Going to the Connecticut River. The numbers which are proposed for this Expedition, seem to be but Small." [20] Although Jeffrey Amherst did not at that time hold any official appointment, he was one of the senior generals in the British Army, and the one most experienced in North American warfare. He was therefore frequently consulted by the king and the Cabinet.

The royal approval for the basic outline of Burgoyne's plan having been given, it remained for Germain, in the absence of any General Staff, to draft the necessary instructions. This he proceeded to do, in consultation with Burgoyne, who knew by early March that he was to command the expedition. His selection would, as he was well aware, place him in a difficult situation vis-à-vis his commander-in-chief in Canada, but ambitious generals must be prepared for occasional awkwardness in the course of their upward progress. He was confident that his relations with Carleton were good enough to withstand such a test, and he was tolerably certain that a man of Carleton's character would never allow personal considerations to affect his official actions.

Germain did not worry about Carleton's reaction. With all the arrogance of an English aristocrat, and remembering his previous brushes with Carleton, he drafted a dispatch for Burgoyne to carry to Canada. If the wording was not as offensive as he perhaps intended, it contained nothing that might have soothed Carleton's injured pride. The dispatch, dated March 26, 1777, informed Carleton of the proposed expedition. He was told that Burgoyne would be the commander. Indeed, Carleton, after making provision for the defense of Canada, was to place the rest of his army at Burgoyne's disposal. Burgoyne, for his part, was to march from Canada with a view to effecting a junction with General Howe, he was *"to force his way to Albany."* A subsidiary expedition was to be organized under Lieutenant-Colonel Barry St. Leger, of the 34th Foot, whose task would be to advance on Albany via the Mohawk river.

I shall write to Sir William Howe from hence by the first packet [wrote Germain], but you will nevertheless endeavour to give him the earliest intelligence of this measure, and also direct Lieutenant-Colonel St Leger to neglect no opportunity of doing the same, that they may receive instructions from Sir William Howe. You will at the same time inform them, that, until they have received orders from Sir William Howe, it is His Majesty's pleasure that they act as exigencies may require, and in such manner as they may judge most proper for making an impression on the rebels and bringing them to obedience; *but that in doing so they must never lose sight of their intended junction with Sir William Howe as their principal objects.*[21]

When he received Germain's letter, Carleton, whose boiling point was low and whose pride was high, reacted as most generals would have. He proceeded to carry out his orders to the best of his ability, but he also submitted his resignation. It was due to the king that this was refused.

During the two months that elapsed between Burgoyne's committing his *Thoughts* to paper and his subsequent discussion of them with Germain, another letter from Howe had arrived in London. It was dated December 20, 1776; Germain received it on February 23. In it Howe proposed a new plan, which virtually discarded the concept of a joint operation with the army operating from Canada. Instead, Philadelphia was to absorb most of the British Army's attention for the 1777 campaigning season.

> By this change [wrote Howe], the offensive plan towards Boston must be deferred until the proposed reinforcements arrive from Europe, that there may be a corps to act defensively upon the lower part of the Hudson's river, to cover Jersey on that side, as well as to facilitate in some degree, the approach of the army from Canada. . . . We must not look for the northern army to reach Albany before the middle of September; of course the subsequent operations of that Corps will depend upon the state of things at the time.[22]

In the same letter Howe proposed a garrison of rather fewer than 4,500 men for New York, which would be too weak a force to undertake offensive operations in the direction of Albany.

Howe's apparent obsession with Philadelphia is not surprising. It was not only the rebel headquarters, but also the second largest city in the British Empire, and probably the most English city in North America. Its wealthiest citizens copied the life style of the English landed gentry, and the enthusiasm of many of them for the revolutionary cause was cool. If one believed, as did Howe, that the majority of the colonists were being dragged along in the wake of the militant few, the capture of Philadelphia might well swing the balance in the moderates' favor.

The British did not have sufficient troops in North America for two such widely divergent operations as the seizure of Philadelphia *and* Albany. They could only undertake one operation at a time, and the mystery is that Germain does not appear to have appreciated this. He was not a stupid man and he had had some experience of war. The only possible conclusion must be that he underestimated the length of time Howe would need to take Philadelphia, while he overestimated Burgoyne's prospects of getting to Albany on his own. Burgoyne may well have contributed to the latter by his eagerness for an independent command. He may have led Germain to assume that he was capable of advancing to Albany unassisted, always provided that he was given the troops he needed for the task.

Germain approved Howe's plan on March 3, 1777. He took no immediate action to warn Howe of Burgoyne's proposed expedition, which had been approved a few days earlier and must therefore have been fresh in his mind. He did, however, instruct Carleton, in the dispatch that Burgoyne carried with him, to inform Howe of Burgoyne's instructions. Carleton in due course did so, but by the time Howe received Carleton's letter, preparations for the Philadelphia operation were far advanced. Germain had also informed Carleton that he would be sending Howe a copy of his instructions to Carleton, but this was not done immediately. His failure to do so has led to much speculation, and the most likely explanation was given by William Knox in 1782. Knox, under-secretary of state for the colonies, and Germain's principal civil servant, was in a better position to know the facts than anyone.

When all was prepared, and I had them [Germain's instructions to Carleton] to compare and make up, Lord Sackville [Germain] * came down to the office to sign the letters on his way to Stoneland, when I observed to him that there was no letter to Howe to acquaint him with the plan or what was expected of him in consequence of it. His Lordship started, and D'Oyley [deputy secretary] stared, but said he would in a moment write a few lines. "So", says Lord Sackville, "my poor horses must stand in the street all the time, and I shan't be to my time anywhere." D'Oyley then said he had better go, and he would write from himself to Howe and enclose copies of Burgoyne's Instructions, which would tell him all that he would want to know; and with this his Lordship was satisfied, as it enabled him to keep his time, for he could never bear delay or disappointment; and

---

* In 1769 Lady Betty Germain had bequeathed her handsome estate at Drayton, and £20,000 a year, to Lord George Sackville on the condition that he took the name Germain. Stoneland Park, in Kent, was yet another of Germain's splendid residences.

D'Oyley sat down and writ a letter to Howe but he neither shew'd it to me or gave a copy of it for the office, and if Howe had not acknowledged the receipt of it, with the copy of the Instructions to Burgoyne, we could not have proved that he ever saw them. I applied on this occasion to D'Oyley for a copy of his letter, but he said he kept none. I then desired he would get one from Howe who had the original, but he would not ask for it, and Lord Sackville did not call upon Howe for it. . . .[23]

It seems clear from this that the confusion was caused by human error; Germain, Knox, and Christian D'Oyley must all bear their share of the blame. The fact that the error had disastrous consequences is of less importance, since it is doubtful whether any earlier receipt of Germain's instructions would have caused Howe to change his plan. His mind was set on Philadelphia, and his preparations for that operation were nearly finished. By the time he acknowledged receipt of Carleton's copy of Burgoyne's instructions, it was June 5, and he had by then decided, because he lacked troops, to make the Philadelphia operation an amphibious one. This would absolve him from having to secure long land communications across New Jersey, and enable him to deploy his maximum strength by way of Delaware and Chesapeake bays.

Why did Burgoyne seemingly fail to realize this before he embarked for Quebec? He was in and out of Germain's office, and must surely have heard about Howe's projected operations, although the secretary of state may well not have chosen to discuss the matter with him. But Clinton was in London, dubbed a knight in exchange for his agreement to return to America as Howe's deputy, and it is hardly conceivable that Clinton had not been told of Howe's proposed plan. He and Burgoyne were friendly, and had been critical about the conduct of the war; surely they must have exchanged confidences while they were together in England, particularly since Clinton had at one stage been considered for the command of the Canadian expedition.

Burgoyne left London for Plymouth on March 27, 1777. Like every general about to be entrusted with an independent command, he probably felt that the prospect of future distinction softened the pangs of departure; indeed, it is an old saying in the army that the greater the danger, the greater will be the glory. John Burgoyne attached great importance to glory, though, oddly enough, he had resisted an attempt to invest him with the Order of the Bath just prior to his departure, and he left explicit instructions with his young relative the twelfth Earl of Derby that if the offer was renewed in his absence overseas, it was again politely to be declined. There has never been a satisfactory explanation for Burgoyne's refusal of a knighthood. It is possible that he hoped for greater things—a viscountcy, or even an earldom, with a seat in the House of Lords.

At Plymouth he discovered that H.M.S. *Albion* was about to sail for New York, and he took advantage of this to send a few lines to Howe.[24] He told him about the aim of the expedition from Canada, and provided him with an outline of his own instructions. The intention may have been merely to provide Howe with some additional information, since Burgoyne would have assumed that Germain had already written to him on the subject, or he may have been trying to dissuade Howe from going to Philadelphia. The latter seems unlikely, because Burgoyne, like Howe, probably thought that he could deal with Philadelphia long before Burgoyne himself could reach Albany. The one thing certain is that Burgoyne reckoned on Howe's assistance and support, once Albany had been taken.

Ambitious politicians and generals in the eighteenth century did not differ to any material extent from their equivalents today. They were just as liable to be overconfident. The responsible minister in Parliament, heckled daily by the Opposition, was just as likely to be anxious for quick success, while the general, equally anxious to achieve fame, was just as likely to underrate the risks. Burgoyne believed that the plan had every chance of success, provided that he was given the troops he had asked for and that Howe fulfilled his part. He was willing to take a calculated risk. Germain was confident that he had found the right man for the job. Similar situations have occurred throughout history, and failure has followed for much the same reason—bureaucratic inefficiency, delay and muddle in intercommunication, overconfidence, lack of mutual understanding, underestimation of the enemy, bad intelligence, failure to appreciate the logistic problem, and sometimes for allowing political considerations to outweigh the harsh military facts.

Germain was lax in not communicating to Burgoyne the consequences of Howe's decision to advance against Philadelphia, but it seems at least possible that he did not himself appreciate the full import of this. He knew nothing of North America, and had a poor understanding of logistics. He was certainly remiss in endorsing Howe's proposals without at the same time insisting that Howe set aside sufficient troops to support Burgoyne's advance. He was even more wrong in so drafting Burgoyne's instructions that the latter took them to mean that he could not act upon his own initiative if necessary. But any general must be prepared to tear up his orders, and act differently, if by so doing he can better contribute to victory. As for Howe, he may have been wrong to select Philadelphia as his objective, but he thought this a more likely way of winning the war than by waiting in New York until Burgoyne advanced from Canada. He also believed that he would be able to deal with Philadelphia long before Burgoyne was anywhere near Albany, and there was, after all, a reasonable chance that Burgoyne would get to Albany without Howe's support. Burgoyne was a good general, commanding good troops, and, if popular report was correct, upper New York was swarming with loyalists only waiting for the arrival of British soldiers to demonstrate their loyalty.

It was only when everything went badly wrong that everyone began to seek excuses. There was insufficient information, faulty intelligence, and not enough transport; the troops were too few, the loyalists too halfhearted, and the instructions from London too stringent. It took too long to gather the ships to transport Howe's army to Head of Elk, and even the winds were disobliging in their contrariness. More depressing still was General George Washington's reluctance to come to grips with Howe, and allow his army to be destroyed. As for Burgoyne, "Faugh, faugh!" laughed Cornwallis, when Erskine * urged Howe to march north to Albany; "Wooly only wants a junction with Burgoyne that he may crack a bottle with him." [25]

Failure was in fact inevitable for two simple, and commonsense, reasons. First, those responsible for preparing the plans overlooked the serious logistic problems. Second, both the planners and those responsible for executing the plans made the serious error of underrating their enemy. This is not the way to win wars.

* Sir William Erskine (nicknamed "Wooly") was Howe's quarter-master-general. Major-General Earl Cornwallis was one of the better British generals to take part in the American War of Independence, although, like Burgoyne, he ended his campaigning in surrender.

Chapter 12

```
┌─────────────────┐
│                 │
│    Preparing     │
│      for        │
│    Disaster     │
│                 │
└─────────────────┘
```

BURGOYNE'S SHIP made a moderately fast crossing to drop anchor at Quebec on May 6, 1777. While he had been on the high seas, Germain received a letter from Howe making it clear beyond any reasonable doubt that Burgoyne's army could expect little help from Howe. Howe informed Germain of his intention to invade Pennsylvania from seaward, dispelling any hopes that the war might be ended that year. He did not have enough troops to do more than one thing at a time.

Enclosed with his letter to Germain was a copy of a letter to Carleton. Howe had written:

. . . having little expectation that I shall be able, from the want of sufficient strength in this army, to detach a corps in the beginning of the campaign to act up the Hudson's River consistent with the operations already determined upon, the force your Excellency may deem expedient to advance beyond your frontiers after taking Ticonderoga will, I fear, have little assistance from hence to facilitate their approach; as I shall probably be in Pensilvania when that corps is ready to advance into this province it will not be in my power to communicate with the officer commanding it so soon as I could wish; he must therefore pursue such measures as circumstances be judged most conducive to his Majesty's service, consistently with your Excellency's orders for his conduct. . . . I flatter myself . . . that it will prove no difficult task to reduce the more rebellious parts of the province. In the meanwhile I shall endeavour to have a corps on the lower part of Hudson's River sufficient to open the connection for shipping through the Highlands, at present obstructed by several forts erected by the rebels for that purpose, which corps may afterwards act in favour of the northern army.[1]

Surely nothing could have been clearer than this. Howe was intending to march *away* from Burgoyne, rather than *toward* him; it was anybody's guess whether the detachment Howe intended leaving to operate on the lower reaches of the Hudson would be sufficiently strong to force its way to Albany. It is equally clear that Howe envisaged no difficulty over the recapture of Ticonderoga; he also considered that the commander of the army from Canada should be able to fend for himself in the northern part of the province of New York. Howe later claimed that he had written to Carleton entirely of his own volition, since, at the time he wrote, he had received no *official* information regarding the northern campaign.

Carleton must have been astonished to receive Burgoyne's instructions, as drafted by Germain, almost simultaneously with Howe's letter. He would have been even more surprised if he had been sent a copy of Germain's letter, in which the secretary of state acknowledged that from Howe.

As you must from your situation and military skill be a competent judge of the propriety of every plan, his Majesty does not hesitate to approve the alterations which you propose, trusting, however, that whatever you may meditate, it will be executed in time for you to co-operate with the army ordered to proceed from Canada and put itself under your command. I have the pleasure to acquaint you that his Majesty entirely approves of your letter to Sir Guy Carleton.[2]

Study of a map, and consideration of the distances involved, would have shown Germain that he was approving nonsense, but he was no judge of time and space. Nor was he the type of man who troubled to consult others. He did his best to have it both ways by approving Howe's plan while at the same time cautioning him about Burgoyne's expedition. With this he rested content. As Fortescue has written: "Howe was left with directions to attack Philadelphia, and Burgoyne with positive and unconditional commands to advance to Albany and there place himself under Howe's orders. . . . Never was there a finer example of the art of organizing disaster." [3]

Both Carleton and Burgoyne were disturbed by the tenor of Howe's letter, and Carleton was angered by the instructions brought by Burgoyne. He had been ordered to place his troops, less 3,000 deemed necessary for the defense of Canada, at the disposal of his former second-in-command. The plan adopted was the one he had himself proposed, but he was not to be allowed to execute it. It is true he was requested to consult with Burgoyne on the plans for the campaign, but Germain had drafted the instructions in such detail that there was scarcely any room for maneuver. A lesser man than Carleton might have refused to co-operate, but Carleton could not have been more helpful. Burgoyne, naturally aware of Carleton's resentment, went out of his way to pay tribute to him. Writing to Germain on May 14, he acknowledged gratefully the assistance he was being given by Carleton, and he did the same in a letter to General Harvey.

Carleton hit back at Germain, claiming that he had been treated with "Slight, Disregard and Censure," and asserting that this was due to Germain's private enmity. He disagreed with Germain on the employment of Indians and put the record straight so far as the enlistment of Canadians was concerned. Carleton knew how difficult the settlers could be, and how lukewarm for the cause, but his warnings fell on deaf ears. Germain knew better. This undignified wrangling continued throughout 1777 and for most of the following year. Carleton's frequent attempts to resign his appointment would almost certainly have met with Germain's agreement (only once in all their correspondence did he see fit to utter a word of praise in Carleton's favor), but the king put a higher value on his general's services than did the minister. Carleton did not return from Canada until June of 1778, when he was welcomed as a hero. His sovereign later recognized his services by raising him to the peerage as Baron Dorchester.

Burgoyne remained in Quebec for only a few days; within a week he was sailing upriver to Montreal, where his troops were assembling. Before leaving Quebec he wrote again to Howe, emphasizing that his orders were to force his way from Canada with a view to placing himself and his troops under Howe's command. He also complained about the inflexibility of his orders and wished he had been given more latitude in their interpretation. For example, he would have preferred to make "a diversion towards Connecticut," if that seemed advisable, but his orders would not permit it. They were precise, and he had no choice but to carry them out equally precisely. They were "to force a junction with his excellency [Howe]."

Satisfied that he had done all he could to keep Howe informed, Burgoyne took a warm farewell of Carleton. There seems to have been a mutual understanding between these two men. Even in the worst times ahead neither blamed the other for his troubles. Nevertheless, Burgoyne was uneasy. Although outwardly brimming with confidence, he was troubled not only by the apparent confusion over the plan of campaign, but also by its inflexibility. Soon after arriving in Montreal, he wrote to Germain: "It is my design, while advancing to Ticonderoga, and during the siege of that post, for a siege I apprehend it must be, to give all possible jealousy on the side of Connecticut." [4]

Obviously he was brooding about this, for he wrote a few days later to Harvey, repeating the sentence, and expanding on his theme: "If I can by manoeuvre make them suspect that after the reduction of Ticonderoga my views are pointed that way, it may make the Connecticut forces very cautious of leaving their own frontiers, and much facilitate my progress to Albany." [5] There was nothing particularly startling about this, since every general seeks to surprise and confuse his enemy, but it is curious that Burgoyne should be so insistent that nothing in this plan should be taken to mean that he was diverging in any way from the orders given him. He seems to have been overanxious to forestall any criticism that might flow from Germain's pen.

There was yet another cause for concern. As soon as he arrived in Montreal, Burgoyne discovered that the projected campaign was common gossip everywhere he went. "I had the surprise and the mortification," he wrote to Harvey, "to find a paper handed about at Montreal, publishing the whole design of the campaign, almost as accurately as if it had been copied from the Secretary of State's letter." [6] He told Harvey that he had not discussed the plan with even his personal staff officers, and he was certain that Carleton would have been equally discreet. There could be only one possible conclusion. "I am therefore led to doubt," he wrote, "whether imprudence has not been committed in private letters from England." [7]

This was a good example of the biter being bit. There was virtually no censorship of mail. While in Boston, Burgoyne had felt free to write letters to his correspondents in England criticizing his commander-in-chief, as well as giving suggestions for alternative plans. He would have known that there had been widespread discussion of the forthcoming operation in London clubs and drawing rooms, and for this reason it is surprising that he should have counted on secrecy.

In his planning paper, Burgoyne had specified a force of 8,000 regulars, which the king in his comments on the plan had reduced by a thousand. Seven British regiments had been allocated to Burgoyne, each about 400 strong. They were organized into ten companies per battalion, but of these one was the grenadier company, and another the light company. In accordance with contemporary practice, these flank companies were taken away from each battalion to form a corps of grenadiers and a corps of light infantry. These two elite corps were further strengthened by the addition of the flank companies of the battalions remaining behind to garrison Canada. The total British rank and file, exclusive of artillery personnel, was 3,724.

Burgoyne had no cause for complaint with the British regiments provided for his campaign. They were well officered and had proud traditions. The uniform consisted of the familiar red coat, loose fitting and buttoned back to form lapels, a tight stock around the neck, waistcoat, tight white breeches, black gaiters reaching just above the knee, and cocked hat. Grenadiers wore a mitered cap, and soldiers in the light companies a cap better adapted to skirmishing than the clumsy cocked hat. Short gaiters were provided for summer wear.

Both officers and men "clubbed" their hair, which meant wearing it long, plaiting it, turning it up, and tying it with tape. Men whose hair was too short to club had to wear a false piece, or switch, and since the hair had to be heavily greased, the backs of tunic collars were usually black and greasy. As if this tight and uncomfortable uniform was insufficient to constrain movement, the soldier was hung about with numerous articles of equipment. A belt around his waist suspended a bayonet and a short sword, while another belt over his left shoulder supported his cartouche box. He also carried a knapsack containing a blanket, extra clothing, and cleaning materials; a haversack with rations; a canteen; and a fifth share of the materials for his bivouac tent, which he shared with four other men. He was expected to carry rations for four or five days, and the total weight of his accouterments, arms, and sixty rounds of ammunition amounted to about sixty pounds. According to Burgoyne, it made "a bulk totally incompatible with combat." [8]

The infantryman's principal weapon was his musket—the famous "Brown Bess," which served the British Army well for nearly 200 years. It was a smooth-bored flintlock with priming pan, three feet eight inches long in the barrel, and it weighed fourteen pounds. It fired a paper cartridge containing a measured amount of powder and a .69-caliber ball. Since the musket's caliber was .75, the undersized ball made for inaccuracy, but it did permit rapid reloading. Battlefield tactics are dictated as much by weapon characteristics as by anything else, and therefore warfare in the eighteenth century took place at short range. There are, in fact, sound tactical reasons to account for the phrase "Don't fire until you see the whites of their eyes!" Accuracy was not essential; what was important was speed of fire. There was no requirement for accuracy or range if the object was to hit a billboard-sized target at a range of fifty yards. A well-trained soldier could load and fire his musket in twelve to fifteen seconds, and this standard was achieved partly by drill hammered home until it became almost second nature, and partly by the design of the weapon and its ammunition.

Fighting usually took place in large open fields between large groups of people at short range. The tactical formation adopted was usually linear, and the troops were deployed into two or three ranks for volley firing. If numbers permitted, there might be a fourth rank to replace casualties in the front ranks. The ranks would advance as if on parade to beat of drum until they were within eighty to one hundred yards of their objective. At this point the enemy's fire would become effective, and it was a severe test of discipline to require men to hold their fire for yet another fifty yards. Badly trained soldiers would fire too early, leaving themselves with an unloaded weapon at the crucial moment, but well-trained troops would continue to advance steadily until they were virtually at point-blank range. Then, on the order and without breaking stride, they would deliver a volley, reload, and fire a second, and sometimes even a third. The rest was left to the bayonet, on which the British Army placed great reliance.

There were rifled weapons, too, which were much more accurate than the musket, and at much greater range. Major Hanger, who fought under Burgoyne, wrote of the American rifle:

I have many times asked the American backwoodsmen what was the most their best marksmen could do; they have constantly told me that an expert rifleman, provided he can draw good and true sight . . . can hit the head of a man at 200 yards. I am certain that provided an American rifleman was to get a perfect aim at 300 yards at me standing still, he most undoubtedly would hit me, unless it was a very windy day. . . .[9]

Such accuracy had its effects on British morale, and it was said of the American riflemen that they were "the greatest widow and orphan makers in the world." But there were also drawbacks, since rifles took a long time to reload, and the British would frequently charge with the bayonet before reloading could be carried out. The riflemen then had no alternative but to run away, usually leaving an embarrassing gap in the line. It did not take the Americans long to discover that although riflemen were usefully employed as skirmishers and scouts, for close-quarter fighting the musket was the better weapon.

The weather also played its part. In high winds the powder would be blown from the pan; in rain it would be soaked and fail to ignite. Then there were the flints. The cheeseparing British provided poor flints, which required resharpening every ten rounds or so. The American flints were much better, and it used to be said that a "Yankee flint was as good as a glass of grog."[10] Cold steel was the British preference, as Burgoyne made clear in his *Orderly Book* on June 20, 1777: "men of half [your] bodily strength and even Cowards may be [your] match in firing; but the onset of bayonets in the hands of the Valiant is irresistible. . . . It will be our glory and preservation to storm where possible."[11]

Other infantry weapons were the fusil, sword, spontoon, and halberd. Fusils were short-barreled muskets, lighter to handle than the Brown Bess, but equally inaccurate; they were carried by soldiers in the light companies and in fusilier regiments. Officers carried swords, as did certain of the soldiers, while many infantry officers were issued with spontoons, or half-pikes. Sergeants carried halberds, which were seven feet long. It would be difficult to conceive a more cumbersome weapon for use in the thick underbrush of American forests.

The balance of Burgoyne's British contingent was completed by 245 artillerymen. In view of his conviction that artillery was the battle-winning weapon, and remembering his reliance on the advice of Major-General Phillips, it is not surprising that the artillery component of his army was larger than normal. He was later to be criticized for restricting his mobility by taking forward so many fieldpieces, but Carleton certainly supported the requirement for a considerable body of artillery. Provision had to be made not only for the reduction of Fort Ticonderoga, but thereafter guns would have to be emplaced in the fort for its defense. From Ticonderoga onward the field train was to consist of four medium twelve-pounders, two light twenty-four-pounders, eighteen light six-pounders, six light three-pounders, two eight-inch howitzers, four five-and-a-half-inch howitzers, two eight-inch mortars, and four royal howitzers.

All these guns had to be transported, first by water, and later along deeply rutted tracks. They had to be dragged by teams of horses, assisted by men struggling to turn the wheels whenever the gun carriages stuck in the mud and sludge, or in some instances carried in carts, which were equally liable to bog down or turn over. Nor was this all, since the guns, without ammunition to fire, were only hunks of useless brass or iron. Cannon balls, and gunpowder to propel them, made up a heavy load, but Burgoyne complained that the ammunition carried was barely sufficient for a day's action. There were only 124 rounds for each light six-pounder, 300 rounds for each light three-pounder, and 90 rounds for each royal howitzer. The movement of artillery caused a sufficiently difficult logistic problem on the North German plain, where the roads were bad but relatively numerous; in the North American wilderness, the logistic problem was multiplied a hundred-fold.

Burgoyne's German contingent was 3,016 strong. It was commanded by Major-General von Riedesel, who had fought at Minden, where, like Phillips, he had distinguished himself; he had also served with Burgoyne under Carleton in the 1776 campaign. Burgoyne thought highly of him, and Riedesel got on well with Burgoyne, although he did complain of being excluded from his commander's inner counsels. His force consisted of five infantry regiments, a light battalion, and a grenadier and Jäger company. There was also the Hesse-Hanau Artillery Company, under Captain Georg Pausch, and the Brunswick Dragoon Regiment von Ludwig, which had arrived at Quebec on June 1, 1776, with everything except their horses. They were to remain horseless throughout the campaign.

The Germans were good soldiers, tough and disciplined, but greatly hampered by their inability to speak English. The lingua franca among officers was usually indifferent French. They wore blue tunics instead of red, but otherwise did not differ much in appearance from the British. There was no marked difference in weapons, equipment, or training. Only the unfortunate dragoons differed markedly from the rest. Since their uniform was designed for service on horseback rather than on foot, they wore jack boots, spurs, and an ornate cocked hat. They carried heavy sabers, which were utterly useless on foot, as well as being a considerable impediment when they had to trudge 200 miles along muddy North American tracks.

Burgoyne organized his Anglo-German army into three divisions. This was merely an instrument for organizing control, and there was nothing standard about the size or composition of a division. The first division was placed under the command of Brigadier-General Simon Fraser and was described as the Advanced Corps. It consisted of the 24th Regiment (Fraser's own regiment), the grenadier and light infantry composite battalions, two companies of Canadian woodsmen, and a company of fifty rangers (or commandos), raised in Canada and known as Fraser's Rangers, commanded by Captain Alexander Fraser, General Fraser's nephew. As the name implies, the function of Fraser's corps was to lead the advance of the main army.

The second division, or right wing, was commanded by Major-General William Phillips, who, with General Fraser, was Burgoyne's closest confidant. His division consisted of two brigades. The third division, or left wing, contained the Germans. They were also divided into two brigades. A Corps of the Reserve was formed under Lieutenant-Colonel Heinrich von Breymann.

The artillery was split up to operate under the command of the various divisions. Fraser's corps was allotted ten pieces, each wing of the army and the center was allotted one brigade of artillery, each of four six-pounders, and the balance of the artillery was held centrally in the artillery park. Nominally, Phillips commanded the artillery, but since in practice he commanded a division (or wing) of the army, the chief artilleryman was Major Griffith Williams, known as "Old Twelve Pounder." *

There were four other elements in Burgoyne's force: the loyalists, the Canadians, the Indians, and the women. Since so much has been made of Burgoyne's "womanizing" on the campaign, it may be advisable to deal with the women first. For much of its history it was standard practice in the British Army, as in most other armies, to take women on campaign. By regulation and custom no more than six wives were authorized to accompany each company of approximately fifty men. The women drew lots as to who should go, and the rule was that they should be legally married. This was as much hon-

* Burgoyne's order of battle is given on pages 333–34.

ored in the breach as in the observance, but it could be said that any woman who was widowed on a campaign would have little difficulty in finding a replacement for her late husband.

The fact that women were allowed to accompany their husbands on active service owed little to the charitable feelings of the government. There was a much more practical reason. Women, quite apart from the physical, performed other useful functions on campaign. They acted as nurses for the wounded, they washed the soldiers' clothes, they provided a humanizing element in what was otherwise a brutish existence. Since, however, they had to be provided with rations, transportation, and, on occasion, cover from the elements, their numbers had to be strictly controlled. This made it all the harder when a battalion was ordered overseas, because only a small percentage of the married women could accompany their husbands. There were heart-rending scenes at the quayside when a woman said good-bye to the husband she would be lucky to see again, and the husband bade farewell to the family he was consigning to the poorhouse.

There is no reason to suppose that the number of women accompanying Burgoyne's expedition greatly exceeded the usual allocation. It may appear foolish to embark on a campaign in the North American wilderness encumbered by numerous women and children, but since this was then the accepted military practice, to have issued orders to the contrary might well have had adverse effects on morale. The fact that among the ladies accompanying his expedition he found one who amused his leisure moments is again nothing to be wondered at. Burgoyne enjoyed female company. His wife was dead and he had no ties. Thus, an attractive wife of a commissary has found a niche in history as John Burgoyne's *chère amie*. Whether she would have done so had she not aroused the dislike of the formidable wife of Major-General von Riedesel is a matter for conjecture. When the prim, blue-eyed baroness Frederika joined her husband in August, 1777, all Burgoyne's notorious charm for the ladies failed to win her over to his side. Another officer's wife who joined the army at about the same time was Lady Harriet Acland.

The total number of noncombatants—including commissariat and transport men, as well as women—is stated to have been about 1,000. This seems to be a reasonable figure, although Burgoyne has been accused of permitting 2,000 women to accompany the expedition. He vehemently denied this, and it seems unlikely he would have agreed to embarrass his commissaries with the task of feeding so many. Nor do we know whether these numbers included children. Baroness von Riedesel, for example, went on campaign with three of hers.

Burgoyne's original plan depended to some extent on his army's being augmented by loyalists, flocking to serve their king and country. Why he should have expected this, after his experiences in Canada the previous year, is hard to say, but most British generals serving in North America seem to have believed that there were more loyal Americans than the reverse. It was typical of the wishful thinking that, in the end, rendered the British position hopeless. In Burgoyne's case two skeleton regiments were formed—the Queen's Loyal Rangers and the King's Loyal Americans—under Lieutenant-Colonels John Peters and Ebenezer Jessup. They were given a fancy uniform of red, with green facings, but they never amounted to more than a company or two. Together with the Canadian hatchet men, their numbers did not exceed 250, nor were they successful in persuading other Americans to join them as they advanced into New York. Prominent among them was Major Philip Skene, a former British officer who had settled at Skenesboro, or Skenesborough, south of Ticonderoga, where he farmed a considerable estate. He had rallied to the king at the outset of the rebellion, and had found it necessary to exile himself to Canada. There he acquired an importance that was more than his advice was worth. He acted for Burgoyne in the capacity of political officer, and was prominent in the general's counsels.

Carleton had managed to provide Burgoyne with his hatchet men only by invoking the *corvée* of French Canada, and men pressed unwillingly into service frequently seek the first opportunity to desert. Although their enthusiasm for the cause was at best lukewarm, some 150 were eventually collected. Burgoyne's original bid had been for 2,000. There was a similar shortfall where the Indians were concerned. Burgoyne had proposed 1,000, but only some 400 assembled under the elderly La Corne St. Luc, a member of Carleton's Council, and Charles de Langlade; they turned out to be very unreliable allies.

The employment of Indians has been the cause of much criticism, but the truth is that both sides were prepared to make use of their services. The king was strongly in favor of employing them, and so was Germain. On several occasions he exhorted Howe to "make use of the friendly Indians." [12] It seems strange that a man like Burgoyne, who had shown himself to be aware of the psychological aspects of the conflict, should have been so foolish as to ignore the resentment that the employment of Indians was bound to cause.

Burgoyne's main problems were logistic. It was one thing to trace an army's progress across a map; this required little more than experience to state the number of troops and the quantity of equipment and supplies required. It was a different matter to conjure up out of Canada, conquered from the French only twenty years previously, and inhabited by many French Canadians who would willingly have seen the British sent to perdition, all the boats, canoes, carts, horses, forage and fodder, supplies, and workmen needed. Carleton did his best, but his agents were commissaries not renowned for their personal honesty. Burgoyne was shocked when he reached Montreal to discover how much still needed to be done, but he does not seem to have been particularly active himself.

He had been in Canada more than a month before he made an official demand for "contracts for an expeditious supply of horses for the artillery, and 500 carts, with two horses each, for other purposes." [13]

Short of requisitioning carts from the unco-operative farmers, there was no alternative but to build them. This took time, and involved the use of green wood, which did not stand up to strain. Labor was short, and horses were worth their weight in gold. They also ate their own weight in hay and corn every day of the march, and all of this had to be carried with them. Canada could not supply all the animals that Burgoyne needed, and of those that it could, more than thirty were set aside to pull the carts allocated for Burgoyne's personal baggage and for the baggage of his staff. This has led to censorious comment, but it was customary for a general to take the field in style; he had to support his personal staff, as well as entertain his subordinates. Burgoyne did not differ from other British generals in this respect.

Chapter 13

"I Have Beat All the Americans"

FORT TICONDEROGA, on the southwestern shore of Lake Champlain, is nearly 200 miles from the Canadian border; it controls the entrance to Lake George, which in turn leads into the Hudson valley. It was therefore a place of some strategic importance, which the French had been quick to appreciate. They built a fortress there, which they called Fort Carillon. In 1758, Montcalm successfully repulsed James Abercrombie's attempt to capture the fort, but in the following year the French lost it. Amherst drove them out, and renamed the fort Ticonderoga. The British considered the place so strong that they provided a negligible garrison; when Ethan Allen and his Green Mountain Boys arrived outside on May 10, 1775, there was only Captain William Delaplace and about forty-five men of the 26th Regiment to oppose them. The garrison might have put up a better fight had they not been tricked into surrender. When the perplexed Delaplace inquired in whose name he was surrendering the fort, he must have been surprised by the thunderous reply: "In the name of the great Jehovah and the Continental Congress!"

A good deal of nonsense has been written about the natural strength of Ticonderoga, which has been described as the "Gibraltar of the North," and even as the "Key to a Continent." The fort was in fact dominated by high ground within artillery range of its walls, and only if this high ground was strongly held could Ticonderoga be considered secure against capture. Nevertheless, Carleton, in the fall of 1776, considered the fortress too strong to be assaulted at such a late stage in the campaigning season. It was because Burgoyne believed that Ticonderoga would be a hard nut to crack that he asked for, and was given, such a large train of artillery. There is no evidence to suggest that he doubted his ability to capture the fort, but he expected to be compelled to fight hard for it. Certainly, without Ticonderoga in British hands any farther advance southward would be virtually impossible.

Burgoyne embarked his army at Saint Johns, on the Richelieu river, in the middle of June, 1777. He had with him some 7,863 men. The soldiers left behind in Canada their leggings and blanket coats in order to reduce transport; the officers had been exhorted to cut down their baggage to a minimum. There was a severe shortage of transport, and this was not helped by the fact that many carriages, hastily constructed of unseasoned timber, fell apart on the rough track from Chambly to Saint Johns, before the expedition had even arrived at the place for embarkation. There was also an acute lack of horses, which had compelled Burgoyne to impress oxen to pull his wagons.

When hopes are high, the sun is shining, and the drums and fifes are playing, few soldiers give much thought to such a mundane matter as logistics. During the long delay in Montreal, Burgoyne had lost no opportunity to impress his personality on his soldiers, and he had won their confidence and affection. Both he and Carleton had taken great care to prepare the troops for what they foresaw would be an arduous campaign. According to Sergeant Roger Lamb, of the 9th Regiment, "the soldiers were in a high state of discipline and had been kept in their winter quarters with the greatest care, in order to prepare them for this expedition." [1] Lieutenant J. M.

Hadden's Orderly Book also provides, in considerable detail, evidence of the care taken to ensure efficiency. Soldiers were to clean and oil their feet and shoes so that they would be fit to undertake long marches, their clothing was to be carefully fitted, all officers were to receive instruction in gunnery, and special attention was to be paid to health and hygiene. The instructions issued for the construction of field latrines have a modern ring: "New and convenient Necessaries are to be made in the Rear of every Cantonment and Encampment every week, and the old ones filled up; at least six inches depth of Earth should also be thrown into the Necessaries in use every Morning." [2]

There can be no greater mistake than to assume that Burgoyne's expedition was ill-found, or organized in a slipshod fashion. The troops were good; the officers were of as high a caliber as any to be found in any army in the world at that time; they were plentifully provided with artillery. Morale could not have been higher, while confidence in the general was absolute. As Lieutenant T. Anburey wrote: "As to our army, I can only say if good discipline, joined to health and spirit among the men at being led by General Burgoyne, who is universally esteemed and respected, can ensure success, it may be expected." [3]

Unfortunately, Burgoyne could not resist the grand gesture. Although he could be natural and approachable with men, as well as charming and winning with women, as soon as he took up his pen, he became stilted and pompous. He was even worse when it came to drawing up proclamations, forgetting, as many other generals have done, that high-sounding declarations issued *before* a campaign or battle may appear ridiculous *after* the event.

His first proclamation was issued on June 20 at Putnam's Creek.[4] It was addressed to the rebellious colonists, and asserted that the purpose of his address was "to hold forth security, not degradation, to the country." He promised clemency to all those who repented of their misdeeds and returned to the path of righteousness. For those who did not, he had only "to give stretch to the Indian forces under my command (and they amount to thousands) to overtake the hardened enemies of Great Britain and America." This was a threat hardly calculated to endear him to the colonists. He went on to denounce "the wilful outcasts." "The messengers of Justice and wrath await them in the field," he thundered, "and Devastation, famine and every concomitant horror that a reluctant, but indispensable prosecution of military duty must occasion, will bar the way of their return."

Horace Walpole described this effusion as a "rhodomontade in which he [Burgoyne] almost promises to cross America in a hop, step and a jump." It earned Burgoyne the title of the "Hurlothrombo of North America," from the Haymarket Theatre burlesque of that name, and the "Chrononhotontholo-gos of War," from Henry Carey's play. One anonymous pamphleteer summed it up admirably: "General Burgoyne shone forth in all the tinsel splendour of enlightened absurd-ity." [5] Francis Hopkinson produced a delightful parody which had London, as well as North America, rocking with laughter. "But what words can express the plenitude of our horror when the Colonel of the Queen's regiment of light dragoons advanced towards Ticonderoga?" asked Hopkinson. "The mountains shook before thee, and the trees of the forest bowed their lofty heads—the vast lakes of the North were chilled at thy presence, and the mighty cataracts stopped their tremendous career and were suspended in awe at thy approach. . . ." [6] This led to Horace Walpole's gleeful admission "I have never seen more humour, nor better kept up." [7] The humor may seem somewhat forced today, but it made its point at the time.

Though Burgoyne's proclamation to the colonists had been greeted with derision, he went on to make an equally pompous and absurd address to his Indian allies. Not the thousands he claimed, but only some few hundred Indians, from four of the six Iroquois nations, had assembled at the mouth of the Bouquet river. There, on June 22, Burgoyne, in the full-dress

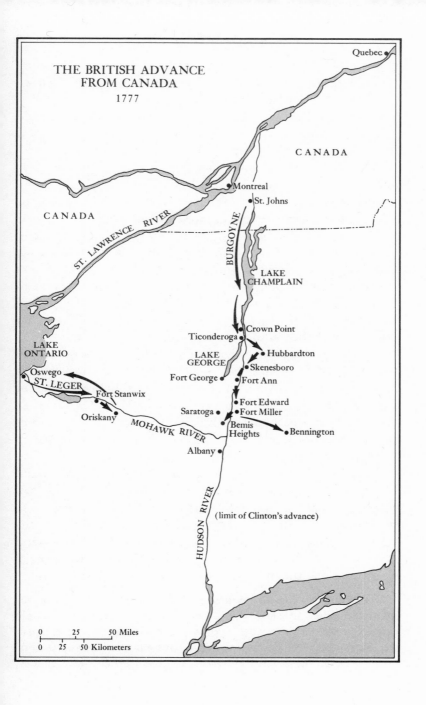

THE BRITISH ADVANCE
FROM CANADA
1777

Quebec

CANADA

Montreal
St. Johns

CANADA

ST. LAWRENCE RIVER

BURGOYNE

LAKE
CHAMPLAIN

Crown Point

LAKE
ONTARIO

Ticonderoga

Hubbardton

LAKE
GEORGE

Skenesboro

Oswego

Fort George

Fort Ann

ST. LEGER

Fort Stanwix

Fort Edward

Oriskany

Saratoga

Fort Miller

MOHAWK RIVER

Bemis
Heights

Bennington

Albany

HUDSON RIVER

(limit of Clinton's advance)

0   25   50 Miles

0   25   50 Kilometers

uniform of a British general, subjected them to an hour-long harangue in his best parliamentary style. He adjured them to avoid bloodshed when they were not opposed in arms. They were to leave unharmed old people, women, children, and prisoners, even in the heat of action. He promised a reward for all prisoners taken, but forbade scalping; scalps could be taken from the dead, when killed in fair fight, but that was to be the limit.

Burgoyne had serious reservations about the wisdom of employing Indians in any capacity other than as scouts or guides. Carleton certainly disliked the idea of employing them, notwithstanding the fact that both the British and the French had used them extensively during the Seven Years' War, and it would seem unlikely that he did not pass on his fears to Burgoyne. It is of course true that the Americans in their turn had toyed with the idea of winning the Indians over to their side—in 1775 the Bostonians actually appealed to the Stockbridge Indians for their active support—but memories of Indian wars were fresh in American minds. It was Germain who was determined that the aid of the Indians should be procured, but nothing did the British cause more harm in American eyes than ill-advised exhortations from London to enlist the aid of Indians and Negroes in order to force the colonists into submission.

The assembly point for the invasion fleet was Cumberland Head, north of Valcour Island, where Benedict Arnold had gallantly fought it out with Carleton the previous year. On the morning of June 25 the drums beat the "General," the sailors and soldiers manned the sides and gave three cheers, and slowly the flotilla got under way. The sight of such a martial scene on a fine summer morning moved Anburey to write:

When we were in the widest part of the lake . . . it was remarkably fine and clear, not a breeze stirring, when the whole army appeared at one view in such perfect regularity, as to form the most compleat and splendid regatta you can possibly conceive. . . . In the front, the Indians went with their birch canoes, containing twenty or thirty in each; then the advanced corps in a regular line, with the gun-boats, then followed the Royal George and Inflexible, towing large booms, which are to be thrown across two points of land, with the other brigs and sloops following; after them the first brigade in a regular line, then the Generals Burgoyne, Phillips and Riedesel in their pinnaces; next to them the second brigade, followed by the German brigades, and the rear was brought up with the sutlers and followers of the army.[8]

There was no sea-borne enemy to combat. The Americans had not attempted to rebuild the fleet burned to the gunwales the previous year, and such ships as they did possess were being conserved to contest possession of Lake George. Burgoyne's flotilla sailed on across the placid waters of Lake Champlain to make its landfall at Crown Point. There Burgoyne landed a small garrison to secure the defenses, and from there he issued a general order on June 30.

The army embarks tomorrow, to approach the enemy. We are to contend for the King, and the constitution of Great Britain, to vindicate Law, and to relieve the oppressed—a cause in which his Majesty's Troops and those of the Princes his Allies, will feel equal excitement. The Services required of this particular expedition are critical and conspicuous. During our progress occasions may occur in which, nor difficulty, nor labour, nor life are to be regarded. This Army must not Retreat.[9]

The wording of this order bears all the evidence of having been drafted by Burgoyne himself. The language was bombastic, but the intention was clear.

On July 1 the expedition hove to beyond gun range of Ticonderoga, and disembarkation began. Burgoyne expected some American resistance, but he had no doubt of his ability to take the fortress. Writing to General Howe two weeks previously, he had given him

intelligence of my situation at the time, and of my expectation of being before Ticonderoga between the 20th and 25th instant; that I did not apprehend the effective strength of the army would amount to above 6500 men; that I meant to apply to Sir Guy Carleton to send a garrison to Ticonderoga when it should be reduced, but that I was apprehensive he would not think himself authorised by the King's orders to comply; that whenever, therefore, I might be able to effect the junction, Sir William need not expect me to bring near the original number. I repeated my perseverance in the idea of giving jealousy on the side of Connecticut, and at the same time my assurances, that I should make no manoeuvre that could procrastinate the great object of junction.[10]

It is hard to conceive what Howe made of this letter. By the time he received it his troops were already embarked and waiting for a favorable wind to sail for Delaware Bay. There is indeed something pathetic in Burgoyne's attempts to keep Howe informed, as if in return he hoped that Howe would either change his plans or annihilate distance from Philadelphia and come thundering up the Hudson to join hands at Albany.

There remained the immediate problem of Fort Ticonderoga, its walls rising steep and sheer above the green meadows that sloped gently down to the waters of Lake Champlain. The trees and underbrush had been cleared to provide a field of fire, and trenches had been dug and abatis constructed to form the outer defenses. The portage between Lakes Champlain and George was protected by a barbette, known as Mount Hope, and across the lake a strong position had been constructed on Mount Independence. A bridge linked the two positions, with guns sited to bombard the British fleet with converging fire as it closed on the fortress. Ticonderoga was formidable, but any fortification can only be as strong as the hearts of those who defend it. In this respect Ticonderoga was lacking.

The American commander in the Northern Department was Major General Philip Schuyler, an American aristocrat of Dutch extraction, who was held in high regard in New York. He was also highly regarded by George Washington, but his reserved manner and wealth did not endear him to those of his countrymen with more egalitarian views. In 1776 he had played a prominent part in resisting Carleton's advance toward Ticonderoga, but in March, 1777, as a result of petty intrigues, engineered largely by General Gates, he was superseded for a time. Intrigue did not, however, deter this high-minded man from continuing to do his utmost to ensure the defense of the Northern Department, and in the spring of 1777 he had even provided food at his own expense for the Ticonderoga garrison.

Brigadier General Anthony Wayne had been largely responsible for improving the fortifications, but he was short of men, ammunition, and guns. He had failed to fortify a hill about a mile from the fort, west of Lake Champlain and south of the connecting channel with Lake George. It was known locally as Sugar Hill or Sugarloaf, although some people referred to it as Rattlesnake; it was also called Mount Defiance. The hill was about 800 feet high, with apparently sheer slopes, but the lame Benedict Arnold, accompanied by Wayne, had scaled Sugar Hill from the northwestern side. Obviously it should have been fortified, but when so much needed to be done, the construction of defenses on Sugar Hill was given a low priority, and for one apparently sound reason: the enemy would be unable to drag their guns up the steep slopes.

After his reappointment to the command of the Northern Department, in May, General Schuyler had sent his ablest subordinate, Major General Arthur St. Clair, to take command at Ticonderoga. St. Clair was a Scotsman who had served in the British Army, and he was unhappy about Ticonderoga. "If the enemy intended to attack us," he wrote to Schuyler, "I assure you, sir, we are very ill-prepared to receive them. The whole amount of Continental troops, fit for duty is one thousand five hundred and seventy-six . . . we cannot reckon upon more than twenty-two hundred men." [11]

Schuyler was disturbed by this information, although he wrote to Washington on June 10 discounting reports that the British garrison in Canada had been increased and that Burgoyne had arrived there in May. He proceeded at once to Ticonderoga to see for himself, and on June 20 reported to Congress.

I was in hopes to have found the post in a better state of defense than it is. . . . I was very disagreeably disappointed to find the troops at Ticonderoga so miserably clad and armed . . . many are literally barefooted and most of them ragged . . . the huts built last campaign . . . consumed in the course of the winter . . . as fire wood . . . the enemy cannot be ignorant how very difficult if not impossible it will be for them to penetrate to Albany unless in losing Ticonderoga we should lose not only all our cannon but most of the army designed for this department.[12]

Schuyler and St. Clair then attempted to improve the defenses, but since neither of them credited reports that the British were preparing to attack Ticonderoga, they did not act with the urgency that the situation demanded. Leaving St. Clair to carry on the work, Schuyler returned to his headquarters at Fort George, informing the New York legislature that he had left Ticonderoga in a better state than he had found it, and that St. Clair did not believe that the British intended to attack the fort.

Schuyler understood the strategic importance of Ticonderoga, but he does not seem to have appreciated the importance attached by the British to its capture. They recalled how bitterly they had fought the French for its possession; and they recalled, equally bitterly, how easily they had been tricked into delivering the place up to Ethan Allen. Ticonderoga was a magnet that attracted the British with compelling force, and Burgoyne knew he would become a popular hero if he took the fort.

His plan depended on the employment of a considerable weight of artillery. Anburey reflected ruefully, "Fortified as the enemy are, nothing but a regular siege can dispossess them"; and Burgoyne proposed to batter the place into submission from both the lake and landward sides. After landing his British troops on the western shore of Lake Champlain, and the Germans on the eastern, the *Royal George,* flying Burgoyne's pennant, accompanied by the *Inflexible,* stood inshore to open the bombardment. Fraser's Advanced Corps was sent on a wide outflanking movement to take Mount Hope, which covered the portage to Lake George. Realizing the danger to this exposed position, St. Clair ordered a sortie to cover the withdrawal of the Mount Hope garrison.

The sortie ran into Burgoyne's Indians. St. Clair's men got away in the resultant confusion with little loss, but his main problem was to control the fire of his own men, who discharged their muskets at random. James Wilkinson, the fort's adjutant, recounts one incident when a sergeant was ordered to shoot a man who was working his way toward the fort. No sooner was the order obeyed than every man on the walls, without command, fired a volley, and two more volleys were fired before the firing could be stopped. The only result of this indiscriminate fire was that the target, a drunken soldier of the 47th Regiment, was not wounded but taken prisoner. With the aid of a bottle of rum, and a little gentle probing, St. Clair knew by nightfall on July 3 the order of battle of Burgoyne's army. He was also left in no doubt that Burgoyne soon intended to assault Ticonderoga.

The significance of the Sugar Hill feature had not escaped the eye of Major-General William Phillips; nor did it escape that of Lieutenant William Twiss, Burgoyne's chief engineer. Twiss reconnoitered the hill and found it was climbable, albeit with difficulty. He also reported that the hill dominated the fortifications of Ticonderoga and Mount Independence at ranges of 1,400 and 1,500 yards respectively. After hearing his report, Phillips is reputed to have said, "Where a goat can go, a man can go, and where a man can go, he can drag a gun." Preparations were made to clear a passage up the slopes for the guns, and a working party constructed gun emplacements on the summit. Work began early on July 5 and proceeded with such energy that two guns were emplaced by the same night. Such activity could not be concealed from enemy observation, but if there had been any intention to surprise the enemy this was given away by the action of some artillerymen who fired at a vessel in the narrow strait leading from Lake Champlain into Wood Creek. Also, the Indians lit fires on the summit, and by last light that day St. Clair knew that the game was up. He could either stand fast and wait to be pounded into inevitable surrender, or he could slip away while there was yet time.

As soon as St. Clair heard the fire from Sugar Hill, he turned to Wilkinson and said, "We must get away from this, for our situation has become desperate." A council of officers was convened, every one of whom agreed that the garrison should withdraw, but the final responsibility was St. Clair's. It was a brave decision, since he knew he would be blamed for abandoning the fort to the enemy. But St. Clair believed his responsibility was to preserve his army as a fighting force—not to hand it over as prisoners to the British. He ordered a bombardment to cover preparations for the evacuation of Ticonderoga, and orders were issued for the withdrawal.

So hurriedly was this done that James Thacher, a doctor serving in the garrison, did not know until he was awakened at midnight that the evacuation had begun. The sick, wounded, and women were loaded into boats, and then sailed down Wood Creek to Skenesboro, confident that the bridge and boom linking Ticonderoga with Mount Independence would delay any pursuit by water. The rest of the garrison slipped across the bridge under cover of darkness, intending to rally on Mount Independence, but their efforts to destroy the bridge behind them were ineffectual. Three of the garrison took advantage of the confusion to desert to the British. They arrived just before daylight, but the American plan had already been given away by an incompetent French adventurer, Roche de Fermoy, who was the commander on Mount Independence. He had made no preparations for withdrawal, and in his efforts to pack his belongings he managed to set fire to his tent. The flames were seen from far away, notably by General von Riedesel, whose Germans were making their way painfully down the eastern shore of Lake Champlain, with the intention of attacking Mount Independence from the east. Realizing that something was afoot, Riedesel roused his troops and had them on the move before sunrise.

Brigadier-General Fraser was equally quick off the mark. As soon as he had received information from the three deserters, he at once advanced to seize the fortress, sending a message to Burgoyne, who had retired to the *Royal George* for the night. Burgoyne received this message just after dawn, by which time the Union Jack was once more flying above the ramparts of Ticonderoga. Fraser informed his commander of his intention to pursue the enemy, and Burgoyne concurred. "Knowing how safely I could trust to that officer's conduct," wrote Burgoyne, "I turned my attention to the pursuit by water, by which route I understood one column were retiring in two hundred and twenty bateaux, covered by five armed gallies." [13]

As St. Clair's weary and dispirited men made off down the rough track leading to Hubbardton, with Fraser in hot pursuit, and with Riedesel coming up fast, Burgoyne's naval commander, Commodore Lutwidge, made short work of the supposedly unbreakable boom. By nine o'clock in the morning a passage had been cleared for the frigates and gunboats, and the pursuit to Skenesboro began. It was a moment of triumph for Burgoyne, who had expected Ticonderoga to hold out for days, perhaps even for weeks. Not even he, with all his self-confidence, could have anticipated such a rapid and virtually bloodless surrender. When the time came, five days later, to write his dispatch to Germain, he did not attempt to conceal his pride, although more than a month passed before that dispatch arrived in London. Rumor of course preceded it, which led Horace Walpole to comment: "I suppose the silent, modest, humble General Burgoyne has not yet finished his concise description of the victorious manner in which he took possession of [Ticonderoga]." [14]

Ticonderoga had fallen; Burgoyne was a popular hero. The king, when he heard the news, burst into Queen Charlotte's bedroom, exulting, "I have beat them, beat all the Americans." John Adams' comment in a letter to his wife, Abigail, was more to the point: "I think we shall never defend a post," he wrote, "until we shoot a general." [15]

Chapter 14

The Dividing of the Ways

THE WATERS of Lake Champlain flow north and are fed by Lake George and South river. Some thirty miles as the crow flies south from Ticonderoga lay Fort George, situated at the southern end of Lake George, which provided the easiest access to the Hudson valley. The importance of this route had been noted by the king, who had written: "If possible, possession must be taken of Lake George, and nothing but an absolute impossibility of succeeding in this, can be an excuse for proceeding by South Bay and Skenesborough." [1] Burgoyne had also emphasized that "the immediate possession of Lake George would be of great consequence, as the most expeditious and most commodious route to Albany. . . ." [2]

There was, however, another route from Ticonderoga to the Hudson valley. This was east of Lake George, via South river, which enters Lake Champlain just below Ticonderoga. South river flows out of a small and swampy lake, South Bay, and used to be navigable for most of its length of twenty miles; near Lake Champlain it narrows into a gorge, which is dominated from the high ground above. Just north of South Bay, another river, Wood Creek, joins South river. Four miles from the junction was the small hamlet of Skenesboro, seat of Philip Skene, Burgoyne's political adviser. Skene had constructed a sawmill and iron foundry on Wood Creek, and had built himself a handsome house. A rough track had been hewn through the forest to Lake Champlain, and another, rougher still, went by way of Fort Anne to Fort Edward, on the Hudson.

By midday on July 6, Burgoyne had launched his pursuit of St. Clair. Leaving the 62nd Regiment to garrison Ticonderoga, and the Brunswick Regiment Prinz Friederich to secure Mount Independence, he sent his gunboats, followed by the *Royal George* and the *Inflexible*, in chase of those Americans who were escaping up South river. Three British regiments were included in this force, and around 3:00 P.M. they caught up with the enemy at Skenesboro. The Americans, confident that the boom connecting Ticonderoga with Mount Independence would long delay the British, were taken by surprise. "We were unsuspicious of danger," wrote Doctor Thacher, "but behold, Burgoyne himself was at our heels." [3]

St. Clair had presumably chosen to evacuate his sick and noncombatants by South river because the British controlled the portage between Lake Champlain and Lake George, but whatever his reason, he played right into Burgoyne's hands. In a short and sharp engagement, most of the American boats were either destroyed or set on fire. Troops were then landed to work their way through the thick forest to Skenesboro, where there was a small fort, but the terrain was so difficult that it took much longer than Burgoyne had anticipated. The Americans managed to set the fort on fire before escaping down the track to Fort Anne. Many of their wounded and almost all their baggage fell into British hands, but some of the sick and supplies were got away by boat up Wood Creek to Fort Anne.

A detachment of the 9th Regiment under Lieutenant-Colonel John Hill was dispatched hotfoot to make contact with the retreating enemy. Because the track was bad and the burning houses at Skenesboro had set fire to the surrounding woods, Hill's men made desperately slow progress. It took them an entire day to cover the seven miles to Fort Anne, and although they succeeded in capturing several boats laden with women and invalids, Hill reached the fort only to discover that he was outnumbered. A supposed deserter, who turned out later to be a spy, informed Hill that the fort was held by nearly 1,000 men. He then promptly decamped with the information for the enemy that the British did not amount to more than 200.

Hill took up a defensive position and sent a message to Burgoyne requesting reinforcements. Attacked by about 400 New York militia, led by Colonel van Rensselaer, the British were hard put to it to hold their ground. This "smart skirmish," as Doctor Thacher called it, lasted for several hours, in the course of which the Americans worked their way through the dense undergrowth, effectively cutting off Hill's retreat. The British position seemed desperate, but suddenly the Americans withdrew. They had heard a succession of war whoops, and had immediately deduced that British reinforcements, preceded by Indian scouts, were approaching. In fact, the war whoops had been made by a solitary British officer, deserted by his Indian companions, who hoped to persuade the Americans that he was approaching at the head of a considerable force.

Burgoyne had meanwhile ordered Hill to withdraw, sending forward Brigadier-General Henry Powell with the 20th and 21st Regiments to cover Hill's retreat. Hill got away successfully with thirty prisoners and the colors of the 2nd New Hampshire Militia. He left behind his wounded, under Sergeant Lamb, who later wrote: "It was a distressing sight to see the wounded men bleeding on the ground; and what made it more so, the rain came pouring down like a deluge upon us." [4] The resourceful Lamb, whose knowledge of medicine was rudimentary, was provided with only a few men to protect his wounded. He was, however, given a letter by Burgoyne which could be handed to the Americans if he was forced to surrender.

Here I remained seven days with the wounded men, expecting every moment to be taken prisoner [he wrote]; but, although we heard the enemy cutting down trees every night during our stay, in order to block up the passages of the road and river, yet we were never molested. Every necessary which we wanted was sent us from the camp at Skenesborough, and all the wounded (except three who died) were nearly fit for duty when we arrived at headquarters.[5]

Burgoyne personally led the pursuit up South river. Fraser was responsible for following up the main American force, which had taken the forest road toward Castle Town; he had with him the light and grenadier battalions of the Advanced Corps, as well as the 24th, his own regiment. Behind came the Germans, moving at a slower pace along the execrable track. The plan was to drive the retreating Americans toward Skenesboro, where Burgoyne would soon be in a position to deal with them. Fraser had set his men in motion about 5:00 A.M. on July 6, and he drove them remorselessly until four in the afternoon, by which time they were exhausted. About then, Riedesel caught up with him, and there arose the delicate question of seniority. Fortunately, Riedesel respected Fraser, and there was no friction. Fraser, it was decided, was to press on ahead, while the Germans advanced at a slower pace. The object was to bring the retreating Americans to battle, and, if possible, to destroy them.

Just before first light on the seventh, Fraser came up with the American rear guard, commanded by Colonel Seth Warner. The Americans had bivouacked for the night about two miles from the hamlet of Hubbardton, on the crosstracks to Castle Town. Warner had with him his own regiment of Green Mountain Boys from Vermont, Colonel Nathan Hale's 2nd New Hampshires, and Colonel Ebenezer Francis' 11th Massachusetts—a total of 900 men, who outnumbered Fraser's force. The two sides were about equally worn down by forced marching through the hot and humid forest, but Fraser's men were the pursuers, and their morale was high. They had surprised the Americans, who were cooking their morning meal before pushing on to join St. Clair's main body, which had not halted at the hamlet of Hubbardton, but had carried on for another six miles to Castle Town.

The 24th Regiment led the British attack, and immediately scattered the New Hampshire men. Warner's Vermonters, many of them skilled woodsmen, were, however, a different proposition. Using cover cleverly, they picked off many of the red-coated British soldiers as they blundered about in the undergrowth. But the British pressed on, and began to climb the slope toward the spot where Warner and Francis stood watching the rout of the New Hampshire militia. Their attention was diverted by a messenger from St. Clair, bringing the news that Burgoyne was in Skenesboro. St. Clair was about to continue his retreat, and he ordered the rear guard to do the same. "We must move with great expedition," said Francis, "or the enemy will be upon us." [6]

The Americans held the tactical advantage, since they still possessed the high ground, but the momentum of Fraser's attack threatened to outflank them and cut off their retreat. The American reply to this was to advance the Massachusetts regiment to the crest of the ridge and pour fire onto the British toiling up the steep slope. Francis was so prominent in encouraging his men that Lieutenant Digby later described him as a "gallant and brave man." [7] He certainly shook the light companies, under Lord Balcarres, who was wounded. They were halted in their tracks. On the British right, Major John Acland's grenadier companies were more successful; they succeeded in scaling Mount Zion, an isolated hill commanding the road to Castle Town. Warner's attempt to force them off the hill was repulsed, as was Balcarres' second attempt to gain the ridge. It was clear to Fraser that the Americans were so strongly posted, and were fighting so stoutly, that he had little hope of flushing them out without reinforcement.

Riedesel's main force was still several hours' marching time

away, but he had started off himself at 3:00 A.M. with about
180 light troops and grenadiers. Breymann's regiment was
close behind. The sound of musketry ahead spurred Riedesel
on, and he came up with Fraser at about the time the second
British attack failed. Without waiting for Breymann's regiment, Riedesel deployed his light troops, at the same time
ordering their band to start playing. He hoped to deceive the
Americans into believing that this was the beginning of a full-
scale brigade attack. As the Germans, singing their battle
songs, came down the slope to attack the American right,
Fraser launched yet another assault on the American position.
Balcarres, nursing his wounded arm and bruised shoulder, led
his men forward to take the crest at bayonet point, if indeed
they lived long enough to get there. They might never have
done so but for the unexpected reinforcement of the German
Jägers and grenadiers. Together, the British and Germans
were irresistible; Francis' Massachusetts militia fell back in
disorder. Francis was killed by a German bullet as he attempted to rally them. The engagement, since known as Hubbardton, was over.

The sound of the firing had been heard at Castle Town,
and St. Clair took immediate steps to send relief. He ordered
two militia regiments to turn back to Warner's aid, but without much avail. Their reluctance to do so was clear; they
redoubled their pace in the opposite direction. Much the
same attitude prevailed in Castle Town. "I perceived a manifest repugnance in the corps to turn about and march upon
the enemy," recorded James Wilkinson; "even one of the
Brigadiers was open in his opposition to the measure." [8] St.
Clair could only wait until the sound of musketry died away
and his aides-de-camp returned with a report of defeat. With
the comment "All is over," St. Clair changed the direction of
his withdrawal, from toward Skenesboro to Manchester and
Bennington; and he made certain that his troops did not
slacken their pace.

They moved fast for fear of their pursuers, but they need

not have worried. Warner and Francis had fought the British to a standstill, in the process killing 50 and wounding 100; they also killed 10 Germans and wounded 14. The action had lasted just under one hour, but to those involved, including Anburey, it had seemed half a lifetime. The day was hot, the forest was dank, and flies were everywhere. Slowly the prisoners were rounded up, dug out at bayonet point from where they were skulking in the woods. It was a good haul; 228, mostly New Hampshire militia, including their colonel, Nathan Hale, and seventeen officers. Hale (not the well-known American patriot) was later released on parole to answer allegations of cowardice, but he was never charged. He returned to British hands, and died a prisoner of war in 1780.

Hubbardton was a hard-fought action. It should have served as a warning to the British that the American militia, when well posted and well led, could be a formidable enemy. The elite corps of Burgoyne's army had been compelled to fight hard, though saved by Riedesel's opportune arrival. Burgoyne's account of the action paid warm tribute to Fraser and his troops; as for Riedesel, "the Germans pushed for a share in the glory, and they arrived in time to obtain it." [9] This was less than just, since without the Germans there might well have been no glory.

All seemed to be going well on July 11 when Burgoyne drafted his dispatch. He was installed with his staff at Skenesboro, with Riedesel's Germans and the British camped nearby. In less than a week he had taken Ticonderoga and driven St. Clair helter-skelter before him. The wounded were on their way back to Ticonderoga, it was expected that loyalists would soon come flocking in to join him, and "General John Burgoyne" was going to be the toast of London. It is not to be wondered at that the wine should flow and the fiddles play as the commander-in-chief celebrated his victory with his officers.

"The country from Albany to Lake George seems good

land but as yet little cleared unless where we had posts during the war," Captain Robert Innes had written to James Grant in August of 1772.[10] Much the same description held true five years later. The land was mostly covered in forest and seamed with rivers and streams that turned all low-lying ground into swamp. Wherever men had hacked a narrow track through the thick underbrush, they had tried as far as possible to stick to the high ground. Where this had proved impossible, they had been compelled to cross streams by narrow and rickety wooden bridges, and swamps by laboriously laying logs side by side across the treacherous ground. These tracks were intended only for the occasional farm wagon or man on horseback; they were not constructed for the passage of an army. Settlements were few and far between. Castle Town, where Riedesel was directed to concentrate his German brigade, was "a wretched place, consisting of only twenty miserable dwelling houses," [11] and Skenesboro was little better. Fort Anne, for all its high-sounding title, was no more than a square wooden palisade, containing a dilapidated barrack and storehouse. Almost everything was made of wood, and it was uncommon to find more solidly constructed buildings. The woods swarmed with violently biting flies and mosquitoes, as well as with game. In winter the cold was extreme; in the summer it alternated between downpours of rain and humid heat. Those who had to travel in those parts chose to do so, whenever possible, by boat or on horseback.

No one was more aware of this than Burgoyne, as he paced the living room of Philip Skene's house, discussing with Fraser and Skene the problem of the advance. The British had outrun their supplies and were short of transport animals. However, Skene was optimistic, claiming that the local inhabitants were loyalists at heart; they waited only for Burgoyne's appearance in their midst to declare their sympathies. This advice may have been due partly to self-interest, but Skene was to some extent supported by Schuyler. Writing from Fort Edward, Schuyler told Washington, "a very great proportion of the inhabitants are taking protection from General Burgoyne, as most of those in this quarter are also willing to do." [12]

The problem facing Burgoyne was whether to retrace his steps to Ticonderoga, and then embark his troops for the passage to Fort George; or to continue his advance overland from Skenesboro, via Fort Anne, to Ford Edward on the Hudson. He decided on the latter, for reasons that at the time seemed to be sufficiently compelling:

I considered not only the general impressions which a retro-grade motion is apt to make upon the minds both of enemies and friends, but also, that the natural conduct of the enemy in that case would be to remain at Fort George, as their retreat could not then be cut off, in order to oblige me to open trenches, and consequently to delay me, and in the mean time they would have destroyed the road from Fort George to Fort Edward. On the other hand, by persisting to penetrate by the short cut from Fort Anne, of which I was then master, to Fort Edward, though it was attended with great labour, and many alert situations, the troops were improved in the very essential point of wood serv-ice; I effectually dislodged the enemy from Fort George with-out a blow; and seeing me master of one communication, they did not think it worth while to destroy the other. [13]

War is an option of difficulties, and every commander has to weigh the difficulty of one course against another. There was much to be said for a return to Ticonderoga followed by passage down Lake George. It was the longest in distance, but it could well turn out to be the shortest in time. On the other hand, it meant a failure to reinforce success, and would un-doubtedly dishearten those loyalists who were daily counting on the arrival of the British. It also meant abandoning the threat to Connecticut, on which Burgoyne set such store as a cover plan.

Burgoyne may well have underestimated the difficulty of the terrain between Skenesboro and Fort Edward. The dis-tance was only twenty-three miles, but the ground was low-lying and swampy. For most of the way, the track ran through thick forest and could easily be blocked. There were numerous bridges, which could be destroyed. A careful reconnaissance by Lieutenant Twiss disclosed the difficulties, but Twiss did not regard them as insuperable. Burgoyne had full confidence in this officer who had distinguished himself in the capture of Ticonderoga. If Twiss's experienced eye, backed by Skene's advice, coincided with the general's preferred option, a decision could the more easily be reached. The army, having rested and received its supplies, would continue the advance from Skenesboro. There was to be no going back to Ticonderoga.

In his dispatch of July 11, Burgoyne reported his troops as "very much fatigued," and short of provisions, tents, and baggage. There were only 180 carts available, many of the Canadian-built ones having disintegrated on the appalling track from Ticonderoga, and the countryside was devoid of either horses or cattle. The rain poured down, turning tracks into quagmires and swelling the numerous streams into torrents. It was necessary, wrote Lamb, "to suspend all operations for some time, and wait at Skenesborough for the arrival of provisions and tents." The interval was employed in improving the communications forward. "This was attended with incredible toil. The Americans, now under the direction of General Schuyler, were constantly employed in cutting down large trees on both sides of every road, which was in the line of march. The face of the country was likewise so broken with creeks and marshes, that there was no less than forty bridges to construct, one of which was over a morass two miles in extent." [14]

Not all of Burgoyne's officers agreed with the decision to continue the advance from Skenesboro. "Many were of opinion the General had not the least business in bringing the army to Skenesborough, after the precipitate flight of the enemy from Ticonderoga," wrote Digby, "and tho' we had gained a complete victory over them, both at Fort Anne and Hubberdton, yet no visible advantage was likely to flow from either except proving the goodness of our troops at the expense of some brave men." [15] This criticism was unfair, since Burgoyne could hardly have been expected to allow St. Clair to get clear away. His pursuit was almost bound to follow the line of the American's withdrawal, and the fact that he had failed to catch St. Clair and utterly destroy him is more a tribute to St. Clair's fleetness of foot than to any lack of determination on Burgoyne's part. That Digby did not necessarily share the views of those who thought Burgoyne was mistaken is clear from his comment that doubtless the general "had his proper reason for so acting, though contrary to the opinion of many." [16]

It was satisfactory to be able to report that several hundred loyalists had joined the British at Skenesboro. Those who had already been in action had fought with spirit. Burgoyne told Germain that he intended to employ them "particularly upon detachments, for keeping the country in awe, and procuring cattle." [17] If provincial troops were seen to be acting vigorously in the king's cause, Burgoyne believed the impression created could only be a favorable one.

He would have wished the same could be said about the Indians. They had lingered overlong looking around Ticonderoga, and Burgoyne had found them to be virtually useless. "If, under the management of their conductors, they are indulged, for interested reasons, in all the caprices and humours of spoiled children, like them they grow more unreasonable and importunate upon every new favour; were they left to themselves, enormities too horrid to think of would ensue, guilty and innocent, women and infants, would be a common prey." [18] It was admitted that these strictures applied to the Indians from Lower Canada; those from farther afield were reputed to be of sterner metal—"they profess war, not pillage." [19] Burgoyne had originally intended to employ them as a feint into New England, but since Schuyler appeared to be employing a scorched-earth policy in the face of the British advance, he thought now to use them "to prevent, if possible, by their terror, the continuance of these operations." [20]

"Your Lordship will pardon me if I a little lament that my orders do not give me the latitude I ventured to propose in my original project for the campaign, to make a real effort instead of a feint upon New England," his letter to Germain continued; "as things have turned out, were I at liberty to march in force immediately by my left, instead of my right, I should have little doubt of subduing before winter the provinces where the rebellion originated." [21]

Burgoyne had his problems, but they must have seemed as nothing compared with Schuyler's. He wrote to Washington on July 7:

I have not been able to learn what is become of General St Clair and the enemy. And what adds to my distress is, that a report prevails that I had given orders for the evacuation of Ticonderoga, whereas not the most distant hint of such an intention can be drawn from any of my letters to General St Clair, or any person whatever. What could induce General Officers to a step that has ruined our affairs in this quarter, God only knows. [22]

Schuyler was not the kind of man to sit idly by wringing his hands. Although he could only muster about 1,500 men, he set up his headquarters at Fort Edward on the Hudson. He sent a detachment to Colonel Long, commander at Fort Anne, and encouraged him to stand firm. Encouragement was not enough, for Long precipitately abandoned Fort Anne, and Schuyler was compelled to report to Washington that "Colonel Long contrary to my express orders evacuated that post. . . ." [23] The only thing Schuyler could do was to make things as difficult as possible for Burgoyne. Urged on by their general, all available woodsmen were set to work destroying bridges, felling trees to block tracks, and damming streams to turn the ground into a swamp. All supplies were removed or destroyed, farms burned, and every horse and cow removed or killed. Boats were burned or sunk at their moorings, fields of corn were laid flat, and the country between Skenesboro and Fort Edward was turned into a desert. In the midst of all these activities, St. Clair unexpectedly turned up at Fort Edward with his travel worn but still intact little army. This brought Schuyler's strength up to 4,000, but a third of them were "not fit for the field, and many of the officers would be a disgrace to the most contemptible troop that ever was collected." [24]

There were enemies in front of Schuyler; there were enemies behind. The loss of Ticonderoga had come as a stunning blow to Congress. The immediate cry was "Treachery!" Schuyler was already suspect in New England, and the rumormongers were busy. Doctor Thacher recorded one of the more malevolent stories in his *Journal:* "It has been industriously reported that Generals Schuyler and St Clair acted the part of traitors to their country and that they were paid for their treason by the enemy in silver balls shot from Burgoyne's guns into our camp and that they were collected by order of General St Clair and divided between him and General Schuyler." [25] Samuel Adams, writing to Roger Sherman, was withering in his contempt for the unfortunate general: "Schuyler has written a series of weak and contemptible things in a style of despondency which alone, I think, is sufficient for the removal of him. . . . He seems to have no confidence in his troops, nor the states whence reinforcements are to be drawn. . . ." [26] John Adams was even more scathing in his letters to Abigail.

Washington remained calm as the hurricane of accusation and counteraccusation whirled around him. With his deep strategic insight, he had seen from the first the dangers implicit in Burgoyne's campaign. On July 2 he had written to Connecticut's governor, Jonathan Trumbull, "If it is not merely a diversion, but a serious attack, of which it bears strongly the appearance, it is certain proof that the next step of General Howe's army will be towards Peekskill, and very suddenly, if possible to get possession of the passes in the Highlands before this army can have time to form a junction with the troops already there." [27] It was a correct appreciation of the original British plan, but what Washington did not yet know was Howe's amendment to it.

As soon as he heard of the fall of Ticonderoga, Washington sent Arnold north to assist Schuyler. In war a single man may sometimes be worth battalions, but Arnold alone, for all his energy, could not hold Burgoyne. Letters were sent to Connecticut and Massachusetts urging the dispatch of reinforcements to Schuyler, and Washington prepared to take his own army north once he could be certain of Howe's intentions. Spies reported the concentration of British troop transports in New York harbor, but they could not establish the intention behind the concentration. Not until July 25 did Washington deduce that Howe's objective was Philadelphia, and not the Hudson highlands and Albany. On the previous day Burgoyne's main body had marched from Skenesboro and camped in the burned-out ruins of Fort Anne.

Washington was still perplexed. "General Howe's in a manner abandoning General Burgoyne is so unaccountable a matter, that, till I am fully assured it is so, I cannot help casting my eyes occasionally behind me," he wrote to General Gates on July 30. [28] By that date Congress had decided to replace Schuyler with Gates, and Howe's fleet was already on the move toward the "Capes of Delaware."

Burgoyne's main body did not arrive at Fort Edward until July 30. Schuyler had by then slipped away down the Hudson to prepare a defensive position four miles north of the village of Stillwater. Hubbardton had been fought twenty-three days before, so, it has been reckoned, Burgoyne's advance to Fort Edward was at the rate of one mile a day. However, this does not take into account his requirement to bring up supplies and ammunition from Ticonderoga to Skenesboro, or the time required for repairs to the track to Fort Edward. It is a poor tribute to Schuyler's skillful delaying tactics for Burgoyne to be blamed for the slow rate of the British advance; greater captains than John Burgoyne have found their best-laid plans frustrated both by the enemy and by logistic factors. Fortescue was right when he wrote, "It was no small feat that Burgoyne should have reached Fort Edward on the 30th of July." [29] It moved Digby to write: "We moved on farther to a rising ground, about a mile south of Fort Edward, and encamped on a beautiful situation, from whence you saw the most romantic aspect of the Hudson's River interspersed with many small islands." [30]

Any feelings of triumph were marred for Burgoyne and his officers by a most unfortunate incident. Miss Jane McCrae, affianced to a young loyalist officer named David Jones, was eagerly awaiting the arrival of her lover at Fort Edward when some Indians, scouting ahead of the British, murdered and scalped her. According to Anburey, the Indians came across her by chance in the woods. "They at first treated her with every mark of civility . . . and were conducting her into camp, when within a mile of it, a dispute arose between the two . . . whose prisoner she was; and words growing very high, one of them . . . fearful of losing the reward for bringing her safe into camp, most inhumanly struck his tomahawk into her skull and she instantly expired." [31]

It was just the kind of incident that can be used to maximum effect for propaganda purposes. The fact that poor Jane McCrae's death was one of those horrifying occurrences inseparable from war made not the slightest impression on public opinion in America or Britain. The murder caused a shudder of revulsion throughout the colonies. Burgoyne was later to be called to account for it in the House of Commons, although he shared to the full the horror and regret of friend and foe alike.

It is said that the distraught fiancé, having rescued Jane's scalp, immediately applied for discharge; when this was refused, he deserted the British camp and returned to Canada, where, for the rest of his life, he lived as a recluse.[32]

As soon as Burgoyne heard of the murder, he went to the

Indian camp and demanded that the murderers should be delivered up. According to Anburey, "The situation of the General, whose humanity was very much shocked at such an instance of barbarity, was very distressing and critical, for however inclined he might be to punish the offender, still it was hazarding the revenge of the savages, whose friendship he had to court, rather than seek their enmity." [33]

Burgoyne's evident anger caused concern among those of his officers who feared the Indians' capacity for mischief. The Earl of Harrington, who was then a captain in the 29th Regiment, testified later that Burgoyne had demanded that the culprit be given up and then executed: "There were many gentlemen of the army, and I own I was one of the number, who feared that he would put that threat into execution. Motives of policy, I believe, alone prevented him from it; and if he had not pardoned the man, which he did, I believe the total defection of the Indians would have ensued, and the consequences, on their return through Canada might have been dreadful. . . ." [34] Harrington also feared that the Indians might go over to the side of the enemy. In the event, Burgoyne was dissuaded by St. Luc from putting his threats into effect, but he insisted that he would "rather lose every Indian in his army than connive at their enormities." [35]

This did not save him from a diatribe from Horatio Gates, who accused him of "hiring the savages of America to scalp Europeans and the descendants of Europeans." [36] Gates went on to allege that Burgoyne paid a price for every scalp taken. "Miss McCrae," he wrote, "a young lady lovely to the sight, of virtuous character and amiable disposition, engaged to be married to an officer in your army, was with other women and children taken out of a house near Fort Edward, carried into the woods, and their [sic] scalped and mangled in the most shocking manner." He concluded his letter by reminding Burgoyne that "the miserable fate of Miss McCrae was partly aggravated by her being dressed to meet her promised husband; but met her murderers employed by you."

Gates's letter hit hard, and he had enjoyed the drafting of it. Before he dispatched it, he showed it to Major General Benjamin Lincoln, and to Wilkinson, his principal staff officer. Both men thought it was couched in too personal terms, whereupon Gates replied, "By God! I don't believe either of you can mend it." [37] He was right, because he was hitting Burgoyne where it hurt most.

"I condescend to inform you," replied Burgoyne, "that I would not be conscious of the acts you presume to impute to me for the whole continent of America, though the wealth of worlds were in its bowels and a paradise on its surface." [38] He went on to recount the events leading up to the woman's death, but the rest of his letter reads rather tamely after such a grandiloquent beginning. Both Gates and Burgoyne were shadowboxing, because, as professional soldiers, they knew well enough the ugliness of war. But Gates was right to take advantage of such an unfortunate incident; just as Burgoyne knew full well that whatever he said would carry no weight in either America or Britain.

Many years later Burgoyne received a letter from Jane McCrae's brother, who had served under him in the campaign of 1777. Burgoyne had succeeded in obtaining a company for McCrae, and was obviously pleased to do him this service. "I had been accused by the malicious of having encouraged the Indians to acts of barbarity," he wrote in the margin of McCrae's letter. "It was a great pleasure to me to be thought of so differently by that lady's brother, as five years afterwards, when he had other and more able supporters, to be singled out as the person whom he wished to act as his patron. From a man of Captain McCrae's character, this selection was not only a pleasing evidence of my innocence, it was one on his mind of my abhorrence of that act." [39]

Chapter 15

The Beginning of the End

A PROBLEM common to all armies in war is the need to provide detachments. Seldom is this taken into sufficient account by those responsible for planning a campaign; wastage from sickness, wounds, and death may be calculated by a rough-and-ready formula, and the necessary provision made for battle reinforcements; but the need to provide detachments is often overlooked, or underestimated. An advancing army marks its onward progress with detachments—here a corporal and three soldiers guarding a bridge; there a battalion of infantry defending a recently captured strong point. As more and more soldiers are left behind to protect the lines of communication, the bayonets in the front line grow fewer.

Burgoyne was acutely conscious of this problem before ever he decided to continue his advance from Skenesboro. On July 11 he wrote to General Carleton requesting him "to take into consideration the expediency of supplying from Canada, a garrison for Ticonderoga." [1] Carleton's reply was courteous but unforthcoming. Burgoyne wrote again, from near Fort Anne, on July 29:

The construction your excellency puts upon the orders of the Secretary of State, is too full and decisive for me to presume to trouble you further upon the subject of a garrison for Ticonderoga from Canada, I must do as well as I can, but I am sure your Excellency, as a soldier, will think my situation a little difficult. A breach into my communication must either ruin my army entirely, or oblige me to return in force to restore, which might be the loss of the campaign. To prevent a breach, Ticonderoga and Fort George must be in very respectable strength, and I must besides have posts at Fort Edward and other carrying-places. These drains added to common accidents and losses of service, will necessarily render me very inferior in point of numbers to the enemy. . . .[2]

He did not exaggerate. As the expedition advanced southward, it grew weaker; the Americans, on the other hand, were hurriedly scraping together all the men they could find and were sending them hotfoot to Schuyler. On July 22, Washington wrote to Schuyler: "From your accounts he [Burgoyne] appears to be pursuing that line of conduct, which of all others is most favourable to us; I mean acting in Detachments."[3] He exhorted Schuyler to use every endeavor to cut off and destroy one of the weaker British posts. Two days later he reminded Schuyler of Burgoyne's increasing predicament: "As they can never think of advancing, without securing their rear by leaving garrisons in the fortresses behind, the force with which they can come against you will be greatly reduced by the detachments necessary for the purpose."[4]

The supply problem was a constant nightmare. "How zealously so-ever a general, in such an undertaking as mine," Burgoyne wrote, "may be served by the chiefs of departments (and much praise is due from me upon that score), for one hour he can find to contemplate *how he shall fight his army, he must allot twenty to contrive how to feed it.*"[5] He had issued a general order at Skenesboro instructing officers to reduce their baggage. Similar orders issued earlier had not been obeyed, and regiments were consequently encumbered with baggage they could not transport once they quit

the lake and rivers. All but essential baggage must be dispatched to Ticonderoga by the returning bateaux: "Such
gentlemen as served in America the last war may remember
that the officers took up with soldiers' tents, and often confined their baggage to a knapsack for months together." [6]

Some baggage was sent back, as is clear from Burgoyne's
letter to Riedesel dated July 18:

I request you to take measures that the spirit of the order respecting the sending back officers' baggage to Ticonderoga may
have due force. The baggage of the British officers is already
gone, and many of them have only retained a small tent and one
cloak bag. It is really for the interests of the officers, in the end,
that I am pressing upon this subject. [7]

Riedesel doubtless did his best to ensure compliance, but
not altogether successfully if General Phillips is to be believed.
Writing from Fort Edward, Phillips expressed his astonishment that the orders concerning baggage were being dis-
regarded, "notwithstanding . . . most serious and positive
orders of the 16th instant that no Carts should be used for any
purpose whatever, but for the Transport of Provisions, unless
by particular orders from the Commander in Chief etc. as
expressed in that order, there are this day about thirty Carts
on the road laden with Baggage. . . ." [8]

When Burgoyne's dispatch of August 22, reporting the
capture of Ticonderoga, reached London, Germain basked
in the glow of Burgoyne's short-lived fame. He had been
Germain's own choice for command of the expedition from
Canada, and how admirably was he justifying that selection.
The one fly in the ointment was Burgoyne's friend Fox, who
hated the war so much that he welcomed only reports of
British defeats.

However, Germain was satisfied and so was the king. Burgoyne's success merited recognition. "His conduct is so meritorious and the approbation of his service is so general,"

wrote Germain on August 29 to Lord Derby, "the King speaks of him as an officer of distinguished merit, and immediately declared he would honour him with the vacant red ribbon. I trust he will hereafter receive more substantial marks of honour." [9] Lord Derby had declined the honor once on behalf of his uncle. Writing a few days prior to the receipt of Germain's letter, he mentioned that he had again heard rumors of the intention to confer the red ribbon on Burgoyne: "From whim, caprice, or some other motive, he has, I know, a strong objection to the honour above mentioned, and though if offered, his respect and gratitude to His Majesty would prevent his refusal of it, I am well convinced he would be infinitely obliged to your Lordship (should such a thing have been thought of) to let it drop in such a manner as your Lordship might think most proper." [10]

Germain replied that the king would certainly not wish to "force" on Burgoyne such a mark of distinction. It was, however, unfortunate, since "it is difficult to reward the services of a general officer who is employed upon the staff, who has [already] a regiment of dragoons, and a government." [11] The mystery of Burgoyne's persistent refusal remains unsolved. The offer was never renewed, and he died plain *Mr.* Burgoyne.

Burgoyne lacked information about Howe's future intentions, as well as news of the progress of the diversionary force in the Mohawk valley. The problem of intercommunication was virtually insuperable. His dispatches to Carleton, Germain, and Howe had to be carried on horseback either to Fort George or Skenesboro, and thence by canoe or boat to Montreal or Quebec. With luck, the time taken might be measured in days rather than in weeks, but from Quebec it depended on available vessels and the Atlantic weather. Overland communication with the British forces in New York was equally undependable and time-consuming. Men on foot, always in hazard of capture, would have to make their way across enemy-held territory; it was impossible to be certain that the message would get through. The co-ordination of such widely separated operations as Burgoyne's, Howe's, and St. Leger's was incredibly difficult.

The Mohawk valley diversion was first conceived in 1776, when Burgoyne was chafing at the bit as a result of Carleton's slow progress down Lake Champlain to Crown Point and Ticonderoga. He had then proposed a diversionary operation down Lake Ontario to Oswego, and thence up the Mohawk valley, but Carleton had decided against it. In his *Thoughts for Conducting the War*, Burgoyne had reverted to the idea, proposing that St. Leger command the operation. He had also specified the number of troops required. Germain, in London, and Carleton, in Quebec, endorsed Burgoyne's recommendations. They also agreed that Lieutenant-Colonel Barry St. Leger, of the 34th Regiment, should command. He was an officer well experienced in North American warfare, and he possessed Burgoyne's full confidence. His force consisted of 200 British infantry from the 8th and 34th regiments; 100 "Jägers"; 133 loyalists formed into a regiment, the Royal Greens, raised and commanded by Sir John Johnson, whose father had played a prominent part in the war against the French; 100 loyalist rangers under Colonel John Butler; and forty artillerists with two six-pounders, two three-pounders, and four mortars, or cohorns. The European component was kept intentionally small, and reliance was placed principally on the Indians, who revered the memory of Sir William Johnson.

Johnson had married an Indian woman, and her brother, Thayendanegea, commanded the Indian contingent. Better known by his anglicized name, Joseph Brant, Thayendanegea was a remarkable man; he had visited England and been lionized in London—by Boswell, among others. Nine hundred Indians from the Mohawk and Seneca tribes, belonging to the Confederacy of the Six Nations, joined St. Leger under Brant.

The expedition left Montreal on June 23, just before Burgoyne launched his force across Lake Champlain, and arrived at Oswego on July 25. The first objective was Fort Stanwix, which had been built to control the portage between Wood Creek and the Mohawk river. It was garrisoned by about 700 American troops under Colonel Peter Gansevoort, with Lieutenant Colonel Marinus Willett as second-in-command. Although no Ticonderoga, the fort presented a stiff problem to a force as weak in artillery as St. Leger's. His efforts to bully Gansevoort into surrender by parading his men in full view of the fort failed. The British then besieged the place and sent back to Oswego for their artillery.

Meanwhile, the news of St. Leger's arrival outside Fort Stanwix spread throughout the valley of the Mohawk. It reached the colonel of the county militia, Nicholas Herkimer, who at once called upon every man able to carry a musket to join him at Fort Dayton. Loyalties in the Mohawk valley were divided, and Herkimer's brother had rallied to the British. Many Americans did not trust Nicholas Herkimer, but some 850 men answered his call. They marched out from Fort Dayton on August 4, on their way to relieve Fort Stanwix. With them went 400 oxcarts carrying supplies for the beleaguered garrison. On the following day they forded the Mohawk at Oriskany. Herkimer sent a message to Gansevoort warning him of their approach, and requesting him to make a diversionary attack in support of the column's advance. By then news of his advance had reached St. Leger, through a message brought by an Indian to Brant from his sister, Molly, Sir William Johnson's widow. St. Leger at once ordered Colonel Guy Johnson, with the loyalist rangers and Royal Greens, to prepare an ambush for Herkimer's militia. This was duly set up about six miles from Fort Stanwix, where the track ran through a narrow ravine at Oriskany. The brook at the bottom, since known as "Battle Brook," was marshy and negotiable only by a corduroy causeway. It was a perfect spot for an ambush, and Herkimer marched straight into it at about 10:00 A.M. on August 6.

He had been uncertain whether to advance any farther without a signal from Gansevoort. His message had requested the firing of three guns to warn him that the diversionary attack was about to be launched, but no shots were heard. Yet, because his men had taunted him with disloyalty, and much against his better judgment, he decided to continue the advance. The result was a near massacre. Herkimer was wounded early, and his subsequent conduct has become an American legend. Propping himself against a tree, he continued to fire his musket. When urged to take cover, he replied, "I will face the enemy." With his pipe clenched firmly in his teeth, he proceeded to shoot down any loyalist or Indian unwise enough to approach within range.

Matters would have gone much worse for Herkimer but for the diversionary attack that did come from the fort. Led by Willett, the Americans swept down on the virtually undefended Indian camp, causing Sir John Johnson to flee so hastily that he left behind his coat and personal papers. According to Willett, "The Indians took chiefly to the woods, the rest of the troops then at their posts to the river." [12] When news of this debacle reached Guy Johnson at Oriskany, he at once withdrew his troops in order to defend his rear. The Indians made off even sooner, leaving Herkimer, still propped against his tree, master of the field. But his losses were appalling—200 killed, 250 wounded, and 200 taken prisoner. He died of his wounds two weeks later. Technically, St. Leger had won the battle of Oriskany, because the Americans had been prevented from relieving Fort Stanwix, but it was to do him little good, since the Indians had suffered severely at the hands of the militiamen, and their camp had been looted by Willett's men. Fort Stanwix still held out, and there was little prospect of battering the place into submission without more artillery. St. Leger sent a messenger to Gansevoort, warning him that Indian tempers were running high as a result of their casualties, and that there could be a massacre in the Mohawk valley unless the fort was surrendered. It was a futile threat and received the answer it deserved. "By your uniform you are British officers," said Gansevoort, to the bearers of St. Leger's message. "Therefore let me tell you that the message you have brought is a degrading one for a British officer to send and by no means reputable for a British officer to carry." [13]

Fort Stanwix was strong enough to resist assault, but it could be starved into surrender. St. Leger knew this, and made his plans accordingly. Gansevoort knew it, too, and sent his second-in-command to inform Schuyler at Albany. For Schuyler, struggling to make bricks without straw, it was just another message of woe. Burgoyne was poised at Fort Edward to cross the Hudson; the promised reinforcements from New England remained no more than promises; and Congress was debating the question of Schuyler's loyalty. His own officers were averse to weakening the troops available to resist Burgoyne's advance, and many of them were active in petitioning their friends in Congress to remove Schuyler. A lesser man would have left Fort Stanwix to its fate and concentrated on Burgoyne.

Washington had sent Benedict Arnold to Schuyler. Major General Arnold was one of the ablest, and certainly one of the most controversial generals on the American side. Only a Washington could have perceived his genius for war. Now, Schuyler, disregarding his council, some of whom suggested that he deliberately intended to weaken the army, sent Arnold to halt St. Leger. Arnold reached Fort Dayton on August 21, together with 950 men under Brigadier General Ebenezer Learned. The locals warned him that with so few troops he had no hope of defeating St. Leger. Arnold was undeterred.

Despite his faults, and they were many, Benedict Arnold possessed in full measure the attributes required by any man who aspires to lead his fellow-men in battle. He had complete confidence in his own ability, as well as a dominating personality. Courageous, he led his men from the front, and was foremost in showing them the way. Although a dashing commander, he was not foolhardy. He was disturbed by the reports from Fort Stanwix, where the British trenches had reached to within 150 yards of the fort's walls; and was not impressed by the American survivors of the Oriskany ambush. He was, however, interested to learn that St. Leger's force was mainly Indian. If only he could detach them from St. Leger, the odds would be more even. The instrument for this was at hand. John Joost Schuyler, a half-witted relative of General Schuyler, better known as "Hon-Yost," had recently been taken into custody, with other local Tories. The charge was that they planned an uprising in favor of the British. They had been sentenced to death. Arnold was aware that Hon-Yost was well known to the Indians in those parts and spoke the language fluently. He also knew that Indians revered the mentally deficient as possessing some means for communicating with the Divine Being. Accordingly, Hon-Yost was told he would be spared execution provided that he visited the Indian camps and spread the story that Arnold was about to advance at the head of thousands of men.

Hon-Yost, his coat riddled with bullets to lend verisimilitude to his story, arrived in the Indian camp spreading alarm and despondency. He was greeted as a messenger of the wrath to come. The Indians, blaming St. Leger for bringing them to such a pass, and still complaining bitterly about the damage done by Willett's sortie, hurriedly decamped. St. Leger had no alternative but to follow. When Arnold arrived at Fort Stanwix on August 24, after a forced march of twenty-two miles, he found the birds had flown. Gansevoort was relieved, and St. Leger was pursued as far as Lake Oneida, where the Americans arrived on the shore in time only to wave derisively at the departing British bateaux. It could not be described as a "famous victory," but it was certainly a convincing one.

Burgoyne wrote to Carleton shortly after his arrival at Fort Edward to explain his reasons for choosing to advance from Skenesboro. He also warned Carleton that he would now have to halt and collect supplies. The letter concluded with the words, "I have no news of Sir William Howe." [14] In a dispatch to Germain dated July 30 Burgoyne had reported at greater length. He again explained his reasons for selecting the Skenesboro–Fort Edward route, from which one may conclude he was aware that some of his officers were critical of this decision. He praised his soldiers and drew attention to the happy outcome of the advance: Fort Edward's occupation without a shot being fired. He reported the enemy "at present in force at Saratoga, where they profess the intention of standing a battle. . . ." He, too, was preparing for battle by bringing up supplies "as quickly as could be arranged." [15]

A personal letter to Germain accompanied this dispatch. In it Burgoyne stressed his ignorance of Howe's intentions and complained of his inability to get in touch with him. "I am in total ignorance of the situation or intentions of that General," [16] he told Germain. He also made it clear that under no circumstances was he prepared to succeed Carleton in Canada. Burgoyne had heard of Carleton's application to resign, and it was quite possible that he might be appointed to succeed him. Neither his "talent nor his constitution were adapted to do due justice in the province of Canada," he told Germain. He must therefore beg to decline any such offer. He sought only to return to Britain at the conclusion of the campaign.

This provides an interesting sidelight on Burgoyne's character. The post of governor of Canada was an important one. If he was as ambitious as so often seems to have been the case, why did he go out of his way to avoid being offered such a distinguished appointment? He was well aware of the problems ahead, and however sanguine he may have appeared outwardly, inwardly he must have had an occasional doubt. It would have been easy to hand over command to Fraser and return to Montreal. But he chose instead the harder path.

Chapter 16

Bennington: The Futile Foray

THE LONGER the British dallied on the wrong bank of the Hudson, the harder it would be for them in the long run. Burgoyne knew this, of course; had he been as reckless a general as some have described him, he would have taken a calculated risk and driven his troops on remorselessly. By so doing he might have kept up the pressure on Schuyler all the way to Albany, leaving him without the time he desperately needed to lick the raw American militia into shape, and preventing him from building the field defenses the Americans required if they were to take on British regulars on anything like equal terms. But Burgoyne was an orthodox soldier at heart and was determined not to outrun his supplies. Inevitably this meant loss of time, and time was not on Burgoyne's side, because the depredations of his Indian allies had so enraged the colonists that they were flocking to join the militia. For a general who prided himself on his light cavalry touch, Burgoyne was failing to keep up the momentum of his advance, and in the end he would pay the penalty for taking too much counsel of his fears.

One cannot entirely blame him, because he was daily confronted by a distracted quarter-master-general, who, with his attendant commissaries, recounted a tale of woe about supplies. As fast as supplies came forward, the troops were consuming them. Soldiers have to be fed, whether at the halt or on the move, and they are less likely to complain about their scanty rations if they are moving forward. There was nothing to be found around Fort Edward. Schuyler's scorched-earth policy was paying handsome dividends. According to one of Riedesel's officers, the Americans had swept the "few cultivated spots of all articles likely to benefit the invaders. . . . All the fields of standing corn were laid waste, the cattle were driven away, and every particle of grain, as well as morsel of grass, carefully removed. . . ." [1] Everything the soldiers and their horses ate had to be transported from Canada. The officers might still have their wine, and the soldiers their rum, but, though this may have been good for their spirits, it did not keep them fit for the rigors of a campaign.

It is not surprising in the circumstances that Burgoyne paid such attention to the advice of Philip Skene, who was, after all, a local inhabitant. Skene pointed out that not so far away, in New England, there was a stretch of country as yet untouched by the ravages of war. It was predominantly a farming district, its fields filled with cattle, its barns with corn. Even more important, it was a horse-breeding area. Burgoyne desperately needed horses—not only to pull his wagons and guns, but also to mount his Brunswick dragoons, who had tramped all the way from Skenesboro in their ridiculous jack boots and clanking spurs, trailing their heavy sabers behind them. For a cavalry general this was a criminal misemployment of *l'arme blanche*, quite apart from the fact that a regiment of cavalry would be invaluable for reconnaissance duties.

Burgoyne has been criticized for mounting an operation virtually at right angles to his line of advance, but there were sound reasons to account for this. In the first place, he always had at the back of his mind the concept of an advance into New England, either as a cover plan ("giving a jealousy," as he described it) or as another means of bringing the Americans to battle and defeating them. Second, General von Riedesel had advocated a raid into New England soon after the engagement at Hubbardton, with the object of obtaining horses for his horseless dragoons. Third, any operation that might be expected to improve the parlous supplies situation was worth trying, since, as Riedesel had written to the Duke of Brunswick, the army was "unable to advance three miles without waiting about eight or ten days for our necessary supplies to be brought up." [2]

As originally conceived, the objective was to be the area of Manchester, in Vermont, and since Riedesel's wing of the army lay nearest to the objective, it is understandable that Burgoyne should have selected the Germans for this operation. Riedesel was, in fact, ordered to plan it, and presumably was asked to nominate the officer in command. Much has been made of the fact that the officer selected, Lieutenant-Colonel Friederich Baum, spoke hardly a word of English, but most of the senior German officers suffered from the same disadvantage. An officer as experienced as Riedesel was unlikely to choose an officer in whom he had no confidence.

Baum's lack of English would in any case be offset by Burgoyne's choice of Skene to accompany him as his political officer. Skene was told that the objects of the operation were "to try the Affections of the Country; to disconcert the Councils of the Enemy; to mount the regt of Riedesel dragoons; to compleat Lieut. Col. Peters's corps, and to procure a large supply of horses for the use of the troops, together with cattle and carriages." [3] The reference to Peters's Corps related to the loyalists, with whom the countryside was swarming, according to Skene. They were to be encouraged to join Baum's expedition; while "Baum is directed to communicate to you the rest of his instructions, and to consult with you upon all matters of intelligence, negotiation with the inhabitants, roads and other means depending upon a knowledge of the country for carrying his instructions into execution." [4] Skene was also enjoined to issue receipts for all animals requisitioned.

These orders were drawn up with great care, but in some haste. Burgoyne personally made several alterations to the original draft, prepared by his adjutant-general, Lieutenant-Colonel Robert Kingston. The haste was due largely to the need for secrecy; the British camp had its full quota of spies, and it would not be long before the Americans came to hear of the expedition. There would be little point in marching all the way to Manchester only to find the stable doors open and the horses gone.

Riedesel did not like any operation that might result in a head-on clash with the Americans with the odds in their favor. The operation he had originally proposed from Castle Town would have been well to the north of rebel concentration, and he had expected to get away with his booty before the Americans could do much about it. He favored a "tip and run" raid, rather than a full-scale military operation. But Burgoyne overruled him, and Riedesel had no alternative but to comply. According to Baroness von Riedesel, her husband thought the expedition "very unadvisable, and against which he emphatically contended." [5] Unfortunately for Riedesel, he received no support from General Fraser, on whom he tended to rely, and Baum was therefore ordered to move his regiment to Fort Miller, preparatory to marching to Manchester. He had with him 175 Brunswick dragoons, 200 grenadiers and Jägers, a few artillerymen from the Hesse-Hanau battery to handle his two three-pounders, and some 300 loyalists and Canadians. Captain Fraser accompanied the expedition with fifty of his picked marksmen; as did Captain O'Connell, to act as interpreter for Baum. A few German wives accompanied their husbands.

Baum was preparing to set out, on the morning of August 11, when Burgoyne rode up and changed both the direction of Baum's march and his objective. He was not to go to Manchester, but to Bennington, a village about thirty miles to the southeast of Fort Edward. It had just been reported that many horses and a considerable quantity of corn had been collected there, guarded by fewer than 400 militia. This meant that Baum would have to march almost due south, leaving his right flank wide open to Schuyler, who was concentrating his troops at Saratoga, on the opposite bank of the Hudson. Riedesel protested when he heard of this change of plan, but he was too late. Baum had already left Fort Edward on his way to Bennington.

Baum's force took the Cambridge road and covered the sixteen miles to that place in twelve hours. This was certainly slow progress, even for heavy dragoons on their feet, but the track was rough and the terrain hilly. Baum was also handicapped by his need for an interpreter in talking with Skene. The track ran through thick forest, where there was always the possibility of ambush. Fraser and his sharpshooters led the column, with a party of Indians, who should have provided ample warning of any trouble ahead, but Baum was excessively cautious. Fraser's party had a brush with a small detachment of militia, but easily drove them back, capturing some men and some ox wagons. They should have taken some horses but the Indians slaughtered them, which must have been particularly irritating for Baum, who was a cavalryman; he promptly sent a messenger to Burgoyne recommending that a price be paid for every horse brought in by such unreliable allies. He also reported that the Bennington garrison was more like 2,000 than 400.

Pushing on from Cambridge on the morning of the fourteenth, Baum was held up by a small party of the enemy at the confluence of Owl Kill and the Hoosic. The place was called St. Croix, known locally as "Sancoik," and the bridge across the river there was destroyed by Eleazer Eggerton and two companions from Bennington. They carried out this task under heavy fire and were lucky to escape unhurt. Baum, who had lost any chance of surprising the enemy, sent another messenger to Burgoyne. He told of the enemy strength at

Bennington, but added that they were unlikely to put up much resistance. He also reported: "people are flocking in hourly, but want to be armed; the savages cannot be controlled; they ruin and take away everything they please." [6]

The activities of the Indians had infuriated the Americans, who poured into Bennington to swell the ranks of the militia. Many of the so-called loyalists who joined Baum at Sancoik were equally outraged. Skene, however, was so unwise as to enlist them without checking their *bona fides*. As Burgoyne later reported:

A provincial gentleman of confidence who had been sent with the detachment, as knowing the country and character of the inhabitants, was so incautious as to leave at liberty such as took the oath of allegiance. His credulity and their profligacy caused the first misfortune. Colonel Baum was induced to proceed without sufficient knowledge of the ground. His design was betrayed; the men who had taken the oaths were the first to fire upon him; he was attacked on all sides. He showed great personal courage, but was over-powered by numbers. [7]

After crossing Owl Kill, Baum advanced cautiously on Bennington. He was within four miles of his objective when he halted for the night. He sent another message to Burgoyne, asking for reinforcements, and he reconnoitered the ground above the Walloomsac valley to select a defensive position. Burgoyne received Baum's message at dawn on August 15, and was perturbed by the contents. He immediately ordered Riedesel to send Breymann, with his regiment of Brunswick grenadiers, to Baum's assistance. Breymann's regiment was bivouacked some twenty-five miles away, on Batten Kill, and they set off at nine that morning, taking with them two six-pounder guns, which were carried on carts because there were no spare horses to drag them. The artillery ammunition was also carried on the carts, while every soldier carried forty cartridges.

From the outset Breymann's advance was dogged by misfortune. Batten Kill was in flood. Since there was no bridge, the river had to be forded. This delayed the advance, and matters were made worse by the rain, which turned the track into a sea of mud, through which the men waded and plodded at less than half a mile in the hour. Carts were overturned and had to be righted. The guide lost his way, and it took an hour or more to find the right path. To add to the delay, Breymann halted the column at regular intervals to dress ranks. By nightfall his sodden grenadiers had covered less than eight miles, and they were still seventeen miles from Baum. Tired, wet through, and tormented by the ceaseless downpour, Breymann halted for the night, sending a messenger to Baum to tell him he was on his way.

Baum was an unlucky officer. Not only was he a stranger to the peculiar conditions of warfare in North America, but he found himself pitted against one of the most experienced, as well as one of the most unorthodox, soldiers on the American side. John Stark was a farmer from New Hampshire who had campaigned with Wolfe at Quebec and marched and fought against the French in the ranks of Robert Rogers' Rangers. He was a lean, cantankerous man, forty-seven years old in 1775, when he recruited his own regiment in New Hampshire and led it to Boston. He took it to Canada during the spring of 1776, and then back again to New Jersey. Stark did not get on with Schuyler, but Washington appreciated his real worth, although not enough, apparently, to obtain for him the coveted promotion to brigadier general. Burning with indignation, Stark returned home in a rage.

Burgoyne's invasion of upper New York, and the "jealousy" offered thereby to Connecticut, brought Stark back into the war almost as soon as he had turned his back on it. On July 18 the New Hampshire General Assembly called upon him to raise a brigade of militia, which he did within a week, but only on condition that he was not required to serve under either Congress or the Continental Army. The independent burghers of New Hampshire, well knowing the trust they could repose in him, willingly agreed to his terms. They furnished him with a special commission and left it to him to deal with Burgoyne—in whatever way he deemed best. Stark then sent his troops to Manchester, and followed after them a few days later.

Major General Benjamin Lincoln was waiting for him at Manchester. That shrewd and obese officer had been dispatched by Schuyler to bring Stark and his men to Stillwater. Stark refused to acknowledge Lincoln as his superior officer. He took his stand upon his commission from the New Hampshire legislature and told Lincoln he was entirely competent to command his own men. Until Congress provided him with a proper commission, and the rank to which he was entitled, the New Hampshire brigade would operate independently. Lincoln realized there was little point in debating the matter; he left Stark in Manchester and returned to Schuyler with the information that Stark was insubordinate. Lincoln had, however, promised Stark that he would do his best to get him his rank. To save Lincoln the trouble of riding all the way back again to Manchester with, as Stark hoped, the news of his promotion, Stark moved the New Hampshire militia to Bennington, halfway to Stillwater. Baum therefore found Bennington more strongly garrisoned than he had been led to believe by Burgoyne.

The steady downpour that impeded Breymann's march on August 15 also delayed Stark's attack on Baum, who made use of the respite to take up a defensive position on a hill overlooking the Walloomsac river, roughly midway between Sancoik Mill and Bennington. This hill, which subsequently became known as "Hessian Hill," was about 300 feet above the valley, and provided a reasonable defensive position. The Germans worked hard to throw up a log-and-earth redoubt, which was held by Baum's dismounted dragoons. About 300 yards farther up the road a bridge crossing the Walloomsac was defended by Fraser's Rangers with one three-pounder; Baum's other three-pounder was sited in the main redoubt.

Just beyond the bridge was a small elevation on which Baum's loyalists entrenched themselves, while the women accompanying Baum's force were gathered together in a wooden hut on the far bank of the Walloomsac. It was as good a position as could be found in that area, and Baum's men spent the wet daylight hours improving their defenses.

Baum expected Breymann to reach him some time on that day. He began to be concerned about his nonappearance only late in the afternoon. He had taken the precaution of sending Skene back up the road to hasten Breymann's advance, and Skene took with him all the available horses to assist in towing Breymann's guns and ammunition wagons. Baum would therefore be completely immobilized if he was forced to retreat. Meanwhile, as the soldiers labored to improve their defenses, parties of local farmers came and went through the positions, pausing to chat with the few Germans who could speak a little English. All these locals wore pieces of white paper in their hats, identifying them as loyalists, although they were regarded with suspicion by those of their countrymen who had marched with Baum from Fort Edward. Lieutenant-Colonel Jessup, who commanded Baum's provincial contingent, bitterly criticized his commander's credulity: "He allowed people to go and come from his camp, readily believing their professions of sympathy with the Royal Cause, and imparting to them most fully and completely all information as to his strength and designs." [8] Since Baum's lack of knowledge of English made it impossible for him to communicate with the local inhabitants, loyalist or otherwise, the real blame for this state of affairs must attach to Skene, and to those other Americans and Englishmen serving under Baum. Skene undoubtedly underestimated the depth of the feeling aroused by the depredations of the Indians and the murder of Jane McCrae.

While Baum and his men were digging their trenches and erecting their log palisades, Stark was restraining the more eager of his militiamen, who were clamoring to attack the hated Hessians and their despised loyalist allies. When Thomas

Allen, the parson and leader of the Pittsfield contingent, arrived at the head of his dripping men on the evening of August 14, demanding to be allowed to attack, Stark asked him, "Would you go out on this dark and stormy night?" He advised the militant cleric to give his men some rest, so that they might fight the better on the morrow. That same night Colonel Seth Warner rode into Bennington, some hours ahead of his Green Mountain Boys, and the American strength increased to more than 2,000.

As far as numbers were concerned, the odds were with the Americans, but they could hardly be described as an army.

To a man they wore small-clothes, coming down and fastening just below the knee, and long stockings with cowhide shoes ornamented by large buckles, while not a pair of boots graced the company. The coats and waistcoats were loose and of huge dimensions, with colours as various as the barks of oak, sumach and other trees of our hills and swamps could make them, and their shirts were all made of flax and, like every other part of the dress, were homespun. On their heads was worn a large round-top and broad-brimmed hat. Their arms were as various as their costume.[9]

A motley collection, perhaps, but united in the determination to defend their homes, and equally determined that no damned German mercenaries and their contemptible Tory friends were going to reach Bennington.

On August 16, which turned out to be fine and dry, the Americans moved out to battle. Stark's plan was simple. Baum's entrenched positions were first outflanked by Colonel Moses Nichols from the north and by Colonel Herrick from the south. In many instances the American militiamen were allowed by Baum's men to approach to within musket range in the mistaken belief that they were loyalists coming to join Baum. Once the fight had become general, Stark led his main body down the Bennington road, and a bitter battle took place around the position manned by Baum's loyalist contingent. Fraser and his rangers were pushed back from the bridge.

Stark, meanwhile, lost his horse, from which he had temporarily dismounted and had hitched to a fence. His troops swept on to attack the main defenses.

Stark described the battle as "the hottest I ever saw in my life. It represented one continued clap of thunder. . . ." [10] But numbers were bound to tell in the end, particularly when the Germans began to run out of ammunition. An ammunition wagon blew up at a critical moment, partly wrecking the main redoubt and stunning its defenders. Baum gathered together those of his dragoons still fit to fight and began a fighting retreat. He was almost immediately hit by a musket ball. The wound was mortal, and the fight went out of the Germans with their commander's death. A few escaped into the forests, but the majority surrendered. They had fought bravely for two long hours, and now for them the war was over.

The day had been hot, and the Americans were as exhausted as the Germans. They had been on the move since dawn and had little more fight left in them; but Stark now learned of the approach of Breymann and realized that the battle was far from over. Although there was no sign of Breymann's column, Stark sent Warner with his Green Mountain Boys down the road toward Sancoik's Mill. Warner's troops were comparatively fresh, and around 4:00 P.M. they ran into Breymann's jaded grenadiers. Breymann had heard nothing of Baum's defeat; he later claimed that if he had done so, he would never have continued his advance. Skene, the eternal optimist, encouraged him to keep advancing, and was certainly not backward in showing him the way; he had two horses shot from under him in less than an hour's encounter battle.

The Germans, whose fire discipline was bad, squandered their scanty ammunition by opening fire at too great a range. They were bewildered by the American tactics and disheartened by rumors of Baum's defeat. Breymann was a capable soldier, but out of his element in forest warfare. He had no confidence in Skene and no way of discovering the strength of the enemy lapping around his flanks. With the sun setting and help far away, he gave the order to withdraw. The retreat, which began as a disciplined movement, soon turned into a *sauve qui peut*. As darkness fell a confused mass of men poured across the bridge at Sancoik Mill, among them their colonel, badly wounded in the leg. Fortunately for them, the Americans were too exhausted by the battle, and too exhilarated by their victory, to do more than speed them on their way by random firing into the darkness.

Bennington was as complete a victory as could possibly have been hoped for by the Americans. The militia of New England, ill-disciplined and ill-equipped, had defeated at least 1,000 regular troops with little loss to themselves. Of Baum's force, only nine escaped out of the more than 375 German soldiers engaged. Between them, Baum and Breymann had had 207 killed. Three hundred eighty-nine were taken prisoner, among them 170 loyalists, who were tied, two to a horse, and led away past their jeering countrymen. "Had daylight lasted one hour longer, we should have taken the whole body of them," reported Stark. "We recovered 4 pieces of brass cannon, some hundred stands of arms, 8 brass barrells, drums, several Hessian swords. . . ." [11]

He went on to give praise where praise was due: "Too much honour cannot be given to the brave officers and soldiers for gallant behaviour. They fought through the midst of fire and smoke, mounted two breastworks that was well fortified and supported with cannon. I can't particularize any officer as they all behaved with the greatest spirit and bravery. Colonel Warner's superior skill in the action was of extraordinary service to me. I would be glad he and his men could be recommended to Congress." [12]

This was a handsome tribute by a brave officer. In his turn, Stark was formally thanked by the New Hampshire General Assembly, and presented with a "compleat suit of Clothes becoming his rank, together with a piece of linen." [13] When this news filtered through to the British, still smarting from the Bennington debacle, Lieutenant J. Hadden commented that "it was remarked upon the above reward that either the General was Stark naked or Congress stark mad." [14] But it was the Americans who had had the last laugh.

Bennington was a stunning defeat, from which Burgoyne never recovered. The causes were the usual underrating of the enemy and the absence of accurate information about him. It may have been a mistake to employ the Germans on such a detached mission. General Fraser had had his doubts when shown the plan and had commented, "The Germans are not very active people." Be this as it may, it was certainly a mistake to have sent the gullible Skene as Baum's political adviser. Breymann, too, had displayed little sense of urgency, although he had fought bravely enough. The Indians had contributed nothing. In the final analysis, however, it was Stark's leadership, and Warner's providential arrival toward the end of a long and exhausting day's fighting, that made the greatest contribution to one of the most significant American victories of the war.

When the news of Bennington reached London, Horace Walpole recorded: "General Burgoyne has had bad sport in the woods." [15] Washington's comment was less sarcastic, but more perspicacious. "Now," he wrote on August 22, "let all New England turn out and crush Burgoyne." [16]

Chapter 17

"This Army Must Not Retreat"

On his arrival at Fort Edward on July 29, Burgoyne had established his headquarters in the Red House, a blockhouse-like building erected some years before by a Doctor Smyth, and he remained there until August 14, when he moved to the Duer House at Fort Miller, eight miles farther down the Hudson. It was there he received the news of Bennington, and on August 20 he wrote two letters to Germain. One was intended for public information; the other was for the secretary of state's eyes alone. Neither letter gave Germain any cause for satisfaction.

Burgoyne's official account of the Bennington disaster was an unconvincing attempt to gloss over unpleasant facts. He reported that both Baum and Breymann had fought gallantly, but the former had reposed too much confidence in the protestations of the so-called loyalists. Burgoyne did not seek to apportion blame when all had fought so well, but it was unfortunate that "four pieces of cannon" had been lost. It was true that about 596 men had been killed or taken prisoner, and that twenty-six officers had fallen into enemy hands, "but men who were dispersed in the woods drop in daily." There is no hint of dejection in this public dispatch, and indeed Burgoyne concluded it with a report that a bridge of boats had been thrown across the river opposite Saratoga, and added that "nothing within my scale of talent shall be left unattempted to fulfill his Majesty's orders." [1]

The private letter told Germain a different story. Burgoyne went out of his way to explain why he had mounted the Bennington operation, and why he had selected German troops to execute it. He severely criticized Breymann for his slow movement; "could Mr Breymann have marked [*sic*] at the rate of two miles an hour any given twelve hours out of the two and thirty, success would probably have ensued, misfortune would certainly have been avoided." He trusted Germain would make this clear to the king.

Nevertheless, he was not unduly disheartened by Bennington, or so he told Germain. There were other reasons to account for his concern. St. Leger was having no success at Fort Stanwix, and in Burgoyne's opinion Johnson's optimistic predictions about the number of loyalists in the Mohawk valley were very wide of the mark. Far from believing Johnson, he had grave suspicions about the loyalists serving with his own force; about 400 of them could be relied upon, but "the rest are trimmers, merely actuated by interest. The great bulk of the country is undoubtedly with the Congress, in principle and in zeal; and their measures are executed with a secrecy and dispatch that are not to be equalled."

This could not have been welcome reading, for Germain had all along maintained that a whiff of gunpowder would soon bring the rebels to heel. "The Hampshire Grants in particular," Burgoyne went on to say, ". . . now abounds in the most active and most rebellious race of the continent, and hangs like a gathering storm on my left." The devastated nature of the countryside rendered it essential to carry all supplies, since none were to be obtained by foraging. Even more disheartening was the absence of any co-operation from Howe. He complained:

Another most embarrassing circumstance is the want of communication with Sir William Howe; of the messengers I have sent, I know of two being hanged, and am ignorant whether any of the rest arrived. The same fate has probably attended those dispatched by Sir William Howe; for only one letter is come to hand, informing me that his intention is for Pensylvania; that Washington has detached Sullivan, with 2500 men to Albany; that Putnam is in the Highlands, with 4000 men. That after my arrival at Albany, the movements of the enemy must guide mine; but that he wished the enemy might be driven out of the province before any operation took place against Connecticut; that Sir Henry Clinton remained in the command in the neighbourhood of New York, and would act as occurrences might direct.

No operation had yet been carried out in Burgoyne's support. The Americans were daily growing stronger, and they now outnumbered the British, he reported. They were well equipped with artillery.

Had I a latitude in my orders I should think it my duty to wait in this position, or perhaps as far back as Fort Edward, where my communication with Lake George would be perfectly secure, till some event happened to assist my movement forward; but my orders being positive to 'force a junction with Sir William Howe,' I apprehend I am not at Liberty to remain inactive longer than shall be necessary to collect twenty-five days provision, and to receive the reinforcement of the additional companies, the German drafts and recruits now (and unfortunately only now) on Lake Champlain. . . .

He had never envisaged that he would be expected to advance through such difficult country, he said, and in the face of such enemy resistance, without Howe's co-operation. Nor had he anticipated being called upon to garrison Ticonderoga, which could not be left defenseless. But despite the difficulties, he did not despond. "Should I succeed in forcing my way to Albany and find that country in a state to subsist my army, I shall think no more of retreat, but at the worst fortify there and await Sir W. Howe's operations." [2]

This is the most significant letter Burgoyne wrote from North America. It makes it abundantly clear that as early as

August 20, and probably even earlier, he knew that Howe would not be moving up the Hudson to join hands with him at Albany. He must also have known that Howe would hardly have moved into Pennsylvania without taking the larger part of his army with him. In fact, Howe's letter, dated July 17, which had been hidden in a quill pen and carried at considerable hazard through enemy territory, made it perfectly clear that Howe expected to fight Washington in Pennsylvania, and only if Washington turned north, presumably to counter Burgoyne, would Howe be operating in New York Province.

It is hard in the circumstances to explain why Burgoyne still stuck to his original intention of advancing to Albany. He may have believed that Clinton would help him by a push northward from New York, but his own knowledge of Howe's strength would have shown him that Clinton's force was unlikely to be strong enough to force a junction. Both Hubbardton and Bennington had demonstrated that the Americans could fight well, and Burgoyne no longer believed that his own strength would be significantly increased by local recruitment. Indeed, he had made it clear to Germain that the countryside was solid for Congress. His Indians were slipping away daily.

He argued later that his orders were positive that he reach Albany, but no general can be expected to adhere to his orders regardless of all consequences. Even in the eighteenth century, generals were expected to display more initiative than this; Burgoyne's subsequent pleadings smack of being wise after the event. Yet it is not easy to turn back when almost within sight of success, particularly when the campaign has opened with a move as striking as the capture of Ticonderoga. It could conceivably seem to be taking counsel of one's fears, and a general's will to win is as essential for success in battle as his skill in maneuvering his troops. John Burgoyne, a proud man to whom honor meant more than public approbation, was ambitious for military glory. If he now turned back, it would mean farewell to glory; worse, it might tarnish his honor. If he went on, he might succeed; and the success would be all his own, because Howe had failed to fulfill his part of the bargain. As an "old gamester," as Gates was later to describe him, Burgoyne put out of his mind any thought of retreat.

It has been suggested that Burgoyne did not learn of Howe's diversion to Pennsylvania until *after* his troops had crossed the Hudson, but his letter to Germain of August 20 makes it clear that this was not the case. At least three weeks elapsed between Burgoyne's receiving Howe's letter and the crossing of the Hudson. Burgoyne could have been under no illusions when he moved his troops. He was on his own.

He made this plain to Germain, who was beginning to grow alarmed. In one of his notes to Under-Secretary Knox, written after receiving Burgoyne's letter, Germain commented: "I am sorry to find that Burgoyne's campaign is so totally ruined; the best wish I can form is that he may have returned to Ticonderoga without much loss. His private letter to me, 20th of August, contains nothing material about the affair at Bennington, but what alarms me most is that he thinks his orders to go to Albany to force a junction with Sir William Howe are so positive that he must attempt at all events the obeying them." [3]

Hudleston, one of Burgoyne's biographers, takes Germain to task for making this comment, but he never attempts to conceal his predilection for Burgoyne, or his dislike of Germain; in this instance his criticism would seem to be both prejudiced and naïve. Surely it is not surprising that Germain should have expected Burgoyne to do the sensible thing in the circumstances? Once he knew that Howe had gone to Philadelphia, an *essential* part of the plan had been jettisoned. What was wrong then in withdrawing to Ticonderoga? It was the most sensible action to take, and it seems clear that this is what Germain expected.

Despite his undoubted zeal for public business, Germain was lamentably casual when it came to considering military operations. He seemed to be incapable of judging time and space and relative strengths in estimating a military problem. Nine days after his note to Knox, Germain was informing the king that Burgoyne was not advancing as rapidly as had been hoped, but that he was coping with his difficulties in an admirable fashion. The king was also told that Burgoyne had complained of not hearing from Howe and that he knew nothing of Howe's operations. Almost immediately after this letter to the king, Germain wrote again to Knox: "I am sorry the Canada army will be disappointed in the junction they expect with Sir William Howe, but the more honour to Burgoyne if he does the business without any assistance from New York." [4]

Germain had placed an each-way bet on Burgoyne. If he managed to get through to Albany, some of the credit would accrue to Germain, since he had selected the horse for the race. If, on the other hand, Burgoyne managed to extricate himself from his predicament, and withdrew successfully to Ticonderoga, he could be congratulated for acting with common sense. All the blame could then be laid on General Howe, for wrecking the plan by electing to go to Philadelphia instead of to Albany. Either way Germain would not be the loser.

Congress appointed a new commander for the Northern Department early in August. He was Major General Horatio Gates, aged fifty, until recently adjutant-general of the Continental Army. Schuyler's steadfastness of purpose and scorched-earth policy had slowed Burgoyne's advance, but Congress found it hard to forgive him for the surrender of Ticonderoga. He had acted with determination but his letters were despondent, conveying the impression that he lacked confidence both in himself and in his troops. He was too aloof and aristocratic to be popular; his detractors in Congress had their way, and he was superseded.

Gates was almost the exact opposite of Schuyler. An Englishman, son of a minor government functionary, he was born into a ducal household, his mother having been housekeeper to the Duke of Leeds. This can hardly have been as menial an appointment as the name suggests, since Gates's godfather was no less a man than Horace Walpole, after whom he was named; nor was his father so poor that he could not afford to purchase his son an ensigncy in an infantry regiment. He was in fact surveyor of customs at Greenwich. Gates was posted early in his career to North America. He was able to purchase a captaincy in 1754 in an independent company, the ranks of which were mainly recruited from Americans, and took part in Braddock's ill-fated expedition in 1755. He was severely wounded in the ambush on the Monongahela and owed his life to a Private Penfold, who carried him to safety. Many years later, when Penfold had fallen on hard times, Gates wrote to him, saying, "Come and rest your firelock in my chimney corner and partake with me; while I have my saviour Penfold shall not want." [5]

Gates was a major in 1762 when the Seven Years' War ended. He had acquired considerable experience as a staff officer and had merited further promotion. He had also married Elizabeth Phillips, an ambitious woman from a better class in society than his own, but he lacked the means to purchase command of a regiment. He retired from the army, disgruntled and at odds with the Establishment. He spoke his mind freely, and was thought to have republican views. It is therefore not surprising that he should have returned in 1773 to the land where he had passed his youth, and where success did not depend solely on money and an aristocratic lineage. He knew George Washington, with whom he had served under Braddock, and on Washington's advice bought a plantation in Virginia, which he named "Traveller's Rest."

He rallied to the colonists' side in 1775, and was welcomed

by Washington, who knew of his experience as a staff officer. He was appointed a brigadier general, and became adjutant-general at Washington's headquarters at Cambridge. As such he played a major part in introducing some order into the early, chaotic months of the formation of the Continental Army. He drafted the regulations and relieved Washington of many administrative chores. It was a sphere in which he excelled, but he aspired to a field command. He was a tireless intriguer, finally achieving promotion to major general in May, 1776, when assigned to command the troops retreating from Canada. He was instrumental in putting Ticonderoga into a state of defense, and in checking Carleton's advance. However, he clashed with Schuyler, also a major general, who claimed that Congress had appointed *him* to command the Northern Department. After months of bickering between the two men, both of whom had their supporters in Congress, Gates finally returned to Philadelphia, leaving Schuyler in command in the north, though he left no stone unturned in his efforts to supplant Schuyler. He was the inevitable choice when Congress decided to supersede Schuyler. On August 19 he rode into Albany to assume command of the Northern Department, while Schuyler retired to his handsome mansion to brood over his wrongs, and to watch his successor reap where he had sown.

Gates was an unimaginative and cautious commander, with a warm personality; his nickname, "Granny," explains much about him. He was careful with the lives of his soldiers, devoting much of his undoubted administrative ability to the improvement of their living conditions. He had a good eye for ground, as well as a healthy respect for the British soldier's skill with the bayonet. The effect of his arrival at Albany was heartening, not altogether unlike the effect of Burgoyne's arrival in Canada to take command of the expedition. According to Sam Adams, admittedly a staunch supporter of Gates, "He . . . has the Art of gaining the Love of his soldiers principally because he is always present with them in Fatigue and Danger." [6]

As a former professional soldier, Gates knew the value of discipline, but he did not make the mistake of underrating the American militia simply because they lacked the discipline of the British Army. In this respect he was like Charles Lee, and for the same reasons. Both men had served during the war against the French in units composed mainly of American colonists, and they knew how well Americans could fight. They also understood how to adapt the pipe-clayed discipline of the British Army to suit the temperament of men who valued personal independence above everything but the loss of liberty. Gates could be firm, but he was also fair. His benevolent and somewhat unassuming outward appearance concealed a good deal of steel, though he was less than bold in the field. Cautious almost to the point of timidity, he was reluctant to take any kind of chance. He quarreled with most of his fellow-generals, and even with his patron and friend George Washington, acquiring a reputation for being both contentious and malicious.

Gates and Burgoyne provided a complete contrast in character. Burgoyne's career in the British Army had been glitteringly successful; Gates ended as a mere major. The cavalry general could affect to despise the plodding infantryman, referring to him contemptuously as "an old midwife"; but Gates believed he had Burgoyne's measure, always provided that he fought him on ground of his own choosing, and kept the British infantry well beyond bayonet distance.

With this object in view, Gates moved his troops forward from the flat terrain at the mouth of the Mohawk. After careful reconnaissance he chose a position sixteen miles farther up the Hudson, near Stillwater. Here the road to Albany is hemmed in, by the river on one side and by steeply rising and heavily wooded ground on the other. It was a natural defile, which Burgoyne would have to clear before continuing his advance to Albany. The ground above the river was rolling downland, seamed with ravines running to the river, their sides and bottoms covered in thick underbrush.

Everywhere was primeval forest, apart from the occasional clearing where a settler had felled the trees to erect a cabin, stoutly constructed to resist an Indian raid. The cleared ground had been sown with corn, and the few tracks existed only for farm wagons to carry the produce down to the Albany road. The names of that handful of settlers who cleared the land above the Hudson are now part of American history—Neilson, Chatfield, Freeman, and Barber—as is that of Jotham Bemis, who kept a tavern on the Albany road just below the defile. His name was given to the heights above, where Thaddeus Kosciusko, the Polish *émigré* now serving as Gates's engineering adviser, constructed a strong point to serve as the anchor for the American defenses.

Gates did not move to this position until September 12, and by then his army was about 7,000 strong. His name had brought the militiamen of New England swarming in, but there had been little time to lick them into shape. Arnold had arrived back from the Mohawk, bringing 1,200 triumphant soldiers with him. An equally important reinforcement was Daniel Morgan, with his 500 riflemen. Washington had sent Morgan north on August 16 with what has been described as "the finest infantry of the day." [7] They were frontiersmen from western Pennsylvania, mostly of Scottish-Irish stock, armed with a long-barreled flintlock rifle, and marching light for considerable distances. As much at home in the forests as the Indians, against whom they had conducted many a bloody foray, they were light troops par excellence. Burgoyne had nothing to compare with them when it came to forest fighting; nor, for that matter, had Howe. It is good evidence of Washington's concern about Burgoyne's expedition that he should have been willing to deprive his own army of the services of such an elite formation, and at a time when he was daily expecting to be attacked by Howe.

Both British and Americans were preparing for battle. Gates needed time to bring some order into his army and to prepare his defenses. Burgoyne needed time to bring forward the supplies he must have to feed his troops and animals until Albany could be reached. The latter part of August and the first two weeks of September were taken up by these activities, and by British efforts to determine the strength and dispositions of the enemy. These attempts to acquire information were mostly thwarted by Gates, whereas on the American side there was a steady stream of information about the British.

On August 15 there arrived at the Red House a dusty cavalcade. It consisted of Baroness Frederika von Riedesel; her three daughters, Gustava, Frederika, and Caroline, aged, respectively, five, three, and one; and two ladies' maids. This was the end of a journey that had begun fifteen months earlier when the baroness set out from Wolfenbüttel, in Germany, to join her husband. She wrote that she owed the reunification to General Burgoyne, who had remarked to General von Riedesel, shortly after Lady Acland had joined her husband at Fort Edward, "General, you shall have your wife here also!" For this kindly action Burgoyne was later to receive scant acknowledgment from the baroness. She had been married in 1762 and was thirty-one when she set up house beside the Hudson. A woman of great determination and character, she spoke no English when she left Germany, nor had she found it easy to adjust herself to English ways while she waited in England for a ship to take her to Canada. She had, however, been kindly received at Court, where she had been presented to the king and queen by Lady Germain. The king had kissed her, inquiring kindly after her husband, and the queen had been particularly friendly. She later visited the queen on several occasions.

The baroness was an acute observer, who not unnaturally saw things through her husband's eyes. They were a devoted couple, simple and straightforward, and did not find it easy to come to terms with a man as sophisticated and pleasure-loving as John Burgoyne. What for him would seem merely being gracious, they regarded as patronizing, and they resented his evident reluctance to include Riedesel in his inner counsels. The baroness found it hard to condone the commander-in-chief's obvious enjoyment of the good things in life and the open manner in which he consorted with the commissary's wife. As provincial in her attitudes as any other member of the German petty nobility, Baroness von Riedesel strongly disapproved of the lax morals of the upper aristocracy, which, so far as she was concerned, were exemplified by the scandalous behavior of her husband's commander-in-chief. She disapproved of General Burgoyne almost from the outset of their acquaintance.

At first, however, all went well.

We led, during these three weeks, a very pleasant life [she wrote]. The surrounding country was magnificent; and we were encircled by the encampments of the English and German troops. We lived in a building called the Red House. . . . It was at this place that I eat bear's flesh for the first time, and found it of capital flavour. We were often put to it to get any thing to eat; notwithstanding this, however, I was very happy and content, for I was with my children, and beloved by those by whom I was surrounded. There were, if I remember rightly, four or five adjutants staying with us. The evening was spent by the gentlemen in playing cards, and by myself in putting my children to bed.[8]

There was also visiting, for there were several other ladies with the army. One of them was Lady Harriet Acland, whose husband was a major in the 20th Regiment. He had commanded the grenadier companies with distinction at Hubbardton, but he failed to win the baroness's approval. He was, she wrote, "a plain rough man, and . . . almost daily intoxicated," but she grudgingly conceded that, this apart, "he was

an excellent officer." As for Lady Harriet, "she was the love-
liest of women." [9]

Baroness von Riedesel was fortunate in arriving when she
did. A few days later and she would have been too late, because Burgoyne, in an effort to concentrate his maximum
strength for the battle for Albany, called in all the detachments that had been protecting his line of communication with
Canada. Only Diamond Island, on Lake George, and Ticonderoga itself remained under guard. From Fort Edward to
Fort George the track ran undefended, open to interruption
throughout its length. The sailors who had accompanied the
expedition from Lake Champlain labored to construct a bridge
across the Hudson. It rained with capricious violence, swelling the river and making it difficult to anchor the clumsy
bateaux, across which planks had to be laid for the wagons
and the guns. Midshipman Edward Pellew, later to become
an admiral, distinguished himself in these bridge-building activities, narrowly escaping drowning on several occasions. On
September 11 the flooded river broke the bridge, but the flood
subsided next day and the troops began crossing on the thir-
teenth. It took two days for the entire army to cross, carrying
provisions for thirty days, and followed by those women who
still remained with the army. Riedesel had wanted to send his
family back to Canada, but was dissuaded by his wife's
pleadings.

She was in high spirits despite the rain and the constant
moves.

We made only small day's marches [she wrote], and were very
often sick; yet always contented at being allowed to follow. I
still had the satisfaction of daily seeing my husband. A great part
of my baggage I had sent back, and had kept only a small summer wardrobe. In the beginning all went well. We cherished the
sweet hope of a sure victory, and of coming into the 'promised
land;' and when we passed the Hudson River, and General Burgoyne said, 'The English never lose ground,' our spirits were
greatly exhilerated.[10]

And so, it appears, were her husband's. "General Burgoyne was so certain of victory that the ladies were in high spirits," he wrote, although he must have shared his wife's concern at the total absence of any kind of security. Plans were freely discussed by officers of high and low rank, often in the hearing of Loyalists, whose loyalty was often barely skin-deep. But the army was on the move again, and heading in the right direction.

The force that crossed the Hudson consisted of 4,646 regular troops, of which 2,635 were British, the rest being Germans. There were in addition about 440 Canadians and loyalists, and 300 sailors, artillerymen, drivers, and bateaux men. Only about 200 Indians remained of all those who had whooped their way across Lake Champlain three months earlier. There were thirty-five guns and six mortars. Washington had been correct when he warned Schuyler of the debilitating effect of detachments on the expedition's strength. This, coupled with the losses at Bennington, had reduced Burgoyne's strength by over 2,000 men, but if Burgoyne had any fears about the future, he kept them to himself. With Generals Riedesel and Phillips beside him, and surrounded by his staff, he reviewed his troops as they paraded past, with colors flying, drums beating, and fifes playing, to cross the bridge. It must have been a brave sight, the scarlet of the British line and the blue of the German, with the trees along the Hudson slowly turning red with the fall. There was a nip in the air, warning of winter. The winter clothing had unfortunately been left behind in Canada, but it should be warm enough in Albany.

While the troops set up their tents on the northern bank of Fishkill Creek, and as Burgoyne's servants took possession of Schuyler's wooden mansion in the hamlet of Saratoga, where their commander-in-chief would sleep that night, the British sailors began to dismantle the bridge. The bateaux were required to ferry supplies down the river, keeping pace with the army as it marched. Burgoyne had now severed his last link with Canada, nearly 200 miles away.

Chapter 18

The Decisive Battle

ONCE ACROSS the Hudson, Burgoyne's principal problem was the lack of reliable information about the enemy. He knew the road to Albany was barred, but he did not know precisely where, or how strongly. His Indians were of little use as scouts since they were operating against men who knew the woods as well as they did. Fraser's sharpshooters had been frittered away at Bennington, and Burgoyne never really trusted his loyalists. His soldiers were suffering from the cumulative effects of short rations and bad meat; dysentery and fever were rife. The days were humid, but the nights cold. The women camp followers were a constant source of anxiety. To add to the general's annoyance, some soldiers plundering a potato field had been caught unawares by American sharpshooters. Fourteen men were killed or missing, and Burgoyne issued the following order:

The Lieut. Genl. will no longer bear to lose Men, for the pitiful consideration of Potatoes, or Forage. The Life of the Soldier is the property of the King, and since neither Friendly Admonitions, repeated Injunctions, nor Corporal punishments have effect, after what has happened, the Army is now to be informed, and it is not doubted the Commanding Officers will do it solemnly, that the first Soldier caught beyond the Advanced Centinels of the Army, will be instantly Hanged.[1]

The Decisive Battle

Anyone who knows the British soldier will doubt the efficacy of any such order, for when soldiers are hungry they will find ways and means to satisfy their hunger, whatever their generals may decree to the contrary. There was a more convincing way of keeping soldiers from straggling. American sharpshooters continued to prowl the woods ahead of the British lines, and any unwary British soldier was shot out of hand. Nevertheless, three soldiers of the 20th Regiment were taken prisoner on September 14; they were closely followed by two Germans, who succeeded in deserting, taking with them information that Gates found useful. Not that Gates was short of information. Lieutenant Colonel James Wilkinson had reconnoitered almost up to the British lines, and Colonel Colborn had been able to count the British tents from the vantage point of a tree with the aid of a spyglass. Both sides suffered from the intermittent downpours, but the Americans welcomed the fact that the rain delayed Burgoyne's advance. While he crawled down the river road, reaching Dovecot (the modern Coveville) on September 15, and the Sword House on the seventeenth, Gates was fortifying his position.

The extent of this position was approximately one and a quarter miles from west to east, and three-quarters of a mile from north to south. As good a description of it as any has been given by Wilkinson:

General Gates's right occupied the brow of a hill near the river, with which it was connected by a deep intrenchment; his camp, in the form of a segment of a great circle, the convex towards the enemy, extended rather obliquely to his rear, about three-fourths of a mile to a knoll occupied by his left; his front was covered from the right to the left of the centre, by a sharp ravine running parallel with his line and closely wooded; from thence to the knoll at his extreme left, the ground was level and had been partially cleared, some of the trees being felled and others girdled, beyond which in front of his left flank, and extending to the enemy's right, there were several small fields in very imperfect cultivation, the surface broken and obstructed with stumps and fallen timber, and the whole bounded on the west by a steep eminence. The extremities of this camp were defended by strong batteries, and the interval was strengthened by a breast-work without intrenchments, constructed of the bodies of felled trees, logs and rails, with an additional battery at an opening left of the centre. The right was almost impracticable; the left difficult of approach.[2]

The position was naturally strong and had been made even stronger by the ingenuity of Kosciusko and the wielding of axes.

The intermediate space between the adverse armies on the low grounds of the river was open and in cultivation [states Wilkinson]. The high land was clothed in its native woods, with the exception of three or four small, newly opened and deserted farms, separated by intervals of woodland, and bordering on the flanks of the two armies, most remote from the river; the principal of these was an oblong field, belonging to a person of the name of Freeman; there was also, exclusive of the ravines fronting the respective camps, a third ravine, about mid-way between them, running at right angles to the river. The intervening forest rendered it utterly impracticable to obtain a front view of the American position, or any part of the British except its left near the river.[3]

Within this position were concentrated about 9,000 men. There should have been at least 800 more, but when John Stark brought in his brigade on September 18, his men immediately clamored for their release from service on the grounds that their time was up. Stark appears to have done little to dissuade them, while all the pleading of Gates and his senior officers fell on deaf ears. In Wilkinson's words, "These citizens had fought once, and having served the term of their engagement, were desirous to tell the tale of 'feats performed,' and look into their private affairs, after which they were ready again to take arms." [4] By midday on the eighteenth they were on their way home.

Gates deployed his army in two wings. On the right, and under his immediate command, were the Continental brigades of Brigadier Generals John Glover, John Nixon, and John

Paterson, whose primary task was to command the river and the road that ran beside it. In the center, and on the left, were the Continental brigades of Brigadier General Learned and Brigadier General Enoch Poor, together with Morgan's riflemen and 300 light infantry under Major Henry Dearborn. This wing was under the command of Major General Arnold. Gates had in addition a number of militia regiments which varied in strength, equipment, and dependability. He placed little confidence in such troops, whose lack of discipline was a constant source of irritation to an old regular soldier like him, but they were useful in preparing defenses. There was also an artillery train of twenty-two pieces. Well prepared, and reasonably confident of his ability to stop Burgoyne, Gates sat back and waited for the "old gamester" to make the first throw.

The first battle, at Freeman's Farm (Saratoga), was fought on September 19, 1777. The history of a battle, wrote the Duke of Wellington, "is not unlike the history of a ball. Some individuals may recollect all the little events of which the great result is the battle won or lost; but no individual can recollect the order in which, or the exact moment at which, they occurred, which makes all the difference to their value or importance." [5] Saratoga was to prove no exception. It began in a fog and ended in darkness. In between, the contestants were blinded for much of the time by the forest, as well as by the smoke of gunpowder. The difficult terrain hampered the movement of artillery and impeded the British and German infantry in their unsuitable uniforms. Their officers, conspicuous by the gorgets hanging around their necks, presented splendid targets for marksmen concealed in the undergrowth, or in the foliage of the trees, which they had climbed.

If there was confusion among the British, whose three columns were incapable for much of the time of supporting each other, due partly to the terrain and partly to the distance between each of them, there was great dissension among the Americans. Gates was all for caution; he wanted Burgoyne to batter himself to pieces against the American entrenchments. Arnold favored a battle in the open, arguing that there were always the entrenchments to fall back on if the British were not stopped. Gates feared the British skill with the bayonet, and believed their superior discipline would prevail out in the open. Arnold had much more confidence in the bravery of his troops. Even the name of the battle is a confusing one, since some call it Saratoga, and others Freeman's Farm.

The one thing on which there seems to be agreement is that the battle marked the climacteric of the Revolutionary War, but even this is debatable. The war continued for nearly five years after Saratoga. Britain had lost the North American colonies long before Cornwallis surrendered at Yorktown, but the king would not acknowledge the fact. It was a war Britain could never have hoped to win once it had lost the sympathy of the majority of its former subjects. There had been too much blood spilled, too many harsh words spoken, long before Burgoyne came upon Gates barring the way to Albany, for any return to the old relationship. Nevertheless, Saratoga was included by Creasey among his sixteen decisive battles of the world, and as such it will always be remembered.

Saratoga was a pure slogging match, with only a part of the forces on either side involved. For Burgoyne, the brunt of the fighting was borne by his four British regiments—the 9th, 20th, 21st, and 62nd; for Gates, it was Morgan's and Dearborn's light troops, and Poor's and Learned's brigades that did the fighting. The remainder were scarcely involved. Gates took so little part, indeed knew so little about what was happening, that it was rumored he contemplated ordering a withdrawal at one stage.

The battle began between 8:00 and 9:00 A.M., when a thick fog and drizzling rain added to the discomfort of British and Americans alike. Burgoyne knew that Gates was blocking the Albany road about three miles ahead of him. He also had a rough idea of the extent of the American position but little information about its strength. His scouts had reported an unoccupied hill lying to the west of Gates's line, and, doubtless with the occupation of Sugar Hill at Ticonderoga in mind, this hill became Burgoyne's objective. Having captured it, he would turn Gates's open flank, with the object of driving him out of his fortifications by the employment of artillery fire alone. Burgoyne has been criticized for these tactics, but in view of his lack of information about the enemy it was as good a plan as any. He would have been equally criticized had he chosen instead to continue down the Albany road to attack Gates frontally. However, had he fully appreciated the difficulty of the terrain, the latter plan might have held more attraction.

After crossing the Hudson, the British deployed into three parallel columns. Riedesel's German brigade was on the left, using as its axis the Albany road; in the center was Brigadier-General James Hamilton, with four British battalions; on the right was Brigadier-General Fraser, with the light and grenadier battalions, his own 24th Foot, and Breymann's light infantry. As a consequence of this deployment, Burgoyne decided to swing Fraser far to the right, with the aim of engaging the American left and establishing himself on the unoccupied hill. Fraser's Advanced Corps was the elite British formation, and Fraser was Burgoyne's most trusted subordinate; it was therefore natural that Burgoyne should select Fraser's brigade for the crucial task. The center would follow after Fraser, but would not swing so wide. Instead, it would turn south and probe forward to determine the American center, and then act in support of Fraser as required. Riedesel, with the regiments Riedesel, Specht, and Rhetz, and the Hesse-Hanau artillery under Captain Pausch, would continue down the Albany road, prepared to assist the center column. Major-General Phillips would move behind Riedesel, with the supply train, and seven guns under Major Williams.

The day began well enough. The fog lifted, the sun came out, and the troops tramped along the rough track running westward from the Sword House. Burgoyne rode with the center column, which, along with the right, made better progress than Riedesel's; the Germans were impeded by broken bridges. Then the terrain started taking a hand, and it is important to remember in this context the tight uniforms and clumsy weapons that impeded rapid movement. There were also the guns and their ammunition to be hauled through the mud, and up and down steep slopes, the axles catching on the trees, and sometimes swinging the guns around in their traces. These were not lightly equipped troops moving rapidly through the forest, but men tightly trussed, who were carrying sixty rounds of ammunition apiece.

The main obstacle lying between Burgoyne and Gates's position was the Great Ravine, which ran roughly from east to west across the front. The sides of this ravine were steep and clogged with brushwood; the bottom was boggy, and tough going for both men and guns. Fraser struck it, and had to turn west to find a suitable crossing point. He did not find it until he had gone two miles away from the center column, which arrived around noon in a clearing by a farm belonging to a settler named Freeman, who had long since fled. Burgoyne halted close by Freeman's cabins in order to give Fraser time to reach his objective. When all were ready, three guns were to be fired as the signal for a general attack.

There was little sign of the enemy, despite the fact that Gates had received early warning of Burgoyne's advance. Gates had no intention of attacking Burgoyne out in the open; he intended to sit tight behind his entrenchments and await developments. This led to a furious dispute between him and Arnold, who was opposed to leaving the initiative to the enemy. After much argument, Gates yielded so far as to permit Morgan, supported by Dearborn's light infantry, to reconnoiter beyond the American defenses. As a result, Morgan arrived at Freeman's Farm almost at the same time as Burgoyne's center column, and just in time to wipe out a

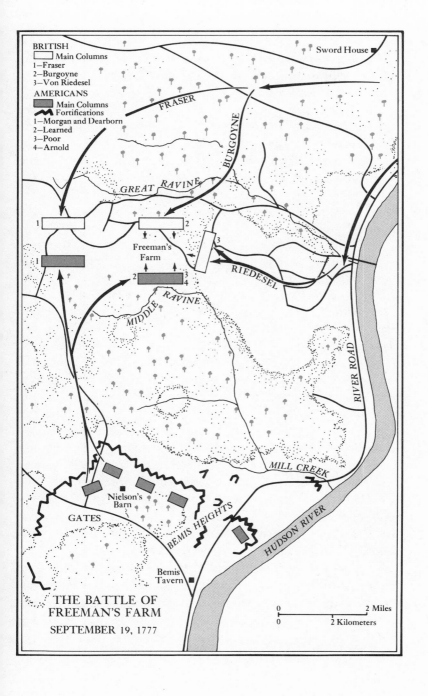

BRITISH
◻ Main Columns
1—Fraser
2—Burgoyne
3—Von Riedesel

AMERICANS
▓ Main Columns
⩙ Fortifications
1—Morgan and Dearborn
2—Learned
3—Poor
4—Arnold

Sword House ■

FRASER

BURGOYNE

GREAT RAVINE

1   2

1   3

Freeman's
Farm

2   3
    4

RIEDESEL

MIDDLE RAVINE

RIVER ROAD

MILL CREEK

Nielson's
Barn

GATES

BEMIS HEIGHTS

HUDSON RIVER

Bemis
Tavern ■

THE BATTLE OF
FREEMAN'S FARM
SEPTEMBER 19, 1777

0   2 Miles

0   2 Kilometers

picket sent forward by the British to investigate the two log cabins. At about 12:30 P.M. the battle of Saratoga began.

The British had been on the move since early morning, the noonday sun was hot, and the soldiers were tired. They were also confused by the forest. There was too much cover for comfort, particularly for soldiers accustomed to volley firing against an enemy who could be clearly seen.

Burgoyne's tactics were complicated by the problem of keeping in touch with his three columns. It was 1:00 P.M. before Fraser came up on the right, and then Burgoyne ordered the three guns to be fired. At this moment Morgan's riflemen, assisted by two regiments from Poor's brigade, were lining the southern fringe of Freeman's fifteen-acre field. The British were drawn up on the northern edge, just clear of the trees, with Burgoyne and his staff on horseback close behind the rear files. The 21st was on the right, the 62nd in the center, and the 20th on the left. The 9th was echeloned back in immediate reserve. For three hours the fighting continued for possession of Freeman's wretched acres. Burgoyne used battering-ram tactics, advancing with measured pace to get close enough to use the bayonet, but he was halted time and again by the withering American fire. American attempts to work around the British right exposed them to flanking fire from Fraser's Advanced Corps, chiefly from Breymann's battalion and the 24th; and when Arnold attempted to drive a wedge between Hamilton's and Fraser's brigades, he was repulsed with heavy loss. Much the worst damage was done by the American sharpshooters, who concentrated with deadly effect on picking off the resplendent officers.

By 3:30 P.M. reinforcements were reaching Arnold—four regiments of Learned's brigade. With these fresh troops, together with Poor's battalions, Arnold concentrated on the destruction of Burgoyne's center column. Fraser, who was clinging to some rising ground on the right, was kept occupied by Morgan to such an extent that he could not intervene to assist Hamilton. The men of the 62nd Regiment bore the brunt of the attack, charging and being countercharged until they were totally exhausted. Their bravery caused Burgoyne to ride forward and shout above the roar of cannon, "Well done, my brave Springers!" The 62nd had gained this nickname in the previous war in Canada, and they had certainly earned Burgoyne's praise, but at a frightful cost: 187 of them were killed or wounded, and twenty-five were taken prisoner. As a regiment they were decimated.

There was little that Burgoyne could do to influence the battle, except to remain with the center column and encourage his soldiers by his personal example. Although he was a staunch proponent of the employment of artillery, his own guns were virtually useless for want of gunners to fire them. Lieutenant Hadden was the only artillery officer serving with the center column who survived the battle; 36 out of 48 artillerymen were either killed or wounded. "The British artillery fell into our possession at every charge," wrote Wilkinson "but we could neither turn the pieces upon the enemy, nor bring them off; the wood prevented the last, and the want of a match the first, as the lint stock was invariably carried off, and the rapidity of the transitions did not allow us time to provide one." [6]

Both sides had fought themselves to a standstill. Had this not been the case, a really determined effort by the Americans might have won them the day. But as Americans and British paused for breath, General Phillips cantered up to Burgoyne, bringing with him four guns and Major Williams, "Old Twelve Pounder." Loaded with grapeshot, Williams' guns did deadly damage among the Americans lurking in the trees on the far side of the clearing. Burgoyne took advantage of the respite to send in the 20th to clear the woods on the left of the field, and to take some of the pressure off the battered 62nd. The only way either Burgoyne or Gates could influence the battle was by throwing in his reserves. Burgoyne's only unused troops were Riedesel's, and they were still some way off. As for Gates, he curbed, rather than encouraged, Arnold's repeated attempts to send more units to the battle. High words passed between the two men, Gates insisting that Arnold was putting the American defenses at risk by denuding them of men. If Gates had permitted Arnold to conduct the battle, it might have ended differently, but Gates feared his subordinate's impetuosity. He even sent to recall him when at one critical moment Arnold galloped off to the sound of the guns.

Then, as at Hubbardton, Riedesel arrived—in the nick of time. He had continued his advance slowly down the Albany road, halting to rebuild bridges and deal with an occasional ambush, until by 2:30 P.M. he had reached the farthest point south that Burgoyne's expedition was to reach as free men. Heavy firing to the west warned him that Burgoyne was engaged with the enemy, and he at once set about organizing a defensive position astride the road. There he left Brigadier-General Johann Specht, with about 800 men and four pieces of artillery; the remainder of the German column, consisting of his own regiment, two companies of the Regiment Rhetz, and Captain Georg Pausch, with two six-pounders, set off posthaste to join in the battle.

Although a staff officer was dispatched ahead of the column to warn Burgoyne of Riedesel's approach, Burgoyne did not call upon Riedesel's services until around 5:30 P.M. It is almost as if he wanted to keep the Germans out of the battle, but by the time he did deploy them, the situation in the center was well-nigh desperate. The 62nd had been bled white, while the soldiers of the 20th were so shaken that one more charge might have broken them. They were saved by Phillips, who personally led a counterattack, supported by Williams' guns, and the 20th Regiment stood firm. According to Riedesel, the battle when he arrived "was raging its fiercest. The Americans, far superior in numbers, had, for the sixth time, hurled fresh troops against the three English regiments—the 20th, 21st and 62nd. The guns on this wing were already silenced, there being no more ammunition and all the artillerymen having been either killed or wounded. The three brave English regiments had been . . . thinned down to one-half, and now formed a small band surrounded by heaps of dead and wounded." [7]

The Germans did not hesitate. They attacked the enemy "on the double quick," ably supported by Pausch's guns, which fired grapeshot at point-blank range. This charge probably saved Burgoyne's center column from defeat, although, since it was fast growing dark, the night might possibly have come to the aid of the hard-pressed British. As it was, the Americans continued to fire sporadically, but their main body drew off and returned to their entrenchments. The British kept their ranks throughout the night, waiting to repel another onslaught. "Sleep was a stranger to us," records Digby, "but we were all in good spirits and ready to obey with cheerfulness any orders the general might issue before the morning dawned." [8]

It was the obstinacy of the Americans, and their readiness to return to the charge, that shook the British. Some of the finest infantry in the world had been thrown back, losing a third of their strength. The 62nd had suffered the worst—only sixty men answered roll call that September night. The killed, wounded, and missing amounted to 556, including thirty-five officers, among whom were two lieutenant-colonels. Burgoyne's army still kept the field, but it had been a Pyrrhic victory. On the British side, it could be said that neither Fraser's nor Riedesel's columns suffered heavily; on the American, it could be argued that Gates's excessive caution had wrecked any prospect of outright victory. Indeed, had Arnold not been present to goad him into action, the likelihood is that Gates would have remained passive behind his defenses. In that case Burgoyne would probably have succeeded in turning the American flank, and the road to Albany would have been wide open. The glory of the day was therefore Arnold's, shared with Morgan and his riflemen, and shared also, of course, with the ordinary soldiers on both sides who had fought with such courage.

In his report on the battle to the secretary of state, Burgoyne paid tribute to the bravery of his officers and soldiers, describing their behavior in general as "exemplary." He singled out for special mention the artillery, and praised the conduct of Generals Phillips, Hamilton, and Fraser. He was somewhat less fulsome when it came to the Germans, whose appearance on the battlefield may not have sealed the victory, but who had certainly averted defeat. "Major-General Riedesel exerted himself to bring up a part of the left wing, and arrived in time to charge the enemy with regularity and bravery," Burgoyne informed Germain, with less than his usual generosity of spirit. He went on to tell the minister that the coming of darkness prevented any pursuit, and that therefore "the prisoners were few." [9] He was rather more critical in his order of the day issued at "Camp at Freeman's Farm" on September 21. After informing all concerned of his general, as well as particular, approbation, his order stated:

> Amidst these general subjects of Applause, the impetuosity and uncertain aim of the British Troops in giving their fire, and the mistake they are still under, in preferring it to the Baynotte [*sic*], is to be much lamented. The Lieut. General is persuaded this error will be corrected in the next engagement, upon conviction of their own experience and reason, as well as upon that general principle of discipline *never* to *fire* but by the *order of an officer.*[10]

Burgoyne did not tell the whole story to his superiors; nor did Gates. In his report to Congress, the latter conspicuously avoided paying Arnold the tribute Arnold rightly considered was owing to him and to his troops. The result was a bitter quarrel between the two men. There has since been some dispute about Arnold's personal involvement in the battle, but

Arnold has become such a controversial character that these arguments are motivated as much by malice as by a conscientious searching for the truth. Nothing can rob Arnold of the credit for persuading Gates to change his tactics, and Arnold's gallantry under fire certainly served as an inspiration for many Americans who were fighting the redoubtable "redcoats" for the first time. Fortescue may have been unduly hard on Gates when later he described him as being "a thoroughly incompetent officer," but he was almost certainly correct when he wrote, "Had Gates sent to Arnold the reinforcements for which he asked, Arnold must certainly have broken the British centre, which, even as things were, could barely hold its own." [11]

Many accounts have been written of the battle of Freeman's Farm, or the first battle of Saratoga. The accounts of those who were present—Digby, Hadden, Anburey, Lamb—have been read and reread in order to discover some fresh information about the tactics. There are many more American eye-witness accounts of the battle, and all tell the same tale. Well-trained and excellently disciplined British troops, fighting in the way they had been taught to fight under European conditions, were held and very nearly defeated by American irregulars who employed entirely different tactics, but tactics well adapted to the terrain. The American skill with their weapons, their use of ground, and their ability to fight as individuals making the best use of cover enabled them to fight to a standstill four of the finest infantry battalions in the British Army.

The British soldier was trained by numbers. He drilled by numbers, fired by numbers, and often died by numbers. His training was designed to fit him for shock action—first, the disciplined volley of musketry delivered at short range, and then, the controlled charge with the bayonet. At Freeman's Farm he met his downfall in Morgan and his backwoodsmen, who were used to fighting individually, each man picking his own target and instinctively making use of cover and ground to ensure that he could kill without being killed. It was a chastening lesson for Burgoyne and the proud regiments he commanded. Unfortunately, they had come a long way from home to learn the lesson, and on September 19, 1777, it was too late to turn back.

Chapter 19

The Gamester's Throw

WRAPPED in his cloak, John Burgoyne lay out on the battle-field, surrounded by his soldiers and kept awake by the howl-ing of wolves and the moaning of the wounded and dying. He wrestled with a problem familiar to anyone who has com-manded soldiers in battle, be it a platoon or a division. His troops had been fought to a standstill; they were exhausted, but so perhaps were the enemy. He at least remained master of the battlefield. The initiative still remained with the British. Should he, then, call upon his soldiers for one supreme effort? Should he attack at dawn? Or should he wait until supplies and ammunition could be brought up, the wounded evacuated, and the dead buried?

Burgoyne's inclination was to attack, and it was unfortunate for him that he was dissuaded from doing so. General Phillips, according to Wilkinson, said that Burgoyne had intended to continue the attack on the morning of September 20, his object being to turn the American left, and that orders for this operation had in fact been sent out. However, Fraser, who had been in favor of the continuation of the operation, at the last minute begged for a postponement for twenty-four hours in order to rest his troops. The projected oper-ation was postponed, and the British fortified the ground on which they stood. Wilkinson had no doubt that a British attack would have been successful. The American camp was in disarray. A thick fog added to men's fear of an imminent onslaught. The left wing was short of ammunition, and a deserter from the 62nd reported that an attack was impending. It came therefore as a surprise that there was no movement from the British lines.

Burgoyne's conduct during the battle was warmly commended by Sergeant Lamb. "General Burgoyne," he wrote, "during this conflict behaved with great personal bravery. He shunned no danger; his presence and conduct animated the troops, for they greatly loved the General. He delivered his orders with precision and coolness, and in the heat, danger, and fury of the fight, maintained the true characteristics of the soldier—serenity, fortitude, and undaunted intrepidity." [1]

The soldiers had fought as well as they had ever done. The heaped American dead on the far side of Freeman's Farm bore witness to the fact. The ammunition had been replenished and fresh supplies had arrived. The most distasteful task was the burial of the dead, and the carrying back of the wounded to the base camp. Their sufferings were indescribable as they were jolted back and forth along the deeply rutted tracks. The arrangements for their reception were primitive. The only treatment was bleeding or amputation; medicines were scarce. The wounded lay on the ground on straw, unable to attend to their slightest need. Here the women played an invaluable part, fetching and carrying water and food, bathing the fevered bodies, and cleansing the wounds. Without their ministrations, many more of the wounded would have died.

Among these women were the wives of Riedesel, Acland, Henry Harnage, and Thomas Reynell. To the house in which they had taken refuge were brought Major Harnage, who had been shot through the bowels, was in excruciating pain, and later died; a lieutenant whose wife Baroness von Riedesel knew well; and a young officer named Young, whose uncle had befriended the baroness during her stay in England. She nursed the wounded Young until he died. "As he occupied an apartment close to mine and the walls were very thin," she wrote, "I could hear his last groans through the partition of my room." [2] So presumably could her three children, who shared the room with her.

It is probable that Burgoyne would have reopened the attack on September 21 had it not been for an event that was to have disastrous consequences. On that day, as he reported to Lord George Germain, "a messenger arrived from Sir Harry Clinton with a letter in cypher, informing me of his intention to attack Fort Montgomery in about ten days from the date of his letter, which was the 12 instant." [3] On the same night, a messenger was sent to Clinton with information about Burgoyne's situation, and requesting him to create such a situation as might compel Gates to divert some of his army to oppose him. Clinton was also to be informed that Burgoyne was prepared to wait in his present position until October 12. Two other messengers, both officers in disguise, were dispatched on the two following days with similar instructions.

Clinton was an old friend of Burgoyne's; he had refused the Canadian command, and to this extent Burgoyne was in his debt. Moreover, Clinton had profoundly disagreed with Howe's plan to go to Philadelphia. As Howe's second-in-command, he had argued against it for as long as he decently could, but unhappily his influence with Howe was negligible—"by some cursed fatality we could never draw together." [4] When Howe sailed south on July 23, he left Clinton in New York with about 7,000 men, many of them unfit for active campaigning. He later wrote to Clinton, regretting his inability to return a brigade he had originally promised, but adding: "If you can in the meantime make any diversion in favour of General Burgoyne's approaching Albany, I need not point out the utility of that measure." [5] The arrival in New York, toward the end of September, of 3,000 recruits, provided Clinton with sufficient troops to do something for Burgoyne. Hence his message of September 12:

You know my good will and are not ignorant of my poverty. If you think 2,000 men can assist you effectually, I will make a push at Montgomery in about ten days. But ever jealous of my flanks if they make a move in force on either of them I must return to save this important post. I expect reinforcements every day. Let me know what you wish.[6]

Burgoyne had sent three messengers to Clinton. Two of them, Captains Scott and Campbell, got through, and Clinton knew of Burgoyne's predicament. He recorded Campbell's statement, including the fact that Burgoyne's provisions

would not last him longer than till the 20th of October, his communication with Canada being entirely cut off; that altogether he had no doubt of being able to force his way to Albany, yet, being uncertain he could subsist after he got there, he wished before he attempted it to know whether I could open a communication with that town, at what time I expected to be there, and whether I could procure supplies from New York for him afterwards, requesting I would send him as soon as possible by triplicate my most explicit orders, either to attack the enemy or to retreat across the lakes while they were still clear of ice. . . .[7]

Burgoyne's message seriously alarmed Clinton. He said it filled his mind "with the most anxious reflections"; the knife may have been turned in the wound by Burgoyne's reported comment that he would never have severed his communications with Canada had he not expected assistance in the taking of Albany. Clinton was not to blame for a situation he had foreseen and warned against, but Burgoyne was clearly in serious straits and it behooved Clinton to do something about it. He positively declined the responsibility for telling Burgoyne what he should do, however; Burgoyne was an independent commander and must make up his own mind.

As far as Burgoyne was concerned, his mind was already made up. He had missed the opportunity to seize the initiative after the battle of Freeman's Farm. He would fortify his present position, husband his rations, and wait until Clinton came within striking distance. He had little alternative, for on September 18 an American force under Colonel John Brown had surprised and taken the British flotilla at Fort George. Brown failed to take Ticonderoga, and was repulsed by two companies of the 47th Regiment at Diamond Island; nevertheless, Burgoyne's communications with Canada were effectively cut. Stark rammed the cork even harder into the bottle when, a few days later, he seized Fort Edward. General Lincoln deserves the credit for these operations against Burgoyne's communications, and he and his men were a welcome reinforcement when they joined Gates in late September.

The position selected by Burgoyne to wait in until Clinton came within reach ran for about a mile and a quarter from the high ground immediately west of the Hudson inland to the rising ground occupied by Fraser during the battle of Freeman's Farm. A series of redoubts was erected along this line, protected by earthworks and log palisades, with abatis making approach difficult. The strongest position was the one nearest the river, which was known as the Great Redoubt. The extreme right of the line was held by the light infantry, whose redoubt was called Balcarres after its commander; echeloned back from this was Breymann's Redoubt, facing southwest. Between these strong points were field defenses, taking advantage of such natural obstacles as the numerous ravines. Riedesel's brigade was on the left, with Hamilton's to its right. Burgoyne established his headquarters behind Hamilton's position. A hospital, artillery park, and supply depot were established on the flat ground by the river, protected by the Great Redoubt, and a little less than two miles from the American position on Bemis Heights.

British soldiers have never displayed much enthusiasm for pick-and-shovel work, but Burgoyne's officers saw to it that they set about their work to some effect. The position was made into a strong one; certainly no less strong than the American. But it suffered from being too dispersed; there were too many covered approaches up which the enemy could creep unobserved. The terrain was so broken and wooded that it was difficult to provide warning of an enemy approach, and it was now that the defection of his Indians really affected Burgoyne. The few who had remained after crossing the Hudson mostly deserted after Freeman's Farm, some to offer their services to Gates. Burgoyne's Canadian and American volunteers did their best as scouts, but they were overworked. Once again the absence of reliable information about the enemy was to confuse, confound, and ultimately destroy Burgoyne and his Anglo-German army.

As his soldiers dug, important events were taking place elsewhere. On September 25 Howe rode into Philadelphia, to the plaudits, it is said, of the most beautiful women in America. It had taken him a long time to get there, and Washington's army was still "in being." About the same date, Clinton's reinforcements began disembarking at New York, and that general moved into the field to begin his operations up the Hudson. Clinton was not a strong character and was inclined to worry unduly, but on this occasion he acted with vigor. Moving rapidly, he descended on Veerplanks Point on October 5. His 3,000 men drove out the garrison, capturing the guns, whereupon Major General Israel Putnam, who was defending the highlands for Congress, moved his troops to defend the passes up to the eastern highlands. This fell in with Clinton's plans: he passed his troops across the Hudson, sent 2,000 of them up the difficult track to the higher ground, and then launched simultaneous attacks on Forts Clinton and Montgomery. Both forts were taken. The American flotilla, unable to escape on account of contrary winds, was burned to prevent its capture.

This was a signal success. Small wonder that Clinton should write exultantly to Burgoyne on October 8: *"Nous y voici,* and nothing between us and Gates. I sincerely hope this little success of ours will facilitate your operations. In answer to

your letter of 28th of September by C.C. [Campbell] I shall
only say I cannot presume to order, or even advise, for reasons obvious. I heartily wish you success." [8] Sergeant Daniel
Taylor was chosen to carry this message to Burgoyne. At
Esopus, on October 10, he fell in with a party of Americans
wearing British uniforms. Thinking he was among friends, and
being told that their general's name was Clinton, he asked
to be taken to him, only to discover that it was the American
General Clinton. He is then supposed to have swallowed the
message, concealed in a silver bullet, but vomited it up after
an emetic; soon afterward he was hanged. Burgoyne never
received the message.

Clinton's relatively easy success encouraged him to press
on up the Hudson, although he had previously sent a message
to Burgoyne by the returning Campbell warning him that he
should not suppose Clinton "had any idea of penetrating
to Albany with the small force he mentioned in his last letter."
Nevertheless, there was no harm in trying, and he sent
General John Vaughan on ahead with 2,000 men, escorted
by naval galleys, and carrying provisions for Burgoyne.
Vaughan's orders were that he was to assist Burgoyne's operations, and even to join him, but he was not to become inex-
tricably committed.

This force managed to reach Livingston Manor, only forty-
four miles from Albany, and eighty miles from Burgoyne, but
the pilots navigating the ships refused to proceed any farther.
The Americans were massing more and more troops to oppose
Vaughan. When Clinton received this information, he wrote,
on October 22, ordering Vaughan's withdrawal. He gave as
his reasons the fact that Vaughan's situation was becoming
desperate and that he had received explicit orders from Howe
directing him to send reinforcements to the commander-in-
chief. Howe had given Clinton a certain amount of discretion
as to when this should be done—"except I should be on the
eve of accomplishing some very material and essential stroke,
being left at liberty in that case to proceed upon it provided

I judged it might be executed in a few days after the receipt of his letters." [9] Clinton appears to have decided that Howe's demand for reinforcements took precedence over any possibility of joining up with Burgoyne. Accordingly, on October 26, Clinton withdrew his troops to New York.

Had he pressed on, he would probably have been too late to save Burgoyne, but it is remarkable that he should not have judged an operation of such magnitude as being a "very material and essential stroke."

Burgoyne was growing increasingly worried. He put on a brave front before his troops, entertaining gaily and incurring Baroness von Riedesel's disapproval of his style of life, but nothing could conceal the fact that nights were drawing in, days were growing colder, and supplies were getting shorter. It was his quarter-master-general who worried Burgoyne—far more than anything Gates did. On October 3 the army was put on half rations—only one pound of flour and a little salt pork each day. As was inevitable, the soldiers took to raiding the supply dumps, or foraging out beyond the lines, where they were soon picked off by the enemy. Dysentery, usually referred to as camp sickness, began to take its toll; as did the results of constant lying out in the cold, damp nights.

Rumors, ever the morale-destroyer of a beleaguered army, grew apace. There was no accurate information about the enemy, who, according to Pausch, were "said to be encamped behind thick woods in an abattis and a fortified camp. It is also said that every day and every hour their numbers are augmented by the arrival of militia from the adjoining provinces." [10] They were said to total more than 12,000, and the activities of their patrols kept the weary troops standing to their arms throughout most of the nights. Burgoyne ordered, "All out Guards and posts not intended to be concealed, are to light fires one hundred yards in their front," [11] in an attempt to detect friend from foe. Anburey recorded that "not a night passes but there is firing, and continual attacks upon the advanced picquets especially those of the Germans. It seems to be the plan of the enemy to harass us by constant attacks. . . ." [12]

Anburey was correct. Gates, whose strength was increasing almost daily, could afford to wait. He had his troubles, it is true, including a furious row with Arnold. The two men behaved like spoiled children, and at one stage Arnold requested permission to leave the army. Gates did not try to prevent this, but Arnold elected to remain, ostensibly because the other general officers had pleaded with him to do so.

Writing to Clinton on October 4, Gates provided an accurate enough description of Burgoyne's dilemma. "Despair may dictate him to risk all upon one throw," he wrote; "he is an old gamester, and in time has seen all the chances." On October 5, Gates went further, in a letter to Washington: "in a fortnight at furthest he must decide whether he will rashly risque at an infinite disadvantage to force my camp or retreat to his den." [13] Gates knew his man; he also knew that time was not on Burgoyne's side.

Burgoyne knew it, too. On October 4 and 5, he held councils of war to discuss and decide future action. Riedesel was in no doubt regarding the army's critical situation; he advocated recrossing the Hudson, occupying the old position behind Batten Kill, restoring the lines of communication with Canada, and waiting there for Clinton's arrival. If Clinton did not come, the army should retreat to Canada. Fraser agreed with Riedesel. Phillips would not give an opinion. All three disagreed with Burgoyne's proposal to launch an attack on Gates's western flank, employing all but 800 of the available troops for this operation. Riedesel did not consider 800 troops sufficient to guard the base camp; he also doubted whether the operation could be concluded in one day, as Burgoyne believed. Burgoyne rejected any idea of retreat for the reasons he gives in his dispatch to Germain dated October 20. Although this was written after he became a prisoner, and to that extent may be regarded as influenced by hindsight, it was sufficiently soon after the surrender for the reasoning to be still clear in his mind. He told Germain that the difficulties of a retreat to Canada were obvious; less obvious, perhaps, was the fact that a British retreat would leave Gates free to operate against Howe.

This consideration operated forcibly to determine me to abide events as long as possible, and I reasoned thus. The expedition I commanded was evidently meant at first to be *hazarded*. Circumstances might require it should be *devoted*. A critical junction of Mr Gates's force with Mr Washington might possibly decide the fate of the war; the failure of my junction with Sir Harry Clinton, or the loss of my retreat to Canada could only be a partial misfortune.[14]

If this really represents Burgoyne's line of thought, it explains a good deal. In effect, what he was telling Germain was that the operation was a chancy affair from the outset. It had all along been a hazardous operation, but intentionally so; indeed, there might well have arisen a set of circumstances in which the expedition should be sacrificed for the sake of British strategy as a whole. Reaching Albany, and joining forces with Clinton, was not the all-important consideration; what mattered was preventing Gates from joining forces with Washington. If this could be achieved, even at the expense of the destruction of Burgoyne's army, the campaign would still have been justified. It is possible that Burgoyne convinced himself of the truth of this by early October, but it is certainly a far cry from the aim he had proposed eight months earlier. He did not know, of course, when he rejected Riedesel's advice to retreat, that Howe was safely in Philadelphia, but he may have reasoned that his troops were playing their part simply by holding Gates at bay.

Whatever his reasoning, it was clear to Burgoyne that of the two courses open—attack or retreat—there could be no attack without first determining the extent and strength of Gates's position. He therefore decided to carry out a recon-

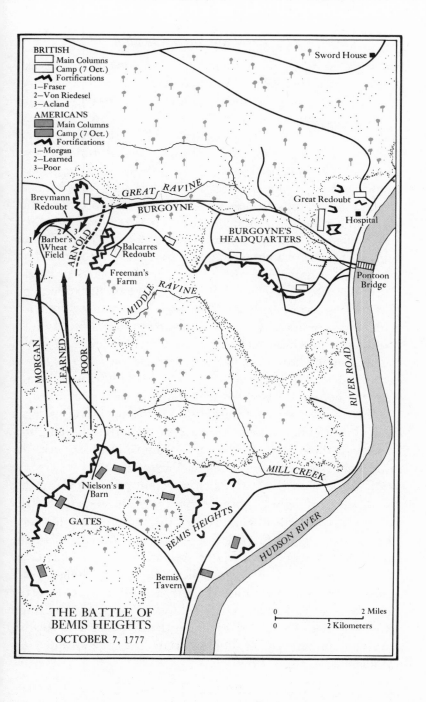

BRITISH
- ☐ Main Columns
- ☐ Camp (7 Oct.)
- ⌇ Fortifications
- 1—Fraser
- 2—Von Riedesel
- 3—Acland

AMERICANS
- ▦ Main Columns
- ▦ Camp (7 Oct.)
- ⌇ Fortifications
- 1—Morgan
- 2—Learned
- 3—Poor

Sword House ■

GREAT RAVINE

Breymann
Redoubt

BURGOYNE

Great Redoubt

Hospital ■

2 3

1

Barber's
Wheat
Field

ARNOLD

Balcarres
Redoubt

BURGOYNE'S
HEADQUARTERS

Freeman's
Farm

MIDDLE RAVINE

Pontoon
Bridge

MORGAN

LEARNED

POOR

RIVER ROAD

1   2 3

Nielson's
Barn ■

MILL CREEK

GATES

BEMIS HEIGHTS

HUDSON RIVER

Bemis
Tavern ■

THE BATTLE OF
BEMIS HEIGHTS
OCTOBER 7, 1777

0   2 Miles

0   2 Kilometers

naissance in force on October 7. In this instance, at least, Baroness von Riedesel could not complain of lack of security. She was living in what she described as "a pretty well built house," since known as Smith House, situated three and a half miles south of Fish Creek. Captain Williams had set about building her a log cabin, which she described as a blockhouse, nearer to General Riedesel's camp, in order that the general could spend the nights there without the long ride back to Smith House. The baroness was to have moved into this cabin on October 8, but, "suddenly . . . on the 7th of October, my husband, with the whole general staff, decamped." She adds: "Our misfortunes may be said to date from this moment. I had just sat down with my husband at his quarters to breakfast. General Fraser, and, I believe, Generals Burgoyne and Phillips, also, were to have dined with me on that same day. I observed considerable movement among the troops. My husband thereupon informed me, that there was to be a reconnoissance, which, however, did not surprise me, as this often happened." [15] On her way back to Smith House after breakfast, the baroness passed "many savages in their war dress." [16]

The troops chosen by Burgoyne for this operation were all picked men. They amounted to 1,500, supported by ten guns. Although there were no separate columns, the force was divided into two wings and a center, Burgoyne with his personal staff riding with the latter. Fraser commanded on the right, with Balcarres' light companies, the 24th, and some Canadians and loyalists. Riedesel commanded the center, with 300 men drawn from all the German regiments, and Breymann's light infantry and grenadiers. Major Acland was in command on the left with the British grenadier companies. Phillips exercised a general control over the left, as well as over the artillery, which was distributed as follows: Fraser, two mortars; Riedesel, two Hessian sixes under Pausch and two British twelves; directly under Phillips, four sixes commanded by Williams.

At 11:00 A.M. on October 7, this force left its entrenchments and began probing toward the American position, directing its advance toward the southwest, with the object of determining where precisely the American defenses lay. Burgoyne would then have the necessary information to plan a full-scale attack for the following day. It has been suggested that his object was to occupy a hill overlooking Gates's western flank, but this would seem to be most unlikely. Burgoyne's view of Gates's position was obscured by the forest; all he knew about it was from scouts, chiefly Indians, Canadians, and loyalists, and therefore not to be relied upon. He had to see the ground for himself before he could plan an attack, and this was why he decided upon a reconnaissance in force. He was being neither foolish nor foolhardy; he was merely taking sensible precautions.

The trouble with a reconnaissance in force is that it may result in overreaction by the enemy. Had Burgoyne carried out his reconnaissance with a couple of hundred men for protection, screened by the Indians and Canadian woodsmen, he would have discovered all he required to know without calling down a hornets' nest around his ears. As it was, the bugles and the drums, the heaving of the horses in their traces as they strove to move the guns, the shouts and the noise inseparable from a large body of men moving through the forest, alerted Gates. His own patrols were quick to report that the British were on the move. If they reported that it was the entire army, instead of only a part of it, why should they be blamed? Men do not stop to count every man they can see when they are in danger of being overwhelmed. The information reaching Gates was that Burgoyne was advancing, and not unnaturally he assumed that his position was about to be attacked.

The battle that followed is known by various names; that of Bemis Heights is the most popular, although the bulk of the fighting took place some distance from Gates's strong point. It took place on a bright autumn day, with consequences that no man present would have believed possible.

The British moved cautiously, preceded by a thin screen of scouts. As soon as their move was reported to Gates, he sent Wilkinson to observe the advance. By the time Wilkinson was in a position to observe the enemy, they had reached a field belonging to a farmer named Barber. This field, in which the wheat was still standing, was about 2,000 yards west of Freeman's Farm, where the Balcarres Redoubt had been constructed, and about the same distance from the western end of the American defenses. The ground to the right and left of the field was thickly wooded; the field itself sloped gently down from its northern edge to the center, and then climbed more steeply to the southern edge.

Wilkinson watched for a good fifteen minutes. The British were resting in the field, drawn up in double ranks, with many soldiers sitting on the ground holding their muskets between their legs. Some appeared to be cutting the wheat. Several officers had climbed to the roof of a nearby cabin, endeavoring to pinpoint the American defenses through their spyglasses. Wilkinson noticed that beyond the British right was a "lofty height," densely covered in forest, from which the British line could be enfiladed. On his return, he reported that the enemy seemed to be foraging, as well as reconnoitering the American position. "I think, Sir, they offer you battle," he told his general. He described the ground, and the fact that the British flanks rested on woods, through which they could be approached unseen. His advice was that Gates should attack. According to Wilkinson, Gates replied, "Well, then, order on Morgan to begin the game."

The plan was simple. Morgan with his riflemen would make a wide circuit to the west to gain the wooded hill on Burgoyne's right. He would then be in a position to outflank the entire British line. Simultaneously, General Poor was to attack the British left, while General Learned was to be held in re-

serve to attack the center as soon as the two flanking operations were under way. Morgan has been given the credit for
proposing this plan, although the final responsibility must be
Gates's. Something like 5,000 troops—Continentals and militia
—were originally committed to the battle; by the end of the
day the figure was nearer 9,000. The odds were never less
than four to one in favor of the Americans.

The British had ended their halt in Barber's field and were
just beginning to advance when Poor fell upon them. He had
approached unobserved, partly because of the forest, and
partly because the British were halted in low ground and had
taken no precautions to cover the dead ground to the south
of the field. At 2:30 P.M. the blow fell, Acland's grenadiers
taking the first shock. They were surprised and badly shaken.
They gave ground, and almost simultaneously Morgan and
Dearborn attacked Balcarres on the right. The 24th was forced
to change front to protect its rear, and the entire British line
reeled under the unexpected onslaught. As the 24th fell back
from the edge of the field, Burgoyne sent his aide-de-camp,
Sir Francis Clarke, with an order to bring away the guns.
Clarke fell, seriously wounded, and the message did not get
through.

Poor's furious assault on the British left had serious con-
sequences. Major Acland was badly wounded, and Major
Williams' beloved guns were taken by the enemy. There was,
therefore, no leadership or artillery support at a crucial moment in the battle. The grenadiers, still firing, fell back
unsteadily, exposing the center, which was still standing firm.
A fresh American attack under Learned was launched against
Riedesel and his Germans. About 300 Germans faced 3,000
Americans and acquitted themselves with great gallantry.
Riedesel maintained that his troops would have stood their
ground had it not been for Balcarres, who fell back on Riedesel's right, but Pausch makes it clear that the German "left
wing retreated in the greatest possible disorder, thereby causing a similar rout among our German command, which was

stationed behind the fence in line of battle." [17] Pausch managed to withdraw his guns, and repositioned them in support of the right of the German line, firing three wagonloads of ammunition before the guns became too hot to load. Not that this mattered; things had gone too far for any artilleryman, however devoted, to influence the battle. Pausch ordered his gunners to save themselves, and personally brought out of battle one of the remaining ammunition wagons; but he was obliged to abandon his guns. He joined "all the different nationalities of our division running pell-mell," and made his way back through the melee to the Great Redoubt.

The British right, although severely mauled, remained firm. Fraser, conspicuous on his gray charger as he rode among his men, calming them by his apparent indifference to fire, endeavored to cover the British withdrawal. Nearly a third of the British force had been lost, and six of their guns had been taken. It was clear to Burgoyne, as it was to his generals, that retreat was the only answer. Burgoyne himself had been prominent throughout the battle; there had been musket balls through his hat and waistcoat. One of his horses had been killed under him, but he still managed to maintain some semblance of control. Even at that critical stage of the battle, something might have been saved from the wreck. This was thwarted by the marksmanship of one of Morgan's riflemen, Timothy Murphy, who mortally wounded General Fraser.

Legend has it that Morgan drew Murphy's attention to Fraser, with the words "There is a gallant officer, but he must die. Take a post in that clump of bushes, and do your duty." The legend has been further embellished by the story that no less a man than Benedict Arnold drew Morgan's attention to Fraser, and proposed his elimination, on the grounds that Fraser was "himself a host." It is a good story but an unlikely one. In the heat of battle, soldiers do not normally concern themselves with the character of those they shoot. A man on a gray horse is a better aiming mark than a man on foot.

It was a grievous shock for Burgoyne. Fraser was his friend

and confidant. As a soldier he stood out from all the officers who had accompanied Burgoyne from Canada. His troops would follow him anywhere; Balcarres, who replaced him in command of the right wing, was a capable and popular officer, but he was not a Simon Fraser. Burgoyne, distressed by the mortal wounding of his friend, and concerned by the increasing number of enemy appearing out of the woods, sent word to Phillips and Riedesel to cover the withdrawal of the rest of the reconnaissance force from the battlefield. It was now 3:00 P.M., and the weary British and Germans had been locked with the Americans in close-quarter fighting for more than thirty minutes. Morale was shaky, but Burgoyne might have succeeded in extricating his troops without further loss had it not been for Benedict Arnold.

That tempestuous character, whose pride was as prickly as his conceit was high, had virtually severed relations with Gates, as Gates had with him. General Mattoon reported to Schuyler after the battle of October 7 that Gates had rejected Arnold's advice to send a strong force to attack Burgoyne, and had even told him that he had nothing for Arnold to do. Another story, told by Colonel John Brooks, is that Arnold was dining with Gates when the news of Burgoyne's approach was reported. He asked if he could ride out to see the situation for himself, but was refused by Gates, with the words "I am afraid to trust you, Arnold." When Arnold promised to behave himself, Gates let him go.

The best story of all is the one that tells of Arnold riding around the American lines in a state of ever-increasing agitation, fretting because Gates would not let him go. At last he could stand it no longer, dug his spurs into his horse, and, hatless and still in undress uniform, galloped to the sound of the guns, waving his sword and shouting hysterically, "Victory or Death!" Whichever of these stories is the correct one, Arnold's arrival on the battlefield had the effect of a thunderbolt. He rallied the scattered units of Poor's and Learned's brigades, sent Morgan off on a wide outflanking movement to the west, and prepared to attack the Balcarres Redoubt, into which many of the British had retreated. Arnold was behaving like a madman, shouting and cursing, galloping from unit to unit to galvanize them into action; at one stage he struck a captain of Dearborn's company on the head with his sword.

Balcarres Redoubt had been well sited, with a clear field of fire, and was far too tough a nut for the Americans to crack. Despite their gallantry, and overwhelming numbers, they were thrown back. The battle might have finished then but for Arnold. Galloping through the fire of both British and Americans, he collected more troops from Learned's brigade, leading them around the rear of the Balcarres Redoubt, and mopping up some Canadians and loyalists who were holding two isolated log cabins. This movement brought Arnold behind Breymann's Redoubt, which was sited on some rising ground a few hundred yards north of the Balcarres Redoubt, and protected on its northern flank by the Great Ravine. Breymann was already hotly engaged to his front by Morgan, and the attack from the rear was entirely unexpected. The Germans fought bravely, but the odds were too great. Breymann was killed. A *sauve qui peut* followed. The redoubt was carried just before sunset, and the battle was over.

Burgoyne had lost 176 men killed; 250 were wounded; and 200 were taken prisoner—out of his 2,000-odd engaged. What was much worse, he had lost Fraser, as well as ten guns. The American losses were lighter—about 50 killed and 150 wounded, but Benedict Arnold was among the latter. His horse was killed, pinning Arnold to the ground and breaking his leg. Luckily for him, the redoubt was captured just as a German soldier was about to shoot him. He was carried on a litter from the battle he had done so much to win, although Wilkinson criticized his conduct as "crazy," saying he had "neither rendered service, nor deserved credit on that day." This must be regarded as the evidence of a prejudiced witness, because Burgoyne never doubted Arnold's influence on the battle.

Without his intervention, the British might have met with a serious setback, but as it was they met with disaster.

Many of the British blamed their German allies for the unfortunate turn of events. Burgoyne did not do this, merely observing, "unhappily the intrenchments of the German reserve, commanded by Lieutenant-Colonel Breymann, who was killed, were carried, and although ordered to be recovered, they never were so, and the enemy by that misfortune gained an opening to our right and rear." [18] Sergeant Lamb was less magnanimous. "The Germans retreated," he wrote, "firing until they had gained their tents in the rear of the entrenchments, but, supposing that the assault was general, they gave one discharge, after which some retreated to the British camp, but others surrendered prisoners." [19] It is difficult to see what else Riedesel could have done in the center, once the British had fallen back and exposed his flanks.

Whoever was responsible for the British defeat, it certainly was not General Gates. He spent the greater part of the action in his tent on Bemis Heights, arguing for much of the time with Sir Francis Clarke, who, after being wounded, was taken prisoner. Gates was kind enough to allow the injured Englishman, who later died, to rest on his bed, but they soon became involved in arguing the rights and wrongs of the war. Strong words passed between them, until Gates lost his temper and stormed out of the tent, commenting angrily to Wilkinson, "Had he ever heard such an impudent son of a bitch!" [20]

Chapter 20

Convention— Not Capitulation

THERE WAS GLOOM that night in the British camp. Anburey reports that Burgoyne came up to him and inquired if he was the officer in command of the quarter-guard, and told him, "You must defend this post to the very last man." [1] It was impossible to describe the anxiety depicted on his general's face. All that night the British withdrew into the defenses of the Great Redoubt, abandoning the battlefield to the enemy. Riedesel found time to slip away to dine with his wife, who wrote:

Finally, towards evening, I saw my husband coming, upon which I forgot all my sufferings and thanked God he had been spared to me. He ate in great haste with me and his adjutant, behind the house. We had been told that we had gained an advantage over the enemy, but the sorrowful and down-cast faces which I beheld, bore witness to the contrary, and before my husband again went away, he drew me to one side and told me that every thing might go very badly, and that I must keep myself in constant readiness for departure, but by no means to give any one the least inkling of what I was doing. I therefore pretended that I wished to move into my new house the next morning, and had every thing packed up.[2]

The wounded General Fraser had been taken to her house that afternoon, where, instead of giving him dinner, as had been the original plan, she had to listen to his death agonies. According to her memoirs, Fraser kept exclaiming, "Oh, fatal ambition! Poor General Burgoyne! My poor wife!" [3] but she is entitled to some poetic license. She had enough to endure, for she had also to console Lady Acland, whose husband had been wounded and captured. When Fraser died at eight o'clock the following morning, his corpse was prepared for burial and laid out, wrapped in a sheet, on a bed that had been brought into the baroness's living room. There she sat throughout the day, with her three small children, keeping the dead Fraser company. It is impossible to withhold admiration from this gallant woman who knew as well as any soldier how to do her duty.

Burgoyne was fortunate to be opposed by a general with an exaggerated respect for the British soldier. Had Arnold been in command, rather than lying impotently in his tent nursing a broken leg, an all-out attack might have been made, and could have finished the British on October 8. Gates chose instead to devote the day to revictualing his troops, while Burgoyne pondered his next move. It might just be possible to retreat to Ticonderoga, but he knew of Lincoln's foray on Lake George, and of Stark's capture of Fort Edward. The dice would be loaded against the British if it came to retreat.

First, Burgoyne must pay his last respects to his old friend Simon Fraser, who had asked to be buried on the Great Redoubt at six o'clock in the evening. He had requested that he be attended to his grave only by his personal staff, but Burgoyne, Riedesel, and Phillips were also present. This congregation of a considerable number of people on the Great Redoubt was reported by American scouts, the inference being that the British were preparing for an attack. The American artillery opened a heavy fire, which may have discomposed some of the mourners but not the Reverend Edward Brudenell, who read the burial service without a tremor, "though frequently covered with dust which the shots threw up on all sides of him." [4] Many "overs" from this cannonade landed

perilously close to the house from which Baroness von Riedesel was watching the ceremony.

The problem facing Burgoyne after the battle of Bemis
Heights is simple to state, but it was difficult to resolve. The
fighting on October 7, during which his 1,500 troops had
resisted attack from four or five times their number for over
five hours, had made it clear that Gates was too strong for
a British attack to have any chance of success. Moreover, the
loss of the Balcarres and Breymann redoubts meant that the
British position had been turned on the right, or western,
flank. Sooner or later Gates must outflank Burgoyne's position. The British could no longer remain where they were,
but what should be their next move? The occupation of yet
another position farther back, or a withdrawal to Ticonderoga?
The case for occupying yet another position was strengthened
by Burgoyne's belief that Clinton was on his way to the
rescue. But where was Clinton? And when would he arrive?
Supplies were running short, and for this reason alone a prolonged defense was out of the question. There was also the
onset of winter to be taken into account.

A retreat to Ticonderoga was equally difficult. The route
up the east bank of the Hudson via Fort Edward was under
threat from the enemy; the west-bank route was along a
muddy track fringed by swamps, and subject to the constant
interruptions of destroyed bridges. There were the women to
be considered; how would they fare in a retreat? And what
about the guns? They must not be allowed to fall into enemy
hands, perhaps later to be turned against Clinton or Howe.
Burgoyne stated the problem in his dispatch of October 20
to Germain.

The army continued offering battle to the enemy in their new
position (based on the Great Redoubt) the whole day of the
8th. Intelligence was now received that the enemy was marching
to turn the right, and no means could prevent that measure but
retiring to Saratoga. The army began to move at nine o'clock

at night, Major-General Riedesel commanding the van-guard, and Major-General Phillips the rear.[5]

Retreat meant abandoning the wounded and breaking up the bridge o' boats across the river; the pontoons were needed to ferry supplies to Saratoga. Heavy rain complicated the arrangements, turning the road into a quagmire and swelling the numerous streams, but it delayed an enemy attack. The withdrawal began after dark in order to confuse the enemy, and Baroness von Riedesel recorded that "the strictest silence had been enjoined; fires had been kindled in every direction; and many tents left standing, to make the enemy believe that the camp was still there. We travelled continually the whole night. Little Frederika was afraid, and would often begin to cry. I was, therefore, obliged to hold a pocket handkerchief over her mouth, lest our whereabouts should be discovered." [6]

Her husband's orders to the vanguard were to march to Saratoga, cross the river by a ford above that village (now known as Schuylerville), and occupy a position north of Batten Kill. It is clear from this that on October 8 Burgoyne was seriously contemplating a retreat to Ticonderoga. It was the weather, as much as anything, that caused this plan to be abandoned. It rained in torrents throughout the night. The road, already badly damaged by the passage of guns and wagons during Burgoyne's advance, was almost impassable. The bridges so painfully rebuilt by Riedesel during his advance had been destroyed by raiding parties and had to be rebuilt again. It was 4:00 A.M. on the morning of the ninth before the British rear guard was finally on the move, and by then the route had been churned into a sea of mud by the passage of the main body. "Our retreat," wrote Anburey, "was made within musket-shot of the enemy, and, though greatly encumbered with baggage, without a single loss." [7]

Between 5:00 and 6:00 A.M. Burgoyne ordered a halt to rest his troops and to check his guns. He also needed time for the bateaux being poled up the Hudson to catch up with the column. Riedesel later criticized him for making this halt, claiming that the advantage the army had gained by breaking contact with the enemy so successfully "was completely lost by this hesitation." Riedesel claims that the halt, lasting until 4:00 P.M., enabled an enemy force to advance up the opposite bank, thereby effectually preventing any British attempt to cross the Hudson; but Burgoyne would not have halted without good reason. He was in fact pressed by Lieutenant-Colonel Nicholas Sutherland, commanding the 47th Regiment and holding the high ground around Dovogat, where the main body had halted, to throw a force across the river to form a bridgehead, but Burgoyne considered that his troops were too tired for such an operation.

The rain continued throughout the day, hampering the retreat but delaying any pursuit. Toward evening Burgoyne yielded to the pleas of Lady Acland that she be allowed to join her wounded and captive husband. The Reverend Brudenell offered his services as escort; Lady Acland's maid and her husband's servant, who also was wounded, went, too. They traveled downriver by skiff, bearing a letter from Burgoyne to Gates:

Lady Harriet Acland, a lady of the first distinction of family, rank and personal virtues, is under such concern on account of Major Acland her husband, wounded and a prisoner in your hands, that I cannot refuse her request to commit her to your protection. Whatever general impropriety there may be in persons in my situation and yours to solicit favours, I can not see the uncommon perseverance in every female grace and exaltation of character of this lady, and her very hard fortune, without testifying that your attention to her will lay me under an obligation.[8]

The journey, which took place at night, lasted eight hours, because the American sentries quite properly refused to allow the party to land until it was light and they could be identified. When finally Lady Acland was taken to Gates, he received her with great courtesy and, after allowing her to rest, sent her on to Albany, where she rejoined her wounded husband.

She was pregnant at the time, and her courage impressed Americans and British alike. Her husband recovered from his wound, but died some years later. The story that she then married her clerical escort is, alas, untrue.

The rain-sodden troops reached Saratoga on the evening of October 9, having taken twenty-four hours to cover only seven miles. They arrived in time to flush out some enemy militia who were establishing themselves in the grounds of General Schuyler's house, beside Fish Kill, a tributary of the Hudson. Schuyler owned a "plantation" at Saratoga, and a small hamlet had grown up around his house, which was appropriated that night by Burgoyne as his headquarters. He described it as "a very good dwelling house, exceeding large store-houses, great saw mills, and other out-buildings, to the value altogether of perhaps ten thousand pounds." [9]

Burgoyne's conduct that night has come in for much criticism, although it is only fair to add that both the witnesses against him were severely prejudiced. Baroness von Riedesel records that she asked General Phillips on her arrival at Saratoga why the retreat was not being continued, and that Phillips replied, "Would that you were only our commanding general! He halts because he is tired, and intends to spend the night here and give us a supper." [10] A remark of this kind does not ring true of Phillips, an old friend of Burgoyne's and a close confidant, but the baroness embroiders the tale by adding, "In this latter achievement, especially, General Burgoyne was very fond of indulging. He spent half the nights in singing and drinking, and amusing himself with the wife of a commissary, who was his mistress, and who, as well as he, loved champagne." [11] The other witness is Captain M. von Eelking, who drew liberally on the baroness's memoirs for his *German Auxiliaries in America*, which was published in 1893.

While the army were suffering from cold and hunger [he wrote], and everyone was looking forward to the immediate future with apprehension, Schuyler's house was illuminated, and rang with singing, laughter, and the jingling of glasses. There Burgoyne was sitting, with some merry companions, at a dainty supper, while the champagne was flowing. Near him sat the beautiful wife of an English commissary, his mistress. Great as the calamity was, the frivolous general still kept up his orgies. Some were of opinion that he had made that inexcusable stand, merely for the sake of passing a merry night. Riedesel thought it incumbent on him to remind Burgoyne of the danger of the halt, but the latter returned all sorts of evasive answers.[12]

It is a good story, with possibly a grain of truth, which has been improved upon with time. Its weakness lies in the fact that no general could have behaved in such a fashion and still retained the affection and respect of the ordinary British soldier. There is ample evidence to show that Burgoyne was successful in retaining his soldiers' trust, even in adversity. Sergeant Lamb was loud in his general's praise, as were those British officers who kept diaries of the campaign. That Burgoyne enjoyed the good things in life, and kept as fine a table as circumstances permitted, is not to be disputed; nor is it surprising that he should have gathered his staff around him and taken dinner with them. If his "belle amie" was present at the occasion, it led to no adverse comments from Lamb and his companions. As for the failure to press on with the retreat, this can be easily explained. The troops were tired, wet through, and disorganized. It would have been unwise in such circumstances to continue the retreat throughout the night, in danger of ambush, and without the support of the artillery, on which Burgoyne placed great reliance. Guns would have been virtually useless in the dark. A general must be left to judge the moment when he can ask no more of his soldiers; in Burgoyne's case, he reckoned they could go no farther on the evening of October 9.

He spent the night in Schuyler's house, protected by Hamilton's brigade (9th, 20th, 21st, and 62nd regiments) and the artillery, which had been unable to ford the swollen stream. Riedesel's brigade and the rest of the army bivouacked north of Fish Kill. The baroness found an abandoned house, and, although soaked to the skin, bedded her family down on some straw. It had been a long and depressing day.

On the morning of the tenth Burgoyne took stock of the situation. It was still raining, and Gates had made no move. The artillery was brought across Fish Kill, followed by Hamilton's brigade. Hamilton set fire to Schuyler's house and outbuildings before fording the kill, because, according to Burgoyne, it obscured the British field of fire. Sutherland, with six companies of his 47th and what was left of Captain Fraser's sharpshooters and some Canadians under Major Mackoy, was sent to reconnoiter the track west of the Hudson. The pioneers went with him to repair broken bridges. The rest of the army was ordered to dig in.

Hamilton's brigade took up a position on high ground north of the Saratoga–Albany road, overlooking Fish Kill. This was the most likely way for the Americans to come, and Burgoyne intended to make them fight hard for the crossing of Fish Kill, still swollen by the heavy rain. About a mile to the north, in Saratoga itself, was Riedesel's brigade. Ferdinand Barner's Jäger company held an outpost position, between Riedesel and the edge of the forest, which approached to within 800 yards of Saratoga. In reserve, were the 20th and 62nd, the latter mustering barely a company; six companies of the 47th, reinforced by ten men from each British battalion, were disposed in a ravine by the banks of the Hudson, protecting the precious bateaux. Eight guns were sited to fire across the Hudson, where the Americans could be seen massing, and the remaining twenty-seven guns covered Fish Kill. It was a reasonably strong position, measuring about one and a half by one and a half miles, but its two weaknesses were the covered approaches through the forest on the western flank and the fact that it could be enfiladed by artillery fire from across the Hudson.

Gates did not make an appearance until the afternoon of October 10, by which time the rain had stopped. Burgoyne hastily recalled Sutherland, still marching up the west bank of the Hudson; he returned, leaving the pioneers hard at work on a bridge, guarded by some provincials, who took to their heels as soon as they were fired on. That ended any further idea of a withdrawal up the west bank, which was just as well, since Stark had thrown a force across the river at Fort Edward, where he occupied a hill dominating the western track. It has since become known as "Stark's Knob."

According to Elijah Fisher, Gates "gave the Enemy three Days to git off with themselves,"[13] for Gates took no risks. Even when he came up with Burgoyne, he delayed his attack until the following day, thinking he had merely caught up with the British rear guard. This miscalculation could have landed him in serious trouble when he continued his advance on the morning of October 11. Sending Morgan, followed by Learned, around wide to approach from the west, Gates led with Nixon's brigade, which moved down to Fish Kill at nine o'clock in the morning. Glover's brigade was to follow Nixon's, little opposition being anticipated from the supposed British rear guard. Saratoga was blanketed in mist, concealing British from Americans, and vice versa. At that critical moment Glover's leading troops picked up a British deserter, who reported that the whole of Burgoyne's army was drawn up on the other side of Fish Kill. At first the story was not believed, but a German deserter corroborated it. There was just time to halt the attack before the mist lifted and the British guns opened fire with grapeshot. It was the narrowest escape Gates had had since he took over command from Schuyler, and he was determined not to repeat it. Henceforward he would shell and starve Burgoyne out; he knew that time was on his side.

Once the American bombardment began it was heavy and continuous. Baroness von Riedesel had to take refuge with her children in the cellars of the house she was occupying. Many women and children had done the same, using the place as a lavatory because they were afraid to go outside. The baroness, with admirable composure, undertook to have the place cleaned out; she then allocated the three rooms among the women already there, some wounded officers, and herself and four other officers' wives, including the notorious wife of the commissary. There they remained throughout six days of bombardment, eleven cannon balls going through the house. General Phillips visited the baroness and was so overcome by her situation that he told General Riedesel, "No! not for ten thousand guineas would I come here again, for my heart is entirely, entirely broken!" The baroness tells us that not all those who shared her refuge deserved sympathy: "There were, also, poltroons in our little company." [14]

The British position was hopeless. Clinton, if indeed he was coming, could never arrive in time. If he did not come, Burgoyne's army had served some purpose by causing Washington to detach troops from his main army to reinforce Gates. All that remained was to find some way out of the mess that would be consistent with the honor of an officer and gentleman. Burgoyne called a council of war in the afternoon of October 12. Generals Phillips, Riedesel, and Hamilton attended. They were asked for their views on five possible courses of action. First, to stand at Saratoga, hoping to repel an enemy attack, and trusting that something might turn up. Second, to launch an attack. Third, to retreat, taking the guns with them, which would mean having to repair bridges en route. Fourth, to withdraw by night, abandoning guns and baggage. Fifth, to take advantage of Gates's extended left, slip past him, and march rapidly on Albany.

It was decided "that the fourth proposition is the only recourse, and that to effect it, the utmost secrecy and silence is to be observed. . . ." [15] No sooner decided, however, than it was abandoned. If it was to have the slightest chance of success, complete secrecy was essential, and Burgoyne's scouts reported that there were so many enemy parties watching his line of withdrawal that secrecy could not be assured. Soon afterward information was received that Stark had blocked both the western and eastern tracks up the Hudson.

The following day another council of war was called. It was attended by "all the general officers and Field Officers, and Captains commanding Corps, on the Heights of Saratoga, October 13." According to Burgoyne's account:

> The Lieutenant-General having explained the situation of affairs, as in the preceding council, with the additional intelligence, that the enemy was intrenched at the fords of Fort Edward, and likewise occupied the strong position on the Pine-plains between Fort George and Fort Edward, expressed his readiness to undertake at their head any enterprise of difficulty or hazard that should appear to them within the compass of their strength or spirit. He added, that he had reason to believe a capitulation had been in the contemplation of some, perhaps of all, who knew the real situation of things; that upon a circumstance of such consequence to national and personal honour, he thought it a duty to his country, and to himself, to extend his council beyond the usual limits; that the assembly present might justly be esteemed a full representation of the army; and that he should think himself unjustifiable in taking any step in so serious a matter, without such concurrence of sentiments as should make a treaty the act of the army, as well as that of the general.
>
> The first question therefore he desired them to decide was, whether an army of 3500 fighting men, and well provided with artillery, were justifiable, upon the principles of national dignity and military honour, in capitulating in any possible situation?
>
> Resolved, nem. con. in the affirmative.
>
> Question 2. Is the present situation of that nature?
>
> Resolved, nem. con. That the present situation justifies a capitulation upon honourable terms.
>
> The Lieutenant-General then drew up the message, marked No. 2, and laid it before the council. It was unanimously approved, and upon that foundation the treaty opened.[16]

Burgoyne took every precaution to consult with his senior officers before committing himself to ask Gates for terms. There seemed to be no alternative. Gates outnumbered them by at least five to one; supplies were virtually exhausted; casualties from wounds and sickness were increasing daily. The expedition from Canada had reached the end of the road, unsupported by Howe, and abandoned by Clinton. All that remained was surrender, but surrender on the best terms possible.

Lieutenant-Colonel Robert Kingston, Burgoyne's adjutant-general, carried a message to Gates on October 14:

After having fought you twice, Lieutenant-General Burgoyne has waited some days, in his present position, determined to try a third conflict against any force you could bring to attack him.

He is apprised of the superiority of your numbers, and the disposition of your troops to impede his supplies, and render his retreat a scene of carnage on both sides. In this situation he is impelled by humanity, and thinks himself justifiable by established principles and precedents of state, and of war, to spare the lives of brave men upon honourable terms. Should Major-General Gates be inclined to treat upon that idea, General Burgoyne would propose a cessation of arms during the time necessary to communicate the preliminary terms by which, in any extremity, he and his army mean to abide.[17]

There can seldom have been a more remarkable request for terms. It is hard to determine whether Burgoyne is requesting terms from Gates or requiring Gates to ask *him* for terms. But Gates knew the "old gamester" and was prepared to play him at his own game. He had already prepared the terms, and they were nothing less than "unconditional surrender." On the face of it these terms were eminently reasonable. Burgoyne's army posed little threat to Gates, but he was uncomfortably aware of Clinton's reported advance. It would not do to defeat Burgoyne only to be defeated later by Clinton. Gates's object was to persuade Burgoyne to capitulate, and then he could deal with Clinton. This can be the only sensible explanation for Gates's subsequent bargaining with Burgoyne. An armistice was agreed upon, to last until sunset on October

14, and Kingston rode back to the British lines, carrying with him the American terms:

I. General Burgoyne's army being exceedingly reduced by repeated defeats, by desertion, sickness, &c. their provisions exhausted, their military horses, tents, and baggage, taken or destroyed, their retreat cut off, and their camp invested, they can only be allowed to surrender prisoners of war.

II. The officers and soldiers may keep the baggage belonging to them. The generals of the United States never permit individuals to be pillaged.

III. The troops under his Excellency General Burgoyne, will be conducted by the most convenient route to New England, marching by easy marches, and sufficiently provided for by the way.

IV. The officers will be admitted on parole; may wear their side-arms, and will be treated with the liberality customary in Europe, so long as they, by proper behaviour, continue to deserve it; but those who are apprehended having broke their parole, as some British officers have done, must expect to be close confined.

V. All public stores, artillery, arms, ammunition, carriages, horses, &c. &c. must be delivered to commissaries appointed to receive them.

VI. The terms being agreed to and signed, the troops under his Excellency General Burgoyne's command may be drawn up in their encampments, where they will be ordered to ground their arms, and may thereupon be marched to the river side, to be passed over in their way towards Bennington.

VII. A cessation of arms to continue until sunset, to receive General Burgoyne's answer.[18]

These terms were unacceptable to Burgoyne and his council of war. Kingston therefore carried back to Gates the following comments:

As for Article I, Lieutenant-General Burgoyne's army, however reduced, will never admit their retreat is cut off, while they have arms in their hands. Article III, This article is answered by General Burgoyne's first proposal, which is here annexed. Article IV. There being no officer in this army under, or capable of being under the description of breaking parole, this article needs no answer. Article V, All public stores may be delivered, arms excepted. Article VI, This article inadmissible in any extremity. Sooner than this army will consent to ground their arms in their encampment they will rush on the enemy determined to take no quarter.[19]

Kingston was instructed to insist on the army being granted the full honors of war in the event of surrender. Gates consented to an extension of the armistice until ten o'clock the following morning, while he considered Burgoyne's rejection of the original terms. There was much coming and going between the American and British lines during the negotiations. Burgoyne was striving to obtain the best terms he could, and to some extent playing for time in the hope that Clinton would arrive to save him; while Gates was nervously looking over his shoulder and hoping to get the matter settled as quickly as possible. It was a game of bluff and counter-bluff, and it says much for Burgoyne's steadiness of nerve that he continued to remain in the game, for Gates held all the cards.

The American reply reached Burgoyne early on the fifteenth. Gates agreed to amend his original terms, but insisted that the British Army should "capitulate" by 3:00 P.M. that day, "grounding their arms" in their encampment before surrender. Burgoyne refused to accept this, again demanding that he should be granted full honors of war, and proposing that his troops should be permitted to return to England, provided that they took no further part in the war. Surprisingly, Gates agreed. The armistice was extended, and Lieutenant-Colonel Sutherland and Captain James Craig were dispatched to Gates's headquarters to negotiate the detailed conditions of surrender.

Sutherland and Craig returned in the evening to Burgoyne, bringing the Articles of Capitulation.* Gates had conceded far more than could ever have been anticipated. A significant second clause had been inserted: "A Free Passage to be granted

* The Articles of Capitulation are included as Appendix II.

to the Army under Lieutenant-General Burgoyne to Great Britain, upon condition of not serving again in North America, during the present Contest; and the Port of Boston is Assigned for the Entry of Transports to receive the Troops whenever General Howe shall so order." [20]

The subsequent repudiation of this clause by Congress resulted in much bitterness, but it is debatable whether any general in the field could be authorized to make such an astonishing concession on his own responsibility. Gates was in effect offering to permit Burgoyne's army to go free, although it is true that he was at the same time requiring that the soldiers should not serve again in the war. There was, however, nothing to prevent the British from employing them elsewhere than in North America in order to release other troops for the war zone. Gates played directly into Burgoyne's hands, since such a concession was inconsistent with an outright capitulation, and Burgoyne was to make much of it later in his defense of his actions at Saratoga.

Burgoyne knew that the Articles of Capitulation were more lenient than he had any right to expect, but he persisted in asking for further concessions. In particular, the word "Capitulation" was unacceptable. It was a word to be used between victor and vanquished, and Burgoyne would not admit that his army came into the latter category. A better word to use would be "Convention," implying an agreement between equals. Accordingly, at eleven o'clock on the night of October 15, Captain Craig wrote to Lieutenant-Colonel Wilkinson, with whom he had been in negotiation for much of the day on the exact drafting of the terms of surrender, saying:

Upon reporting the Proceedings of this evening to Lieut. General Burgoyne, I was happy to receive his approbation of and ready concurrence in every article that has been agreed on between us. It however appears upon a retrospect of the Treaty, that our zeal to compleat it expeditiously has led us into the admission of a Term in the Title, very different from his meaning and that of the principle Officers of his Army, who have been consulted on this important occasion. We have, Sir, unguardedly called that a Treaty of Capitulation, which the Army means only as a Treaty of Convention; with the single alteration of this word Lieut. Col. Sutherland and myself will meet you at the stipulated time tomorrow morning, with the fair Copy signed by General Burgoyne. I hope, Sir, you will excuse my troubling you so late; but I thought it better than by any delay to prevent the speedy conclusion of a Treaty, which seems to be the wish of both parties, and which may prevent the effusion of blood between us.[21]

Burgoyne's effrontery seems to have escaped Gates. A brief note from Gates's adjutant-general closed the matter: "Col. Wilkinson's compliments to Capt. Craig; Major General Gates will admit the alteration."

Gates retired to bed a contented man; Burgoyne was still torn by doubts. Was Clinton as close as reported? There had been news that British troops had reached Esopus, on the Hudson, which was only sixty miles from Albany. If help was near, was it consistent with British honor—and with Burgoyne's own honor—to surrender? The council of war was summoned yet again to debate the old arguments. It was probably to this council that General von Riedesel was summoned, for his wife records that she woke him in the middle of the night to speak to someone from Burgoyne's headquarters. The message did not please the general, for he eventually returned to bed "considerably out of humour."

The questions put by Burgoyne to this council are a curious mixture of shrewdness and naïveté; he may even have drafted them with a view to a future inquiry into his conduct. By their phrasing, he may have hoped to cover himself both ways, although he must have known the answers before he put the questions.

"General Gates having, in answer to General Burgoyne's message, given a solemn affirmation on his honour, that no detachment has been made from his army during the negociation of the treaty," did the council consider that the treaty as presently drafted was binding on the army, "or is the general's honour engaged for the signing it"? All those consulted were required not only to vote, but also to sign. By 14 to 8 they voted in the affirmative. Burgoyne then made his own position clear. "The lieutenant-general's opinion being clear, that he is not bound by what has passed," he recorded, "he would not execute the treaty upon the sole consideration of the point of honour, notwithstanding the respectable majority *against* him." He then expanded on his argument. "He is likewise far from being convinced that this army, by great exertions and by great enduring in point of provisions, might not yet be relieved; but he is compelled to yield on the following considerations."

So much for the future; it was now necessary to be practical. The terms were as good as could possibly be obtained; indeed, only the rumors of Clinton's advance threw doubts on the advisability of their acceptance. But Gates had given assurance that he had not reduced the strength of the army opposing Burgoyne in order to deal with Clinton, while the reports on Clinton were founded on hearsay and unreliable. Even if Clinton was as far up the Hudson as had been reported, it was unlikely that Burgoyne's army could hold out until help arrived. Burgoyne then gave several reasons why continued defense was impracticable: one officer considers that desertions will increase; the 47th are not to be relied upon; the 62nd's morale is poor; the general opinion among the troops is that the convention should be accepted; many of the best officers have been wounded or are sick; although the soldiers will probably defend themselves if attacked, they lack the spirit to go over to the offensive; if the present treaty is not accepted, it is highly unlikely that a similar one can be negotiated later.

The two concluding sentences summed up the position as Burgoyne saw it: "A defeat is fatal to the Army. A victory does not save it, as they have neither provisions to advance nor retreat against an enemy who by experience we know are capable of rallying at every advantageous post. And that the life and property of every provincial and dependant of this army depends upon the execution of this treaty." [22]

Surrender of his army to the enemy is the most awesome decision any general can take, and no one was more aware of this than John Burgoyne. He was doing his utmost to put off the evil day; almost to the very end he tried to avoid committing himself. Riedesel, when consulted yet again, counseled against breaking a treaty so laboriously negotiated; Hamilton was of the same mind; and so apparently were the eight officers who had given as their opinion only a few hours previously that Burgoyne was not bound to abide by the treaty. Phillips would not offer any counsel. He would do his duty whichever way his commander-in-chief decided; the decision, however, must be Burgoyne's alone. The army was *his* responsibility.

Almost at the eleventh hour Burgoyne again drew back, but Gates was growing impatient. According to Wilkinson, who may not be the most reliable of witnesses, it was the fact that Craig's letter had already committed Burgoyne to agreeing to the convention that finally decided Burgoyne to sign. It was a point of honor. If Wilkinson is correct, Gates was about to reopen hostilities when Wilkinson returned to the American camp, carrying with him the convention signed by Burgoyne. It was dated "Camp at Saratoga, October 16, 1777."

Baroness von Riedesel thought that Burgoyne had acted wisely, and she was probably repeating her husband's views: "this was fortunate for us," she wrote, "as the Americans said to us afterwards, that had the capitulation been broken we all would have been massacred; which they could have done the more easily, as we were not over four or five thousand men strong, and had given them time to bring together more than twenty thousand." [23]

It was a tragic moment for Burgoyne, but he could at least console himself with the knowledge that he had retained throughout the respect of his soldiers. On the morning of October 17 the officers of the army were called together, and Burgoyne addressed them. He explained the reason for his actions "since he had the honour of commanding the army but he was too full to speak." At ten o'clock the army paraded in the camp, and then marched out with colors flying and with drums and fifes playing. None of those taking part felt in the mood for ceremonial, and Digby admits he was close to tears—"though we beat the Grenadiers' march, which not long before was so animating, yet then it seemed by its last feeble effort as if almost ashamed to be heard on such an occasion." [24] Gates, to his credit both as a man and as a soldier, did his utmost to avoid rubbing salt into the wounds. The British marched to a previously assigned place on the banks of the Hudson, close by the ruins of old Fort Hardy, and there they piled their arms. Conscious of the shame his former comrades must have felt, Gates confined the majority of his troops to camp; only one officer from his staff was there to witness the ceremony.

Burgoyne himself, wearing the full-dress uniform of a British general officer, accompanied by Major-Generals Phillips and von Riedesel, together with their staffs, rode across Fish Kill to Gates's headquarters. That general, dressed in a plain blue frock, came out of his tent to greet them. Burgoyne saluted by raising his hat and bowing. "The fortunes of war, General Gates," he said, "have made me your prisoner." To which Gates replied, in the most courteous fashion, "I shall always be ready to bear testimony that it has not been through any fault of your Excellency." [25]

Chapter 21

Qui s'excuse s'accuse

THE TWO PRINCIPAL antagonists in the war of words that followed Saratoga were Burgoyne and Germain, the one attempting to justify his actions, the other seeking a scapegoat. Few British generals have succeeded in exculpating themselves from the blame for military disasters, but Burgoyne was more successful than most—partly on account of his influential friends, and partly because most people knew that the real cause for failure was Germain's inability to comprehend the hard facts of campaigning in North America.

Burgoyne could have had no complaints about his treatment by Gates. In the combat zone there was mutual respect between victors and vanquished, but farther back this tolerance was replaced by hostility. After Burgoyne had surrendered his sword to Gates, which Gates returned without a word, there was, according to the Boston *Continental Journal and Weekly Advertiser* of January 14, 1779, a special dinner.

The table was only two planks laid across two empty beef barrels. There were only four plates for the whole company. There was no cloth, and the dinner consisted of a ham, a goose, some beef, and some boiled mutton. The liquor was New England rum, mixed with water, without sugar; and only two glasses, which were for the two Commanders-in-Chief; the rest of the company drank out of basins. After dinner, General Gates called upon General Burgoyne for his toast, which embarrassed General Burgoyne a good deal; at length he gave *General Washington;* General Gates, in return, gave *the King.*

According to the returns prepared by Burgoyne's adjutant-general at the time of surrender, 1,905 British and 1,594 Germans laid down their arms. The American strength on that same day, as presented by Gates to Burgoyne, was 13,216. The arms having been piled, the troops marched away to the tune of "Yankee Doodle," struck up by an American band, on the first stage of their long march to Cambridge, in Massachusetts, which they reached on November 6. With them went 297 women (215 British and 82 German), a motley collection of camp followers, and a miscellaneous assortment of pet animals, ranging from a bear to a raccoon. Neither the officers nor the soldiers appear to have blamed the sad end of their enterprise on their general. If later there was to be criticism of his conduct of the campaign, it would not come from them. "He possessed the confidence and affection of his army in an extraordinary degree," wrote Sergeant Lamb, "that no loss or misfortune could shake the one, or distress or affliction the other . . . not a voice was heard throughout the army, to upbraid, to censure or blame their general." [1]

Gates was naturally elated by his success. He wrote to his wife and son on the night of the surrender:

The voice of fame, ere this reaches you, will tell how greatly fortunate we have been in this department. Burgoyne and his whole army have laid down their arms and surrendered themselves to me and my Yankees. Thanks to the Giver of all victory for this triumphant success. If Old England is not by this lesson taught humility, then she is an obstinate old slut, bent upon her own ruin. Tell my dear Bob not to be too elated at this great fortune of his father. He and I have seen days adverse as well as prosperous. Let us through this life endeavour to bear both with equal mind. [2]

Although Gates's attitude seems humble, his treatment of his commander-in-chief was cavalier. He reported his victory direct to Congress, rather than to Washington, who, when he wrote to Gates to congratulate him on his signal success, went on to say, "I cannot but regret that a matter of such magnitude and so interesting to our general operations, should have reached me by report only, or through the channel of letters, not bearing that authenticity, which the importance of it required, and which it would have received by a line under your signature, stating the simple fact." [3] Yet, despite his justifiable annoyance, Washington knew that Saratoga had been a "famous victory."

So did many a humbler American. "Rebellion, which a twelvemonth ago was really a contemptible pigmy," wrote Enos Stevens, New York loyalist, "is now become a giant more dreadful to the minds of men than Polyphemus of old, or the sons of Anak." [4] Ralph Cross, who shouldered a musket under Gates, was even more graphic: "The Grand Army of Gen Burgoin Capillelated & agreed to be Prisoners of War, A Grand Sight as ever was beheld by Eye of Man in America"; [5] while Henry Dearborn commented on the "Greatest Conquest ever known," when "the Great Mister Burgouyn with his whole army surrendered themselves as Prisoners of War with all their Public stores." [6]

Burgoyne's host in Albany was Philip Schuyler, who had made such a significant contribution to his defeat. It was Schuyler's scorched-earth policy that had slowed down Burgoyne's advance, giving the Americans time to gather together an army that eventually outnumbered the British. No one could have shown greater consideration for the defeated British general and his staff than Schuyler did. His house was made available to Burgoyne and twenty of his officers as a lodging, and when Burgoyne apologized for the destruction of Schuyler's property at Saratoga, Schuyler replied, "That is the fate of war . . . let us say no more about it." [7]

He showed equal courtesy to Baroness von Riedesel, who records that she was "received in the most friendly manner by the good General Schuyler, his wife and daughters, who showed us the most marked courtesy, as, also, General Burgoyne. . . ." [8]

It was from Schuyler's house that Burgoyne sent his letters to rally support in London; it was also from there that he wrote on October 20 officially informing Lord George Germain of the convention of Saratoga.

His official dispatch to Germain was a chronological account of events since the army crossed the Hudson on September 13 and 14. The battles of Freeman's Farm and Bemis Heights were reported, as well as the withdrawal to Saratoga and the events leading up to the convention. Burgoyne emphasized the importance he attached to preventing Gates's army from taking part in the campaign against Howe, as could have been the case had the expedition retreated to Canada. He did *not* explain why Gates should have chosen to march south, rather than to follow after the retreating British and recapture Ticonderoga. He paid tribute to the bravery of the British officers, and mentioned that he, too, had had his narrow escapes. "It depends upon the sentence his Majesty shall pass upon my conduct," he concluded; "upon the judgement of my profession, and of the impartial and respectable parts of my country, whether I am to esteem them blessings or misfortunes." [9] His private letter to Germain, accompanying the official dispatch, reads much more like an apologia.

I rest my confidence, [he wrote], "in the justice of the King and his councils, to support the General they thought proper to appoint to as arduous an undertaking, and under as positive a direction, as perhaps a cabinet ever framed. It will, I am sure, be remembered, my Lord, that a preference of exertions was the only latitude given to me, and that to force a junction with Sir William Howe, or at least a passage to Albany, was the principle, the letter, and the spirit of my orders. [10]

It was obvious to Germain that Burgoyne intended to take his stand on the inflexibility of his orders, which provided no option but to force a passage to Albany. Burgoyne expanded on this argument in the second paragraph of his letter, maintaining that if he had not made the attempt, his conduct would have been held "indefensible by every class and distinction of men in government, in the army and in the public." Then came the apologia.

The expediency of advancing being admitted, the consequences have been honourable misfortunes. The British have persevered in a strenuous and bloody progress. Had the force been all British, perhaps the perseverance had been longer. But as it was, will it be said, my Lord, that in the exhausted situation described, and in the jaws of famine, and invested by quadruple numbers, a treaty which saves the army to the state, for the next campaign, was not more than could have been expected? *I call it saving the army*, because if sent home, the state is thereby enabled to send forth the troops now destined for her internal defence; if exchanged, they become a force to Sir William Howe, as effectually, as if any other junction had been made.

This curious argument, that surrender rather than retreat was justified because in due course it would permit the reinforcement of Howe's army by fresh troops, overlooked the effect on both British and American morale of the surrender of such a substantial body of troops. It was an attempt to gloss over failure, and was the only excuse that Burgoyne could offer.

He went on to report favorably on Gates's army.

The standing corps which I have seen, are disciplined. I do not hazard the term, but apply it to the great fundamental points of military institution, sobriety, subordination, regularity and courage. The militia are inferior in method and movement, but not a jot less serviceable in woods. My conjectures were very different after the affair of Ticonderago [*sic*], but I am convinced they were delusive; and it is a duty to the state to confess it.

In regard to myself, I am sunk in mind and body; but while I have a faculty of either, it shall be exerted for the King's service.[11]

Burgoyne in Albany was beaten and depressed. He believed he had been let down by Howe, and also by Clinton. He blamed Germain for his misfortunes because that minister had not provided sufficient latitude in the orders he had drafted. He knew that the ministers would close ranks to defend themselves, and that his struggle to justify his actions was likely to be hard and long. A copy of his dispatch went to Lord Derby by the same ship as bore his official report to the secretary of state. He also wrote to a personal friend, Colonel Richard Philipson, who was one of the king's equerries.

If my letters of the beginning of Sept reached you, the events which succeeded will not appear to you extraordinary; tho' unfortunate, I foresaw, & believe expressed to you, that passing Hudsons River, was putting the fate of the Army upon a chance, *but the precision of my Orders*, the Season of the Year, and other Circumstances of the time, made the steps unavoidable. I inclosed to Lord Derby, a Copy of my dispatches to Lord George, in Order that it may be published by him, in case that Ministry should Mangle or Curtail any part of it, in their Gazette; I desir'd him also to Communicate it to you, in the first instance, and I refer you to that public account, trusting indeed, that the fairness of ministers, will make the manuscript unnecessary, or the detail of as difficult, as deversified and as bloody a progress, as the space of time in any Campaign, has produced; I shall subjoin hereto, extracts of Paragraphs of my private Letters, to Lord George & Lord North, and I do it to furnish you with means of Defending your Friend against the Attacks that necessarily follow unsuccessful Events. I expect Ministerial Ingratitude will be display'd, as in all Countries, and all times it is usual to remove the blame from the Orders, to the Execution; and the first Trumpeters of my Accusation will be the Cunninghams, the Smyths and the Keens, should such a return be made for the Zeal with which I have pursued their purposes, it will be the part of my Friends to place the foundation of my Defence, on the Principle, and Letter of my Orders.

It was the will of the State to risque a Corps of Troops to Assist the great General arrangement of the Campaign; if the State thought it necessary to Devote a Corps of Troops for General purposes; it was no more the Generals duty to decline proceeding upon motions of Prudence, and upon Speculation of Consequences, than it would be justifiable in a Serjeant, who heads a forlorn hope, at the Storm of a Breach, to recede, because his distruction was probable; mine was a Forlorn hope; with this difference, that it was not supported. This Army has been deminished by a scandalous desertion, in the Collateral parts, by the heavy drain of the Garrison of Ticonderago, and by great loss of Blood, and it has been totally unsupported by Sir William Howe; when my conduct for proceeding so far as to leave my Communication with Canada is arraigned, face the accusation with the wording my Instructions; and ask the accusers what they would have said, had I remained Supine in a Camp at Fort Edward. Is there a man that would have held me defensible had I left exertions untried in the circumstances I then was, at Hubberton, at Ticonderago, at Skeensburg and at Fort Ann; The ascendancy of British Troops had been apparent against superiour numbers, The junction of large Corps of Loyalists had been engaged for as the Army should advance, Schuyler, who then Commanded the Enemys Army was then retreating and no possibility was then suggested by either Friends or Foes of a Collection of a quarter of the Forces which has since appeared.

The Contempt of my own Army, the Condemnation of Government and the World would have been inevitable and deserved consequence of inaction; my head would have been answerable for it, And I should have left my Friends (had I any remaining) the painful task of defending, a disobedience of Orders upon Cowardly principles. Instead of which, I thank God! it will be now their only trouble to vindicate a Spirited exertion of Orders; the utmost that Malevolence can say will be, that I have been too bold. Upon the whole/ my Friend, if I do not deceive myself, my Friends may maintain the following ground. A principle of Duty engaged me to accept a Command of which I foresaw the difficulties and Dangers respecting the public Service, and Personal reputation. Orders in the construction of which, there was neither Latitude nor alternative; compelled me to lay by (of consequence) the general maxims of military reasoning, upon securing a retreat. I twice fought, and once Conquered double my numbers: and I afterwards Courted an action from more than a quadruple my numbers with which I was invested. And at last with only three Days provision for the men (upon a short allowance) and not a particle of Forage, the troops gall'd with the Cannonading into all parts of their position, and exhausted with watchfulness of many Days and nights under Arms, the Germans dispirited, and ready to Club their Arms at the first Fire, Under all these circumstances of Distress, amongst all these Causes of Dispair I dictated Terms of Convention, which saves the Army to the state for the next Campaign—

The Consolation I have received from the public view of Gates's Army is, I confess extreem. I have now the Stubborn Fact witnessed by every Officer and Soldier of my Army, that I was not much deceived by intelligence, and that I have not over-stated his numbers in calling them 16000. Sorry I am to add, that a better disciplined, a more alert, or better prepared Army in all essentials, is hardly to be found on our side of the question—

When all these facts are notorious, I am clear, I shall receive Honour, not Disgrace from the Public. I am Impatient, you may imagine, to be at home, to undertake my own Cause, but I think it indispensible to be directed by Sir W. Howe—I certainly shall wish to precede the Embarkation, if he approves of it.

As to myself, I am exhausted in mind and Body, the agitation of the One, and the Fatigues of the other are too much for me. An American Winter, should that be my Fate, will be decisive of my Health, possibly of my life—To the last moment be assured of the inviolable affection of Dear Phillipson yours. J. Burgoyne.[12]

This letter displays clearly Burgoyne's mental distress at the time, and also clearly sets out the instructions for his defense *in absentia*. It is not entirely honest, because he could have declined command of the expedition, but it illustrates the lines along which his mind was working. The blame for failure lay not with Burgoyne—but with others. He had done his utmost; and so had his troops.

Bad news travels fast, but it is hard to imagine the grounds for Horace Walpole's statement on October 26: "Burgoyne is said to be beaten"; Burgoyne's dispatch only reached the secretary of state in early December. Germain assured Parliament on November 20 that "there was every reason to hope for success in America." [13] Unofficial reports must have reached London before official confirmation was received. On November 18, Shelburne had described the "issue of Mr. Burgoyne's expedition" as "too melancholy to be made a subject of conversation," but he did not know the full story. Shelburne thought Burgoyne might have been able to retreat, or possibly have joined with Clinton and reached New York, but he considered that neither possibility would have any effect on the war: "what end would this answer, but that at the expense of many millions, and two campaigns, he has reached a place by land, which he could without the least trouble or interruption have reached by sea, in almost as many weeks." [14]

Germain was hard put to defend the government in the absence of firm news. On November 18 he was savagely attacked in Parliament by Fox, who laid the entire blame on the minister: "There was a fundamental error in the proceedings which would for ever prevent our generals from acting with success; that no man with common sense would have placed the two armies in such a position as from their distance made it absolutely impossible that the one should receive any assistance from the other." [15]

The government's tactics became clear when Germain made his statement on November 20. He stressed the fact that the plan was Burgoyne's, who had been authorized by Carleton to discuss it in London; "little Alteration was made and the Instructions sent to Carleton were seen and approved by the General who was to execute them." [16] Germain said it was wrong to suppose that Burgoyne was under orders to fight his way to New York to join Howe. On the contrary, he was given Albany as the limit of his expedition; only if circumstances rendered it desirable was he to co-operate with General Howe, "to the utmost of his power." [17]

The Opposition had not yet seen the orders given to Burgoyne; Germain was therefore free to interpret them as he chose. He did not tell the House that Burgoyne had complained about the inflexibility of his orders; or that Burgoyne had been ordered "to *force* his way to Albany." Germain was fighting for his political life, just as Burgoyne was fighting for his military reputation, and they were equally concerned about their personal honor. It was fortunate for Burgoyne that his principal opponent was so heartily disliked, but unfortunately he had the ear of the king. George III wanted no dissension within the government. Germain was his stoutest supporter and anyone trying to unseat him could reckon on the king's opposition. Had Burgoyne returned quietly, wearing an air of repentance, his sovereign would probably have found a way in due course to recompense him for his silence, but Burgoyne had other plans.

Germain was in good spirits on December 2, but on the following day confirmation of the disastrous events at Saratoga was received from General Carleton. What had happened was a realization of Carleton's worst fears, if his letter of November 12 to Burgoyne is any guide:

I received your letter of the 20th of October, with your public dispatches by Captain Craig, the 5th instant, and heartily condole with you upon the very disagreeable accounts they contain, all which I sincerely lamented, both on the public account and your own.

This unfortunate event, it is to be hoped, will in future prevent ministers from pretending to direct operations of war, in a country at three thousand miles distance, of which they have so little knowledge as not to be able to distinguish between good, bad, or interested advices, or to give positive orders in matters, which from their nature, are ever upon the change; so that the expedience or propriety of a measure at one moment, may be totally inexpedient or improper in the next.[18]

Germain's first requirement was to find a scapegoat, and who better than Howe? "Howe's going round to Chesapeak instead of going to join Burgoyne, is censured much," [19] wrote Thomas Hutchinson in his diary; but Fox, for reasons of his own, partially absolved Howe, in his speech of November 18, when he said: "An army of 10,000 men destroyed through ignorance, the obstinate willful ignorance and incapacity of the noble Lord [Germain] called loudly for vengeance. . . . Burgoyne's orders were to make his way to Albany, there to wait the orders of Sir William Howe and to cooperate with him; but General Howe knew nothing of this matter, for he had gone to a different country, and left the unhappy Burgoyne and his troops to take care of themselves." [20] Fox wanted Germain's head on a charger, but not at the expense of the two Howes, admiral and general, who had allied themselves with the Opposition.

Burgoyne had been careful not to blame Howe for his failure. He had reported the surrender to Howe, and the events leading up to it, in a letter dated October 20. He also sought Howe's permission to return to England to present his case in person. Only three days after signing the convention he was asking Howe to allow him to "precede the troops if it can be done with propriety." [21] Five days later he was calling upon Howe as a personal friend to furnish him with the means to return to England, and after a month he returned to the attack, saying his "business and his health" necessitated an immediate return home.

Howe was careful not to commit himself. He had his own quarrel with Germain, and was careful to protect his own position in a letter written to the minister on October 22. He made it clear that Burgoyne had been forewarned that he could expect no assistance from him. And not only Burgoyne. Because the king had approved Howe's letter containing the warning, presumably, therefore, so had Germain. In the same letter, Howe submitted his resignation, on the grounds that he had lost the confidence of the government. Clinton was more outspoken on behalf of his old friend. He hated Howe and despised his military abilities. He told Burgoyne of his efforts to prevent Howe from going south to Philadelphia, and deplored his own inability to come to Burgoyne's assistance. He could never have responded to Burgoyne's request for orders, since he had no knowledge of the orders for the campaign. Clinton's statement smacks of special pleading; he may not have seen Burgoyne's orders, although this is improbable, but he was undoubtedly aware of the plan of campaign.

Germain was Howe's and Burgoyne's target, as he was the Opposition's. He defended himself lamely in Parliament, wilting under Fox's attack, and protesting his unwillingness for office in the first place. Lord North came to his defense and was able to outmaneuver Fox's motion for "Copies of all Instructions and Papers, relative to the expedition from Canada under lieutenant general Burgoyne. . . ." [22] He then succeeded in having Parliament adjourned for Christmas earlier than usual, providing the harassed ministers with a breathing space.

The king was as shocked as the country by the news from America. Germain might keep Burgoyne's dispatch from Parliament, but he could not keep it from the king. Yet he managed to get in his own word first by enclosing a covering note with the dispatch; in this note he reminded the king that "the positive orders which Lt. General Burgoyne refers to, your Majesty will remember, but it was never understood that at such a distance any order would be positive, in the present case the words of the order will not bear the strict construction the General puts upon them." [23]

In Cambridge, Massachusetts, to which he had been removed from Albany, Burgoyne was busily lobbying for permission to return home to face his accusers. He seems to have suffered some kind of nervous breakdown, being reported as "indisposed and depressed in spirits." Colonel Elisha Porter, who had been present with Gates at the surrender, was so moved by his condition, "well-nigh helpless with illness," that he extended to him the hospitality of his house. [24]

Burgoyne spent much of his time as a prisoner arguing with his captors for better treatment of his soldiers. Congress was desperately short of funds and reluctant to spend money on their prisoners of war, whose condition became so desperate that Burgoyne was compelled to advance £20,000 from his personal funds in order to provide his troops with the necessities of life. To add to Burgoyne's worries there was bitter wrangling with Congress over the terms of the convention; for Congress, not surprisingly, was taken aback by the lenient terms agreed to by Gates. On November 14 Burgoyne wrote a letter to Gates, protesting about the failure to comply with the terms of the convention. "I am sorry I cannot speak with satisfaction upon what happened and still passes here," he complained. "The officers are crowded into the barracks, six & seven in a room about ten feet square & without distinction of rank. The General Officers are not better provided for. . . ." He absolved Major General William Heath, charged by Congress with looking after the prisoners, from any blame for such a sorry state of affairs; however, he went on to say, "while the supreme powers of the state are unable or unwilling to enforce their authority, & the inhabitants want the hospitality or indeed the common civilisation to assist us, without it the public faith is broke, & we are the immediate sufferers." [25]

Gates forwarded the letter to Congress, and the storm broke. Congress, which believed in any case that Gates had been weak in granting Burgoyne such favorable terms, took offense at the charge that they were not honoring the treaty. At 3:00 P.M. on Friday, January 2, 1778, the delegates passed a resolution, by 14 votes to 7, stating that "the charge made by Lieutenant General Burgoyne in his letter to Major General

Gates of 14 November, of a breach of public faith on the part of these states, is not warranted by the just construction of any article of the convention of Saratoga; that it is a strong indication of his intention, and affords just grounds of fear that he will avail himself of such pretended breach of the convention, in order to disengage himself and the army under him of the obligation they are under to these united states, and that the security which these states have had in his personal honour is hereby destroyed." [26] On the following day, by 16 votes to 1, with two abstentions, it was resolved, "That the embarkation of Lieutenant General Burgoyne, and the troops under his command, be suspended till a distinct and explicit ratification of the convention of Saratoga shall be properly notified by the court of Great Britain." [27]

As a consequence of a few ill-considered remarks, written while under stress, Burgoyne had effectively sealed the fate of his army. He provided Congress with the excuse they were looking for. That he was able personally to escape the worst consequences was due more to George Washington than to anyone else. Most of the soldiers who surrendered at Saratoga remained prisoners of war "for the duration," and by the time the conflict ended many of them had chosen to become American citizens. So much for Burgoyne's claim that he had saved his king an army by surrendering it on October 17 on the heights of Saratoga.

Washington had not failed to note the weakness of the convention. "I do not think it to our interest to expedite the passage of the prisoners to England," [28] he had written to Heath, pointing out that the arrival of the prisoners in England would immediately release an equivalent number of troops for service in North America. He also insisted that Boston should be the port of embarkation, as stated in the terms of surrender, and not some other port more convenient for the British. Suspicion and devious dealing are inseparable from war; certainly neither the British nor the Americans were guiltless in this respect. A "Secret" letter from Howe to Burgoyne, dated November 16, 1777, directed the latter to sail his British troops to New York after their embarkation at Boston. Howe then intended to exchange an equivalent number of American prisoners of war in return for them; the Germans were to be sent back to Europe. He was aware that he would be acting in moral breach of the convention, although perhaps he could have argued that any increase in the strength of his own army would have been balanced by an equivalent increase in Washington's; he warned Burgoyne "to use every possible precaution to keep the Enemy ignorant of my Intentions, as on the least suspicion the Troops will be infallibly stopt." [29]

Congress meanwhile continued to debate the problem of what to do about the convention and Burgoyne's army. There were sharp interchanges between Henry Laurens, president of Congress, and General Gates. Congress wanted to know why the British had not surrendered their colors and their cartouche boxes; why was there a discrepancy between the numbers of men who surrendered and the muskets and bayonets given up; what had happened to the military chest? Gates replied that it was not always possible in the excitement of victory to dot all the i's and cross all the t's. Burgoyne had told him the colors had been left behind in Canada, and if Gates's experience in the British Army was anything to judge by, the military chest had either been left in Canada or its contents dispersed in the reckoning of accounts by Burgoyne after the surrender. He regretted that nothing specific had been mentioned about cartouche boxes in the convention; some had been handed over, while others had been traded by British soldiers for drink on their march to Boston. Muskets and bayonets would inevitably be fewer than the number of prisoners because officers and sergeants did not carry them; moreover, a large quantity had been plundered by militiamen. "I believe," he wrote, "there was no Destruction of Military Stores after the Convention, by, or with the privity of, General Burgoyne, or his officers.

"It is so extraordinary for a British Army to Surrender their Arms," Gates continued, "that we ought not to wonder at the Violent and Disappointed, for Committing some Irregularities; but I do not conceive that anything of sufficient Consequence was done to justify our Charge of their having violated the Convention." He then reminded Laurens that at the time of the convention there were reliable reports of the approach of a British force up the Hudson. It was stated to be within "a few hours' sailing of Albany," and it therefore behooved Gates to conclude the surrender terms as speedily as possible. "When things of such importance must be done in a Hurry, some Articles of seeming Importance never fail to be omitted," he wrote.[30] When all this was taken into account, Gates considered he had acted correctly.

Burgoyne had in fact sent his military chest back to Canada prior to the surrender.[31] The fate of the colors is more obscure. Those of the German regiments were hidden by Baroness von Riedesel in her mattress, and subsequently found their way to Canada. Lieutenant-Colonel John Hill, commanding the 9th Regiment, concealed his regiment's colors about his person, and took them with him on his return to England. He presented them personally to the king, who rewarded him by making him an aide-de-camp and by promoting him to colonel. Burgoyne is reputed to have secreted the colors of the other British regiments in his baggage and conveyed them safely to England. As for the cartouche boxes, the most reliable evidence is that of Lieutenant-Colonel Kingston. He was asked at the subsequent inquiry in London: "Was it by consent of General Gates that the soldiers after the convention retained their cartouche-boxes?" He replied, "They retained their belts, and I really don't recollect whether their cartouch boxes were in general retained or not; but talking with Mr Gates when the king's troops marched by with their accoutrements on, Mr Gates asked me (we had

been old acquaintances formerly) whether it was not customary on field days for arms and accoutrements to go together?
I told him there was nothing said in the convention that I
had agreed to with him relating to the accoutrements, and
that he could have no right to any thing but what was stipulated in that treaty. He replied, 'You are perfectly right;'
and turned to some of the officers in their service by, and
said, 'If we meant to have had them, we ought to have inserted
them in the convention.' " [32]

Burgoyne also took exception to a requirement by Congress
that "the name and rank of every commissioned officer, and
the name, former place of abode and occupation, size, age and
description of every non-commissioned officer and private
soldier, and all other persons comprehended in the Convention" should be furnished to the American authorities in order
that it could be ensured that they did not hereafter take up
arms again in North America. This requirement was passed
on to him by General Heath in a somewhat peremptory
general order. It elicited a sharp reply.

I have received a paper, dated Head Quarters, Boston, Nov.
20th, purporting to be founded upon express orders from the
honourable Continental Congress, which paper I return as inadmissible, because extending to matters in which the Congress
have no right of interference. A list of names and ranks of every
commissioned officer, and the numbers of the non-commissioned
officers and soldiers may be necessary to you, Sir, for the purpose
of fulfilling the Convention in the quartering officers, and the
regular delivery of provisions, fuel, etc. Such lists shall be prepared at your request; but before any other lists can be granted,
I must be assured of the purposes for which they are intended,
and the word *Order* must neither be mentioned nor implied.[33]

Heath's reply was a model of tact. He made it clear that
Congress required the list in order to ensure that none of the
convention troops, after their release, should again be employed in North America. If they were, and were apprehended, they would be punished according to the law. Heath

added that he also required the list in order that the administration of the convention troops could be properly organized. Then he gently reminded Burgoyne of their respective situations. "I shall at all times endeavour to found my orders on the principles of honour, reason and justice, and not to infringe those delicate principles in others," he told him, "but my orders for the purposes of order and regularity must be obeyed by every man and all bodies of men placed under my direction; and fully determined I am, that offenders shall not pass with impunity." [34]

Heath's situation was difficult. It had not been possible in the short time available to provide adequate accommodation for a surrendered army totaling nearly 5,500 men with many dependents. Boston had been ravaged by war and supplies were short. The North American winter had arrived and fuel was hard to come by. Boston was the heart of the rebellion, as well as the city where British troops were most disliked. Jane McCrae's murder was still fresh in men's minds. Chance had to some extent dictated that the prisoners should be quartered in the most anti-British city in North America, and in the one that had so far suffered the most from the ravages of war.

The British made things no easier by their attitude. The convention was not a capitulation, they claimed, and they behaved accordingly. Burgoyne conducted his dealings with Heath as if he still commanded a battleworthy army. He was too experienced a politician, and too courteous a man, to behave arrogantly or rudely, but he watched constantly for slights. His behavior at the time was probably the result of nervous exhaustion, for he was anxious about his health, worried about his enemies in England, and fearful for his military future. In such circumstances men become seized with obsessions, and Burgoyne's was to get back to England just as soon as he could. It dominated his thoughts and his correspondence.

But his own problems were not allowed to override his concern for his troops. In a letter to Howe on November 26 he recommended certain noncommissioned officers for officers' commissions, "upon my personal observation of distinguished conduct before the enemy." [35] During the following January, he involved himself personally in the court-martial of an American officer who was accused of wounding a British soldier. On January 7, a British soldier had attacked an American sentry and made off with his musket. A search was ordered by Colonel David Henley, commandant of the prisoners of war, to identify and apprehend the culprit. A pitched battle followed between the British and their guards, in the course of which Henley ordered his men to charge with fixed bayonets, and he personally pricked a British soldier. Thirty of the prisoners were taken and incarcerated in a guardship in Boston harbor, whereupon Burgoyne wrote to Heath demanding their immediate release and an apology. Heath suspended Henley, held a court of inquiry, and decided, on the recommendation of the court, that "it would be most for the honour of Colonel Henley, as well as for the satisfaction of all concerned, that the judgement of a court martial should be taken on his conduct, during his command at camp." Accordingly a court-martial was convened on January 20 and sat, after various adjournments, until February 25.

Burgoyne appeared in person to conduct the case on behalf of the prisoners. According to the arraignment, " Lieutenant General Burgoyne accuses Colonel Henley of a general tenor of language and conduct, heinously criminal, as an officer and unbecoming a man; of the most indecent, violent, vindictive severity against unarmed men; and of intentional murder." [36] The British general, in full-dress uniform, attended by his personal staff similarly attired, opened the proceedings with an impassioned address, in which he reminded the court "you are trustees for the honour of an infant state, and, therefore, evasion, subterfuge and law-craft, were any man hardy enough to offer such at your tribunal, would be of no avail." [37] According to Anburey, Burgoyne was referring to the American judge advocate general, who was present at the trial, "a little, vain, conceited fellow."

The evidence showed that Colonel Henley had been greatly provoked by the British soldier, who had refused to lay down his arms when ordered to do so. However, Henley had lost his temper and seized a firelock with bayonet from a sentry, with which he pricked the soldier. Burgoyne made an eloquent speech on the subject, and then wrangled with the judge advocate general about the law. After much disputation, Henley was acquitted of the charge, as might have been anticipated. General Heath could not forbear commenting on the appearance of a commanding general as prosecutor in a court-martial. This "may be warranted by some like precedents in British court martials," he wrote, " yet it is altogether novel in the proceedings of any general court martial in the Army of the United States of America." [38] He considered the practice tended "to render courts martial both tedious and expensive," and recommended that Burgoyne's personal appearance should not be taken as a precedent in the future.

Burgoyne may have failed to obtain the conviction of the much-disliked Colonel Henley, but his presence at the trial in defense of one of his own soldiers, as well as being the prosecutor of an officer so greatly disliked, increased his popularity. It was unusual for an officer as senior as Burgoyne to take up the cudgels so publicly on behalf of his soldiers. They loved him the more for doing so.

A combination of malice and suspicion had decided the fate of Burgoyne's soldiers a month or more before Henley's court-martial. At 3:00 P.M. on Thursday, January 8, Congress considered the following resolutions. First, "That, as many of the cartouch boxes and several other articles of military accoutrement, annexed to the persons of the non-commissioned officers and soldiers, included in the convention of Saratoga, have not been delivered up, the convention, on the part of the British army, has not been strictly complied with." This was carried by 14 votes to 4. Second, "That the refusal of Lieutenant General Burgoyne to give descriptive lists of the non-commissioned officers and privates belonging to his army, subsequent to his declaration that the public faith was broke, is considered by Congress in an alarming point of view; since a compliance with the resolution of Congress could only have been prejudicial to that army in case of an infraction of the convention on their part." And third, "That the charge made by Lieutenant General Burgoyne, in his letter to Major General Gates, of the 14 November, of a breach of public faith on the part of these states, is not warranted by the just construction of any article of the convention of Saratoga; that it is a strong indication of his intention, and affords just ground of fear, that he will avail himself of such pretended breach of the convention, in order to disengage himself, and the army under him, of the obligation they are under to the United States; and that the security, which these states have had in his personal honor, is hereby destroyed."

Whereupon, Congress resolved: "That the embarkation of Lieutenant-General Burgoyne, and the troops under his command, be suspended till a distinct and explicit ratification of the convention of Saratoga shall be properly notified by the court of Great Britain to Congress." [39] This resolution has been described as "a sordid story of meanness and ill faith, an indelible blot on the reputation of Congress," [40] and it is hard to justify if treaties are to mean anything. Burgoyne declared that it caused him "an astonishment that no occurrence ever before occasioned." [41] George Washington feared that it might lead Burgoyne and his officers to decide they were no longer bound by their paroles. It is easy to understand why Congress was astonished by Gates's leniency at Saratoga, but it is less easy to condone the reasons given for repudiating the terms of the convention. Congress broke faith with both Gates and the enemy. It could have refused to ratify the convention on the grounds of public expediency, but by acting as it did, it destroyed whatever case it might have had.

Burgoyne redoubled his efforts to return home. He wrote to Washington, to Gates, and to the president of Congress. He received courteous commiseration from the first two and consideration from the latter, to whom he had enclosed a paper defending his conduct and dealing with the charges set out against him in the resolution of January 8. On March 3, 1778, his efforts were rewarded when Congress passed a resolution "That Lieutenant General Burgoyne, on account of his ill state of health, have leave to embark for England by Rhode Island, or any more expeditious route, with the officers of his family and his servants; that General Heath furnish the necessary passports, accepting a parole from Lieutenant General Burgoyne, Lieutenant Colonel Kingston, and Dr Wood, That should the embarkation of the troops of the convention of Saratoga be by any means prolonged beyond the time apprehended, these officers will return to America upon demand and due notice given, and will re-deliver themselves into the power of Congress, unless regularly exchanged." [42]

General Heath received Burgoyne's parole on April 2, and the two men took leave of each other. Heath had treated Burgoyne throughout with courtesy and consideration, and no blame could be attached to him for the misfortunes of the convention troops. Burgoyne, according to Phillips, "sick in body and in mind," [43] appears to have given little thought to the criticism he might expect for returning home while his officers and men remained prisoners. By eighteenth-century standards, perhaps, there was no reason why the thought should have crossed his mind; but for an officer who spoke so often of honor, it is not easy to excuse.

Chapter 22

Scapegoat

DEFEATED GENERALS can usually advance several good reasons to account for their failure. Burgoyne was no exception. But governments prefer to muzzle them lest their defense disclose ministerial incompetence and bureaucratic bungling. Lord North's government did its best to silence Burgoyne, and failed only because he was a member of Parliament. Denied a forum in a court-martial, he found one in the House of Commons.

There had been plenty of time to prepare his case, and he brought home with him Robert Kingston, his principal staff officer. Kingston, both loyal and thorough, had been privy to his commander-in-chief's inner thoughts. The two men landed at Portsmouth on May 13, 1778, determined to justify Burgoyne's every action. As a first step, a letter was dispatched to Germain requesting a personal interview.[1] But Burgoyne knew he would have to be cautious in his choice of tactics. The king strongly supported North and Germain, and Burgoyne had no desire to fall out with his sovereign. He owed a great deal to royal favor—his colonelcy of the 16th Light Dragoons, his governorship of Fort William, and his selection to command the expedition from Canada. Moreover, he was to some extent identified with the court party, despite his Whig sympathies, and had even been seen riding in Hyde

Park in company with the king. To attack Germain would mean attacking North, and behind North stood George III.

Therefore it might be wiser to single out Howe as the prime cause of failure. If Howe had carried out his part of the plan, Burgoyne would be returning home a hero instead of as a prisoner of war on parole. According to Thomas Hutchinson, Burgoyne was advised to abandon this line of attack. "It is said that when Burg[oyne] arrived, Charles F[ox] asked him his plan?" wrote Hutchinson. "To charge Howe with leaving him to be sacrificed [replied Burgoyne]. 'If that's y'r plan we must forsake you: we are determined to support H[owe].' The next news—that [the] Ministry is chargeable; and his [Burgoyne's] speech in the H[ouse], and his new publication, are conformable to this account." [2]

This was recorded some time later, but it confirms the report that Fox intercepted Burgoyne on his way to London and persuaded him to switch his attack from Howe to Germain.[3] This meant throwing in his lot with the Opposition. Since at this stage Burgoyne still hoped for a court-martial to clear his name, he preferred to keep his options open, at the same time seeking assurances from Fox that he could count on his support, which was unlikely to be withheld. Fox had moved a vote of censure on March 16, 1778, on Germain's conduct of the war; it was lost, by 164 votes to 44. This so infuriated Fox that, "taking the resolution of censure out of his pocket, [he] tore it in pieces and immediately quitted the House." [4] The solicitor-general then moved "that it does not appear . . . that the failure of the Expedition from Canada arose from any neglect in the Secretary of State," and the resolution was agreed to by the committee although it was not reported to the House. The government was closing its ranks.

Tempers were high, and the administration was under constant attack—by Chatham, Burke, and Fox. According to Fox, "ever since the day that nobleman [Germain] forced himself into administration, our affairs began rapidly to decline." [5]

Lord George Germain badly needed a scapegoat. To public mortification was added personal tragedy for him: Lady Germain died, of the measles, on January 15. Nevertheless, he did not lose his grip, but kept his determination that Burgoyne should not be given the opportunity of stating his case before a court-martial. He did, however, take care to shelter behind the king. "Your Majesty will be pleased to give the orders you shall think proper with regard to any enquiry that may be made into the conduct of Lieutenant General Burgoyne," he wrote on May 13, 1778.[6]

He was affable enough at his first meeting with Burgoyne, soon after the latter's arrival in London. Burgoyne gave his version in *A Letter from Lieut. Gen. Burgoyne to His Constituents.*

I was received with apparent kindness. Explanations passed, but they were friendly; I was heard attentively, through a report of all the transactions subsequent to the Convention of Saratoga, and I was led by degrees, and without suspicion of insidiousness, to the most confidential communication, on my part, of facts, observations, and opinions, respecting very important objects. . . . It was not until after the matter of my communication was exhausted, that the Secretary of State drew from his pocket an order, that I should prepare myself for an enquiry; at which I expressed my fullest satisfaction, till he followed the order with the information, of the *etiquette* I before mentioned, that I was not to appear at Court.[7]

Burgoyne had claimed his rights as a soldier to be tried by court-martial. Germain had refused. There would be an inquiry, but held *in camera* on the grounds of public interest. Since the war continued, it could not be permitted that the enemy be provided with confidential information. By denying Burgoyne a court-martial and the right to appear at Court, Germain had gone a long way toward muzzling him. All that remained was to prevent his using Parliament as a forum in which to air his grievances. With the aid of Alexander Wedderburn, the solicitor-general, Germain attempted to stop Burgoyne from taking his seat as a member for Preston.

A board of five senior generals was convened "to examine and enquire into the causes of such failure" at Saratoga. General Gage was one of them, and Charles Gould, the judge advocate general, presided. The board met on May 22. Despite their requirement to examine and inquire into the events leading up to the convention, the board concentrated instead on determining whether Burgoyne, as a prisoner of war on parole, could legally be examined on his actions.

Burgoyne claimed that he was not a prisoner of war. He explained "that he has never been considered as Prisoner of War, and that he holds himself a free man in every Circumstance except that he is restricted by the Convention of Saratoga not to serve in America during the War; with the further Parole on his leaving America, that should the Embarkation of the Convention Troops be by any means prolonged beyond the time apprehended, he will return to America upon demand and due notice given by Congress, and will redeliver himself into the Power of the Congress, unless regularly exchanged." [8]

The board decided otherwise. On the twenty-third, in a lengthy judgment, the generals ruled that they were not empowered to examine Burgoyne so long as there were any restraints upon his person. Three days later the king signed a warrant approving their conclusion and discharging the board. Germain had successfully checkmated Burgoyne's efforts to be interrogated by his military peers, and had avoided the issue of a court-martial. He was less successful in preventing Burgoyne from taking his seat in Parliament.

There were rumors going about London that Burgoyne did not intend to take his seat until after a court-martial. He put an end to this gossip in a letter to Germain on May 18. On the twenty-first he took his seat without anyone challenging his right, though Wedderburn was searching for legal precedents to prevent him from doing so. A somewhat similar situation had arisen in the case of Lord Frederick Cavendish, who had been captured by the French at Saint-Malo, but who had sat and voted in the House while on parole. Cavendish had asked the French before accepting his parole whether they would object to his resuming his place in Parliament. He had pointed out that he would certainly vote in favor of measures for prosecuting the war, whereupon the French had replied that they might as well object to his conceiving a child lest it grew up to fight against them.[9]

In his efforts to muzzle Burgoyne, Wedderburn was supported by Richard Rigby, who had made a fortune as paymaster-general. When another member, Robert Vyner, rose on May 23 and announced that he wished to put certain questions to Burgoyne, a furious argument ensued regarding Burgoyne's right to reply. On the previous evening Burgoyne had informed the speaker of his intention to answer questions put to him in the House, arguing that "I could not be supposed to entertain a doubt that any part of my situation precluded me from a right to exercise at full, every privilege of a member of parliament."[10] The stage was set for a public confrontation with Germain.

On May 26 Burgoyne replied to Vyner. Horace Walpole records that the House was so crowded that "they were forced to turn out the strangers, although Burgoyne begged that they might stay and hear his defense."[11] The questions having been put, they were answered by Burgoyne in forthright fashion. Then Vyner moved for a committee to inquire into his conduct. Burgoyne seconded the motion, and gave a brief account of the campaign, avoiding any criticism of Howe, praising the fighting ability of the Americans, but complaining bitterly of being refused permission to appear at Court. The moment had now come for Wedderburn to contest Burgoyne's right to appear in the House. This he did with some skill, supported by Rigby, but he was overruled by the House, ever jealous for the privileges of its members. Charles Fox then intervened to extend the inquiry to cover the entire expedition, providing Burgoyne with the opportunity to enlarge on his previous statement.

Burgoyne began by disclaiming sole authorship for the plan of campaign. "The plan as originally drawn I have no reason to be ashamed of," he told the House, "because it underwent the inspection of some of the first and ablest officers of this country; but the plan, as it stood when orders were framed, can with no more propriety be called mine, than others framed by the cabinet for the distant parts of America or any other quarter of the globe where I had no participation or concern." [12] He complained that the plan was too inflexible; it had only one object—"the forcing of a passage to Albany." He made it clear that "the orders framed upon that plan could in no wise be understood than as positive, peremptory and indispensable." [13]

As for Howe, Burgoyne had expected co-operation, and had had no reason to expect otherwise. "That [letter] to sir Guy Carleton had never weighed on my mind; because it was dated early in April, and consequently long before the secretary of state's instructions, which I must have supposed to relate to cooperation, could be received." In other words, Burgoyne gave the House of Commons every reason to assume that he had expected Howe to abandon his projected operation against Philadelphia once Howe learned from Germain of the planned advance from Canada, and to operate, instead, up the Hudson from New York in order to join forces with Burgoyne at Albany.[14]

He explained his return to England ahead of his troops as being necessary in order to settle very complicated accounts, to restore his health, and to enable him to explain his actions to Parliament. He read out George Washington's letter authorizing his departure. He also defended his decision to advance via Skenesboro, and denied that his army was overloaded with baggage or overprovided with artillery.

In his peroration he left the House in no doubt of where in his opinion the blame lay. His unfortunate experience, as well as the experiences of Carleton, Howe, and Gage, would serve as a warning, he trusted, for "all those who might be hazardous enough to attempt to serve their country under the auspices of men who were obliged to cover their ignorance and inability, and screen themselves from ignominy and contempt, by throwing blame upon the men who were unwise enough to act as they were instructed." [15]

Burgoyne sat down amid scenes of uproar. Walpole, writing on May 31, described Burgoyne as "bullying," and said that "Lord G. Germain scolded like two oysterwomen." [16] Sir Alexander Leith queried Germain's fitness to be a minister; Temple Luttrell went even further, accusing Germain of being "a minister whose loss of a nation's confidence and his own character is a matter of public record." The reference to Germain's behavior at Minden was too obvious to be missed. He jumped up in his seat, clapped his hand to his sword hilt, and virtually challenged Luttrell to a duel. Amid increasingly disorderly scenes, Luttrell left the House, but returned unrepentant, refusing to recant. Lord North tried to pour oil on the troubled waters, Germain apologized, and the honors undoubtedly rested with Luttrell. "Lord George grasped his sword—and then asked pardon for having been so grossly insulted," recorded Walpole.[17] It was clear when the day was done that Burgoyne was master of the field, despite the fact that Vyner's motion was lost, by 144 votes to 96.

The king had made his feelings clear when he had thought it "rather particular that Mr Burgoyne should wish to take a lead in Opposition when his own situation seems to me to be far from either pleasant or creditable." [18] There were others who held the same opinion. Burgoyne may have felt that he had been let down by his political masters, but was it consistent with his duty to his soldiers that he should have accepted parole? Lord Pembroke may have summed up contemporary opinion when he wrote: "Burgoyne in my mind always carried more sail than ballast, but he is gallant and honest; and such ought not to be sacrificed to a Minden B . . . g Hero." [19]

The secretary-at-war signed a letter on June 5, 1778, directing Burgoyne to return to America "as soon as you have tried the Bath waters, in the manner you propose." [20] Barrington made it clear that the order was by the king's command, and referred to Burgoyne's letter to Howe in which he had trusted that a "short time at Bath" would enable him to return to New England.

Burgoyne replied to Barrington on June 22. He acknowledged receipt of the minister's letter and requested him to lay certain particulars before the king. The first of these concerned his health.

My letter to Sir William Howe, referred to in your Lordship's letter, was writ in the fulness of zeal to renew my service in arms during the ensuing campaign. Deprived of so animating a support and visited by new and unexpected anxieties, I have now recourse only, as far as the mind is concerned, to a clear conscience, perhaps a more tardy, but I trust as efficacious an assistance. The present season of the year, always favourable to me, gives me the appearance, and indeed in some degree the sensation, of health; but much care is still wanting to restore me to my former state. The remedies prescribed are repose, regimen of diet, and repeated visits to Bath. My intention was to remain some time in the country, to repair to Bath for a short time next month, and to return thither for a longer space in the proper season, the autumn. But whatever may be the benefit of all or any part of this plan, I am persuaded that to expose my constitution to the next American winter is in all probability to doom me to the grave.[21]

He went on to plead his past record. "I am confident that the King will admit, when in his grace he shall recollect how often at His Majesty's call in this war, I have relinquished private duties and affections more imperative upon the heart than any we owe to existence." He doubted whether his return to America would improve the morale of the prisoners of war;

indeed, he thought it might well have the opposite effect, since they might deduce from it "that Government either thought it inexpedient to ratify the Convention of Saratoga or despaired of the ratification effectuating the redemption of that army." The troops would scarcely conceive it possible for the king to act so harshly as to send "an infirm, calumniated, unheard, complainant across the Atlantic merely to inspect the embarkation." [22]

Burgoyne was careful to point out that he was appealing against the king in council, and not against the king in person. It was not only his health, but also the vindication of his honor that required his presence in England. "Until that, by full and proper trial, is cleared to my Sovereign and to my country," he wrote, "I confess I should feel a removal from hence, though enforced by the term duty, the severest sentence of exile ever imposed. . . ." [23]

Burgoyne had now taken his stand, and *ipso facto* it would be taken to mean that he had thrown in his lot with the Opposition. As he explained in his letter to his constituents, "Though it bore the King's name, it was avowedly a Letter of the Cabinet, and there remained no longer a doubt in my mind that my ruin was a measure of state." [24] The only course left was open war with Germain. Barrington's reply was short and to the point. On June 27 he wrote to acknowledge Burgoyne's letter, emphasizing that it was the king's pleasure "that you return as soon as you can, without any risk of material injury to your health." [25] The fact that the matter was left open was probably due to the king's reluctance to apply too much pressure on a general who had formerly enjoyed his confidence, and for whose misfortunes he may still have had some sympathy.

Had Burgoyne remained quietly in Bath all might have been forgiven and forgotten. But this would have suited neither him nor Fox. Germain and the administration were to be hounded out of office, and in this endeavor they would soon be gaining influential supporters. Howe, tired of wrangling with Germain and weary of the war, handed over his command to Clinton and sailed for England on May 25, 1778. He and his brother had old scores to settle with Germain, as had Carleton, who arrived in London in the early summer and was cordially welcomed by the king. Carleton was less concerned to call on Germain, who wrote querulously to Knox: "I conclude he will do me the honour of reporting the state of his late Government [in Canada] before he has related all his grievances to his Majesty." [26]

Burgoyne spent the remainder of the year recovering his health and spirits at Bath, preparing his case against Germain, and paying court to a young singer, Susan Caulfield. He could afford to wait while the aggrieved Howe took up the cudgels against Germain. The government had failed to make Burgoyne the scapegoat for Saratoga, and most people thought him more sinned against than sinning. Germain therefore switched the attack to Howe, claiming he had botched the operation by failing to support Burgoyne as Germain had directed him to do.

Howe arrived in England in July and spent the rest of the year marshaling his supporters. Germain was in some difficulty preparing his attack, partly because the king sympathized with Howe, and partly because North wanted Admiral Lord Howe to join his ministry. It was not until February 17, 1779, that General Howe proposed a motion in Parliament requiring that all the correspondence that had passed between him and Germain from August 2, 1775, to May 16, 1778, be laid before the House. Although the motion was agreed to, no correspondence was produced, but on April 29 a committee of the whole House began an inquiry into Howe's conduct of the campaign. By clever parliamentary tactics Germain succeeded in quashing this inquiry before any damaging revelations were produced, but he made the great error of complaining when all was over that he had not been heard. He also commented that "he did not think that the Howe conduct had been quite right." [27] This angered Rigby, hitherto Germain's henchman, but also a close friend of Howe. He had avoided voting on the original motion for an inquiry, but he now rose to defend Howe's rights to an inquiry, on the grounds that Howe had been accused publicly by a member of the administration. He therefore proposed there should be an inquiry, and, to everyone's surprise, his motion was seconded by Lord North.

Howe's opportunity was also Burgoyne's, and he made better use of it than the slower-witted Howe. "Burgoyne thrust himself into the altercation with his usual self-sufficiency and ill-success," wrote Walpole.[28] Hansard tells a different story, claiming that "it [the inquiry] went uniformly to place the character of General Burgoyne in a very high point of view." [29] Burgoyne had been waiting nearly a year for this moment. He had prepared his brief with great care, and had selected his witnesses with similar attention. Better acquainted with parliamentary procedures than Howe, he delivered his speeches with considerable eloquence and skill. In his opening address, on May 20, he disputed Germain's contention that the orders drawn up for the expedition had left him with considerable latitude regarding their execution. He contrasted Germain's attitude with that of the Count of Lippe during the campaign in Portugal in 1762. At a critical moment in that campaign, Lippe had instructed Burgoyne to hold a certain pass, even if it meant that Burgoyne's troops would be cut off and forced to surrender. In such an eventuality, Burgoyne had no fear for his reputation, since Lippe would accept full responsibility for issuing the order. How different, Burgoyne implied, had been the behavior of Lord George Germain in not altogether dissimilar circumstances.

Burgoyne then proceeded to give a narrative of the campaign up to October 7, 1777. He told of the letters he had sent Howe, stressing the fact that his orders left him with no alternative but to force a junction with Howe. He paid tribute to the assistance he had received from General Carleton, but pointed out that the force provided fell far short of the numbers he had expected. He described his first conference with the Indians, emphasizing that their behavior during the initial stages of the campaign had given him no cause for concern. He protested that he had not taken with him an excessive number of artillery pieces, nor were they too heavy for the task required of them. They were required for use against blockhouses, for the arming of gunboats, and for the defense of the camp at Albany when the expedition arrived there. He had noted that Howe had made a similar requisition for artillery in one of his letters to the secretary of state.

He gave his reasons for continuing the advance from Skenesboro instead of returning to Ticonderoga, and dealt at some length with the Bennington foray. He explained why German troops were employed instead of British, and pointed out that the British detachment provided may have been small, but it consisted of picked men, commanded by Captain Fraser, "one of the most distinguished officers in his line of service that ever I met with." [30] It was regrettable to have to admit that his cautions were not observed, nor had the reinforcements advanced with the speed he had expected. The delay, if delay there was, in crossing the Hudson was due to the requirement to build up supplies. It was untrue that either General Fraser or General Phillips was opposed to crossing the Hudson, and the Hudson once crossed, the enemy was brought to battle at the earliest possible moment. He paid tribute to the gallantry of his troops during the action on September 19, and observed that this "ought not to lose its due applause, because it is said, their opponents were irregulars and militia." [31]

Burgoyne claimed a victory on September 19; only nightfall had prevented his troops from following up the advantage. Reports the next day showed that the enemy was strongly posted, while the British casualties had been heavy. Since no further action had followed until October 7, it might well be asked why did he not retreat if unable to follow up his victory? He explained the delay by the report he had received of Sir Henry Clinton's advance up the lower Hudson. He believed that he and Clinton operating jointly would be able to dislodge Gates; or, alternatively, that Gates would be compelled to divert part of his force to contain Clinton, thereby providing Burgoyne with the opportunity to storm the American entrenchments. There was also the state of his sick and wounded; this imposed delay until they were again fit for service. And, finally, there was the prospect that St. Leger might join him with reinforcements from Ticonderoga, after the abortive operation in the Mohawk valley.

When action was again joined on October 7, it was Arnold, Burgoyne claimed, who turned the scales against him. Had Gates had his way, he would have remained in his entrenchments, which Burgoyne would undoubtedly have stormed. It was disagreeable, but necessary, to pay tribute to the bravery and tenacity of the enemy. Few officers had battled against heavier odds than Lord Balcarres had done to withstand the attacks. Burgoyne promised to provide detailed evidence of the events of October 8, and argued that even as late as October 11 there was a possibility of turning the tables on the enemy. Information from a deserter had led to an American withdrawal; otherwise a general action would have developed, which Burgoyne was confident he would have won.

He disposed of the contention that the enemy's strength fell short of the numbers he had claimed, producing a return signed by General Gates, and claiming this would be supported by witnesses. Finally, he regretted his inability to produce as witnesses "a most confidential friend in Major General Phillips; zealous advocates, I trust, in Major General Riedesel and Brigadier Hamilton." [32] They were still in America with the convention army; regrettably, two other witnesses were dead—General Fraser and Colonel Acland, a former member of the House.

Burgoyne concluded his opening remarks by saying: "I trust my zeal, in promoting this enquiry, as I have done, will

[303]

be one mark of the sense I bear of the general character of this house; that however men may be biassed by political attachments upon common occasions, when the honour of an individual is committed to their hands, they will be guided by truth and justice. And the next inference I should wish to be drawn, from my earnestness for a public appeal, is this; that however others may impute errors to my conduct, I am myself conscious of the rectitude of my intentions." [33] It was an excellent appeal to the indulgence of the House of Commons, which has always been sensitive to the privileges and honor of its members. The next step would be to produce witnesses to testify to the accuracy of Burgoyne's account of his actions. They were not to fail him.

His witnesses were Lieutenant-General Sir Guy Carleton; the Earl of Balcarres; Captain John Money, Burgoyne's deputy quarter-master-general; the Earl of Harrington, of the 29th Regiment and supernumerary aide-de-camp; Major Gordon Forbes, of the 9th Regiment; Captain Thomas Bloomfield, of the Artillery; and Lieutenant-Colonel Robert Kingston. Carleton was the first to be called.

He agreed about the amount of artillery provided, regretted he had been unable to garrison Ticonderoga, and approved Burgoyne's decision to advance directly from Skenesboro. "I had no reason to disapprove of any part of his conduct while under my command," he replied to a questioner. He was recalled twice, and when asked whether Burgoyne had received positive orders to march to Albany, he replied: "The orders have been published I understand— Every gentleman in this House must be a judge of those orders whether they were positive or not." He was also asked whether in Burgoyne's situation he would have felt obliged to carry out his orders to the letter, or whether he would have felt at liberty to deviate from them. "I should certainly have thought myself bound to have obeyed them to the utmost of my power," he said, "but, to say as a military man, that in all cases possible, I must have gone on, is a very nice thing to say indeed. . . . Every man must decide for himself. What I should have done, I really don't know; the particular situation, and a man's own particular feelings, must determine the point. . . ." [34]

Carleton was cautious in his replies, but his evidence supported Burgoyne. He declined to criticize Howe and refused to say whether Burgoyne's army was strong enough for its task. In answer to a question about the employment of the Indians, he replied, "I don't recollect that I said anything about them." [35]

Lord Balcarres, who followed, was more partisan. He praised the soldierly qualities of the enemy and he denied that General Fraser had disapproved of the crossing of the Hudson. The Americans had "behaved with great obstinacy and courage" on September 19, but the British were the "masters of the field of battle"; only nightfall prevented a pursuit. He considered that Burgoyne had been right to withdraw after the battle on October 7, and he endorsed the decision to conclude a convention.

Balcarres praised Burgoyne, both in battle and after the surrender. "It appeared to me," he said, "that General Burgoyne always possessed himself in every situation of danger and difficulty, and, I may venture to say, it appeared so to the army." There had been no criticism of Burgoyne for returning ahead of his troops, and he added, "General Burgoyne, at all times, shared the dangers and afflictions of that army in common with every soldier; as such they looked on him as their friend, and certainly would have received him in person, or any accounts of him, with every mark of affection." [36]

Captain Money, and the others who followed, supported Balcarres' testimony. Bloomfield gave evidence on the employment of the artillery; Forbes described the situation as seen by an ordinary regimental officer; and Kingston described the negotiations leading up to the surrender. The witnesses and Burgoyne had between them built up a formidable case, as Burgoyne was to make clear when he came to review the evidence.

He attacked Germain for failing to support him and for refusing him a court-martial. He also hotly denied the report that he had schemed against Carleton in order to obtain command of the expedition. He defended his actions step by step from Ticonderoga to Saratoga and explained why he had returned to England. His reluctance to go back to America should not be understood as disobedience of the king's commands. It was not the king's wish that he should do so, but, rather, the king's ministers'. He must remain in England to defend his honor, and he reminded the committee that "he who obeys at the expense of fortune, comfort, health and life, is a soldier; he who obeys at the expense of honour is a slave." [37] He was the unfortunate victim of circumstances; the blame lay with Germain. It now remained for Parliament to exonerate Burgoyne completely.

Howe followed after Burgoyne. He, too, attacked Germain for incompetence and meddling. Germain acted independently of his colleagues, and he had approved the plan for Philadelphia. "Had I," said Howe, "adopted the plan of going up the Hudson's River, it would have been alleged that I had wasted the campaign . . . merely to ensure the progress of the northern army, which could have taken care of itself, provided that I made a diversion in its favour by drawing off to the southward the main army under General Washington." [38]

Howe's witnesses corroborated his evidence and concurred with him in deploring the continuance of the war. Whenever Germain attempted to intervene in the inquiry, his interventions were usually unfortunate and sometimes lamentable. Carleton left the committee in no doubt that he regarded Germain as the principal architect of the disaster. Barrington was so critical of North's and Germain's mismanagement of the debate that he wrote, "even their warmest and best friends supported them with great reluctance, and openly blamed their conduct." [39] Surely the government must resign, but North did nothing. Neither he nor Germain would answer questions, and although some ministers resigned, the government struggled on without them. After Spain's declaration of war had diverted attention, the inquiry petered out "without coming to a single Resolution on any part of the Business." [40]

Howe retired briefly from the public eye before resuming his military career in less demanding appointments than the American command. He had never quite lost the confidence of the king, despite the fact that he had undoubtedly lost America, and his progress up the military ladder was steady if not spectacular. He succeeded his brother as viscount in 1799 and died in 1814 at the age of eighty-five.

As for Burgoyne, he had come out of the inquiry with a better reputation than Howe and had soundly defeated Germain. But the king found his conduct hard to forgive. He may have pressed his attack too hard, but it is more likely that his open adherence to the Opposition was regarded as treachery. He would have to pay the penalty for his intransigeance. Charles Jenkinson, Barrington's successor as secretary-at-war, was directed to take the necessary action. On September 24, 1779, he wrote to Burgoyne: "I am commanded by the King to acquaint you that your not returning to America, and joining the troops prisoners under the Convention of Saratoga is considered as a neglect of duty and disobedience of orders transmitted to you by the Secretary-at-War in his letter of 5th June, 1778." [41]

Burgoyne was angry. "The time in which I am charged with neglect of duty has been employed to vindicate my own honour, the honour of the British troops and those of his Majesty's allies, under my late command," he replied, "from the most base and barbarous aspersions that ever were forged by malignity supported by power." How was it, he asked, that he could be refused a court-martial on the grounds that as a prisoner on parole he was not amenable to military law, and yet still be *ordered* to return to North America? The government's intention was to bury "my innocence and their guilt, in the prisons of the enemy, and by removing my person to the other side of the Atlantic Ocean, to remove the means of renewing Parliamentary proceedings which they have reason to dread." If the government was determined to refuse him a court-martial, then he would have no alternative but to resign his appointment on the American staff, his colonelcy of the Queen's Light Dragoons, and the governorship of Fort William. He wished only to retain his rank of lieutenant-general "to render me the more clearly amenable to a court martial hereafter, and enable me to fulfil my personal faith, should I be required by the enemy to do so." [42]

On the same day that he wrote to Jenkinson, October 9, Burgoyne also wrote to Germain, complaining of his treatment and appealing to the minister's personal honor. He expressed concern over the delay in ratifying the convention, and reminded Germain, "There are many accounts to settle between your Lordship and me before the tribunal of the world; I give you this notice of one particularly intended; I am persuaded you will not willingly conspire to remove a man who thinks you have injured him; you will not willingly decline to face an enquiry into your duty to the State." [43]

Germain did not deign to reply. Jenkinson wrote instead, on October 15:

Having laid your letter before the King, I am commanded to acquaint you, that for the reasons submitted to his Majesty by the Board of Officers, in their report, dated May 23, 1778 (which reasons subsist in the same force now as they did at that time) his Majesty does not think it proper that any part of your conduct should be brought before a military tribunal, so long as you shall continue engaged to re-deliver yourself into the power of Congress upon their command and due notice being given by them. Nor does his Majesty think proper, in consequence of the representations contained in your said letter, to restore you, circumstanced as you are, to a capacity of service. Neither of these requests can therefore be granted.[44]

He went on to say that, in the king's view, Burgoyne's letter was a clear indication of his disobedience to a royal command. The resignation of his various appointments would therefore be accepted. He would, however, be permitted to retain his rank for the reasons already given.

Burgoyne wrote back, on October 17, denying that he had disobeyed the king's command and once more asking for a court-martial. Five days later Jenkinson replied curtly: "I have the honour to acknowledge the receipt of your letter . . . and to acquaint you that I took the first opportunity of laying it before the King." [45]

That was to be the end of Burgoyne so far as the government was concerned. He had failed in America but had then refused to go quietly. He had joined the Opposition, disobeyed the king, and made himself a popular hero in the eyes of all those who were disaffected and troublesome. But the government had prevailed. Lord North was still prime minister, Germain remained in office, and the war dragged drearily on. A campaign that might have succeeded had failed because of somebody's incompetence. A scapegoat had to be found, and if it had to be Lieutenant-General John Burgoyne, the more was the pity.

Burgoyne believed that his conduct had been vindicated, but at the cost of halving his income and virtually eliminating his prospects for future military employment. It can be argued that Burgoyne, his task in England accomplished, should now have returned to his captive army, but there is nothing to suggest that he shared this view. He may have considered he could do more to secure the release of the convention army by remaining in England than by surrendering his parole. Whatever his reasons, the one thing certain is that his former soldiers did not feel bitter about his nonreturn. They may have felt that "Gentleman Johnny" at large held out more hope for them than "Gentleman Johnny" confined.

When *A State of the Expedition from Canada as laid before the House of Commons* was published in January, 1780, Burgoyne dedicated it to Major-General Phillips and his officers. He also told the story of his victimization in a letter to "the Gentlemen, Clergy, and other Voters of the Town of Preston," complaining bitterly of the "etiquette" that had been invented to prevent his presenting his case in person to the king. Although both publications contain, as might be expected, a fair measure of special pleading, they nevertheless provide a favorable impression of Burgoyne, both as a man and as a soldier. At least he did not attempt to gloss over the heavy responsibility of high command, or the confusion and cross-purposes inseparable from war.

Part Three

Life Still Had
Much to Offer

"*With these celestial wisdom
calms the mind,
And makes the happiness
she does not find.*"

—Samuel Johnson, *Vanity
of Human Wishes*

Chapter 23

Politician and Playwright

No MEMBER of the "Triumvirate" had added to his reputation in North America, but Burgoyne, unlike Howe and Clinton, was not content to slip quietly into obscurity. He continued to be an active politician and still had military ambitions, although he realized that by identifying himself with the Opposition he had seriously compromised his chances. He was also able to indulge his interest in the theater, by writing plays as well as attending them. He went out much in London society, accompanied by Susan Caulfield. Although he never married her, she bore him two sons and two daughters.

There was little he could do until the vexed problem of his being a prisoner of war on parole could be resolved. General Washington had informed Congress that Burgoyne's rank made him difficult to exchange. Matters might have rested there but for the fact that in August, 1780, the British captured Henry Laurens, on his way across the Atlantic to negotiate a treaty with the Dutch. They had thrown him into the Tower of London, which had so infuriated the Americans that in April, 1781, Thomas Bee and Thomas McKean moved in Congress for Burgoyne's surrender of his parole. Edmund Burke, among others, took up Burgoyne's case, and he wrote to Benjamin Franklin in Paris urging Burgoyne's release and citing his love for "generosity and humanity." After a good deal of haggling, it was agreed that Burgoyne should be exchanged in return for more than 1,000 Americans who were prisoners in British hands, and this Burke described as "taking a quantity of silver in exchange for gold." [1]

Burgoyne was now a free man. He could go where he was sent, always provided that it was not to North America. The fall of Lord North's ill-fated administration in March, 1782, and its supersession by a government headed by Lord Rockingham, which included Burgoyne's friends Fox and Burke, resulted in his selection to command the army in Ireland. The appointment carried with it membership of the privy council of Ireland. This was not Burgoyne's own preference. He had hoped for the semipolitical lieutenant-generalship of the Ordnance, with plenty of pickings from contracts, but that went to General Howe. Burgoyne was sent to Dublin instead.

Ireland was, as usual, in a state of turmoil, and Dublin was far from the gossip of Westminster. Burgoyne was unhappy as commander-in-chief, although Susan joined him there after the birth of their first child in the late summer of 1782.* Lord Temple, who became lord lieutenant of Ireland not long after Burgoyne's arrival in Dublin, was anxious to appoint his own nominee as commander-in-chief, and therefore did nothing to hinder Burgoyne's obvious desire to resign the appointment. It was two years before Burgoyne did so, mainly because his political friends, Edmund Burke among them, did their best

---

* John Fox Burgoyne, named after Charles James Fox, entered the army at the age of fifteen and died a field-marshal and a baronet. He was Pakenham's chief engineer at New Orleans in 1814, chief famine commissioner during the disastrous Irish "Potato Famine," and chief engineer to General Lord Raglan during the Crimean War. He is commemorated by a statue in London, which is often mistaken for his father's, a better but less distinguished soldier. The field-marshal's only son, a captain in the Royal Navy who won the Victoria Cross in the Crimea, lost his life when the experimental ironclad H.M.S. *Captain* turned turtle in the Bay of Biscay in 1870.

to persuade him to remain in Ireland. But by the end of 1783 his mind was made up, and on January 18, 1784, he resigned his appointment, thereby terminating his active career in the army. He gave as his reason the fact that his political opinions were incompatible with the holding of an appointment that was as much political as military—in other words, he was out of sympathy with the current administration—but it is quite clear that his real feeling was that he was out on a limb at a time of great change on the British political scene.

His friends may not have succeeded in persuading him to stay in Ireland, but they had done their best for him in other ways. In June, 1782, he was given the colonelcy of the 4th (King's Own) Regiment, which was as good as a pension at that time, and Fox only just failed to add to this the colonelcy of the 8th Dragoons. He had omitted to establish that the existing colonel was still alive, and he apologized profusely for his mistake. However, Burgoyne, whose style of life was expensive, was hard pressed for money when he returned from Dublin and was forced to turn to an old friend, Nathaniel Day, for the temporary loan of £500. Burgoyne offered to secure this loan not only by a bond, but also by lodging with Day the diamond he had been given by the King of Portugal, "valued upon occasions when such large jewels are in demand at about £1000. . . ."[2]

Day was an old comrade from the 16th Light Dragoons who had acquired a considerable fortune in Canada as commissary-general. He sent Burgoyne the £500, and with the money a letter. "My dear Sir, The continuance of your health gives me infinite pleasure, and being able to accommodate you with the sum you mention makes me truly happy; but it must be accepted *without* that which you have mentioned. . . ."[3] Day had responded handsomely to the request of his former commanding officer, and Burgoyne had recourse to him again when his expenditure exceeded his income. Burgoyne responded by leaving Day £2,000 in his will.

Seventeen-eighty-four was an election year, and Burgoyne had to spend liberally to retain his seat at Preston. His opponent was a Mr. Elton, who was so unwise as to play a practical joke on the general. The two men were staying at the same inn, and Elton waylaid Burgoyne's servant, placed his gold watch on a tray, and told the servant to take it to Burgoyne and ask him "if he could tell the time of day." Burgoyne responded by placing a pair of pistols on the tray beside the watch and then sought out Elton, who was in the inn parlor with his friends. Burgoyne asked who owned the watch, but Elton thought it wiser not to reply; whereupon Burgoyne said that since no one claimed the watch, he was appropriating it. Turning to his servant, he told him, "Take this watch and fob it in remembrance of the Swan Inn at Bolton." [4] Elton lost both his watch and the election.

Returned to Parliament with a handsome majority, Burgoyne became an assiduous attender of the House of Commons. He spoke often, usually on foreign affairs, defense, and India, and although inclined to be prosy, he was heard with respect. He was one of the committee selected by the House to frame the charges for the impeachment of Warren Hastings in 1788, but he played little part in the proceedings that followed. Fanny Burney attended the opening day of the trial in Westminster Hall with her brother James, a captain in the Royal Navy who had traveled to America in the same ship as Burgoyne, and she has recorded:

When the Managers were all arranged, one from among them whom I knew not came up into the seats of the House of Commons and said, "Captain Burney, I am very glad to see you." "How do you do, Sir," answered James, "here I am come to see the fine show." Upon this the attacker turned short upon his heel and abruptly walked away. I inquired who he was: "General Burgoyne," James told me. "A Manager!" cried I, "and one of the chargers! and you treat the business of the Hall with such contempt to his face!" James laughed heartily at his own uncourtly address but would not repent, though he acknowledged he saw the offence his slight, and slighting speech, had given.[5]

Burgoyne's interest in military affairs never flagged, and his contributions to defense debates in the House of Commons were sensible and sometimes radical. He continued to be a military reformer, determined to improve the lot of the common soldier and junior officer. He found it hard to accept the fact that he could no longer expect to play an active part as a soldier. In 1789 war with Spain seemed likely, and he wrote to the prime minister to offer his services. "I intend, Sir, to take an early opportunity to make to the King in person a humble tender of service in the ensuing war," he told Pitt. He went on to say that he had held "great and important commands" and had known "the vicissitudes of military life in their extremes." He explained his conduct, both in Parliament and in the Army, and reminded Pitt: "I had the honour, Sir, to receive from your father many obligations. To him I was indebted for my Regiment of Dragoons; to him I was indebted for a more distinguished honour, his applause for my services at the head of it." He would not have been John Burgoyne if he had not made great play of his devotion to principle, which had on occasion led him to oppose Pitt in Parliament, but he trusted this would not be held against him. "I hope then it will not be construed a professional rant, or appear in any degree a forced sentiment in an old soldier to say that should his period in the destination of Providence be near, he would rather meet it in the duties of the field than amidst the sorrows and afflictions of the sick bed." [6] Fortunately, the threat of war passed, and Pitt was thereby excused from the disagreeable task of declining the services of the elderly Burgoyne.

Burgoyne had earlier been a member of a commission under the Duke of Richmond to survey the national defenses. Invasion by France was much in men's minds, and the commission was to advise on the best way to defeat it. This it did, with no obvious sense of urgency: "When it visited Portsmouth it sat from six A.M. to four P.M., had a three-hours dinner, and then sat again from seven to ten." [7] Lord Cornwallis found the proceedings intolerably tedious and formed a poor opinion of Burgoyne, whom he described as both a blockhead and a sycophant. But Burgoyne had more sense than the majority of his colleagues, who recommended that large sums of money should be expended in fortifying the naval dockyards. Burgoyne, Lord Percy, and John Jervis (later Earl St. Vincent) dissented from the majority view. They claimed that the first defense of the dockyards was the fleet, and they found it inconceivable that the fleet would be elsewhere when invasion threatened. In the debate that followed in Parliament, Burgoyne complained of the Duke of Richmond's "rage for fortification." [8] The commission's recommendations were not accepted.

The well-being of the army was Burgoyne's chief concern. He warmly supported the proposal that there should be a commander-in-chief, arguing that one of his principal duties would be "to bring military merit to the foot of the throne and to draw it forth from places where ministers never looked for it—the field of actual service." [9] On March 12, 1792, he told the House of Commons that the subaltern's stipend was "barely adequate to his situation at its first allotment, [and] was rendered so much worse by the increase of price in every article of life, that it was impossible for a gentleman to subsist on it. . . ." [10] In the same debate he criticized the delay in settling officers' accounts, and defended the honesty and sense of duty of the great majority of officers.

When it was proposed in 1791 to increase the strength of the army by raising several independent companies, Burgoyne was opposed; he said the more sensible course would be to increase the strength of existing units. "If there was to be no Commander-in-Chief, there was yet a Board of War," he said, "a most respectable board of General Officers, not one of whom, excepting the unworthy individual then speaking, was

not qualified to give sound and sufficient opinion in the greatest points of the military establishment. The Board was frequently summoned; it was frequently employed to consider
of hats and halberts, and other very necessary but small objects of service; but it could not pass without observation that
when a consideration of the magnitude of a levy of fifteen
thousand men was in question, a Board of War-Office clerks
seemed to have been thought the more proper Council." [11]
The last speech he made in Parliament was devoted to the
army. He asked for an increase in the pay of junior officers
and "the private men," and, as so often before, he was sternly
critical of the War Office's penny-pinching policies. Pitt's
economy measures had reduced both the navy and the army
to a parlous state, leading the adjutant-general to comment:
"The addition of a shilling a day to the subaltern's pay will,
I fear, seem too considerable for the Government to grant,
but something must be done for privates and subalterns." [12]
Burgoyne refused to accept such a defeatist attitude, and
spoke eloquently about the hardships suffered by the junior
ranks. His oratory sufficiently impressed the government for
it to take steps to improve the lot of the soldiers, but it continued to ignore the plight of junior officers. Burgoyne went
to his grave without accomplishing anything on their behalf,
but it was not for want of trying.

It is not unusual for generals to write their memoirs or to
contribute their views on strategy. It is, however, uncommon,
if not unique, for a general to acquire fame as a playwright.
This happened to be the case with John Burgoyne after his
retirement from the army. His interest in the theater had begun long before, when he was a young man-about-town in
London, and it grew with the years until it became almost his
ruling passion. He was a regular attender at the Green Room
of the Drury Lane Theatre and numbered among his acquaintances most of the leading actors and actresses of the
day. It is hardly surprising, therefore, that he should have

toyed with the idea of writing plays, particularly in view of the fact that his nephew, the twelfth Earl of Derby, was a patron of the drama and a regular producer of amateur theatricals at his country seat in Lancashire. But it was not until 1774 that Burgoyne's first play was produced in London.

Maid of the Oaks, as it was called, owed its origins to a masque written and produced by Burgoyne to celebrate the nuptials of his young nephew, then Lord Stanley, and Lady Betty Hamilton, daughter of Lady Charlotte Burgoyne's friend the Duchess of Argyll. Walpole wrote on June 8, 1774, to tell Sir Horace Mann: "This month Lord Stanley marries Lady Betty Hamilton. He gives her a most splendid entertainment tomorrow at his villa in Surrey and calls it a *fête champêtre*. It will cost £5,000. Everybody is to go in masquerade but not in mask. He has bought all the orange-trees around London, and the haycocks, I suppose, are to be made of straw-coloured satin." [13]

Burgoyne spared neither effort nor expense to make the fête a success. He called in Robert Adam to design a splendid temporary ballroom in the garden of the Derby mansion near Epsom, and consulted with David Garrick on the writing of the masque. Lord Stanley went as Rubens and Lady Betty as Rubens' wife. There was "an orangerie, a concealed band of music, swains in fancy dress playing nine pins, shepherdesses swinging, with shrieks of apprehension and tempestuous petticoats . . . archery, dancing, and nymphs kicking at a *tambour de basque* suspended from a tree." [14] The theme was rustic simplicity amid lavish profusion, and Burgoyne was the master of ceremonies. "Ye *fête* appeared to him as if Colonel Burgoyne had planned it and Lord Stanley paid for it," commented George Selwyn. [15]

Even the staid *Gentleman's Magazine* could not pass it by without notice. "Those who may think the repitition of this rural festival beneath the notice of a periodical work intended to record the principal transactions of the times, will, perhaps, be of another opinion, when they reflect that it is from the

gravest authors we learn the diversions of the ancients." [16]
There was something for everyone, including a Druid (Captain Pigott) who made a speech about "The Oaks," and minuets composed especially for the occasion by the Earl of Kelly. There were fireworks, "Tables spread with the most costly dainties," and dancing went on all through the night for five successive nights. "Nothing but Betty cd have stood it all," wrote the mother of the bride-to-be.[17] Burgoyne was "the principal manager and conductor . . . for whose skill and abilities on the occasion the greatest compliments are due . . ." reported the *Gentleman's Magazine*.[18]

The wedding took place on June 23, and Burgoyne was included in the small family party that attended the ceremony. Despite its magnificent beginning, the marriage turned out to be a failure. After startling society with the splendor and extravagance of their entertainments, the young couple drifted apart, the countess attaching herself to the Duke of Dorset, nephew of Lord George Germain, who refused to marry her. The young earl consoled himself by paying court to Miss Elizabeth Farren, a well-known actress, who eventually married him after the countess's death in 1797.

The enthusiastic reception that greeted the *fête champêtre* gave Burgoyne the idea of adapting it for the London stage. After doing this he sent it to Garrick for his opinion, emphasizing his desire for anonymity and saying he would send a servant to collect it if Garrick turned it down. Garrick must have found some virtue in the script, because the preface to the 1774 edition of the *Maid of the Oaks* records: "Mr Garrick, after perusing the outlines of the two original acts, thought he discovered in the writer some talents for the higher species of comedy, and encouraged him to extend his play [to five acts]." [19] Garrick continued to preserve Burgoyne's anonymity when he wrote on September 26, 1774, to Frances Abington, one of the leading actresses of her day:

I shall write to the Author of the piece tomorrow night, which I read to you—I have yet obey'd but half his command, as he

wrote the character of *Lady Bab* for your Ladyship, I must beg
of you to speak your thoughts upon that—which after I had read
it to you I promis'd to let him know your sentiments—I could
wish if you say anything to me of our stage business you would
send it separately from your opinion of the *Maid of the Oaks*
and Lady Bab—with your leave I would wish to inclose what you
say of the last to the Author.[20]

With Garrick to help him, Burgoyne revised both plot and
dialogue, and the play was put on at the Drury Lane Theatre
on November 5, 1774. It had a modest success, due largely to
Frances Abington in the part of Lady Bab Lardoon. Garrick
did not like her, describing her as "the worst of bad women,"
but Lady Bab suited her to perfection. The plot was flimsy,
being the story of a woman-about-town outwitting the gentlemen intent on her virtue, but there were one or two good
songs,* and a masquerade to round off the performance. The
Maid of the Oaks was given a respectable reception, and
Frances Abington's performance was widely acclaimed. Walpole was less impressed, writing on November 12: "There is a
new puppet-show at Drury Lane, as fine as scenes can make
it, called the *Maid of the Oaks*, and as dull as the author could
not help making it." [21] But Walpole was in a minority, and
Burgoyne had no reason to be disappointed with the reception
of his first play. It soon became known that he was the author.
His reputation as a playwright then followed him to Boston,
where he enlivened the tedium of the beleaguered garrison by
writing and producing a farce, *The Blockade of Boston*.

Burgoyne did not return to playwriting until 1780, explaining that he did so then in order "to relax a mind which had
been engaged in more intense application." [22] He unasham-
edly plagiarized the plot of a play by Sylvain, called *Mar-*

* A popular song of the day, "The World Turned Upside Down," is
reputed to have been first performed in the *Maid of the Oaks*, but no
justification has been found for this. It was the tune played by British bands
when the garrison marched out to surrender at Yorktown on October 19,
1781.

montel, and wrote a comic opera entitled *The Lord of the Manor*. Sheridan, then at the height of his fame as the author of *The School for Scandal* and as manager of the Drury Lane Theatre, collaborated with Burgoyne in the writing of *The Lord of the Manor* and produced it at the Drury Lane on December 27, 1780. Once again it was produced anonymously, but as soon as success was assured Burgoyne admitted authorship. He also paid Sheridan a neat compliment in the preface of the play: "As an author he is above my encomium; as a friend it is my pride to think we are exactly upon a level." [23]

The theme was life in the army, and the principal character, Moll Flagon, was played by a man. Mr. Jackson of Exeter composed the music, and Burgoyne himself provided some sickly sentimental lyrics. The libretto is difficult to read today, partly on account of the heavy humor and irritating dialogue, and partly because the jokes, being topical, have entirely lost their point. When *The Lord of the Manor* was revived in 1812 a critic wrote: "The plot is very meagre and unnatural, and the manner of the characters have ceased to exist. The Fop of 30 years ago is no longer remembered. The music however is extremely beautiful. . . ."

Two London productions gave Burgoyne something of a reputation as a playwright. He had this in mind when he paid his customary annual visit to the Derbys' Lancashire seat at Knowsley in 1784. There he embarked upon the writing of his third play, and the result was *The Heiress*, dedicated to the Earl of Derby in a letter dated February 1, 1786:

My Dear Lord, Our connection and friendship, as well as the partiality I know you will entertain in favour of any attempt at regulated Drama, mark you as the person, to whom, with most propriety and inclination, I can inscribe the Comedy of *The Heiress*. It also comes to your Lordship's hand with a secondary claim to your acceptance, as owing its existence to the leisure and tranquility I enjoyed during the last two summers at Knowsley.

I long intended, as your Lordship can witness, to keep the name of the author concealed. After the success with which the Play has been honoured, I must expect that the change of my design will be imputed to vanity. I shall submit, without murmuring, to that belief, if I may obtain equal credit for the sincerity of another pride which this discovery gratifies—that of testifying in the most public manner, the respect and affection with which I have the honour to be, My Dear Lord, Your most obedient, and most humble servant.[24]

Burgoyne offered *The Heiress* to Sheridan, who agreed to produce it at the Drury Lane. "It is very privately reported in Drury Lane that *The Heiress* will soon make its appearance, and it is whispered that General Burgoyne is the author of it . . ." reported one newspaper on November 25, 1785.[25] Elizabeth Farren was to be the leading lady, and the opening night had to be postponed because of her illness. *The Heiress* finally appeared on January 14, 1786, taking London by storm and having the surprisingly long run, for those days, of thirty performances. "*The Heiress* & General Burgoyne, the author, may rejoice," was one comment; "if he proceeds as he has done, advancing as much beyond his *Lord of the Manor* as that was beyond his *Maid of the Oaks* he will rejoice not without good reason." [26]

Horace Walpole described *The Heiress* as "the genteelest comedy in the English language." He went to see it twice in one day and thought it better than any play he had seen since the *Provoked Husband*. "Burgoyne's battles and speeches will be forgotten," he wrote, "but his delightful comedy of *The Heiress* still continues the delight of the stage and one of the most pleasing domestic compositions." [27] One newspaper compared *The Heiress* favorably with *The School for Scandal* and Cibber's *Careless Husband* as "the only genteel comedies the English stage can boast of." [28] The play ran through ten editions during its first year of publication, was translated into French and German, and was performed in both France and Germany.

The plot was thin, being dependent on a series of contrived misunderstandings, but the dialogue was considered to be beautifully written, the wit elegant, and happily there were "no unchaste allusions." Some considered the play to be far too long, but all praised Elizabeth Farren as Lady Gayville and Thomas King as Sir Clement Flint. The last lines of the play, spoken by King, contain much of Burgoyne's philosophy of life:

"If you think me a convert, you are mistaken: I have ever believed self to be the predominant principle of the human mind; my heart, at this instant, confirms the doctrine. There's my problem for yours, my dear Emily, and may all who hear me, agree in this solution: To reward the deserving, and make those we love happy, is self interest in the extreme." [29]

Burgoyne enjoyed his triumph. There was even talk that he would out-Sheridan Sheridan:

> Burgoyne, perhaps, unchill'd by creeping age,
> May yet arise and vindicate the stage;
> The reign of nature and of sense restore,
> and be whatever Terence was before.[30]

However, it was not to be. He was aging fast, and there was no time left for him to become a great playwright. He had to be content with his success with *The Heiress*, which had brought him more fame than money. He received £200 for the play when it was published. This absence of financial reward did not prevent him from trying again, and he next adapted an opera by André Grétry for the English stage. It was called *Richard Coeur de Lion*, and the original libretto had been written by Sedaine. Burgoyne's version, described as "A historical Romance in 3 Acts," was produced at the Drury Lane Theatre on October 24, 1786. It made little impression and is chiefly interesting for the fact that a Mr. Caulfield had a part in it, though it has not proved possible to identify him positively with the Susan Caulfield with whom Burgoyne was living.

[325]

It was fortunate for Burgoyne's reputation as a playwright that death overtook him before he was able to complete his most ambitious venture for the stage. This was the production of a modern version of *As You Like It*, turning Shakespeare into an opera, and substituting Georgian English for Tudor. A few of the lyrics were written before the project was abandoned. It is most unlikely that Burgoyne could ever have improved on *The Heiress*, and it is on that play that his reputation as a playwright will always depend.

Epilogue

JOHN BURGOYNE died on August 4, 1792, soon after returning home from attending the play at the Little Theatre in the Haymarket. He was crippled by gout and was aged sixty-nine. The end when it came was swift, and Susan Caulfield was at his bedside. The *Gentleman's Magazine* recorded:

Died on the 4th of August, at his house in Hertford Street, Mayfair, the Right Honourable John Burgoyne, a Privy Councillor, Lieutenant-General in the army, Colonel of the 4th Regiment of Foot, M.P. for Preston, and author of the much celebrated comedy entitled *The Heiress*. The regret for his death will be extended and lasting. He has died richer in esteem than in money; in the saving or securing of that he had no talent. Of all the gay, the witty, and the fashionable, who eagerly sought his acquaintance, and whose minds were impressed by the elegance of his conversation, and the variety of his talents, very few were present to drop the tear over departed genius. One coach only attended with four gentlemen; a lady was likewise present, whose convulsive agitation showed her to have that within which passeth show.[1]

The unostentatious funeral was by Burgoyne's own request. The agitated lady was, of course, Susan Caulfield, who had lived with him for twelve years and who had borne him four children without being made his wife. Her origins are obscure; she may have been a singer or dancer. She is reputed to have been a friend of Elizabeth Farren, who became countess of Derby five years after Burgoyne's death. Burgoyne referred to Susan as "Dearest Sue" and obviously loved her, but not enough to allow her to take the place of the much-lamented Lady Charlotte. After the will had been read, and Burgoyne's last bequests had been attended to by Lord Derby, he assumed the responsibility for bringing up his uncle's children, and Susan Caulfield disappears into oblivion.

Burgoyne drew up his will, as he had lived his life, in the grand style. He did this in Dublin on September 18, 1783, naming as his executors Major-General Richard Philipson, the Reverend Geoffrey Hornby, and David Stephenson, then residing with Lord Derby. He wished to be buried as near as possible to Lady Charlotte in the Westminster Abbey cloisters. Ten Hertford Street was to be sold and the mortgage of £3,000 owing to General Philipson redeemed. Any money remaining would go to Susan and their son. Hornby was to examine all Burgoyne's papers and "destroy or dispose of [them] in whole or in part." A niece, Mrs. Horton, was to have the portraits by Ramsay of Lady Charlotte and himself. Another niece, Mrs. Warburton, was to receive the miniature of Lady Charlotte, "always about his person," and also his "repeating watch and seals. . . ." There were various other bequests, notably two volumes of the *Antiquities of Herculaneum* to his cousin Major-General Sir John Burgoyne, and a horse to his aide-de-camp. Everything else, apart from the diamond given him by the king of Portugal, was to be sold by auction. Lord Derby was to have the diamond, and Mr. Day, who had come to Burgoyne's financial rescue more than once, was to receive £2,000.

The will, as was customary at that time, contained a fair measure of sententious platitudes. "During a life too frequently blemished by the indulgence of one predominant passion, it has been a comfort to me," said Burgoyne, "to hope that my sensualities have never injured, nor interrupted the peace, of others." [2] Susan Caulfield, gazing into an uncertain future for herself and her children, may well have held other views. The general, who had for so long been noted for his enjoyment of ceremony, made a special point in enjoining that his funeral should be as simple as possible: the hearse bearing his body to the Abbey should be drawn by "four horses only, and attended by one coach only with the same number of horses, for the conveyance of my manservants out of livery and my housekeeper, and no attendants on horseback except my footman, George Gosling, or should he not be in my service, the footman who shall have been longest in my service at the time of my decease." [3] His funeral was, above all, to be private.

In his will, proved on August 22, 1792, Burgoyne had left to Susan, for herself and the education of their son John, the sum of £4,000. A codicil, dated June 1, 1788, had added Maria, Caroline, and Edward, all "having equal claims to his care and protection." But when the estate was examined, and after the various creditors had made their claims, it was clear that John Burgoyne had died, as he had lived for most of his life, in debt. He was insolvent.

He was buried, as he had requested, in the North Cloister of the great Abbey, at less expense than Lady Charlotte's interment, and they engraved on the coffin plate, "the Rt Hon John Burgoyne, Lieutenant-General of His Majesty's Forces, Colonel of 4th Regiment of Foot, and one of His Majesty's most honourable Privy Council of the Kingdom of Ireland." [4]

John Burgoyne was a man of many talents who has on the whole been treated harshly by history. It has been too easily accepted that by his surrender at Saratoga he lost the war in North America, and everything else about him has been overshadowed by this climactic fact. But he came very close to defeating Gates. Indeed, he would probably have

Epilogue

done so but for the fortuitous intervention by Benedict
Arnold at the critical moment; and if he had conquered, the
course of history might well have been changed. With Burgoyne in control of Albany, could Howe have lingered in
Philadelphia; or could Washington have continued to refuse
a major battle? Burgoyne was well aware of the risk he was
running when he chose to cross the Hudson and try his luck
against Gates; and the odds were not so heavily weighted
against him as may seem to be the case when one looks at the
situation with the benefit of hindsight. There has never been a
general worth his salt who was not prepared to take a calculated risk. Burgoyne risked all because he hoped more
from Howe and Clinton than either of them was prepared to
venture on his behalf; because of this the expedition from
Canada turned out to be a failure. It also proved to be the
turning point of the war in North America, but no one could
have known this at the time.

Few generals' reputations survive defeat. Carlyle, in his life
of Frederick the Great, wrote that "the Burgoyne who be-
gins in this pretty way at Valencia d'Alcantara, is the same
who ended so dismally at Saratoga within twenty years.
Perhaps with other war offices, and training himself in something suitabler than parliamentary eloquence, he might have
become a kind of general, and ended far otherwise than he
did." [5] Lord Anglesey, writing a century after Carlyle, says
in his *History of the British Cavalry:* "In command of a
cavalry regiment he was excellent. As a general he was a
failure." [6] But there have been other verdicts, no less authoritative than those quoted above. General J. F. C. Fuller
has recorded, "though as a general Burgoyne does not stand
in the front rank, few British overseas expeditions have been
commanded by an abler man." [7] And in Sir John Fortescue's
opinion it seemed "that no more honourable attempt of
British officers and men to achieve the impossible is on
record." [8]

Macaulay described Burgoyne as "a man of wit, fashion

and honour, an agreeable dramatic writer, an officer whose courage was never questioned, and whose skill was at that time [1773] highly esteemed." [9] Lord Mahon wrote of him: "In war his bravery was never questioned, and in civil life he was gifted with many fine accomplishments; a fluent speaker in Parliament and an agreeable writer of plays." [10] These are high tributes, and the man who receives them must be something out of the ordinary. John Burgoyne was an unusual man—talented, ambitious, brave, and gifted with both political and strategic insight. He was also a military reformer, far in advance of his times in his care for his troops. They were well aware of his consideration and repaid him by their steady loyalty and affection in the bad times as well as in the good. The nickname they gave him—"Gentleman Johnny"—speaks volumes, and sums up their feelings for him; as do some lines from the poem *Marmion* by Sir Walter Scott:

> They love a captain to obey,
> Boisterous as March, yet fresh as May;
> With open hand and brow as free,
> Lover of wine and minstrelsy;
> Ever the first to scale a tower,
> As venturous in a lady's bower . . .

This is how John Burgoyne would best wish to be remembered, but there is a reverse side to the coin. He was an extremely ambitious man, bent on military glory, who had fallen behind in the race because of his voluntary exile at a critical stage in his army career. He was fully prepared to intrigue for preferment and freely used his "interest" to obtain the places he coveted. In Parliament he was both pompous and prolix, and his persecution of Clive showed that he could at times be vindictive. As a gambler and as a womanizer he was no better and no worse than most men of his class and times, and his affair with the commissary's wife during the march to Saratoga has been blown up out of all proportion. It is much harder to forgive his treatment of

Susan Caulfield. It will never be proved whether or not he intrigued with Germain to obtain the Canada command from Carleton in the winter of 1776, although he stoutly denied that he had ever done so; and there must always be mixed feelings regarding his return to England in 1778 in order to clear his name, thereby abandoning to their fate the soldiers he had led into captivity. The least he could have done was to return to them once his object had been accomplished.

As a general he was unlucky rather than incompetent. He possessed imagination, resolution, and personal magnetism. He had the ability to get the best out of his troops and he was not afraid of making difficult decisions. It is not easy to decide whether the decisions he made were determined by a consideration of the military factors alone, or whether they were influenced by his overweening ambition and the desire for glory; probably a bit of both. His justification for taking them is that he came very close to succeeding in his aim. This would almost certainly have been held to his credit by the king and his ministers had he not chosen to justify his actions in public debate, and Shaw was correct when he wrote, in *The Devil's Disciple:* "Burgoyne's surrender at Saratoga made him that occasionally necessary part of our British system, a scapegoat."

For this, Burgoyne was, at least in part, himself to blame.

Order of Battle— The Expedition from Canada—1777

Commander-in-Chief: Lieutenant-General John Burgoyne
Adjutant-General: Lieutenant-Colonel Robert Kingston
Deputy Quarter-Master-General: Captain John Money

ADVANCE CORPS

Brigadier-General Simon Fraser
Grenadier Battalion: Major John Acland, 20th Regiment
Light Battalion: Major the Earl of Balcarres, 53rd Regiment
24th Regiment: Major Robert Grant
Marksmen: Captain Alexander Fraser

RIGHT DIVISION

Major-General William Phillips

First Brigade
Brigadier-General James Hamilton
20th Regiment: Lieutenant-Colonel John Lind
21st Regiment: Major George Forster
62nd Regiment: Lieutenant-Colonel John Anstruther

Second Brigade
Brigadier-General Henry Powell
9th Regiment: Lieutenant-Colonel John Hill
47th Regiment: Lieutenant-Colonel Nicholas Sutherland
53rd Regiment: Major William Hughes

Appendix 1

LEFT DIVISION

Major-General Baron Friedrich von Riedesel

First Brigade

Brigadier-General Johann Specht
Regiment von Rhetz (Brunswick): Lieutenant-Colonel Johann von Ehrenkrook
Regiment von Specht (Brunswick): Major Carl von Ehrenkrook
Regiment von Riedesel (Brunswick): Lieutenant-Colonel Ernst von Spaeth

Second Brigade

Brigadier-General W. R. von Gall
Regiment Prinz Friederich (Brunswick): Lieutenant-Colonel Christian Praetorius
Regiment Erb-Prinz (Hesse-Hanau)

Reserve

Lieutenant-Colonel von Breymann
Grenadier Battalion: Lieutenant-Colonel Heinrich von Breymann
Light Battalion: Major Ferdinand von Bärner
Jäger Company (Brunswick): Captain von Geyso
Dragoon Regiment von Ludwig (Brunswick): Lieutenant-Colonel Friederich Baum

ARTILLERY

Major Griffith Williams
Four Companies Royal Artillery
Detachment Royal Irish Artillery
Detachment 33rd Regiment
One Company Hesse-Hanau Artillery: Captain Georg Pausch

ENGINEERS

Lieutenant William Twiss

NAVAL DETACHMENT

Lieutenant John Schank, R.N.

Appendix 2

Articles of Convention between Lieutenant General Burgoyne and Major General Gates

1st.

The Troops under Lieut. Genl. Burgoyne to march out of their Camp with the Honours of War, and the Artillery of the Intrenchments, to the Verge of the River, where the Old Fort stood; where the Arms and Artillery are to be left. The Arms are to be piled by Word of Command of their own Officers.

2nd.

A free Passage to be granted to the Army under Lieut. General Burgoyne, to Great Britain, on Condition of not serving again in North America during the present Contest; and the Port of Boston is assigned for the Entry of Transports to receive the Troops whenever General Howe shall so order.

3rd.

Should any Cartel take place by which the Army under General Burgoyne, or any part of it, may be exchanged, the foregoing Article to be void, as far as such exchange shall be made.

4th.

The Army under Lieut. Genl. Burgoyne to march to Massachusetts Bay by the easiest, most expeditious and convenient Routes; and to be quartered in, near, or as convenient as possible, to Boston, that the march of the Troops may not be delayed when Transports arrive to receive them.

5th.

The Troops to be supplied on their March and during being in Quarters, with Provisions, by General Gates's Orders, at the same Rate

[335]

of Rations as the Troops of his own Army; and if possible, the Officers' Horses and Cattle are to be supplied with Forage at the usual rates.

6th.

All Officers to retain their Carriages, Bat Horses, and other Cattle, and no baggage to be molested nor searched, Lieut. General Burgoyne giving his Honour that there are no public Stores secreted therein. Major General Gates will of course take the necessary measures for the due performance of this Article. Should any carriages be wanted during the March for the Transportation of Officers' Baggage, they are if possible to be supplied by the Country at the usual Rates.

7th.

Upon the March and during the Time the Army shall remain in Quarters in the Massachusetts Bay, the Officers are not, as far as Circumstances will admit, to be separated from their Men. The Officers are to be quartered according to Rank, and are not to be hindered from assembling their Men for Roll-Callings, and other necessary purposes of Regularity.

8th.

All Corps whatever of General Burgoyne's Army, whether composed of Sailors, Batteau Men, Artificers, Drivers, Independent Companies, and Followers of the Army, of whatever Country, shall be included in the fullest Sense, and utmost Extent of the above Articles, and comprehended in every Respect as British Subjects.

9th.

All Canadians and Persons belonging to the Canadian Establishment, consisting of Sailors, Batteau Men, Artificers, Drivers, Independent Companies, and many other Followers of the Army, who come under no particular Description, are to be permitted to return there; they are to be conducted immediately by the shortest Route, to the first British Post on Lake George; are to be supplied with Provisions in the same Manner as the other Troops, and are to be bound by the same condition of not serving during the present Contest in North America.

10th.

Passports to be immediately granted for three Officers not exceeding the Rank of Captain, who shall be appointed by Lieut. General Burgoyne to carry Dispatches to Sir William Howe, Sir Guy Carleton and to Great Britain, by the Way of New York; and Major General Gates engages the publick Faith, that the Despatches shall not be opened. These Officers are to set out immediately after receiving their Despatches, and are to travel the shortest Route, and in the most expeditious manner.

Appendix 2

11th.

During the stay of the Troops in Massachusetts Bay, the Officers are to be admitted on Parole, and are to be permitted to wear their Side Arms.

12th.

Should the Army under Lieutenant General Burgoyne find it necessary to send for their Cloathing and other Baggage to Canada, they are to be permitted to do it in the most convenient Manner, and the necessary Passports granted for that Purpose.

These Articles are to be mutually signed and exchanged tomorrow Morning at 9 o'clock, and the Troops under Lieut. General Burgoyne are to march out of their Intrenchments at three o'clock in the Afternoon.

Camp at Saratoga, 16th Oct. 1777

(Signed),

HORATIO GATES,
Major General

To prevent any Doubts that might arise from Lieut. General Burgoyne's name not being mentioned in the above Treaty, Major General Gates hereby Declares that is understood to be comprehended in it as fully as if his name had been specifically mentioned.

(Signed),

HORATIO GATES.

(*Orderly Book of Lieut. Gen. John Burgoyne*, edited by E. B. O'Callaghan, and published by J. Munsell of 78 State Street, Albany, New York, in 1860, pages 144–148.)

Bibliography

THE LIST of books given below represents only some of those consulted in the writing of this biography. The main sources were the papers of the Historical Manuscripts Commission; the works of Sir John Fortescue, E. B. de Fonblanque, and F. J. Hudleston; and *A State of the Expedition from Canada*, published by Burgoyne in 1780 (quotations are from the original version).

Any biographer of Burgoyne has two main problems to deal with. First, the absence of any original letters and memoranda. The most diligent search has failed to disclose anything of real value; even the archives of the Earls of Derby have failed to produce anything of consequence. De Fonblanque may have had access to Burgoyne's correspondence when writing his biography in 1876, but the papers have since disappeared except for those lodged in the Public Records Office, and the conclusion must be that Burgoyne's immediate descendants, conscious of their illegitimacy, destroyed their father's personal correspondence.

The second problem is that Burgoyne's life lends itself to fictional treatment. He was the archetype of the eighteenth-century English gentleman, and several of his biographers have failed to differentiate between the fiction and the facts. They may well have reasoned that to do otherwise would spoil a good story. In this biography I have tried to stick strictly to the facts, and where I have been unable to substantiate the facts, and have therefore had to draw the most probable conclusions from the available evidence, I have said so. In the absence of authoritative documents there must inevitably be a certain amount of conjecture, but I have done my best to be objective, and wherever possible I have drawn upon my own military knowledge and experience.

[339]

Bibliography

Ann Arbor, Mich. William L. Clements Library. Papers of Gen. Sir Henry Clinton.

Anburey, Lt. Thomas. *Travels through the Interior Parts of America.* 2 vols. London: William Lane, 1789; Boston: Houghton Mifflin Co., 1923.

Argyll, Duke of, ed. *Intimate Society Letters of the Eighteenth Century.* 2 vols. London: S. Paul, 1910.

Atkinson, C. T., ed. "Some Evidence from Burgoyne's Expedition." *Journal of the Society for Army Historical Research* 26:132–42.

Bakshian, Aram, Jr. "General John Burgoyne." *History Today*, July 1972, 473–80.

Batchelder, Samuel F. *Burgoyne and His Officers in Cambridge 1777–1778.* Boston: Cambridge Historical Society, 1926.

Billias, George A., ed. *George Washington's Generals.* New York: William Morrow & Co., 1964.

———. *George Washington's Opponents.* New York: William Morrow & Co., 1969.

Bingham, Madeleine. *Sheridan: The Track of a Comet.* London: George Allen & Unwin, 1972; New York: St. Martin's Press, 1972.

Bird, Harrison. *March to Saratoga.* New York: Oxford University Press, 1963.

Brown, Gerald S. *The American Secretary: The Colonial Policy of Lord George Germain 1775–1778.* Ann Arbor, Mich.: The University of Michigan Press, 1963.

Burgoyne, John. *A Letter from Lieutenant General John Burgoyne to his Constituents upon his late Resignation, with the Correspondences between the Secretaries of War and him relative to his return from America.* London: J. Almon, 1779.

———. *The Lord of the Manor, Maid of the Oaks, The Heiress, Richard Coeur de Lion.* In vol. 8 of *Jones's British Theatre*, edited by William Jones. 10 vols. Dublin: W. Jones, 1794–1795.

———. *A State of the Expedition from Canada as laid before the House of Commons by Lieutenant-General Burgoyne.* London: J. Almon, 1780. Reprint. New York: Arno Press, 1969.

Clark, Jane. "Responsibility for the Failure of the Burgoyne Campaign." *American Historical Review* 35 (April 1930): 543–49.

Cannon, Richard. Regimental histories of the 9th, 20th, 21st, 24th, 47th, 53rd, and 62nd regiments. London: John W. Parker, 1836 *et seq.*

Connell, Brian. *Portrait of a Whig Peer: The Intimate Papers of Viscount Palmerston.* London: Andre Deutsch, 1957; (as *Portrait of a Golden Age*) Boston: Houghton Mifflin Co., 1958.

Creasy, Sir Edward. *Fifteen Decisive Battles of the World.* Reprint. London: J. M. Dent & Sons, 1960. Reprint. Harrisburg, Pa.: Stackpole Books, 1957.

Curtis, Edward E. *The British Army in the American Revolution.*

Bibliography

New Haven: Yale University Press, 1926. Reprint. London: EP Publishing, 1972.

de Fonblanque, Edward B. *Political and Military Episodes in the Latter Half of the 18th Century, derived from the Life and Correspondence of the Right Honourable John Burgoyne.* London: Macmillan & Co., 1876.

Digby, William. *The British Invasion from the North: The Campaigns of Generals Carleton and Burgoyne from Canada, 1776–1777, with the Journal of Lieutenant William Digby.* Edited by James P. Baxter. Albany, N.Y.: Joel Munsell, 1887. Reprint. New York: Da Capo Press, 1970.

Eelking, Max von. *German Allied Troops in the North American War of Independence 1776–1783.* Translated by William L. Stone. Albany, N.Y.: Joel Munsell, 1893.

Fleming, John. *Robert Adam and His Circle.* London: John Murray Publishers, 1962; Cambridge, Mass.: Harvard University Press, 1962.

Fortescue, Sir John. *History of the British Army.* 19 vols. London: Macmillan & Co., 1899. Reprint. New York: AMS Press, 1970.

Fuller, J. F. C. *The Decisive Battles of the United States.* 2 vols. London: Eyre & Spottiswoode, 1939–1940.

Furneaux, Rupert. *Saratoga: The Decisive Battle.* London: George Allen & Unwin, 1971; New York: Stein & Day, 1971.

Graham, H. *History of the Sixteenth, The Queen's, Light Dragoons (Lancers) 1759–1912.* Devizes: Privately printed, 1912.

Hadden, James M. *Journal and Orderly Books: A Journal kept in Canada and upon Burgoyne's campaign in 1776 and 1777: also Orders kept by Him and issued by Sir Guy Carleton, Lieut. General John Burgoyne and Major General William Phillips in 1776, 1777, and 1778.* Edited by H. Rogers. Albany, N.Y.: J. Munsell, 1884. Reprint. Freeport, L.I.: Books for Libraries, 1970.

Hargreaves, Reginald. *The Bloodybacks.* London: Rupert Hart-Davis, 1968.

Historical Manuscripts Commission. The papers of Dartmouth, Dropmore, Knox, and Stopford-Sackville.

Hudleston, F. J. *Gentleman Johnny Burgoyne.* Indianapolis, Ind.: The Bobbs-Merrill Co., 1927; London: Jonathan Cape, 1928.

Lamb, Roger. *An Original and Authentic Journal of Occurrences during the Late American War, from Its Commencement to the Year 1783.* Dublin and London: Wilkinson & Courtney, 1809.

Lancaster, Bruce. *Guns of Burgoyne.* New York: Frederick Stokes & Co., 1939.

Lee, Charles. *The Charles Lee Papers.* 4 vols. New York. The New-York Historical Society, 1872–75.

Lewis, Paul. *The Man Who Lost America.* New York: The Dial Press, 1973.

Bibliography

London. Public Record Office. Papers of General Guy Carleton, Colonial Office and War Office Correspondence.

Mackesy, Piers G. *The War for America, 1775–1783*. Cambridge, Mass.: Harvard University Press, 1964; London: Longmans Green & Co., 1964.

Namier, Lewis, and Brooke, John, eds. *History of Parliament: The House of Commons 1754–1790*. London: Her Majesty's Stationery Office, 1964.

New-York Historical Society, The. Papers of Major General Horatio Gates.

Nickerson, Hoffman. *The Turning Point of the Revolution*. Reprint. Port Washington, N.Y.: Kennikat Press, 1968.

O'Callaghan, E. B., ed. *Orderly Book of Lieut. Gen. John Burgoyne*. Albany, N.Y.: J. Munsell, 1860.

Paine, Lauran. *Gentleman Johnny*. London: Robert Hale, 1973.

Pausch, Georg. *Journal of Captain Pausch 1776–1777*. Translated by William L. Stone. Albany, N.Y.: J. Munsell, 1886. Reprint. New York: Arno Press, 1971.

Pemberton, W. B. *Lord North*. London: Longmans Green & Co., 1938.

Peterson, Harold L. *Arms and Armor in Colonial America*. New York: Bramhall House, 1956.

Riedesel, Baroness Fredericka von. *Letters and Journals Relating to the War of the American Revolution*. Translated by William L. Stone. Albany, N.Y.: J. Munsell, 1867. Reprint. New York: Arno Press, 1968.

Riedesel, Baron Friedrich von. *Memoirs and Letters and Journals of Major-Gen. Riedesel During His Residence in America*. Edited by Max von Eelking. Translated by William L. Stone. Albany, N.Y.: J. Munsell, 1868. Reprint. 2 vols. New York: Arno Press, 1969.

Roberts, Kenneth. *Rabble in Arms*. New York: Doubleday & Co., 1947; London: William Collins Sons & Co., 1939.

Rossiter, Clinton. *Seedtime of the Republic*. New York: Harcourt, Brace and Co., 1953.

Scheer, George, and Rankin, Hugh F. *Rebels and Redcoats*. Cleveland: World Publishing Co., 1957.

Shaw, George Bernard. *The Devil's Disciple*. London: Constable & Co., 1901.

Stone, William L. *Ballads and Poems Relating to the Burgoyne Campaign*. Albany, N.Y.: J. Munsell, 1893. Reprint. Port Washington, N.Y.: Kennikat Press, 1970.

———. *The Campaign of Lieut. Gen. John Burgoyne and the Expedition of Lieut. Col. Barry St. Leger*. Albany, N.Y.: J. Munsell, 1877. Reprint. New York: Da Capo Press, 1970.

Sweetman, John. *Saratoga, 1777*. Reprint. New York: Hippocrene Books, 1973.

Bibliography

Thacher, James. *A Military Journal During the American Revolutionary War from 1775 to 1783.* Boston: Richardson & Lord, 1823.

Valentine, Alan. *Lord George Germain.* New York and Oxford: Oxford University Press, 1962.

Walpole, Horace. *The Last Journals of Horace Walpole 1771–1783.* Edited by A. F. Steuart. 2 vols. London: John Lane, 1910.

———. *Letters on the American War of Independence.* Edited by W. H. D. Rouse. London and Dublin: Blackie, 1908.

Watson, John S. *The Reign of George III: 1760–1815.* New York and Oxford: Oxford University Press, 1960.

Wickwire, Franklin and Mary. *Cornwallis and the War of Independence.* Boston: Houghton Mifflin Co., 1970; London: Faber & Faber, 1970.

Wilkinson, General James. *Memoirs of My Own Times.* 3 vols. Philadelphia: Abraham Small, 1816.

Willcox, William B. "Too Many Cooks: British Planning before Saratoga," *Journal of British Studies* 2 (November 1962): 56–90.

Wraxall, Sir Nicholas William. *Historical Memoirs of My Own Time 1772–1784.* 2 vols. London: T. Cadell & W. Davies, 1815.

Wrottesley, G. *Life and Correspondence of Field Marshal Sir John Burgoyne.* 2 vols. London: R. Bentley & Sons, 1873.

Source Notes

Chapter 1

1. *Dictionary of National Biography*. 1885. Vol. IV, p. 259.
2. E. B. de Fonblanque, *Political and Military Episodes in the Latter Half of the 18th Century, derived from the Life and Correspondence of the Right Honourable John Burgoyne*, p. 5.
3. *Ibid.*, pp. 6–8.
4. John Sergeaunt, *Annals of Westminster School* (London: Methuen & Co., 1898), pp. 167–168.
5. J. C. Miller, *Triumph of Freedom, 1775–1783* (Boston: Little, Brown and Co., 1948), p. 9.
6. F. J. Hudleston, *Gentleman Johnny Burgoyne*, p. 351.

Chapter 2

1. Hudleston, *Gentleman Johnny*, p. 6.
2. de Fonblanque, *Political and Military Episodes*, pp. 9–10.
3. John Fleming, *Robert Adam and His Circle*, p. 118.
4. Brian Connell, *Portrait of a Whig Peer*, p. 41.
5. John Fleming, "Allan Ramsay and Robert Adam in Italy," *The Connoisseur*, March 1956, pp. 79 ff.
6. Alastair Smart, "The Genuine Portrait of General Burgoyne by Allan Ramsay," *Apollo*, September 1971, pp. 199 ff.

Chapter 3

1. de Fonblanque, *Political and Military Episodes*, p. 11.
2. Alan Valentine, *Lord George Germain*, p. 39.
3. *Ibid.*
4. *Ibid.*, p. 40.

5. *Ibid.*, p. 41.
6. Hudleston, *Gentleman Johnny*, p. 8.
7. Sir John Fortescue, *History of the British Army*, vol. III, p. 343.
8. de Fonblanque, *Political and Military Episodes*, pp. 12–14.

Chapter 4

1. Fortescue, *British Army*, vol. II, p. 568.
2. H. G. Parkyn, *A Short History of the 16th/5th Lancers* (Aldershot: Gale & Polden, 1934), p. 5.
3. de Fonblanque, *Political and Military Episodes*, pp. 15–22.
4. Shute Wildman, *The Political Life of William Wildman, Viscount Barrington* (London: Bulmer & Co., 1814), pp. 51–57.

Chapter 5

1. de Fonblanque, *Political and Military Episodes*, p. 24.
2. *Ibid.*, p. 25.
3. Lewis Namier and John Brooke, eds., *History of Parliament: The House of Commons 1754–1790*, vol. III, p. 645.
4. de Fonblanque, *Political and Military Episodes*, p. 28.
5. *Ibid.*, pp. 28–29.
6. Richard Cannon, *Historical Record of the Sixteenth Lancers* (London: John W. Parker, 1842), p. 18.
7. de Fonblanque, *Political and Military Episodes*, p. 45.
8. Fortescue, *British Army*, vol. II, p. 546.
9. de Fonblanque, *Political and Military Episodes*, p. 49.

Chapter 6

1. Fortescue, *British Army*, vol. III, p. 11.
2. *Ibid.*
3. Horace Walpole, *The Last Journals of Horace Walpole*, A. F. Steuart, ed., vol. I, p. 304.
4. Connell, *Portrait*, p. 43.
5. Grenville manuscripts, in possession of Sir John Murray; Namier and Brooke, *History of Parliament*, vol. II, pp. 141 ff.
6. Connell, *Portrait*, p. 37.
7. *Ibid.*, p. 38.
8. *Ibid.*, p. 62.
9. *Ibid.*
10. de Fonblanque, *Political and Military Episodes*, p. 56.
11. *Ibid.*, p. 83.
12. *Ibid.*, pp. 65–82.
13. *Ibid.*, p. 68.
14. *Ibid.*, p. 73.

15. *Ibid.*, pp. 72–73.
16. *Ibid.*, p. 81.
17. *Ibid.*, p. 82.

Chapter 7

1. Sir Nicholas William Wraxall, *Historical Memoirs of My Own Time 1772–1784*, vol. II, p. 47.
2. "Junius," *Letters of Junius*, John Wade, ed., Bohn's Standard Library (London: Bell, 1890), Letter 34, December 12, 1767.
3. Namier and Brooke, *History of Parliament*, vol. II, pp. 141 ff.
4. Walpole, *Last Journals*, vol. I, p. 203.
5. Wraxall, *Memoirs*, vol. II, p. 48.
6. Hudleston, *Gentleman Johnny*, p. 28.
7. de Fonblanque, *Political and Military Episodes*, p. 93.
8. J. Almon, ed., *The Parliamentary Register: History of the Proceedings and Debates of the House of Commons 1743–1780*, 17 vols. (London: J. Almon, 1774–1780), vol. X, p. 71.
9. *Ibid.*, p. 275.
10. *Ibid.*, p. 281.

Chapter 8

1. de Fonblanque, *Political and Military Episodes*, p. 116.
2. Almon, *Parliamentary Register*, vol. IX, p. 151.
3. de Fonblanque, *Political and Military Episodes*, p. 118.
4. Almon, *Parliamentary Register*, vol. I, pp. 253–254.
5. Walpole, *Last Journals*, vol. I, p. 433.
6. de Fonblanque, *Political and Military Episodes*, pp. 119–120.
7. George A. Billias, ed., *George Washington's Opponents*, pp. 156–157.
8. Hudleston, *Gentleman Johnny*, p. 53.
9. de Fonblanque, *Political and Military Episodes*, pp. 120–132.
10. *Ibid.*, p. 134.

Chapter 9

1. Hugh F. Rankin, *The American Revolution* (New York: Capricorn Books, 1965), p. 20.
2. *Ibid.*, p. 21.
3. *Ibid.*, p. 20.
4. Connell, *Portrait*, pp. 118–120.
5. Reginald Hargreaves, *The Bloodybacks*, p. 248.
6. Clarence E. Carter, ed., *The Correspondence of General Thomas Gage*, 2 vols. (New Haven: Yale University Press, 1931–1933), vol. II, pp. 686–687.
7. de Fonblanque, *Political and Military Episodes*, pp. 142–153.

8. *Ibid.*, pp. 140–141.
9. Fortescue, *British Army*, vol. III, p. 167.
10. *Ibid.*, p. 169.
11. de Fonblanque, *Political and Military Episodes*, pp. 191–199.
12. Hudleston, *Gentleman Johnny*, p. 20.
13. Walpole, *Last Journals*, vol. I, pp. 404–405.
14. George Scheer and Hugh F. Rankin, *Rebels and Redcoats*, pp. 86–87.
15. John C. Fitzpatrick, ed., *The Writings of George Washington*, 39 vols. (Washington: Government Printing Office, 1931–1944), vol. IV, pp. 82–83.
16. de Fonblanque, *Political and Military Episodes*, pp. 161–167.
17. Hudleston, *Gentleman Johnny*, pp. 83–84.
18. *Ibid.*, pp. 80–81.
19. de Fonblanque, *Political and Military Episodes*, pp. 174–179.
20. *Ibid.*, pp. 180–183.
21. *Ibid.*, p. 195.

Chapter 10

1. W. E. H. Lecky, *A History of England in the Eighteenth Century*, 8 vols. (London: Longmans Green & Co., 1882), vol. IV, p. 71.
2. William Digby, *The British Invasion from the North*, pp. 156–157.
3. de Fonblanque, *Political and Military Episodes*, p. 209.
4. *Ibid.*, p. 208.
5. Fortescue, *British Army*, vol. III, p. 176.
6. Edward E. Curtis, *The British Army in the American Revolution*, p. 53.
7. de Fonblanque, *Political and Military Episodes*, p. 213.
8. *Ibid.*, pp. 212–213.
9. Billias, *Washington's Opponents*, p. 164.
10. Digby, *British Invasion*, p. 157.
11. Billias, *Washington's Opponents*, p. 164.
12. de Fonblanque, *Political and Military Episodes*, pp. 218–221.
13. Billias, *Washington's Opponents*, p. 167.
14. Sir John W. Fortescue, ed., *The Correspondence of King George the Third from 1760 to December 1783*, 6 vols. (London: Macmillan and Co., 1894), vol. III, p. 405.
15. *Ibid.*, pp. 406–407.

Chapter 11

1. de Fonblanque, *Political and Military Episodes*, pp. 225–226.
2. *Hansard Parliamentary History of England* (London: Longman Hurst and others, 1810 ff.), vol. XX, p. 684.
3. Valentine, *Germain*, p. 166.
4. de Fonblanque, *Political and Military Episodes*, p. 227.

5. Hudleston, *Gentleman Johnny*, p. 119.
6. Valentine, *Germain*, pp. 164–165.
7. *Ibid.*, p. 166.
8. *Ibid.*
9. Fortescue, *Correspondence of George Third*, vol. I, p. 421.
10. Fortescue, *British Army*, vol. III, p. 206.
11. J. F. C. Fuller, *Decisive Battles*, p. 26.
12. John Burgoyne, *A State of the Expedition from Canada*, p. v.
13. *Ibid.*
14. *Ibid.*, p. vi.
15. *Ibid.*, p. iii.
16. *Ibid.*, p. v.
17. *Ibid.*
18. *Ibid.*, p. vi.
19. de Fonblanque, *Political and Military Episodes*, p. 487.
20. Fortescue, *Correspondence of George Third*, vol. III, p. 444.
21. Fuller, *Decisive Battles*, p. 26.
22. Public Record Office, CO/5, vol. 253, pp. 278 ff.
23. Valentine, *Germain*, p. 284.
24. Burgoyne, *State of the Expedition*, p. 6.
25. Franklin and Mary Wickwire, *Cornwallis and the War of Independence*, p. 100.

Chapter 12

1. Public Record Office, CO/5, 92–103, pp. 299–303.
2. *Ibid.*, p. 292.
3. Fortescue, *British Army*, vol. III, p. 208.
4. Burgoyne, *State of the Expedition*, p. xi.
5. *Ibid.*, p. xxi.
6. *Ibid.*, p. xxxi.
7. *Ibid.*, p. xxxii.
8. *Ibid.*, p. 112.
9. Harold L. Peterson, *Arms and Armor in Colonial America*, p. 198.
10. Edward E. Curtis, *The British Army in the American Revolution*, p. 21.
11. E. B. O'Callaghan, ed., *Orderly Book of Lieut. Gen. John Burgoyne*, p. 3.
12. Valentine, *Germain*, p. 188.
13. Burgoyne, *State of the Expedition*, p. xxx.

Chapter 13

1. Roger Lamb, *An Original and Authentic Journal of Occurrences during the Late American War, from Its Commencement to the Year 1783*, p. 135.

2. James M. Hadden, *Journal and Orderly Books,* H. Rogers, ed., p. 256.
3. Thomas Anburey, *Travels through the Interior Parts of America,* vol. I, pp. 202–203.
4. Hudleston, *Gentleman Johnny,* pp. 145–147.
5. *Ibid.,* p. 148.
6. *Ibid.,* p. 151.
7. *Ibid.,* pp. 151–152.
8. Anburey, *Travels,* vol. I, pp. 304–305.
9. de Fonblanque, *Political and Military Episodes,* p. 245.
10. Burgoyne, *State of the Expedition,* p. 7.
11. William H. Smith, *Life and Public Services of Arthur St Clair,* 2 vols. vol. I, pp. 399–400.
12. Schuyler Letter Book, 1775–1778, New York Public Library, p. xxi.
13. Burgoyne, *State of the Expedition,* p. xvi.
14. Mrs. Paget Toynbee, *The Letters of Horace Walpole, Fourth Earl of Orford.* 16 vols. (Oxford: Clarendon Press, 1902–1905), vol. X, p. 113.
15. Charles Francis Adams, ed., *Familiar Letters of John Adams and His Wife Abigail Adams, during the Revolution* (New York, 1876; reprint, Freeport, N.Y.: Books for Libraries Press, 1970), pp. 292–293.

Chapter 14

1. George III, Remarks of "The Conduct of the War from Canada," holograph manuscript, British Museum.
2. Burgoyne, *State of the Expedition,* p. v.
3. James Thacher, *A Military Journal During the American Revolutionary War,* p. 100.
4. Lamb, *Journal,* p. 143.
5. *Ibid.*
6. Furneaux, *Saratoga,* p. 79.
7. Digby, *British Invasion,* p. 211n.
8. General James Wilkinson, *Memoirs of My Own Times,* vol. I, p. 187.
9. Burgoyne, *State of the Expedition,* p. xviii.
10. Register House, Edinburgh, GD 248, 201/2.
11. Baroness Fredericka von Riedesel, *Letters and Journals Relating to the War of the American Revolution,* p. 96n.
12. Furneaux, *Saratoga,* p. 90.
13. Burgoyne, *State of the Expedition,* p. 12.
14. Lamb, *Journal,* p. 144.
15. Digby, *British Invasion,* p. 227.
16. *Ibid.,* p. 228.

17. Burgoyne, *State of the Expedition,* p. xxi.
18. *Ibid.*
19. *Ibid.*
20. *Ibid.*
21. *Ibid.*
22. Schuyler Letter Book, 1775–1778, New York Public Library, p. xxv.
23. *Ibid.*
24. *Ibid.*
25. Thacher, *Military Journal,* p. 103.
26. *Warren-Adams Letters,* 2 vols. (Boston, Massachusetts Historical Society, n.d.), vol. I, p. 353.
27. Fuller, *Decisive Battles,* p. 33.
28. *Ibid.*
29. Fortescue, *British Army,* vol. III, p. 226.
30. Digby, *British Invasion,* p. 240.
31. Anburey, *Travels,* vol. I, pp. 369–370.
32. "A Scrap of Unwritten History," *Catholic World* 36 (December 1882).
33. Anburey, *Travels,* vol. I, p. 370.
34. Burgoyne, *State of the Expedition,* p. 49.
35. *Ibid.*
36. Hudleston, *Gentleman Johnny,* p. 164.
37. *Ibid.*
38. *Ibid.*
39. de Fonblanque, *Political and Military Episodes,* p. 259.

Chapter 15

1. Burgoyne, *State of the Expedition,* p. xlii.
2. *Ibid.*
3. Fuller, *Decisive Battles,* p. 34.
4. *Ibid.*
5. Burgoyne, *State of the Expedition,* p. 99.
6. *Ibid.,* p. 73.
7. *Ibid.*
8. Hadden, *Orderly Books,* pp. 314–315.
9. de Fonblanque, *Political and Military Episodes,* p. 248.
10. *Ibid.*
11. *Ibid.,* pp. 252–253.
12. Furneaux, *Saratoga,* p. 111.
13. *Ibid.,* p. 112.
14. de Fonblanque, *Political and Military Episodes,* p. 269.
15. *Ibid.*
16. *Ibid.,* p. 270.

Chapter 16

1. Henry Steele Commager and Richard B. Morris, *The Spirit of Seventy-Six* (Indianapolis: Bobbs-Merrill, 1958), p. 570.
2. Furneaux, *Saratoga*, p. 117.
3. Burgoyne, *State of the Expedition*, p. xxxix.
4. *Ibid.*, p. xl.
5. Baroness von Riedesel, *Letters and Journals*, p. 96.
6. Burgoyne, *State of the Expedition*, p. xxxix.
7. *Ibid.*, p. xxii.
8. Furneaux, *Saratoga*, pp. 125–126.
9. Frederick Kidder and Augustus Gould, *History of New Ipswich* (Boston: Gould & Lincoln, 1852), p. 95.
10. Furneaux, *Saratoga*, p. 128.
11. *Ibid.*, p. 131.
12. *Ibid.*, p. 132.
13. Hudleston, *Gentleman Johnny*, p. 171.
14. *Ibid.*
15. *Ibid.*
16. Fitzpatrick, *Writings of Washington*, vol. IV, pp. 466–501.

Chapter 17

1. Burgoyne, *State of the Expedition*, p. xxiv.
2. *Ibid.*, pp. xxiv–xxv.
3. Hudleston, *Gentleman Johnny*, p. 175.
4. Valentine, *Germain*, p. 239.
5. Hezekiah Niles, *Principles and Acts of the Revolution in America* (Baltimore: W. O. Niles, 1822), p. 496.
6. Edmund C. Burnett, ed., *Letters of Members of the Continental Congress*, 8 vols. (Washington: Carnegie Institution, 1921–1936), vol. II, p. 413.
7. Fuller, *Decisive Battles*, p. 45.
8. Baroness von Riedesel, *Letters and Journals*, pp. 92–93.
9. *Ibid.*, p. 120.
10. *Ibid.*, p. 113.

Chapter 18

1. O'Callaghan, *Orderly Book*, p. 113.
2. Wilkinson, *Memoirs*, vol. I, pp. 235–236.
3. *Ibid.*, p. 236.
4. *Ibid.*, p. 249.
5. Anthony Brett-James, *Wellington at War* (London: Macmillan, 1961; New York: St. Martin's Press, 1961), p. 319.
6. Wilkinson, *Memoirs*, vol. I, p. 241.

7. Baron Friedrich von Riedesel, *Memoirs and Letters and Journals*, vol. I, p. 149.
8. Digby, *British Invasion*, p. 274.
9. Burgoyne, *State of the Expedition*, p. xlix.
10. O'Callaghan, *Orderly Book*, p. 116.
11. Fortescue, *British Army*, vol. III, pp. 232–233.

Chapter 19

1. de Fonblanque, *Political and Military Episodes*, pp. 285–286.
2. Baroness von Riedesel, *Letters and Journals*, p. 115.
3. Burgoyne, *State of the Expedition*, p. xix.
4. William B. Willcox, *Portrait of a General: Sir Henry Clinton in the War of Independence* (New York: Alfred A. Knopf, 1964), p. 160.
5. *Hansard*, vol. XX, p. 695.
6. Burgoyne, *State of the Expedition*, p. xlix.
7. Valentine, *Germain*, pp. 245–246.
8. *Ibid.*, p. 247n.
9. *Ibid.*, p. 250.
10. Georg Pausch, *Journal of Captain Pausch 1776–1777*, p. 146.
11. O'Callaghan, *Orderly Book*, p. 127.
12. Anburey, *Travels*, vol. I, p. 431.
13. James M. Hadden, *Journal and Orderly Books*, p. lxxxiv; Furneaux, *Saratoga*, p. 214.
14. Burgoyne, *State of the Expedition*, p. xlix.
15. Baroness von Riedesel, *Letters and Journals*, pp. 115–116.
16. *Ibid.*
17. Pausch, *Journal*, p. 167.
18. Burgoyne, *State of the Expedition*, p. li.
19. Hudleston, *Gentleman Johnny*, p. 196.
20. Fuller, *Decisive Battles*, p. 42.

Chapter 20

1. Anburey, *Travels*, vol. I, p. 441.
2. Baroness von Riedesel, *Letters and Journals*, p. 120.
3. *Ibid.*, p. 119.
4. de Fonblanque, *Political and Military Episodes*, p. 296.
5. Burgoyne, *State of the Expedition*, p. li.
6. Baroness von Riedesel, *Letters and Journals*, p. 122.
7. Anburey, *Travels*, vol. I, pp. 450–451.
8. Hudleston, *Gentleman Johnny*, p. 200.
9. Almon, *Parliamentary Register*, vol. X (1778), p. 221.
10. Baroness von Riedesel, *Letters and Journals*, p. 125.
11. *Ibid.*

12. *Ibid.*, p. 125n.
13. Fuller, *Decisive Battles*, p. 42.
14. Baroness von Riedesel, *Letters and Journals*, p. 133.
15. Burgoyne, *State of the Expedition*, p. lvi.
16. *Ibid.*, p. lvii.
17. *Ibid.*
18. *Ibid.*, pp. lvii–lviii.
19. *Ibid.*
20. de Fonblanque, *Political and Military Episodes*, p. 308.
21. O'Callaghan, *Orderly Book*, pp. 149–151.
22. Burgoyne, *State of the Expedition*, p. lx.
23. Baroness von Riedesel, *Letters and Journals*, p. 133.
24. Hudleston, *Gentleman Johnny*, p. 211.
25. *Ibid.*, p. 212.

Chapter 21

1. Lamb, *Journal*, p. 183.
2. Frank Moore, ed., *Diary of the American Revolution*, 2 vols. (New York: Charles Scribner's Sons, 1860), vol. I, p. 157.
3. Hudleston, *Gentleman Johnny*, p. 214.
4. Rankin, *American Revolution*, p. 149.
5. Furneaux, *Saratoga*, p. 272.
6. *Ibid.*
7. Baroness von Riedesel, *Letters and Journals*, p. 137.
8. *Ibid.*, p. 136.
9. Burgoyne, *State of the Expedition*, p. liii.
10. *Ibid.*
11. *Ibid.*, p. liv.
12. de Fonblanque, *Political and Military Episodes*, pp. 313–316.
13. *Hansard*, vol. XIX, p. 434.
14. *Ibid.*, p. 384.
15. J. Wright, ed., *Speeches of the Right Honourable Charles James Fox*, 6 vols. (London: Longmans Hurst, 1815), vol. I, p. 93.
16. Holograph memorandum, Papers of Lord George Germain (Ann Arbor, Mich., The William L. Clements Library), vol. VII, 8/67.
17. *Hansard*, vol. XIX, p. 434.
18. Burgoyne, *State of the Expedition*, p. xxvii.
19. P. O. Hutchinson, ed., *Diary and Letters of His Excellency Thomas Hutchinson*, 2 vols. (London: Sampson Low, 1883–1886), vol. II, p. 169.
20. Wright, *Speeches of Fox*, vol. I, p. 94.
21. Historical Manuscripts Commission, *Report on American Manuscripts in the Royal Institution of Great Britain*. 2 vols. (London: His Majesty's Stationery Office, 1904), vol. I, p. 140.
22. *Hansard*, vol. XIX, pp. 541–542.

23. Fortescue, *Correspondence of George Third*, vol. III, p. 514.
24. Hudleston, *Gentleman Johnny*, p. 248.
25. *Ibid.*, p. 255.
26. *Journals of the Continental Congress, 1774–1789* (Washington: Government Printing Office, 1904–1937), vol. X (1778), p. 13.
27. *Ibid.*, p. 35.
28. Hudleston, *Gentleman Johnny*, p. 258.
29. Jane Clark, "Responsibility for the Failure of the Burgoyne Campaign," *American Historical Review* 35 (April 1930), 543–559.
30. Hudleston, *Gentleman Johnny*, pp. 265–267.
31. *Ibid.*, p. 202.
32. Burgoyne, *State of the Expedition*, p. 91.
33. Hudleston, *Gentleman Johnny*, pp. 261–262.
34. *Ibid.*, p. 264.
35. *Ibid.*, p. 260.
36. Captain William A. Rounds, "The First Judge Advocate General 'of the American Army Tries a Case," *The Quartermaster Review* (Jan.–Feb. 1930), pp. 22–24.
37. *Ibid.*
38. *Ibid.*
39. *Journals of the Continental Congress*, vol. X (1778), pp. 33–35.
40. Fortescue, *British Army*, vol. III, p. 241.
41. Hudleston, *Gentleman Johnny*, pp. 282–283.
42. *Journals of the Continental Congress*, vol. X (1778), p. 218.
43. de Fonblanque, *Political and Military Episodes*, pp. 332–333.

Chapter 22

1. R. G. Adams, ed., *The Papers of Lord George Germain* (Ann Arbor, Mich., The William L. Clements Library, 1928), vol. VIII, p. 43.
2. Hutchinson, *Diary and Letters*, vol. II, p. 210.
3. de Fonblanque, *Political and Military Episodes*, p. 351.
4. Wright, *Speeches of Fox*, vol. I, p. 121.
5. *Ibid.*, p. 94.
6. Fortescue, *Correspondence of George Third*, vol. IV, p. 214.
7. John Burgoyne, *A Letter from Lieutenant-General J. Burgoyne to his Constituents*, pp. 8–9.
8. Public Record Office, CO/5, p. 253.
9. de Fonblanque, *Political and Military Episodes*, p. 351.
10. *Ibid.*, p. 352.
11. Walpole, *Last Journals*, vol. II, p. 176.
12. *Hansard*, vol. XIX, pp. 1178 ff.
13. *Ibid.*
14. *Ibid.*, vol. XX, pp. 796–797.
15. Wright, *Speeches of Fox*, vol. I, p. 128.

16. Toynbee, *Letters of Walpole*, vol. X, p. 354.
17. *Ibid.*
18. W. B. Donne, ed., *Correspondence of George III with Lord North*, 2 vols. (London, 1867), vol. II, p. 198.
19. Valentine, *Germain*, p. 299.
20. Burgoyne, *Letter to his Constituents*, p. 21.
21. *Ibid.*, pp. 22–23.
22. *Ibid.*, p. 24.
23. *Ibid.*
24. *Ibid.*, p. 10.
25. *Ibid.*, p. 25.
26. Valentine, *Germain*, p. 329.
27. *Ibid.*, p. 352.
28. Walpole, *Last Journals*, vol. II, p. 219.
29. *Hansard*, vol. XX, pp. 801–802.
30. Burgoyne, *State of the Expedition*, p. 13.
31. *Ibid.*, p. 16.
32. *Ibid.*, p. 19.
33. *Ibid.*
34. *Ibid.*, pp. 21, 24.
35. *Ibid.*, p. 27.
36. *Ibid.*, pp. 33, 34.
37. *Ibid.*, pp. 136–137.
38. Public Record Office, CO/5, vol. 94, p. 353.
39. Historical Manuscripts Commission, *Lothian Papers*, Barrington to Buckinghamshire, May 17, 1779, (1905), p. 351.
40. *Hansard*, vol. XX, p. 818.
41. Burgoyne, *Letter to his Constituents*, p. 26.
42. *Ibid.*, pp. 27, 31.
43. de Fonblanque, *Political and Military Episodes*, p. 385.
44. Burgoyne, *Letter to his Constituents*, p. 34.
45. *Ibid.*, p. 37.

Chapter 23

1. *Hansard*, vol. XXII, p. 860.
2. de Fonblanque, *Political and Military Episodes*, p. 437.
3. *Ibid.*, p. 438.
4. Hudleston, *Gentleman Johnny*, p. 309.
5. *Ibid.*, p. 317.
6. de Fonblanque, *Political and Military Episodes*, p. 452.
7. Hudleston, *Gentleman Johnny*, p. 309.
8. John Debrett, *The Parliamentary Register* (London, 1790), vol. XXVII, p. 477.
9. Hudleston, *Gentleman Johnny*, p. 312.
10. Debrett, *Parliamentary Register*, vol. XXXII (1792), p. 45.

11. *Ibid.*, vol. XXIX (1791), p. 28.
12. Fortescue, *British Army*, vol. III, p. 521.
13. A. T. Bolton, *The Architecture of Robert and James Adam*, 2 vols., vol. 2, p. 68.
14. Hudleston, *Gentleman Johnny*, p. 324.
15. Bolton, *Architecture*, vol. 2, p. 237.
16. *The Gentleman's Magazine* 44, 263.
17. Bolton, *Architecture*, vol. 2, p. 237.
18. *The Gentleman's Magazine* 44, 263.
19. David Mason Little and George M. Kahrl, eds., *The Letters of David Garrick*, 3 vols. (London: Oxford University Press, 1963; Cambridge, Mass.: Belknap Press, Harvard University Press, 1963), vol. III, p. 963.
20. *Ibid.*, p. 962.
21. Hudleston, *Gentleman Johnny*, p. 325.
22. de Fonblanque, *Political and Military Episodes*, p. 398.
23. Hudleston, *Gentleman Johnny*, p. 329.
24. John Burgoyne, *The Lord of the Manor*, Preface, p. xx.
25. John Burgoyne, *The Heiress*, p. iii.
26. The Enthoven Collection, Victoria and Albert Museum, London.
27. de Fonblanque, *Political and Military Episodes*, p. 401.
28. The Enthoven Collection, Victoria and Albert Museum, London.
29. Burgoyne, *The Heiress*, p. 118.
30. *Chatham Correspondence*, W. S. Taylor and J. H. Pringle, eds., 4 vols. (London, 1838–1840), vol. 2, p. 429.

Epilogue

1. de Fonblanque, *Political and Military Episodes*, pp. 465–466.
2. *Ibid.*, p. 463.
3. *Ibid.*, p. 464.
4. Westminster Abbey Burial Book 1783–1810, p. 91.
5. de Fonblanque, *Political and Military Episodes*, p. 46.
6. The Marquess of Anglesey, *A History of the British Cavalry 1815–1850* (London: Leo Cooper, 1973), vol. I, p. 43.
7. Fuller, *Decisive Battles*, p. 43.
8. Fortescue, *British Army*, vol. III, p. 241.
9. Thomas Babington Macaulay, "Lord Clive," *Historical Essays of Macaulay*, Samuel Thurber, ed. (Boston: Allyn & Bacon, 1892), p. 632.
10. de Fonblanque, *Political and Military Episodes*, p. 1.

Index

Abercrombie, Gen. James, 147
Abington, Frances, 321–22
Acland, Lady Harriet, 144, 212–14,
    232, 251, 254–55, 331
Acland, Maj. Sir John, 165, 213–14,
    242, 245, 251, 254
Adam, Robert, 15–17, 61, 320
Adams, Abigail, 160, 173
Adams, John, 160, 173
Adams, Samuel, 81, 95, 173, 209–10
Albany, 117, 120–27 *passim*, 129,
    130, 133; Burgoyne's orders
    concerning, 125, 134, 205–6, 234,
    272–74, 278–79, 296, 304; strategic
    importance of, 114, 123, 161, 220,
    227–28, 240
Allen, Ethan, 80, 100, 147, 156
Allen, Rev. Thomas, 197–98
Americans in the British army, 171,
    192, 194, 197, 215, 236; American
    resentment of, 200; Burgoyne's
    estimate of, 144, 216, 243
Amherst, Gen. Lord Jeffrey, 124,
    147
Anburey, Lt. Thomas, 149, 152–53,
    156, 167, 175–76, 229, 238–39,
    250, 253, 288
Ancaster, Duchess of, 48

Anglesey, Marquis of, 330
Anne, Fort, 162–63, 168, 169, 172,
    174
Annual Register, 38
Antiquities of Herculaneum, 328
Argyll, Duchess of, 320–21
Arnold, Maj. Gen. Benedict, 80,
    100-101, 107, 108, 110, 152, 155,
    174, 211; importance in history,
    185–86, 227–28, 248–49, 303, 330;
    legends about, 246–47; Saratoga
    performance, 219–29, 246–48, 251;
    temperament, 185–86, 226, 227,
    247, 277
Articles of Convention. *See*
    Saratoga Convention
As You Like It (Shakespeare-
    Burgoyne), 326
Augusta, Princess of Brunswick, 50

Balcarres, Earl of, 165–66, 242, 245,
    247, 303, 304, 305
Barber's field, 244–45
Barner, Ferdinand, 257
Barrington, Lord, 30, 34–36, 70–71,
    99, 100, 298–99, 305–6, 307
Bath, England, Burgoyne's visits to,
    117, 120, 298, 300

Index

Bath, Order of the, 119, 120, 129, 181
Baum, Lt.-Col. Friederich, 191–201; Burgoyne's estimate of, 202–3
Bedford, Duke of, 69
Bee, Thomas, 313
Belknap, Jeremy, 90
Belle-Ile expedition, 37–38
Bemis, Jotham, 211
Bemis Heights, battle of (see also Saratoga), 231–49; British retreat from, 253–57; evaluation of, 249, 252–53
Bennington, 192–94, 196, 198–201, 202–3, 205, 215, 216, 302
Benson, Harriott. See Bingley, Lady Harriott
Benson, Robert. See Bingley, first Lord
"Benson, Robert," proposed as name for Burgoyne, 5
Bingley, Lady Elizabeth, 3–4, 5, 7
Bingley, Lady Harriott, 3, 5, 6
Bingley, first Lord (Robert Benson), 3–7
Bingley, second Lord, 6
Blaquière, Sir John, 76
Bligh, Lt.-Gen. Thomas, 23–26
Blockade of Boston, The (Burgoyne), 89, 322
Bloomfield, Thomas, 304–5
Bolingbroke, Lord and Lady, 48
Boston, 67, 70–79, 81, 88, 95–103 passim, 126, 286
Bouquet Indian address (Burgoyne), 150–52
Braddock, Gen. Edward, 208
Bramham (estate), 3
Brant, Joseph (Thayendanegea), 182, 183
Breed's Hill, battle of, 82
Breymann, Lt.-Col. Heinrich von, 142, 166, 194–201 passim, 221, 224, 242, 247–49; Burgoyne's estimate of, 202–3
Brooks, Col. John, 247

Brown, Col. John, 235
"Brown Bess," 137–38, 139
Brudenell, Rev. (Lady Acland's escort to American camp), 254–55
Brunswick, Duke of, 105, 191
Brunswick, Prince of, 22, 50
Brunswick Dragoon Regiment von Ludwig, 141, 190–92, 199
Brunswick grenadiers, 194–95
Brunswick Regiment Prinz Friedrich, 162
Bunker Hill, battle of, 82–85, 92
Burgoyne, Anna Maria Burnestone (mother), 4–5, 7, 14
Burgoyne, Caroline (daughter). See Parker, Caroline
Burgoyne, Lady Charlotte (wife), 8, 12–16, 39, 61, 62, 67, 79, 83; Burgoyne's feelings for, 37, 49–50, 71–72, 106, 109; character of, 49; death of, 109, 111; letters of, 13, 15, 47, 48–49, 50–51
Burgoyne, Charlotte Elizabeth (daughter), 15, 50, 61
Burgoyne, Edward (son), 329
Burgoyne, Lt.-Gen. John, personal life: birth, 4, 6; children, 6, 14–15, 60, 313, 314, 328, 329; concern for honor, 206, 278, 290, 306–10 passim; Continental tour, 51–54; death and funeral, 61n, 327–29; elopement, 12–14; exile, 14–18, 331; "go-getter" qualities, 19–20, 34–36, 205–6; grandson, 314n; intelligence, 94; last will and testament, 315, 328–29; manners, 286; marriage, see Burgoyne, Lady Charlotte (wife); monetary fortunes of, 10–11, 17–18, 309, 315, 325, 327–29; parentage, 3, 4, 5–7; personal appearance, 6, 61; personal magnetism, 6, 160, 307, 309–10, 332; pomposity and prolixity, 46, 63, 64, 68, 81, 149–53, 331; portraits of, 15, 16–17, 61, 328; refusal of knighthood, 120, 129,

[358]

Index

181; reputation as a gambler, 7, 11, 14–15, 59–61, 69, 219, 239, 331; reputation as an intriguer, 34–36, 37, 43–44, 56, 68–79, 94, 112–13, 331–32; reputation as a womanizer, 142–43, 213, 256, 331; schooling, 7–9; social life, 14–18, 31, 61, 117, 118, 146, 213, 238, 255–56

Burgoyne, Lt.-Gen. John, *military career* (*see also* Bemis Heights; Bennington; Freeman's Farm; Ticonderoga): attitude toward American colonists, 67–87 *passim*, 120–21, 144, 216, 243; attitude toward military life, 19–22, 31–34, 106, 117–18; behavior as prisoner of war, 280–81, 186–88, 290, 294, 298–300, 308, 313–14; Boston assignment under Gage, 67–96; Canadian assignment under Carleton, 104–12; Canadian independent command, *see* Canada, expedition from; concern for glory, 129, 156, 187–88, 205–6, 331–32; concern for welfare of junior officers and troops, 281, 287–88, 290, 317, 319, 331, 332; Foot Guards commission, 26; Fourth (King's Own) Regiment commission, 315; governorship of Fort William, 59n, 60, 62, 308, 309; Horse Guards commission, 9–11; Ireland command, 314–15; Light Dragoons commission, 29–47; military ambition, 38, 61, 67, 96, 112, 126–27; military talent, 40–41, 96, 108–9, 130, 131, 189–91, 201, 329–32; nicknames, 32, 150, 206, 219, 239, 310, 331; popularity with fellow officers, 187; popularity with public, 307, 309–10; popularity with troops, 107–8, 148–49, 167, 256, 268, 270, 272, 288, 331; Portugal campaign, 38–44; promotion to major-general, 65; resignation from army, 315; Royal

Dragoons commissions, 11, 14, 18–26; steadiness of nerve, 263; strategy for American war, 101–2, 114–15, 120–24, 135–36, 205–6, 239–40; strategy for breaking Boston impasse, 86–89, 95; views on religious discrimination in army, 55

Burgoyne, Lt.-Gen. John, *political career*: elections to House of Commons, 45–47, 56–58, 61, 316; political principles, 47–48, 56, 61–64, 291–92, 301, 307–8; post-Saratoga career in Parliament, 291, 293–95, 316–19; trial for incitement to violence, 58–60

Burgoyne, Lt.-Gen. John, *theatrical career* (*see also* Burgoyne, John, writings), 319–26; reputation as a playwright, 322–23, 326

Burgoyne, Lt.-Gen. John, *writings*: *As You Like It* adaptation, 326; *Blockade of Boston, The*, 89, 322; Bouquet Indian address, 150–52; *Heiress, The*, 323–26; letter charging Continental Congress with breach of faith, 281, 289; *Letter from Lieut. Gen. Burgoyne to His Constituents*, 293; letter to Gates requesting protection for Lady Acland, 254; letter to "the Gentlemen, Clergy, and other Voters of the Town of Preston," 310; *Lord of the Manor, The* (with Sheridan), 323; *Maid of the Oaks*, 320–22; *Observations and Reflections upon the Present Military State of Prussia, Austria and France*, 51–54; ode on Palmerston's wedding, 13; *Reflections upon the War in America*, 101, 102, 104; *Richard Coeur de Lion*, (with Grétry and Sedaine), 325; *State of the Expedition from Canada as laid before the House of Commons*, 310; *Thoughts for Conducting the*

Burgoyne, John, *writings* (*cont.*)
  War from the Side of Canada, 120,
  125, 182; tribute to the officers and
  soldiers at Saratoga, 228; verse to
  Lady Charlotte, 37; *Zara* prologue,
  89
Burgoyne, John (father), 4–5
Burgoyne, John Fox (son), 314n,
  328
Burgoyne, Sir John (first cousin),
  11n, 328
Burgoyne, Sir John, third Baronet
  of Sutton (grandfather), 4
Burgoyne, Maria (daughter), 329
Burgoyne, Roger (ancestor), 4
"Burgoyne's Light Horse." *See*
  Light Dragoons, 16th
Burke, Edmund, 45, 313–15
Burnestone, Anna Maria. *See*
  Burgoyne, Anna Maria Burnestone
  (mother)
Burney, Fanny, 316–17
Burney, James, 316–17
Bute, third Earl of, 44, 55, 94

Cambridge, Mass., 193, 270, 280
Campbell, Capt. C., 234, 237
Canada, expedition from (*see also*
  Bemis Heights; Bennington;
  Freeman's Farm; Saratoga; Ticonderoga): American tactics, 162–65,
  228–30; artillery, 122, 225, 228,
  242, 245–46, 302; Burgoyne's
  account of the expedition, 272,
  301–7; Burgoyne's plan for the
  expedition, 87n, 118, 120, 124,
  126–37, 169–74, 205, 296; camp
  followers, 216; communication
  problems, 181–82, 187, 203–4;
  detachments problem, 178–79, 201,
  204, 215; discipline, 216-17;
  division organization, 141–42;
  historical significance of the expedition, 330; hygiene problems, 216,
  238; intelligence and security

problems, 136, 212, 215–17 *passim*,
  220-21, 236, 238, 240, 282;
  logistical problems, 145–46; non-
  combatant allotment, 144; opera-
  tional efficiency, 149; spy problem,
  192, 194, 212, 215; supply problem,
  179–80, 189–90, 203, 216–17, 252;
  termination of the expedition,
  260–61, 330; terrain problems,
  167–70, 195, 204, 211; troop
  allotment, 136–40, 286; troop
  morale, 148, 149, 170; weapons,
  137–41, 222; women on the
  expedition, 142–44, 232
Canada, governorship of, 119, 187
Canadians in the British army, 145,
  243, 258
Carey, Henry, 150
Carillon, Fort, 147
Carleton, Gen. Sir Guy, 100–104,
  107–17, 148, 152; Burgoyne's
  relations with, 111–13, 119, 124,
  134–36, 178, 209, 277–79, 301,
  304–5; estimate of American fighting ability, 120; feud with Germain, 101, 134, 300; George III's
  estimation of, 124, 134–35; orders
  concerning Burgoyne's expedition
  from Canada, 124–25, 127, 132–35,
  296
Carlyle, Thomas, 330
Carnot, Lazare, 103
cartouche boxes, disappearance of,
  283–84, 288
Castle Town, 164–66, 168, 192
Catherine, Empress of Russia, 105
Caulfield, Susan, 300, 313, 314, 325,
  327–29, 331–32
cavalry, light. *See* Light Dragoons
Cavendish, Lord Frederick, 294–95
Champlain, Lake, 108, 109, 110, 153,
  161
Chanteloup (estate), 14
chaplain, Burgoyne's request for,
  34–35

Charles I, 4
Charles Edward, Prince, 56–57
Charleston, attack on, 118
Charlotte, Queen, 160, 212
Chatham. *See* Pitt, William, the Elder
Cherbourg, attack on, 22–23
Choiseul, Duke of (Comte Etienne de Stainville), 14–15, 38, 53
civil war, professional attitude toward, 67
Clarke, Sir Francis, 245, 249
Clinton, Fort, 236–37
Clinton, Lt.-Gen. Henry: Burgoyne's hope of help from, 128, 204–5, 233–40, 252, 259, 261, 263, 265–66; Burgoyne's relationship with, 109, 233, 274, 280, 303, 330; personality and character, 118–19, 120, 233, 236; reputation as a general, 68, 71, 104, 111, 117, 234, 330; service under Gage, 67, 68, 71, 81–84; service under Howe, 128, 204–5
Clinton, Gen. James, 237
Clive, Lord Robert, 60, 62–64, 331
Colborn, Col., 217
Coldstream Regiment, 26
Cole, William, 38
Coleville (Dovecot), 217
colors, disappearance of, 283–84
Concord, battle of, 80, 84
Continental Army, Gates's role in formation of, 209
Continental Journal and Weekly Advertiser (Boston), 269
Conway, Gen. Henry, 48
Cornwallis, Earl, Maj.-Gen. Charles, 131, 220, 318
court-martial, Burgoyne's request for, 291–94, 308–9
Coventry, Lord, 48
Craig, Capt. James, 263, 264–65, 267
Creasey, Sir Edward, 220
Cross, Ralph, 271

Crown Point, 100, 109–12, 117, 118, 123, 153
Crozat, Louise, 14n
Cumberland, Duke of, 11, 29
Cumberland Head, 152

Danvers, Charles, 93
Dartmouth, Lord, 65, 73, 74–77, 80, 95, 114
Day, Nathaniel, 315, 328
Dayton, Fort, 183, 185
Deane, Silas, 94
Dearborn, Maj. Henry, 220, 222, 245, 271
Defiance, Mount, 155
Delaplace, William, 147
Derby, Earls of, 9, 12, 30, 57, 62
Derby, eleventh Earl of, 6, 7, 13, 16, 17, 57–58
Derby, twelfth Earl of, 62, 111, 181, 274, 320–21, 323–24, 328
desertion, problem of, 217, 258, 266
Devil's Disciple, The (Shaw), 332
Devonshire, Duke of, 50
diamond (gift to Burgoyne from King of Portugal), 315, 328
Diamond Island, 214, 235
Dickinson, John, 69
Digby, Lt., 100, 107, 165, 170–71, 175, 227, 229, 268
Dorchester, Baron. *See* Carleton, Sir Guy
Dorset, Duke of, 321
Dovecot (Coleville), 217
D'Oyley, Christian, 127–28
dragoons. *See* Brunswick Dragoon Regiment; Light Dragoons; Royal Dragoons
Drayton (estate), 127n
Drury, Gen. Alexander, 26
Drury Lane Theater, 319, 322, 323, 324, 325
Dublin, Burgoyne's residence in, 314–15
Duperron, Cornet, 33n

Index

East India Company, investigation of, 62–64

Edward, Fort, 162, 168, 169, 172, 174–76, 185, 202, 235, 251, 260

Eelking, Capt. M. von, 255–56

Effingham, Earl of, 67

Eggerton, Eleazer, 193

Egremont, Charles Wyndham, second Earl of, 49

Eliott, Maj.-Gen. George, 30, 35

Elliott, Sir Gilbert, 74

Elton (Burgoyne's opponent at Preston), 316

Erskine, Sir William ("Wooly") 131

Esopus, 237, 265

Evelyn, Capt., 95–96

Farren, Elizabeth, 321, 324–25, 327

Ferdinand, Prince of Brunswick, 22, 50

Fermoy, Roche de, 158–59

Finch, Lady Elizabeth. *See* Bingley, Lady Elizabeth

Fisher, Elijah, 258

Fish Kill, 255–58, 268

Foot Guards, 2nd (Coldstream) Regiment, 26

Forbes, Gordon, 304, 305

Fortescue, Sir John, 24, 120, 134, 175, 229, 330; comment on confusion of British war plans, 134

Fourth (King's Own) Regiment, 315

Fox, Charles James: relationship with Burgoyne, 20, 56, 58, 60, 62, 69, 277, 292, 314, 315; stand on American war, 66, 118, 180, 279, 280, 292, 295–96, 299

Francis, Col. Ebenezer, 164–66

Franklin, Benjamin, 314

Fraser, Capt. Alexander, 142

Fraser, Brig.-Gen. Simon, 108, 141, 142, 157, 159, 164–68, 192–93, 201; Burgoyne's estimate of, 221, 228, 302; death of, 246–47, 250–52; Saratoga performance of, 221–25, 231, 239, 242, 246–47

Fraser's Rangers, 142, 196, 198, 216, 257

Frederick the Great, 52, 53; Carlyle's life of, 330

Freeman's Farm (*see also* Saratoga, first battle of), 218–29, 232; Burgoyne's account of, 228; evaluation of, 227–30; Gates's account of, 228–29

Fuller, Gen. J. F. C., 330

Gage, Lt.-Gen. Thomas, 65–67, 75, 78, 80–83, 86, 88, 91–92, 95, 294

Gansevoort, Col. Peter, 183–86

Garrick, David, 61, 320, 321–22

Gates, Bob, 270

Gates, Elizabeth Phillips, 208

Gates, Maj. Gen. Horatio: ability as an officer, 207–11, 218–20, 226, 227, 229, 273, 276, 303; background and character, 155, 176, 177, 208–10; opinion of Burgoyne, 239, 268, 269; performance at Saratoga, 217–22, 225–27, 244–45, 249, 252, 258–66, 268–72, 276, 284; relationship with George Washington, 208–9, 210, 271; respect for the British soldier, 251, 268; row with Arnold, 239, 247; testimony at Saratoga congressional hearing, 281–84

Gaunt, John of, 4

Gentleman's Magazine, 9, 320–21, 327

George I, 10, 39

George II, 10, 17, 29

George III, 56, 62, 71, 90, 112, 125, 212; attitude toward war, 46, 66, 159; conduct of American war, 105, 114–15, 123, 124, 145; opinion of Burgoyne before Saratoga, 64, 76–77, 99, 104, 106, 118, 119, 120; reaction to Saratoga surrender, 278, 280, 291–93, 297–99, 307

George, Fort, 161, 169, 235

Index

George, Lake, 122, 147, 153, 161, 214, 251

Germain, Lady (Lord Germain's wife), 212, 293

Germain, Lady Betty (Lord Germain's benefactress), 127n

Germain, Lord George (Lord George Sackville), 62, 89, 95, 187, 321; background and character, 20–21, 124–25, 127, 133, 207; concern for personal honor, 278; early friendship with Burgoyne, 73–74, 77, 89, 100, 111–12, 117–19, 136, 180–81; efforts to discredit Burgoyne, 291–93, 295, 297, 299, 300–301, 306–9, 321; instructions to Burgoyne on expedition from Canada, 105–6, 206–7, 274; performance at Minden, 21, 297, 298; performance at St. Malo, 21–23; reaction to Burgoyne's losses, 206–7, 269, 272–74, 277–80, 293–94, 297–98; relations with Carleton, 101, 134–35; relations with Fox, 279, 280, 292; relations with Howe, 21, 103; war policies, 73, 99, 104, 114–16, 123–30, 132–36, 145, 152, 206–7, 269, 278

German Auxiliaries in America (Eelking), 255–56

Germans in the British army, 105, 123, 141, 166, 167, 191, 193, 199, 201; Burgoyne's feelings about, 123, 203, 226, 228, 249, 273, 276, 302; performance of, 226–28, 245–46, 249; popular resentment of, 197, 198, 249

Glover, Brig. Gen. John, 218–19, 258

gorgets, 219

Gosling, George, 329

Gould, Charles, 294

Gower, Lord, 48, 76

Grafton, third Duke of, 50, 58–59, 60

Grant, Abbé, 16

Grant, James, 167–68

Graves, Adm. Thomas, 89, 95, 101

Green Mountain Boys, 147, 164, 198, 199

Grenadiers' march, 268

Grenville, George, 47–48, 55–56

Grétry, André, 325

Hadden, Lt. J. M., 148–49, 201, 225, 229

Haldimand, Gen., 75

Hale, Col. Nathan, 164, 167

Hamilton, Lady Betty, 320–21

Hamilton, Brig.-Gen. James, 221, 224–25, 228, 256–59, 267, 303

Hampshire Grants, 203

Hancock, John, 81

Hanger, Maj., 138–39

Hanover, as source of German mercenaries, 105

Hansard, comment on Saratoga inquiry, 301

Hardwicke, Earl of, 77

Hardy, Fort, 268

Harley, Robert, 3

Harnage, Maj. Henry, 232

Harrington, Earl of, 176, 304

Harvey, Gen. Edward, 77, 88–89, 104–5, 134, 135, 136

Hastings, Warren, 7, 316

Head of Elk, 131

Heath, Maj.-Gen. William, 281, 282, 285–88, 290

Heiress, The (Burgoyne), 323–26

Henley, Col. David, 287–88

Henry, Prince, 52

Herkimer, Col. Nicholas, 183–84

Herrick, Col., 198

Hesse, Landgrave of, 105

Hesse-Hanau Artillery Company, 141, 192, 221

"Hessian Hill," 196

Hill, Lt.-Col. John, 162–63, 284

Hinde, Robert, 14

Historical Memoirs (Wraxall), 60

History of the British Cavalry (Anglesey), 330

Hodgson, Maj.-Gen. Studholme, 38

Index

Hoghton, Sir Henry, 57–58
Hope, Mount, 154, 157
Hopkinson, Francis, 150
Hornby, Geoffrey, 328
Horse Guards, 9–11
horses, problems of supplying, 146, 148, 190–92
Horton, Mrs. (Burgoyne's niece), 15, 328
Howe, Cmdre. Richard, 7, 21, 23–26, 95, 104, 279
Howe, Lt.-Gen. Sir William: Boston assignment, 67, 81–82, 84, 89; character and reputation, 68, 69, 95; failure to communicate with Burgoyne, 127–35, 153–54, 173–74, 181, 187, 203–7, 237–38, 261; failure to effect a junction with Burgoyne, 121–30, 272–73, 278–80, 292, 296, 300, 330; historical significance of failure to aid Burgoyne, 330; leadership of British in America, 95, 102–3, 104, 109, 114–19; performance at Belle-Ile, 38; performance at Heights of Abraham, 28; performance at St. Malo, 21; Philadelphia campaign, 116, 117, 126–30, 134, 174, 206, 236, 280, 290; relationship with Burgoyne, 71, 75–78, 92, 274, 275, 276, 279, 283, 292, 298; resignation and retirement, 280, 300, 307, 314; testimony to Parliament concerning American campaign, 279–80, 300–301, 306–7
Hubbardton, 159, 164–67, 174, 205, 226
Hudleston, F. J., 206
Hudson River, Burgoyne's crossing of, 206, 214–15, 216, 221, 272, 274, 302, 330
Hutchinson, Thomas, 77, 120, 279, 292

Independence, Mount, 154, 157, 158, 159, 162

Indians in the British army, 134, 157, 158, 163, 171, 175–76, 184–86, 201; American resentment of, 150, 189, 194, 197; Burgoyne's opinion of, 150–52, 302; George III's feelings about, 123; reliability of, 145, 193, 197, 205, 215, 216, 236, 243
Innes, Robert, 167-68
Ireland, Burgoyne's command in, 314–15
Irunibeni, Don Miguel de, 41
Irwin, Gen. John, 88–89

Jackson, Mr., of Exeter (composer), 323
Jacobite Rebellion, 11
Jägers, 192, 257
"jealousy" tactic, 190–91, 195
Jefferson, Thomas, 107
Jenkinson, Charles, 70, 73, 307–9
Jervis, John, 318
Jessup, Lt.-Col. Ebenezer, 144, 197
Johnson, Guy, 183–84
Johnson, Sir John, 182–84
Johnson, Mary, 5
Johnson, Molly Brant, 183
Johnson, Sir William, 182
Jones, David, 175
Joseph I of Portugal, 38–39, 41, 315, 328
Joseph II of Austria, 52
"Junius," 58–60, 69

Kelly, Earl of, 321
Keppel, Adm. Augustus, 7, 67
King, Thomas, 325
King's Loyal Americans, 144
Kingston, Lt.-Col. Robert, 192, 261–63, 284–85, 291, 304, 305
Knowsley Hall, 12, 320, 323
Knox, William, 118, 120, 127–28, 206, 207, 300
Kosciusko, Col. Thaddeus, 110, 211, 218

Index

Lamb, Sgt. Roger, 148, 163–64, 170, 229, 232, 249, 256, 270
Langlade, Charles de, 145
Laurens, Henry, 282, 284, 313
Learned, Brig. Gen. Ebenezer, 185, 219, 220, 224, 244–45, 247–48, 258
Lee, Arthur, 68–69
Lee, Lt.-Col. Charles, 42–43, 89–95, 210
Leicester, Sir Peter, 57
Leith, Sir Alexander, 297
Lexington, battle of, 80, 83, 84
Light Dragoons, formation of, 29–30, 35–36
Light Dragoons, King's and Queen's, 47
Light Dragoons, 16th, 29–36, 37–44, 46–47
Lincoln, Maj. Gen. Benjamin, 177, 196, 235, 251
Lippe-Buckeburg, Count of, 39–44, 301
Livingston Manor, 237
Long, Col., 172
Long Island, Howe's victory on, 118
Lord of the Manor, The (Burgoyne-Sheridan), 323
Louden, Lord, 39
Luttrell, Temple, 297
Lutwidge, Cmdre., 159

Macaulay, Thomas, 330–31
McCrae, Jane, murder of, 175–77, 197, 286
McCrae, Capt. (brother of Jane), 177
McKean, Thomas, 313
Mackoy, Maj., 257
Mahon, Lord, 331
Maid of the Oaks (Burgoyne), 320–22
Manchester, Vermont, 191–92, 196
Mann, Sir Horace, 320
Marlborough, third Duke of, 20–23
Marmion (Scott), 331
Marmontel (Sylvain), 322–23
Mattoon, Gen., 247

Meredith, Sir William, 47
Midhurst (Burgoyne's first constituency), 45, 57
military chest, disappearance of, 283–84
Miller, Fort, 192, 202
Minden, battle of, 21, 28, 106, 141, 297–98
Mohawk valley diversion, 181–85, 211
Money, John, 304, 305
Montcalm, Marquis de, 28, 147
Montgomery, Fort, 233–34, 236–37
Montgomery, Brig. Gen. Richard, 100–101
Moore, Sir John, 34
Morgan, Daniel, 100, 211, 219–20, 222–25, 228–29, 244–48, 258
Morning Herald, 6
Mostyn, Brig.-Gen. John, 22
Murphy, Timothy, 246

Negroes, military employment of, 152
Newcastle, Thomas, first Duke of, 20
New England cover plan, 190–91
New England militia, 200, 211, 219
New York, strategic importance of, 114, 126, 130, 174, 233–34, 278
New York governorship, 72–78 *passim*
Nichols, Col. Moses, 198
Nixon, Brig. Gen. John, 218–19, 258
North, Lord, 61–62, 76, 78, 89, 94, 105, 112, 114, 274, 314; war policies, 66–73 *passim*, 280, 291–92, 297, 300–301, 307, 309
Northampton, Burgoyne's recruiting activities in, 30–31
Nunnery, Cheshunt (estate), 5

Observations and Reflections upon the Present Military State of Prussia, Austria and France (Burgoyne), 51–54

Index

O'Connell, Capt., 192
ode on Palmerston's wedding
 (Burgoyne), 13
Official Gazette, 118
O'Hara, James (Lord Tyrawley), 39
Oneida, Lake, 187
Oriskany ambush, 183–84, 186
Oswego, 123, 182, 183

Palmerston, Lady. *See* Poole, Frances
Palmerston, second Viscount, 13, 15,
 47, 48–49, 50–51, 82–83
Parker, Caroline, 6, 14–15, 329
parole, Burgoyne's acceptance of,
 290, 309–10, 332
Paterson, John, 218–19
Pausch, Capt. Georg, 141, 221, 226–
 27, 238, 242, 245–46
Peekskill, 173
Pellew, Edward, 214
Pembroke, Lord, 297–98
Penfold, Pvt., 208
Pennel, Capt., 105
Percy, Lord, 80–81, 83, 93, 318
Peters, Lt.-Col. John, 144, 191
Pharsalus, battle of, 84
Philadelphia campaign. *See* Howe,
 Maj.-Gen. Sir William
Philipson, Col. Richard, 274–76, 328
Phillips, Elizabeth (Mrs. Horatio
 Gates), 208
Phillips, Maj.-Gen. William, 106–7,
 110–11, 117, 140–42, 157, 290;
 performance at Bemis Heights, 231,
 239, 242, 247, 251, 259, 267, 268;
 performance at Freeman's Farm,
 221, 225, 226, 228; relationship
 with Burgoyne, 228, 255, 303, 310
Pigott, Capt., 321
Pitt, William, the Elder (Earl of
 Chatham), 18, 20, 22, 28–29, 39, 49,
 51, 55, 56, 292
Pitt, William, the Younger, 317
Pittsfield contingent, 198
Pombal, Marquis de, 39, 41

Poole, Frances (later Lady Palmer-
 ston), 13, 51
Poor, Brig.-Gen. Enoch, 219, 220,
 224, 244–45, 247
Porter, Elisha, 281
Portugal campaign, 38–44
Powell, Brig.-Gen. Henry, 163
Pownall, John, 74, 77, 88
Preston (Burgoyne's constituency),
 56–60, 69, 294, 310
Putnam, Maj.-Gen. Israel, 204, 236
Putnam's Creek proclamation, 149–50

Quebec, 28, 100–102, 122
Queen's Light Dragoons, 308, 309
Queen's Royal Rangers, 144

Ramsay, Allan, 15, 16, 218
Rattlesnake Hill, 155
Red House, 202
red ribbon. *See* Bath, Order of the
*Reflections upon the War in
 America* (Burgoyne), 101, 102,
 104
Reynell, Mrs. Thomas, 232
Reynolds, Sir Joshua, 61
Rhetz regiment, 221, 226
Richard Coeur de Lion (Grétry-
 Burgoyne), 325
Richmond, Duke of, 317–18
Riedesel, Baroness Frederika von,
 143–44, 192, 212–15, 242, 253,
 258–59, 265, 272, 284; care of
 wounded, 232–33, 250–52, opinion
 of Burgoyne, 213, 238, 255;
 opinion of Saratoga surrender, 267
Riedesel, Maj.-Gen. Baron Friedrich
 von, 106, 141, 159, 164–68, 191–92,
 194, 215, 221; at Bemis Heights,
 239, 242, 245, 247, 249, 251–54,
 256; at Freeman's Farm, 221–22,
 225–28; at Saratoga, 257–59, 268;
 at Ticonderoga, 159; relations with
 Burgoyne, 141, 213, 228, 256, 265,
 267, 303

Riedesel family, 212, 233, 253, 258
Rigby, Richard, 295, 301
Rocheford, Earl of, 76, 83–88, 95
Rockingham, second Marquis of, 7, 56, 58, 314
Rogers Rangers, 195
Roman Catholics, eligibility for military service, 53, 105
Royal Dragoons: 1st, 11, 14, 19; 11th, 18, 19–26
Royal Marriage Bill, 62

Sackville, Lord George. *See* Germain, Lord George
Saint-Cast, 24–26
St. Clair, Maj.-Gen. Arthur, 155–59, 162, 165–66, 171, 172, 173
Saint-Johns, 148
St. Leger, Lt.-Col. Barry, 125, 182–86, 203, 303
St. Luc, La Corne, 145, 176
Saint-Malo expedition, 20–22, 23, 103
Sancoik (St. Croix) Mill, 193, 194, 196, 199–200
Sandwich, Lord, 77, 105
Saratoga, 187, 193, 203, 215; American strength at, 303; American tactics at, 229, 238–39; British arrival at, 255; British defeat at, *see* Bemis Heights, battle of; British surrender at (*see also* Saratoga Convention), 269–70; British tactics at, 220–25, 231–32, 240–43; casualties at, 227, 232–33; first battle of, *see* Freeman's Farm, battle of; fortifications at, 235–36; morale at, 227, 238; terrain at, 217–22, 224, 225, 235–36, 257
Saratoga Convention, 263–68; Articles of (text), 335–37; Burgoyne's justification of, 264, 265–66, 272–80, 291–98, 301–7; congressional inquiry on, 218–86, 288–90; Howe's proposed breach of, 283; parliamentary inquiry on,

264, 265, 269, 272–80, 294–310; significance of, 329
Savile, Sir George, 47, 62
Schuyler, John Joost ("Hon-Yost"), 186
Schuyler, Maj.-Gen. Philip, 154–56, 168–74, 185, 193, 195, 196; scorched-earth policy, 189–90, 207–9, 271–72
Schuyler mansion, 247, 255–57, 271, 272
Schuylerville, 253
Scott, Capt., 234
Scott, Sir Walter, 331
Sedaine, Michel, 325
Selwyn, George, 320
Seven Years' War, 18, 152, 208
Shakespeare, William, 326
Shaw, George Bernard, 32, 332
Shelburne, Lord, 277
Sheridan, Richard Brinsley, 61n, 323, 324
Sherman, Roger, 173
Skene, Maj. Philip, 144, 161–62, 168, 170, 190–94, 197, 199–201
Skenesboro, 122, 144; American retreat to, 158–59; battle of, 161–62; British installed in, 164, 165, 167, 168, 170, 171; strategic importance of, 187, 296, 302, 304
Smith, Rev. John, 37
Smyth, Dr. (builder of Red House), 202
South Bay, 122, 161
Spain, threat of war with, 207, 317
Specht, Brig.-Gen. Johann, 226
Specht regiment, 221, 226
Springers (62nd Regiment), 224–25, 227, 266
Stainville, Comte Etienne de (Duke of Choiseul), 14–15, 38, 53
Stamp Act, 55–56; Burgoyne's reaction to, 56, 66
Standish, Sir Frank, 57
Stanley, Lady Charlotte. *See* Burgoyne, Lady Charlotte (wife)

Stanley, Lord. *See* Derby, twelfth Earl of
Stanley, house of. *See* Derby, Earls of
Stanwix, Fort, 183–86, 203
Stark, Brig.-Gen. John, 195–201, 218, 235, 251, 258, 260
Stark's Knob, 258
Staten Island, 109
State of the Expedition from Canada as laid before the House of Commons (Burgoyne), 310
Stephenson, David, 328
Stevens, Enos, 271
Stillwater, 174, 196, 210–11
Stoneland Park, 127
Strange, Lord James, 7–9, 12, 13, 14, 17, 43–44, 62
Stuart, Charles, 94
Suffolk, Lord, 76, 77
Sugar Hill (Sugarloaf), 155, 157–58, 221
Sullivan, Maj.-Gen. John, 107, 204
Sutherland, Lt.-Col. Nicholas, 154, 157, 163, 265
Sutton, third Baronet of. *See* Burgoyne, Sir John (grandfather)
Sylvain (author of *Marmontel*), 322–23

Taylor, Sgt. Daniel, 237
Temple, Lord, 314
Thacher, Dr. James, 158, 162, 163, 173
Thanet, Lord, 93
Thayendanegea (Joseph Brant), 182, 183
Thoughts for Conducting the War from the Side of Canada (Burgoyne), 120, 125; 182
Ticonderoga, 100, 103, 109–11, 117, 120, 209, 214, 235, 251–53; Burgoyne's capture of, 148, 153–60, 169, 170, 174, 205, 207, 273, 275; strategic importance of, 121, 122, 123, 132–33, 140, 147–48, 156, 173, 235

"tip and run" raid, 192
Townshend, Charles, 43–44
"Traveller's Rest," 208
"Triumvirate of Reputation," 69, 79, 80–81, 313
Trois-Rivières, battle of, 108
Trumbull, Jonathan, 173–74
Twiss, Lt. William, 157, 170
Tyrawley, Lord (James O'Hara, Viscount Tyrawley), 39
Tyron, William, 72–73, 75

uniform: American, 198; British, 137, 141, 215, 219, 222, 224; German, 215, 219

Valcour island, 110, 152
Valencia de Alcántara, 40–41, 330
Van Rensselaer, Col., 163
Vaughan, Gen. John, 237
Veerplanks Point, 236
Villa Velha, 41–43
Vyner, Robert, 295

Walpole, Horace, 3, 4, 7, 12, 31, 62, 109, 208, 295; comments on Burgoyne, 46, 68, 150, 159–60, 201, 277, 297, 301; comment on Clinton, 68; comments on Germain, 20–21, 22, 297; comment on Howe, 68; reactions to Burgoyne's plays, 322, 324
Walpole, Sir Robert, 7
Warburton, Lady Elizabeth, 6
Warburton, Miss (descendant of Lord Derby), 6, 14–15
Warburton, Mrs. (Burgoyne's niece), 328
Warde, Maj., 19–20
Warner, Col. Seth, 164–67, 198–201
War of the Austrian Succession, 11
Washington, George, 90, 91, 103, 154, 185, 205, 209, 259, 271; comment on confusion of British war plans, 174; reaction to Congress's repudiation of Saratoga

Index

convention, 289; respect for Burgoyne, 201, 211, 282, 296, 313; strategic insight, 115, 116, 131, 173–74, 179, 185, 195, 201

Wayne, Brig.-Gen. Anthony, 155

Wedderburn, Alexander, 60, 64, 293–95

Wellington, Duke of, 26, 219

Westminster School, 7–9, 21

Wilkes, John, 47

Wilkinson, James, 157–58, 217–18, 231–32, 244, 248, 264, 267

Willett, Lt.-Col. Marinus, 183–85

William, Fort, Burgoyne's governorship of, 59n, 60, 62, 308, 309

Williams, Maj. Griffith, 142, 221, 226, 242, 245

Williams, Capt. Sir William, 37, 38, 45, 42

Wolfe, James, 28, 29, 100

Wood, Dr., 290

"World Turned Upside Down, The," 322n

Wraxall, Sir Nathaniel, 56, 60

"Yankee Doodle," 270

Yates, Joseph, 58

Yorktown, British surrender at, 220, 322n

Young (British officer), 232–33

Zara, Burgoyne's prologue for, 89

Zion, Mount, 165